JAPAN'S
⇥ COMPETING ⇤
MODERNITIES

D1498794

JAPAN'S
⇒ COMPETING ⇐
MODERNITIES,

Issues in Culture and Democracy 1900–1930

Edited by

SHARON A. MINICHIELLO

University of Hawai'i Press
HONOLULU

Publication of this book has been assisted by a
grant from the Kajiyama Publications Fund
for Japanese History, Culture, and Literature at
the University of Hawai'i at Mānoa.

©1998 University of Hawai'i Press

Printed in the United States of America

03 02 01 00 99 98   5 4 3 2 1

Library of Congress Cataloging-in-Publication Data

Japan's competing modernities : issues in culture and democracy,
1900–1930 / edited by Sharon A. Minichiello.
p. cm.
Includes bibliographical references and index.
ISBN 0–8248–1931–4 (alk. paper).—ISBN 0–8248–2080–0 (pbk. :
alk. paper)
1. Japan—Civilization—1912–1926. 2. Japan—
Civilization—1868–1912. 3. Japan—Politics and
government—1912–1926. 4. Japan—Politics and
government—1868–1912.
DS822.4.J36   1998
952.03—dc21   98–6077
CIP

University of Hawai'i Press books are printed on acid-free
paper and meet the guidelines for permanence and durability
of the Council on Library Resources

Designed and typeset by Northeastern Graphic Services, Inc.

❧ Contents ❧

✦ II ✦

Cosmopolitanism and National Identity

✦ III ✦

Diversity, Autonomy, and Integration

Contents

❧ *Foreword* ❦

The first three decades of Japan's twentieth century constituted largely unexplored terrain in English-language scholarship when Bernard S. Silberman and H. D. Harootunian invited nineteen Japanese and American scholars to Quail Roost, North Carolina, in January 1970, for the first conference on Taishō Japan. On the twentieth anniversary of the publication of papers from that trailblazing symposium (*Japan in Crisis: Essays on Taishō Democracy,* 1974), twenty-two scholars representing a new generation of modern Japan scholarship gathered on Maui, Hawai'i, for the second Conference on Taishō Japan. Organized by Sharon A. Minichiello and Germaine Hoston, the conference yielded this volume, representing the fruits of a collective effort to push further into the critical era preceding cataclysmic war in Asia.

Although both conferences focused on the question of democracy, the Maui conference set out broader parameters that encouraged the breaking of traditional academic boundaries and intellectual paradigms. The call for papers defined topics in terms of "geographical and cultural space; cosmopolitanism and national identity; and diversity, autonomy and integration."

Accordingly, one distinguishing characteristic of the Maui conference was the presence of China, Manchuria, and Korea specialists whose research on East Asia transcended national borders. Their research not only contributed to our understanding of the nature of Japan's imperial expansion in Asia but lent a valuable comparative dimension to the understanding of modernity in Taishō-era Japan. Modernity was happening in the colonies—in architecture, in popular culture, in technology, and in the formulation of national identities, though, as the papers in this volume reveal, there were multiple constructions of modernity. Exciting and unexpected linkages connecting many of the papers demonstrated mutual influences across all of Northeast Asia. The conference established the value, if not the utter necessity, of dealing with modern Japan in this larger geographical context.

The exploding interest in gender studies over the past two decades contributed a second new ingredient to the Maui conference. Several participants presented research on women, studied not only as political actors and thinkers but also as symbols used to represent competing cultural values.

The new look of Taishō scholarship, especially in the post–World War I period, was also disclosed in studies of popular culture, mass media, and mass consumer society, which drew on new and innovative research materials, such as photographs, cartoons, songs, radio broadcasts, and architectural drawings. A Japanese film made in the early 1920s, a group of Japanese *enka* singers born in that period, and a separate exhibit in the Honolulu Academy of Arts of Taishō-era paintings and decorative items further served to bring alive early twentieth-century popular culture.

Finally, the Maui conference enjoyed participation by scholars from outside of the United States and Japan. Its broad call for papers resulted in invitations to participants from Canada, Australia, Denmark, and Korea.

Similarities in the two conferences are also noteworthy. Although Quail Roost dwelled more on the sense of crisis and political fragmentation that seemed to characterize the Taishō era, concern with issues of nationalism and national identity and continuing efforts to comprehend the meaning of Japan's modern experience characterized discussion at both gatherings. But above all, what holds the two conferences together in my memory of them is the excitement generated by the fellowship of dedicated academic specialists helping each other to produce scholarship of lasting significance.

Gail Lee Bernstein

❧ *Preface* ❦

This volume has been a project of the Northeast Asia Council of the Association for Asian Studies (NEAC). It was a unique experiment in that a democratically elected body held an open competition for papers that would result in an interdisciplinary volume offering fresh perspectives on early twentieth-century Japan. The general themes that would treat the period 1900 to 1930 were three: geographical and cultural space; cosmopolitanism and national identity; and diversity, autonomy, and integration. Moreover, the project Planning Committee for NEAC encouraged the integration or "mainstreaming" of issues that cut across the above-mentioned themes, such as gender and cultural values. While the Japanese experience would be at the core of the project, the Planning Committee held that the experience of the neighboring peoples in Korea, Taiwan, the Pacific Islands, and the Chinese mainland was vital to the understanding of the late Meiji, Taishō, and early Shōwa periods. The committee therefore solicited proposals from specialists on the colonial periods in Korea, Taiwan, and the Pacific Islands and from China specialists on topics related to Japanese expansion on the mainland.

The purpose of this preface is to provide a brief history of this project, and to acknowledge those who made its conceptualization and actualization possible. For both history and acknowledgment, one must mention first the Japanese publishing house of Maruzen Co., Ltd. In May 1994, the Meiji Studies Conference was held at Harvard University—inspired, in part, by Maruzen's gift to Harvard of the invaluable Meiji Microfilm Set that it had produced. The Northeast Asia Council sent Germaine Hoston and Sharon Minichiello as representatives to the conference, at which time they solidified an idea that Meiji Conference organizer Helen Hardacre had suggested earlier—that there be a follow-up to the Meiji Conference that would focus on the Taishō era. By the end of 1994, a Planning Committee was in place, consisting of Hoston and Minichiello as co-chairs, Gail Lee Bernstein, Donald N. Clark, Tetsuo Najita, and J. Thomas Rimer. John W. Dower agreed to serve as consultant and later Miriam Silverberg as NEAC representative.

The call for papers for the Taishō conference went out in November/ December 1994. It would be held November 1–5, 1995, in Maui, Hawai'i—twenty-five years after that held in Quail Roost, North Carolina, which resulted in the first Taishō volume, *Japan in Crisis, Essays on Taishō Democracy* (edited by Bernard S. Silberman and H. D. Harootunian), appearing in 1974. There was an enthusiastic response to the call for papers, with approximately sixty applications. The work of the Planning Committee was exceedingly difficult when it met in February 1995 to make its decisions. John Dower and Tetsuo Najita could not be there for the three-day meeting. Still, Dower wrote detailed comments from Cambridge, noting the conspicuous absence in the applicants' abstracts of more traditional research themes and approaches: "Apparently the state has been finished off, and the capitalists too (almost), along with all those bourgeois chameleons in the Diet, not to mention the bureaucracy and military. *Requiescat in pace Kindaika-ron*—and whatever-the-Latin-is-for-becoming-undead to ethnicity and gender."

In an extended telephone call, Najita made similar observations. He further advised that we not try to fill in what was missing; rather, we should capitalize on the wealth of what we had, considering it a commentary on new scholarship in the field as of 1995, and try to produce with the chosen essays an exceptional volume.

When the conference convened at the Westin-Maui on November 1, 1995, the participants had read in advance each of the participants' papers. Each day's meetings could proceed, therefore, in a workshop format, with the goal of promoting the cross-fertilization of ideas. Professors Shin'ichi Kitaoka (Rikkyō University, and now the University of Tokyo) and Osamu Mihashi (Wakō University) participated in the discussions as Japan observers and Professor Takie Lebra (University of Hawai'i at Mānoa) as our Western observer. At the end of the conference, Professor Kitaoka commented on the three themes the Planning Committee originally chose in 1994—geographical and cultural space; cosmopolitanism and national identity; and diversity, autonomy, and integration. These, he suggested, had collectively facilitated a fresh examination of Japan's periphery during the early twentieth century, which was constituent to a deeper understanding of her center during the same period.

In addition to Professors Hoston, Bernstein, Clark, Najita, Rimer, Dower, and Silverberg, along with the conference observers I have named above, I wish to thank many others who contributed to this project.

Our sponsors were many, beginning with the tremendous support from the Northeast Asia Council of the Association for Asian Studies and Maruzen Co., Ltd. The Korea Research Foundation, Japan-United States Friendship Commission, Kamigata Cultural Foundation, Central Pacific Bank of Hawai'i, and The Westin-Maui all supplied crucial funding. The project would not have been possible without the sustained support of the Kajiyama Publications Fund and many units within the University of Hawai'i at Mānoa. The Japanese Studies Endowment Fund of the University of Hawai'i (through a grant from the Japanese government) provided both start-up and ongoing funding.

Those who contributed to the richness of events surrounding the original Maui Conference included Professor Lucy Lower, the Honolulu Academy of Arts, and the Taishō Singers of Honolulu. Thanks also go to the many individuals and organizations involved in the outreach component of the conference. The Hawai'i Committee for the Humanities provided much of the funding. Gay Satsuma, outreach director, coordinated the interisland appearances of our speakers—Professors Barbara Brooks, Elaine Gerbert, Jeffrey Hanes, Roy Starrs, and E. Patricia Tsurumi. Our assistants on site at the conference were invaluable, and appreciation goes to Angela Carbonaro, Marcia Hoston-Barra, and Gay Satsuma.

The production of this book would not have been possible without Patricia Crosby, executive editor of the University of Hawai'i Press, Masako Kobayashi Ikeda, our managing editor, and Brian Masshardt, editorial assistant at the Center for Japanese Studies, University of Hawai'i at Mānoa. I want to thank these and all of the above for their important roles in conceiving this project and moving it forward.

❧ Introduction ❧

Sharon A. Minichiello

The years 1900 through 1930 bracket the reign years of Japan's Taishō emperor (1912–1926). It was a short reign compared to that of his father, the Meiji emperor (1868–1912), and his son, the Shōwa emperor (1926–1989). For a time, scholars, Japanese and non-Japanese alike, studied the Taishō era within the framework of *Taishō demokurashii*, or "Taishō democracy." As one writer who used this framework, I have suggested elsewhere:

> The period was a time of social, political, and economic ferment in which some Japanese were attempting to become world citizens in line with universal post–World War I democratic trends. In Japan this current found expression in two ways: the *spirit* of democracy, as was manifest in the liberalistic mobilization of the people through various democratic movements; and the *structure* of democracy through establishment of party cabinets and recognition thereby of the parties as a major constituent of political power. Although brief, the period from 1924 to 1932 became known as that of *kensei no jōdō*, or "constitutional government as the normal way of running the state." (Minichiello 1984, 6–7)

While "Taishō democracy" continues to be a useful concept, students of the period in more recent years have sought alternative ways of understanding the late Meiji-Taishō era.[1]

In *Japan's Competing Modernities*, we have used the idea of Taishō to mean "Greater Taishō"—that is, the approximate period 1900–1930 (see Carlile essay). Tetsuo Najita and J. Victor Koschmann's edited volume,

1

Conflict in Modern Japanese History: The Neglected Tradition (1982), also identified this period as a singular "moment" worthy of analysis "as a system of events containing a coherent set of internal identities" (11). My first goal in this introduction, therefore, is to suggest the reasons why 1900–1930 constitutes a coherent historical period. The second is to situate Japan during this period—both through a profile of its internal system and its relation to East Asia and the outside world. My third is to identify the broader thematic tensions that tie the essays together.

To begin, I offer the following working definitions for "modernity," "culture," and "democracy." First, we stress the *ideas* of modernity—progress, science, and rationality (Garon 1994, 350). We take "culture" to mean the sum total of the attainment of learned behavioral patterns of any specific period, race, or people, regarded as expressing a traditional way of life—and its gradual but continuous modification by succeeding generations. And while we use "democracy" generally in its political sense, meaning a constitutional system based on competitive parties in which the governing majority respects the rights of minorities and in which the ordinary citizens exert a relatively high degree of control over leaders, we do not deny its nonpolitical by-products including social democracy, economic democracy, and industrial democracy, as well as an international orientation.

GREATER TAISHŌ, 1900–1930

One could say that this period represents a generation of Japanese experience during which Japan rose in the international community as a world power and experimented with what the early twentieth-century world had to offer, including political philosophies, new technologies, imperial possibilities, economic systems, art, and cultural forms. A major symbol of some of these new developments was the Universal Exposition of 1900 in Paris. This grandiose undertaking attracted visitors ranging from the most exalted figures of Europe, America, and Asia to citizens of every class and culture. The exposition ushered in a period of miraculous inventions and developments, including electricity, the cinema, the motorcar, and the airplane; and little of this was lost on the Japanese as they entered into their own millennium.

As Tetsuo Najita has written, there was no one anchoring event for the 1900–1930 moment, as the Meiji Restoration had been for the earlier Bakumatsu Meiji period of 1850–1880 (Najita and Koschmann 1982, 11). I suggest that a series of events and benchmarks collectively anchored Greater Taishō, with a clear beginning and ending. Japan began the millennium with serious pollution problems resulting from Meiji industrial policies. The year 1900 also saw the alignment of the oligarch Itō Hirobumi with the party system in the formation of the Seiyūkai (Political Fraternity). This juxtaposition of social problems with establishment politics underscored the dilemma of balancing the greater polity with the individual in effecting a harmonious and productive society. The question was how to resolve the problem of combining individual freedom and human rights with the social order—how to totalize without depersonalizing, how to save the assemblage and units at the same time. The question would beg solutions throughout Greater Taishō. The same may be said for the role of the emperor. On May 10, 1900, Crown Prince Yoshihito (1879–1926), then twenty-one, married Sadako, the fourth daughter of Prince Kujō Michitaka, herself only sixteen. As I shall suggest later, the persona of Yoshihito, to become the Taishō emperor, would leave an indelible stamp on the era that bears his reign name.

Of course, this generation of Japanese experience was intertwined with the experience of East Asia as a whole, and a leitmotif in East Asian thought throughout these three decades was a growing disenchantment with the West. While China, Japan, and Korea each felt the escalating encroachment of Russia, China opened the century with an outright challenge to the West in the Boxer Rebellion. The defining events in this East Asian disenchantment came with World War I and the Versailles settlement. In addition to the Western nations' revealing their weaknesses in the war itself, Woodrow Wilson's slogans of "making the world safe for democracy" and the "self-determination of peoples" proved hollow promises. There was no self-determination for Korea; China felt betrayed by Japan's Twenty-one Demands of 1915 and the series of treaties Japan and the Western nations concluded during the war and refused to sign the peace settlement; and Japan would not forget that it did not get the racial equality clause it desired in the Covenant of the League of Nations—even though it emerged from Versailles as one of the top five in that League.

East Asian disenchantment had peaked by 1930. It appeared that while Western forms of democracy were failing, Western capitalism also had failed. With the Wall Street crash of 1929, the Great Depression began, and Japan especially feared the encroachment of "bloc economics." In fact, Japan's own economic system was in deep trouble with a banking crisis by 1927. And even though party government would continue until 1932, one could signify the ending of Greater Taishō by 1930. At the London Naval Conference that year, Japan's civilian government under Premier Hamaguchi Osachi agreed to limitations on naval construction that were extended to include a ratio for heavy cruisers of 10:10:7 among Britain, the United States, and Japan. This evoked a strong reaction at home, with heated dispute over violation of the "prerogative of the supreme command." By late 1930, a chorus of protest had reached shrill levels and found expression in an assassination attempt on Hamaguchi. This rendered him incapacitated for months, finally resulting in his death in 1931, which was also the beginning of Japan's "Fifteen-year War." That war defined the next generational experience for Japanese.

JAPAN, 1900–1930

Marius Jansen has summarized well the complex mood of the Japanese people on the eve of the twentieth century. With Japan's victory in the Sino-Japanese War of 1894–1895, chauvinism reigned. "After decades of weakness, it was good to be a Japanese and to humble the mighty neighbor that had dominated the horizon for so long" (Jansen 1975, 71–72). At the same time, the blow of the Triple Intervention, which deprived Japan of some of the fruits of victory, resulted in a slogan calling for future sacrifices from the people—*gashin shōtan,* "persevering through hardship [for the sake of revenge]." This did not, however, prevent the growth of antigovernment thought and activity. In the wake of economic dislocations following the war, an organized socialist movement emerged; and in 1901, the Socialist-Democratic Party was established.

Still, the people continued to sacrifice when war broke out between Japan and Russia in 1904 over spheres of influence in Manchuria and Korea. Japan "won," but the 1905 Portsmouth peace settlement produced neither the territory nor the indemnities the people expected. The Hibiya Riot that erupted on September 5, 1905, in protest of the peace settlement was also a sign of a growing mass consciousness concerning social inequities. There had been increased taxation levied to finance the war, and a by-product of this was a considerable expansion of the voting population. Having met the tax qualification to receive the franchise, that same population came to feel entitled to a greater voice in public matters. Hibiya and other demonstrations occurred because the oligarchs had failed to keep the people properly informed about how the war was proceeding. Unwittingly, they had allowed others to shape and lead public opinion.[2]

We may call these "others" outside activists—lawyers, journalists, professors, members of nationalist societies, and politicians of the opposition parties, who often resorted to demagogic tactics to capture the growing political consciousness. An integral element in this consciousness would be changes taking place in the class structure after the Russo-Japanese War, especially migration from the countryside and the changing appearance of the labor market. In the years between 1905 and 1918, Japan's economy would take on the modern characteristics of growth, with the nation shifting from an agricultural to an industrial economy. The Russo-Japanese War stimulated industry connected with the war effort. Increased imports, inflation, and foreign loans supported expansion, as did government military expenditures and those for the nationalization of the railroad trunk lines.

This modern industry was beginning to find an export market for certain commodities in Japan's new empire; for as Peter Duus has argued so lucidly, the Russo-Japanese War was a true "takeoff point" for Japanese imperialism: "The peace settlement and the international agreements that followed secured for Japan a new sphere of influence in Korea and southern Manchuria," and the "maintenance and enhancement of this sphere of influence became the central goal of Japanese foreign policy over the next four decades" (Duus 1983, 154). Having already won Taiwan in the Sino-Japanese War, the Japanese felt sufficiently secure by 1910 to annex Korea outright, following the Korean nationalist An Chung-gǔn's assassination of Itō Hirobumi in 1909. Ultimately, Japan's highest leadership decided that Korea would serve the three purposes of purchaser of Japanese manufactured goods, supplier of agricultural products, and emigration territory—all of which meshed well with Japan's vision of her position in the world economy (Duus 1984, 141). Her participation in World War I also would earn for her a mandate over the German islands in the Pacific, as well as rights on the China mainland. A colonial empire was in place under Yoshihito, the Taishō emperor.

~

As is well known, Yoshihito was sickly with meningitis from childhood.[3] When Meiji died, the Privy Council and cabinet members met to select the new reign name. They settled on Taishō, meaning "Great Righteousness," based on a passage from the ancient Chinese text *The Spring and Autumn Annals.* The name invited the meaning of imperial benevolence, thereby indicating a continuity with the spirit of Meiji (Large 1997, 67). But because of illness and other problems, Taishō could not and did not provide the symbol of strength and leadership that Meiji did. As Stephen Large has suggested, "Taishō was not 'mad' as such." However, his poor health and weakness of character—and later his womanizing, drinking, and eccentric behavior—made him a parody of the ideal that the emperor was a "manifest deity" (91).

As a youth, Yoshihito attended Gakushūin (also known as the Peers' School). There, in an interesting way, he encountered some of the internationalist atmosphere that became a hallmark of his reign years. A classmate in 1887 and 1888 was Isaac Harbottle (1871–1948), whom King Kalākaua of Hawai'i had chosen to go to Japan for study. Harbottle and his brother, who accompanied him to Japan, were descendants of Hawaiian *ali'i* (nobility) and were part of Kalākaua's plan to draw knowledge from abroad so as to strengthen his kingdom and profit from the international experience of future Hawaiian leaders (Quigg 1988, 170, 196). From 1886 to 1887, Harbottle also had been in the same class as Prince Morimasa Nashinomoto,

Mr. Issac Harbottle
in Gakushuin
School

1883:   Entered the 4th Year of "Lower Elementary School"
                            (4th Grade)

            --- School Regulations Changed ---

1884:   2nd Year of "Junior Middle School"   (5th Grade)

1885:   3rd Year of the same school.   (6th Grade)

            --- School Regulations Changed ---

1886, Aug.:   5th Grade of "Ordinary Middle School"
                                    (1st Year of Jr. High)

1887, Aug.:   4th Grade of the same school

1888, Aug.:   Left School, undated.

From 1887 to 1888, until when he left school, Mr. Isaac
Harbottle was in the same class with Emperor Taisho.

From 1886 to 1887 Prince Morimasa Nashinomoto was in the
same class with Mr. Isaac Harbottle.

Emperor Taisho entered 5th Grade of Preparatory School
(i.e. 2nd Grade of Elementary School) in September in
1887.

*Gakushūin profile of Isaac Harbottle. (Courtesy of Myron Thompson, Honolulu.)
Isaac Harbottle at Gakushūin circa 1887 as a fellow student of Yoshihito, who became
the Emperor Taishō. (Hawai'i State Archives.)*

though little is known of the young Hawaiian's relations with either of the Japanese royals.

Simply, it is worth noting that during Yoshihito's formative years, a two-way process was taking place with Japanese turning to the West for knowledge and others turning to Japan with the same goal. One wonders about the young crown prince's cognizance of the long-range significance of this process. What we do know is that he did not fare well in academics and was ultimately physically and mentally unfit for most of his reign. As emperor, he began to suffer a series of strokes in 1919. Finally, on November 25, 1921, the Imperial Family Council and the Privy Council instituted a regency to be assumed by Crown Prince Hirohito.

Despite the emperor's condition, there still was a tremendous vitalism to the Taishō reign years, which witnessed the results of developments underway since the years leading up to the Russo-Japanese War. The population grew from 43,847,000 in 1900 to 64,450,000 in 1930 (Japan Statistics Bureau 1986, 4). The agricultural population patterns remained relatively constant, but there was a marked increase in the growth of commercial and industrial cities like Tokyo, Yokohama, Nagoya, Osaka, and Kobe. This increase in the city population was partly the result of migration from the country to the city; it also was a result of the natural increase of the urban population.

Kazushi Ohkawa and Henry Rosovsky have suggested that beginning about 1906, and continuing until 1930, the new feature of accelerated growth of the modern economy entered into Japanese economic development.[4] For these scholars, "modern" equals "non-agriculture"; and "traditional" equals "agriculture." The gap that began to grow between these two sectors from about 1906 created a "differential structure" between them. Thereafter, there existed also a growing wage differential and productivity gap, and the share of modern industry (especially in terms of output) became much larger. In short, "The widening gap between the traditional and modern sectors perpetuated a deep cleavage in Japanese economic life." For one thing, two living standards developed, with important political, social, and economic consequences.

The reasons for the growing sectorial disparity in Taishō are complex. First, it appears that agriculture reached its maximum output owing to traditional small farm size, technology, and the village structure. For greater efficiency and income, farming would have had to change to large-scale agriculture; but this would have conflicted with Japanese social structure. Second, the economic consequences of imperialism for the countryside were significant. Since the colonies produced food, this competed with Japanese food production, thereby depressing Japanese agricultural prices—and the potential for larger numbers of consumers in Japan for the goods produced by the modern economy. Third, despite advances made by tenancy unions into the 1920s, the power of landlords remained strong and the tenancy problem critical. All of these factors had implications for Japan's continuing dependence on Western markets for her goods.

During World War I, exports expanded because of increased markets in areas where European competition was temporarily eliminated. Japan experienced inflation, partly as a result of the export boom and also because of inadequate governmental financial policy. In the aftermath of World War I, exports fell, and increasing inflation (caused in part by the dual economy) triggered falling prices. The Rice Riots of 1918 were a prime example of the "highly skewed distribution of economic power" that had become an ingrained characteristic of the Japanese economy (Yamamura 1974, 300). In addition to rural-urban disparities, the dual economic structure exacerbated the social tensions of industrialization—including dislocation and alienation. Between 1914 and 1917, the number of labor disputes accelerated, reaching a record-breaking 2,388 in 1919 (Duus 1968, 124–125). While the wealth and power of the *zaibatsu* and *zaikai* continued to grow, so too did the misery of factory life in the textile mills in late Taishō. One need only read the ballads in Hosoi Wakizō's *Jokō aishi (The Sad History of the Women Factory Hands)* to understand the extent of that misery (Silverberg 1990, 106).

As economic unrest and opposition to the governing classes continued to grow, public dissatisfaction had taken on new intensity as early as 1913 when the people's energy exploded with the first "movement to safeguard constitutionalism." In December 1912, the cabinet of Saionji Kimmochi, with backing from the Seiyūkai, refused to create two additional army divisions. Under severe army opposition the cabinet collapsed, to be succeeded by the third Katsura Tarō cabinet. On February 10, 1913, a mass meeting was held at the instigation of certain newspapers and political party leaders to "safeguard the constitution." Large-scale demonstrations followed, denouncing the high-handedness of the military and the excessive power of the *han* cliques. Katsura did resign, marking the first time mass pressure had brought down a cabinet (Minichiello 1984, 15). This growing popular demand for a voice in public affairs would culminate ultimately in insistent activity for electoral reform and universal manhood suffrage.

The ideas of Yoshino Sakuzō, a professor at Tokyo Imperial University, fed the escalating popular demand for political rights and participation.[5] In his university lectures, Yoshino stressed the three concepts of racialism, democracy, and socialism—and the coordinating element of freedom ran throughout them all (Rōyama 1951, 151–152, 160–164). His theory of democracy, *minponshugi*, contained two basic propositions, as set forth in his writings for *Chūō kōron (Central Review)*: broad political participatory rights to the people through universal suffrage; and true parliamentarianism, locating the base of politics in the Diet as the people's representative organ.[6]

"The people." The phrase was especially volatile during the years 1917–1920, a period of major upheaval at home and abroad. World War I and the tumultuous decisions made at Versailles, the Russian Revolution, the May Fourth Movement in China, widespread aspirations for the self-determination of peoples, the Rice Riots in Japan—these and other developments set concerned Japanese to thinking about future directions and questioning established norms. In this atmosphere, the Shinjinkai (New Men's Society) came into being in December 1918. An important precipitating event was the debate Yoshino Sakuzō had a month earlier on November 23 with the Rōninkai (Society of Rōnin), a right-wing group descended from the Kokuryūkai (Amur River Society) (Smith 1972, 43–44, 50–51). Against this group, Yoshino "debated for democracy," generating tremendous excitement among young students, laborers, and liberal intellectuals in general. The event provided the catalyst for some of the Debating Club members of Tokyo Imperial University, in concert with Yoshino, to found the Shinjinkai. Activities began in earnest in January 1919, followed by the founding of similar organizations in other universities.

The dual platform of the Shinjinkai was the "liberation of mankind" and the "rationalistic reform of present-day Japan." In the organization's earlier stages, intellectual diversity was its hallmark, with issues of its paper *Democracy* focusing on Lincoln, Rousseau, Marx, Lenin, the anarchist Kropotkin, and the Communist Rosa Luxemburg. The influence of English social democracy was strong, natural in light of the group's commitment to parliamentary democracy and pacifism, tendencies characteristic of twentieth-century English socialism. But by 1920, the Marxist prominence within the Shinjinkai was becoming evident, and English socialist influence all but disappeared from later versions of *Democracy*.

A student of Yoshino's during these years was Rōyama Masamichi, who later would become a professor of political science at Tokyo Imperial University and in the 1930s a founder of the Shōwa Kenkyūkai (Shōwa Research Association), the brain trust to Prince Konoe Fumimaro. I introduce him here for three reasons. First, he is representative of a significant split within the Shinjinkai. No Marxist, Rōyama broke with the group in 1920 and helped form the Shakai Shisō Sha (Association for Social Thought). Evolutionary social reform rather than revolution was the focus of this new association, which remained active throughout the 1920s. Rōyama saw no contradiction between a nondoctrinaire socialism and liberal democracy, and very likely might have agreed with a statement by the Fabian governor of Jamaica that "Socialism is merely individualism rationalised, organised, clothed, and in its right mind" (Catlin 1950, 651).

The second reason for mentioning Rōyama concerns Yoshino's advice to him for study abroad. Yoshino had been invited to China during the closing years of the Qing dynasty and later conducted research on the 1911 revolution from the perspective of global history. When Rōyama decided to join a summer 1919 student excursion to Siberia and northern Manchuria and consulted with Yoshino as to possible research there, the latter suggested two subjects: the problem of Chinese workers in Manchuria and the racial interaction of Japanese, Russians, and Chinese in northern Manchuria. Thereafter, Rōyama could not get the importance of the Manchurian problem out of his mind. Convinced that the Chinese movement for unity would have profound implications for Japan, he continued to study and write about Manchuria over the next decade; in the late 1920s, he also would represent Japan's position on Manchuria at meetings of the Institute of Pacific Relations (Taiheiyō Mondai Chōsakai; IPR), which had been founded in Honolulu in 1925.

The third reason for introducing Rōyama concerns his ideology. Like other Taishō intellectuals of a liberalistic bent, he basically supported Japan's involvement with the outside world, especially with Great Britain and the United States. Also like others, he realized that Japan's economic future was linked to the West and that a compromise had to be worked out with the West (one of the reasons for Japan's "cooperative policy" at the Washington Naval Conference and with China until the later 1920s). Second, he realized also that Japan had to be seen as "Western" and advanced, and especially that Western concerns about "democracy" had to be addressed. But when the atmosphere of Taishō *demokurashii* evaporated in the early 1930s, largely because Japan's economic ties with the West were threatened by worldwide depression and tariff barriers, how quickly did Rōyama and other Taishō intellectuals reject much of the Anglo-American international order for other options.

Still in 1920 Rōyama was envisioning Japan's problems at home and abroad as a race between reform and revolution. It was a year of tremendous social ferment in Japan. Mass gatherings of proletariat groups, formation of the National Universal Suffrage League, the Hachiman Ironworks strike involving 224,000 workers, and the celebration of Japan's first May Day were only symptoms of the widespread unrest that had been building since World War I. In the midst of increasing tenancy disputes, the agrarian movement organized in 1920 into the Japan Farmers' Union (Nihon Nōmin Kumiai). Also that year, the women's movement, which had been spurred on by the 1911 organization of author Hiratsuka Raichō, the Blue Stockings (Seitōsha), built up momentum in the New Women's Society (Shin Fujin Kyōkai). In 1922, the Leveling Society (Suiheisha) formed for the liberation of Japan's social outcasts, the *burakumin.* Also in 1922, the Japan Communist Party organized. Peter Duus has captured the mood of these years and their meaning well:

> The explosion of labor disputes in 1919–1920, the radicalization of students at imperial universities and other middle-class recruiting

grounds, the return of the old socialists to public prominence, the stirrings of discontent in rural areas—all suggested that the problem of social conflict was more profound than it had been at the beginning of the Taishō period, when constitutional palliatives or social policy meliorism seemed adequate to deal with it. (Duus 1982, 425)

Indeed the "consensual or integrative model of society" had come under attack and had begun to lose its persuasiveness as socioeconomic problems and activity heightened.

Many in Japan viewed these developments and the influx of foreign thought with alarm. As early as 1922, Justice Minister Ōki Enkichi and Home Minister Tokonami Takejirō introduced antisubversive legislation into a committee of the House of Peers. This "Law to Control Radical Social Movements" did pass the House of Peers, but the Seiyūkai cabinet did not push it through the lower house owing to a pervasive feeling of dissension both within and outside the Diet. The police used existing laws to suppress the Communist Party in July 1923. Then, in the wake of the Great Kantō Earthquake in September 1923, which killed more than 130,000 persons and destroyed close to 600,000 homes, police took advantage of an emergency ordinance to track down those they had marked as radicals—including the anarchist Ōsugi Sakae. There also was the widespread assassination of Koreans throughout Japan shortly after the quake, owing to rumors of an impending uprising by the Koreans within the country—thereby instigating the formation of self-appointed vigilante committees. Then, on December 27, 1923, the anarchist Namba Daisuke attempted to shoot the Regent Hirohito, on his way to the Diet. Namba had been outraged by the atrocities committed against Koreans, socialists, and labor leaders during the Kantō earthquake and saw himself as an advocate for social justice. The shot missed Hirohito, but Namba was executed.

Social criticism also found its way into the growing popular culture. In 1920, Director Minoru Murata (1894–1937), an early pioneer of the Japanese cinema, joined the new Shōchiku studios. His first production, *Souls on the Road (Rojō no reikon,* 1921), was one of the first outstanding Japanese films and one of the earliest to approach the subject of social criticism. Breaking with the tradition of filming historical dramas, it presented a modern story derived mainly from Western sources—the novel *Children on the Street* by Wilhelm Schmidtbonn and the play *Lower Depths* by Maxim Gorky. It also had a Western type of storytelling. In the first of two intertwined stories, a wealthy but prodigal son leaves home to study violin in Tokyo. When he finally returns home, he is penniless and brings with him his wife and sick child. The reception he receives from his father is extremely hostile. In the second story, two ex-convicts wander through the countryside, penniless and hungry, searching for a way to make a livelihood. Unlike the prodigal son, they find understanding, kindness, and help along the way, especially from an old caretaker at a peer's country villa. The two stories come together when the two wanderers, who set off full of hope and courage for the future, find the rejected son dead in the snow. *Souls on the Road* has become a classic in terms of its execution, its message, and its success in capturing the mood of a moment in Taishō.

Much of Taishō era culture was far less serious. Popular novels, magazines, newspapers, and the new media of radios, motion pictures, and gramophones spread "culture" into the countryside and to all levels of the intellectual spectrum. In many ways, Taishō culture resembled that of Europe during *la belle epoque* (the beautiful era), which flourished from the middle of the 1890s until the Great War. European affluence based on booming business formed the background to *la belle epoque*, but for many European rich and even middle class, "the beautiful era" was the paradise that was to be lost after 1914 (Hobsbawm 1987, 46, 55). In Japan, those who had risen economically during the Great War—the *narikin,* or nouveaux riches, were very much in evidence from 1918 on. Especially during the mid-1920s, the stage was set for a popular culture that the *modan gaaru* (modern girl) symbolized, and in which many different classes participated.

In the painting *Moga* (*Modern Girl*) as seen in the cover of this volume, artist Wada Seika depicts this popular new subject for artists and illustrators of her day. The dainty shoes and "Marcelled" hair were the Parisian rage, and the dangling earrings, opera pearls, fur-collared velvet sweater, and short skirt all represented the latest in imported fashions. The room furnishings also suggest the new, Western influences on the Japanese lifestyle.[7] As Miriam Silverberg has written, "To talk about the Modern Girl was to talk about Modernity. During the 1920s, her defenders, who saw her at the vanguard of a new imperial reign—the Shōwa era—were optimistic" (1991, 266). Her critics perceived her to be challenging traditions that served as a "repository of the past" (263–264); and those critics, as Mariko Tamanoi's essay shows, were often from the countryside.

In concluding this overview of Japan, 1900–1930, I focus on the interplay of national and international matters from 1924. In that year, the United States passed the Immigration Act that in effect banned Japanese from immigration into the United States until the passage of the so-called McCarran-Walter Act of 1952. This was a tremendous blow to the Japanese, exacerbating strained relations following the failure of the racial equality clause at Versailles. Tsurumi Yūsuke, critic and writer (and later politician) who had long been an admirer of the United States and President Woodrow Wilson, went on an extended lecture tour of the United States soon thereafter to plead

Japan's cause. I quote from his lecture of October 22, 1924, at length, for it captures well the mood of many concerned Japanese.

> To my Oriental mind the procedure of Congress is inexplicable. But my personal opinion is unimportant. The grave consequences flow from the fact that it is now very difficult for any Japanese liberal to convince the conservatives and the nationalists that the process by which the immigration bill was passed was not intended to serve notice on Japan that she need expect no more co-operation from America and that the ruthless pursuit of national interests without respect for the feelings of others is not a high and noble quality of patriotism. In saying this I am uttering no criticism of America. The grave consequences to which I refer will affect the social development of Japan far more than the destiny of America.

He also explained that it had been the timing of the Immigration Act that made it so difficult for Japanese to understand and accept:

> By a curious coincidence, the Immigration Act broke in upon the meditations of the Japanese people at a moment when the nation was bleeding from the wounds inflicted by the greatest calamity ever visited upon mankind by earthquake and fire. A tremendous amount of the national capital lay in utter ruin, more than two hundred thousand people had been killed by falling buildings or burnt to death in a raging whirlwind of fire, industries were prostrate, vast regions devastated, and national economy subjected to awful strains at every point. In the midst of our afflictions, the nation that had literally shaken open our gate, introduced us to the family of nations, sent Christian missionaries to teach us the ways of brotherhood and peace, and given us friendly counsel and advice at every turn, waived aside a long standing agreement with us and slammed its own gate shut in our face. It may be said that all this is mere sentiment. That is true. But sentiment is one of the great forces in the world with which statesmen must reckon. (Tsurumi Papers)

Tsurumi's interest in people-to-people diplomacy and in the development of the Pacific region had led him to help organize the Japan Committee of the Institute of Pacific Relations. The IPR was a research institute founded in Honolulu in 1925 by citizens from a number of Pacific countries, including the United States and Japan, to improve mutual relations among Pacific peoples. Prominent members of the various member organizations included Ray Lyman Wilbur, Henry R. Luce, Nitobe Inazō, Takagi Yasaka, George Sansom, Arnold Toynbee, and Hu Shih. Their early meetings dealt with U.S. immigration legislation, Japan's policy in China, and the Manchurian question (Takagi Papers; Tsurumi Papers). Also in 1925, there was in Japan the promulgation of the Universal Manhood Suffrage Law, which increased the electorate from approximately three million to 12.5 million by granting the vote to all male citizens over the age of twenty-five who had resided in their districts for one year and who were not indigent. This may well have been the central accomplishment of Taishō democracy.

About this same time, the Taishō emperor was becoming increasingly ill. As Hirohito took on almost all of his father's duties, we find two strands rejuvenating the late Taishō monarchy. One was the growing popularization of Hirohito—and along with that, the ongoing commercialization of the monarchy, which had begun in the late Meiji period. The second was a more militant imperial loyalism. This was evident in the passing of the Peace Preservation Law of 1925, which guaranteed heavy penalties for anyone plotting to overthrow the national polity *(kokutai)*. Stephen Large has summarized well the greater meaning of Taishō's death on December 25, 1926: "[It] provided the perfect ritual occasion to promote this idealized vision of the monarchy on a national scale. Manipulated to the very end, Taishō ironically did more in death to enhance the prestige of the monarchy than he had ever done in life" (1997, 88–89).

This defensive imperial loyalism would escalate over the next five years, beginning with the controversy over the so-called Tanaka Memorial. The memorial is said to be a 13,000-word secret petition that Prime Minister Tanaka Giichi presented to Emperor Hirohito on July 25, 1927. It outlined a program of economic penetration into Manchuria, China, and Mongolia—which in turn would prepare the way for Japan's subjection of Asia and Europe. Circumstantial and textual evidence strongly support the theory that the memorial is a forgery. Its impact was profound, however, for it "served as a potent means to mobilize international sentiment against Japan in the 1930s much as the 'Twenty-one Demands' had done two decades earlier" (Stephan 1973, 733). The Zhang Zuolin Incident of June 4, 1928, wherein members of the Japanese Kwantung Army blew up the Manchurian warlord Zhang's train as it was returning to Mukden, further heightened suspicion of Japan's motives in the international arena. This incident also foreshadowed the Manchurian Incident of 1931, the beginning of Japan's fifteen-year war.

THEMATIC TENSIONS

In *Imagined Communities*, a study into the origin and spread of nationalism, Benedict Anderson analyzes the concept of "official nationalisms" and their consequences for the rise of twentieth-century Asian and African nationalisms. Looking at the Anglicization of non-British in the British Empire, he posits that "Nothing more sharply underscores the fundamental contradiction of English official nationalism, i.e. the inner incompatibility of empire and nation" (Anderson 1983 and 1991, 93). Focusing a part of his study on Japan's "official nationalism," he concludes:

> It remains only to add that, as the empire expanded after 1900, Japanification ñ la [Thomas Babington] Macaulay was selfconsciously pursued as state policy. In the interwar years Koreans, Taiwanese and Manchurians, and, after the outbreak of the Pacific War, Burmese, Indonesians and Filipinos, were subjected to policies for which the European model was an established working practice. And just as in the British Empire, Japanified Koreans, Taiwanese or Burmese had their passages to the metropole absolutely barred. They might speak and read Japanese perfectly, but they would never preside over prefectures in Honshū or even be posted outside their zones of origin. (98–99)

The tension between nationalism and empire is a significant theme that weaves throughout the essays in this book, as do others. After extended discussions at the Maui Conference itself, as well as at additional meetings and through much correspondence, the authors have identified at least the following:

- National Identities/Ethnic Identities
- Empire/Ethnicity
- The Center/The Periphery
- *Naichi/Gaichi*
- Migrations of Peoples/Barriers
- The Urban/The Rural
- The Public/The Private
- High/Low Culture in Cultural Production and Dissemination

But there are other foci, including gender rights and responsibilities, new technologies, and institutional transformation.[8] The following summary of the authors' essays is an introduction to all of the above.

Geographical and Cultural Space

In her opening essay, Barbara Brooks shows how Koreans and Taiwanese, while in the ranks of the colonized in their own societies, "fell into grayer, often impermanent, categories, when displaced to other realms of the Japanese empire." Her examination centers on the implications of such status for Koreans on the lower rungs of Japanese ruling society in Manchuria before 1931. Joshua Fogel focuses on the Japanese communities that formed in the multicultural metropolises of Shanghai and Harbin during the late nineteenth and early twentieth centuries. His central question is "how the Japanese fit into Shanghai and Harbin, if indeed they tried." In the process of answering this larger question, he also explores the role these cities played for the Japanese preceding the concerted military invasion of the 1930s. In both of these essays, one sees the problems of Japanese fitting into non-Japanese spaces and vice versa.

Elaine Gerbert suggests the various tendencies that emerge when one considers the role of aesthetic space in Taishō-period literature: the "place-haunted" quality of the *shishōsetsu* and the enclosed space in the work of some writers during the early cosmopolitan phases of their careers. Her thesis is that during Taishō, "a certain cosmopolitan literariness was pursued in enclosed spaces, which functioned as incubators for the artistic imagination. . . ." Mariko Tamanoi's spatial dimension is the rural/urban dichotomy, and she centers her argument on the issue of gender in investigating rural modernity in early twentieth-century Japan. Her search for the notion of modernity is in the discursive space of village newspapers.

Julia Adeney Thomas begins her essay with the statement that "Modern nationhood has been portrayed as profoundly unnatural." In the early twentieth century, however, some nations, including Japan, evoked the close tie between nature and nationhood. She argues that in Japan, this close tie may be understood as a "reaction against Meiji conceptions of nature and the form of semimodernity they represented." Her intriguing example is that of shrine space. Helen Hardacre closes this section with an examination of spiritualism in early twentieth-century Japan. Her analysis of a Japanese intellectual who dabbled in spiritualism, Asano Wasaburō, reveals one responsible for a "rapprochement between the spiritualism of bourgeois salons and Japan's indigenous shamanic tradition." Further, her account of Asano's relationship with Ōmotokyō is suggestive concerning the connection between the learned and the "new religions" in late twentieth-century Japan.

Cosmopolitanism and National Identity

Exploring the complex relationship of citizenship, national identity, and imperialism, Tessa Morris-Suzuki analyzes the tensions of identity through the indigenous people of southern Sakhalin (Karafuto). Her penetrating analysis concludes with suggestions concerning the problem of "Japanese-ness" today: "To meet the challenges of the future, . . . it may first be necessary to give those many groups who form (and have always formed) 'the Japanese' a choice of pasts." Kevin Doak's essay dovetails well with that of Morris-Suzuki. He explores the evolution of the ethnic nationalist challenge. Especially, his analysis of "Ethnic Nationalism at the Height of Taishō Democracy, 1920–1930" is strongly suggestive of Japan's problems in early Shōwa and thereafter.

The other three writers in this section individually examine examples of cultural nationalism—one through literature, the second through architecture, and the third by way of song. Roy Starrs shows how Meiji Japanese recognized early on the "nation-building function" of the Western novel, seeing it as a standard feature of the modern nation state. Surveying Japanese literature over the decades from late to Meiji to early Shōwa, Starrs sees a "marked decline in writers' interest in or commitment to Meiji-style nation-building—at least, in strictly political terms." The Bunriha, the group of young architects who launched Japan's first modernist architectural movement in 1922, is the focus of Jonathan Reynolds' article. He analyzes this "Secessionist Architectural Group's" treatment of history in their writings and then their efforts to synthesize a new identity through architectural design. Finally, Christine Yano examines popular representations of nationhood found in songs from Taishō into the early 1930s. Her textual analysis of these songs provides a unique lens through which to observe Taishō cultural production and consumption.

Diversity, Autonomy, and Integration

The generic foci of Jeffrey Hanes' essay are again the processes of cultural production and cultural consumption. In 1920, the social scientist Ōbayashi Sōshi, began a comprehensive survey of "popular recreation" in Osaka, releasing his 380-page study in 1922. Hanes retraces the "space" of Ōbayashi's survey, providing colorful insights into the "media culture" of Taishō Osaka—and "what sells," and who gets taken by the process. The role and character of the modern sector of business appear again in Lonny Carlile's study of the *zaikai*'s evolution over the period 1900–1930, an evolution that showed significant institutional transformation. In this research on the modes and dynamics of supra-industrial interest representation, Carlile argues that the *zaikai* had little reason to "buy into" Taishō party platforms, ultimately helping to "undermine the ability of established political parties to forge lasting social coalitions and thereby take firmer root in the political order."

Sheldon Garon's essay on savings and frugality campaigns expands on some of the themes of the previous two essays. He contends that "Taishō democracy" and "Taishō culture" should not be equated merely with the liberation of society from state management. Using vivid savings and frugality campaign posters, Garon shows the continuing Meiji influence of "character-building," as well as the ongoing tension between public and private.

The last two essays in this section exemplify well the themes of diversity, autonomy, and integration. E. Patricia Tsurumi's essay focuses on a famous aspect of the *ana-boru* debate between champions of anarcho-syndicalism and advocates of Marxian socialism—the dispute between the humanist feminist Yamakawa Kikue on the Marxian socialist side and gynocentrist Takamure Itsue in the anarchist camp, which occurred mainly during 1928. Her analysis concludes with the meaning of the debate for later generations of Japanese feminists—as well as the global significance of the ideas of Takamure and Yamakawa today.

The final essay in this volume takes us once again to the relationship between *naichi* (the homeland) and *gaichi* (the overseas lands). Michael Robinson recasts the story of Korean radio within the colonial experience. He shows how radio was part of a "complicated colonial hegemony constructed of both physical coercion and cultural/political attraction." The challenge for the Japanese was to spread the new medium of radio as a tool for acculturating Koreans to Japanese values; but in the end, "they inadvertently created a space for Korean cultural construction that undermined their original intent."

As a whole, these essays have their basis in original, new research, and open up alternative avenues of exploration for the twentieth century. Even though our cutoff point has been 1930, the authors are in step with the latest scholarship in Japanese studies, which treats the twentieth century as a continuous historical entity. If, as Sheldon Garon contends in his "Rethinking Modernization and Modernity in Japanese History," the imperative "is to understand more fully the historical forces that made Japan what it is today" (Garon 1994), then this group of studies on "Japan's Competing Modernities" in the early twentieth century may shed light on some of the most challenging questions for her history in the whole century.

NOTES

The editor expresses special appreciation to the two anonymous readers of this manuscript for their valuable suggestions and insights.

1. An outstanding example is Gordon 1991.
2. On September 9, 1905, the Milan newspaper *Il Secolo* ran the following account of the Hibiya uprising: "REVOLUTION IN JAPAN. Against the peace —Sensational dispatches—Attack on British legation—State of siege confirmed. Crowd, infuriated by conditions of peace with Russia, turns to violence. Japanese journalists, all belonging to ancient samurai families, meet the crowd in front of the editorial offices, sword in hand" (Mondadori 1978).
3. It is our regret that owing to illness, Professor Stephen S. Large could not participate in this project. He has, however, remained in contact with the editor, sharing his ideas and ongoing research on Taishō the person, as well as the greater meaning of the reign years.
4. For this section, I have drawn on Ohkawa and Rosovsky 1965, 77–81; the essays by Napier 1982 and Waswo 1982; and the insightful suggestions of an anonymous reader.

5. The attention to Yoshino Sakuzō and his contributions to Japanese political thought continues to this day. Two recent examples are Mitani 1995 and the *Yoshino Sakuzō zenshū*, 1995–1997.

6. As Tetsuo Najita has pointed out, there was an important shift in Yoshino's view of democracy following his study tour of Europe (1910–1913), a shift from an earlier, more paternalistic view of government to one greatly supportive of popular participation. The change involved a revision of his phrase for democracy from *minshushugi* (government centered on the people) to *minponshugi* (government based on the people) (Najita 1974, 39).

7. The Honolulu Academy of Arts, which houses this painting, has learned that the model was Ueda Terue, the wife of Ueda Minoru, a professor of astronomy at Kyoto Imperial University. My appreciation to former curator Annie Van Assche at the Honolulu Academy.

8. My thanks to Professor Theodore Bestor for his thoughts on institutional transformation.

REFERENCES

Anderson, Benedict. 1983, 1991. *Imagined Communities: Reflections on the Origins and Spread of Nationalism.* London: Verso.

Catlin, George. 1950. *A History of the Political Philosophers.* British ed. London.

Duus, Peter. 1968. *Party Rivalry and Political Change in Taishō Japan.* Cambridge: Harvard University Press.

———. 1982. "Liberal Intellectuals and Social Conflict in Taishō Japan." In *Conflict in Modern Japanese History: The Neglected Tradition,* edited by Tetsuo Najita and J. Victor Koschmann, 412–440. Princeton: Princeton University Press.

———. 1983. "The Takeoff Point of Japanese Imperialism." In *Japan Examined: Perspectives on Modern Japanese History,* edited by Harry Wray and Hilary Conroy, 153–157. Honolulu: University of Hawai'i Press.

———. 1984. "Economic Dimensions of Meiji Imperialism: The Case of Korea, 1895–1910." In *The Japanese Colonial Empire, 1895–1945,* edited by Ramon H. Myers and Mark R. Peattie, 128–171. Princeton: Princeton University Press.

Garon, Sheldon. 1994. "Rethinking Modernization and Modernity in Japanese History: A Focus on State-Security Relations." *Journal of Asian Studies* 53.2:346–366.

Gordon, Andrew. 1991. *Labor and Imperial Democracy in Pre-war Japan.* Berkeley: University of California Press.

Hobsbawm, E. 1987. *The Age of Empire, 1875–1914.* New York: Pantheon Books.

Jansen, Marius B. 1975. *Japan and China: From War to Peace, 1894–1972.* Chicago: Rand McNally College Publishing Co.

Japan Statistics Bureau, Management and Coordination Agency. 1986. "Population of Japan."

Large, Stephen S. 1992. *Emperor Hirohito & Shōwa Japan: A Political Biography.* London: Routledge.

———. 1997. *Emperors of the Rising Sun: Three Biographies.* Kodansha.

Minichiello, Sharon A. 1981. "Changing Japanese Perceptions of Democracy." Working paper, Japan Forum, Harvard University (April 30).

———. 1984. *Retreat from Reform: Patterns of Political Behavior in Interwar Japan.* Honolulu: University of Hawai'i Press.

Mitani Taichirō. 1995. *Taishō demokurashii ron: Yoshino Sakuzō no jidai.* New ed. Tokyo Daigaku Shuppankai.

Mondadori, Arnoldo, ed. 1978. *La Belle Époque: Fifteen Euphoric Years of European History.* New York: William Morrow.

Najita, Tetsuo. 1974. "Some Reflections on Idealism in the Political Thought of Yoshino Sakuzō." In *Japan in Crisis: Essays on Taishō Democracy,* edited by Bernard S. Silberman and H. D. Harootunian, 29–66. Princeton: Princeton University Press.

———. 1993 "Presidential Address: Reflections on Modernity and Modernization." *Journal of Asian Studies* 52.4:845–853.

———. 1994. "Commoner Economic Thought and Practice in Modern Japan: Legacies for Japanese Democracy." Working paper, Burns Chair Lecture Series, University of Hawai'i at Mānoa (April 21).

Najita, Tetsuo, and J. Victor Koschmann, eds. 1982. *Conflict in Modern Japanese History: The Neglected Tradition.* Princeton: Princeton University Press.

Napier, Ron. 1982. "The Transformation of the Japanese Labor Market, 1914–1937." In *Conflict in Modern Japanese History: The Neglected Tradition,* edited by Tetsuo Najita and J. Victor Koschmann, 342–365. Princeton: Princeton University Press.

Ohkawa Kazushi and Henry Rosovsky. 1965. "A Century of Japanese Economic Growth." In *The State and Economic Enterprise in Japan,* edited by William W. Lockwood, 47–92. Princeton: Princeton University Press.

Quigg, Agnes. 1988. "Kalākaua's Hawaiian Studies Abroad Program." *Hawaiian Journal of History* 22:170–207.

Rimer, J. Thomas, ed. 1990. *Culture and Identity: Japanese Intellectuals During the Interwar Years.* Princeton: Princeton University Press.

Rōyama Masamichi. 1951. "Waga shi Yoshino Sakuzō sensei." In *Waga shi o kataru,* edited by Shakai Shisō Kenkyūkai, 151–174. Shakai Shisō Kenkyūkai Shuppanbu.

Silberman, Bernard S., and H. D. Harootunian, eds. 1974. *Japan in Crisis: Essays on Taishō Democracy.* Princeton: Princeton University Press.

Silverberg, Miriam. 1990. *Changing Song: The Marxist Manifestos of Nakano Shigeharu.* Princeton: Princeton University Press.

———. 1991. "The Modern Girl as Militant." In *Recreating Japanese Women,*

1600–1945, edited by Gail Lee Bernstein, 239–266. Berkeley: University of California Press.

Smith, Henry Dewitt, II. 1972. *Japan's First Student Radicals.* Cambridge: Harvard University Press.

Stephan, John J. 1973. "The Tanaka Memorial (1927): Authentic or Spurious?" *Modern Asian Studies* 7.4:733–745.

Takagi Yasaka. Takagi Yasaka Papers. University of Tokyo.

Tsurumi Yūsuke. Tsurumi Yūsuke Papers. National Diet Library.

Waswo, Ann. 1982. "In Search of Equity: Japanese Tenant Unions in the 1920s." In *Conflict in Modern Japanese History: The Neglected Tradition,* edited by Tetsuo Najita and J. Victor Koschmann, 366–411. Princeton: Princeton University Press.

Yamamura, Kozo. 1974. "The Japanese Economy, 1911–1930: Concentration, Conflicts, Crises." In *Japan in Crisis: Essays on Taishō Democracy,* edited by Bernard S. Silberman and H. D. Harootunian, 299–328. Princeton: Princeton University Press.

Yoshino Sakuzō. 1995–1997. *Yoshino Sakuzō zenshū.* Edited by Matsuo Takayoshi, Mitani Taichirō, and Iida Taizō. 16 vols. Iwanami Shoten.

❯❯ I ❮❮

Geographical and Cultural Space

❧ 1 ❧

Peopling the Japanese Empire: The Koreans in Manchuria and the Rhetoric of Inclusion

BARBARA J. BROOKS

In Dunhua, Jilin province, in China's northeast, on May 1, 1930, a demonstration by a band of Chinese and Korean leftists—suspected Communists—escalated into violence. In retaliation, Chinese authorities under the command of the warlord Zhang Xueliang sent in troops that exceeded their mission, brutally attacking local Korean residents. Innocent farming families scattered to the hills in terror of torture and atrocity while Chinese soldiers ransacked their homes for possessions and livestock. The Chinese took into custody more than two hundred Koreans; in late August the majority were released. On September 5, however, fifteen were executed outside the walls of the city. Most of these men headed families, indicating their settled agricultural life, and among them some were known not to have participated in the violence (Japanese Foreign Ministry Archives [hereafter JFMA], A.6.1.5.6).

At this juncture, Consul General Ishii Itarō, the Japanese official most clearly responsible for the welfare of the Korean community in Jilin province, cabled his superior in Tokyo, Foreign Minister Shidehara Kijūrō, to request permission to lodge a formal protest with the Chinese authorities: "Although as yet Japan has taken no public action regarding the arrest and detention of the Koreans, now it is time to question the Chinese authorities about the situation and simultaneously lodge a protest that makes clear our policy regarding Koreans (*Chōsenjin ni taisuru waga hō no tatemae*)." By policy Ishii referred to Japan's official position that denied Korean (and other colonial) individuals the right to change citizenship, insisting that ethnic Koreans were organically Japanese subjects. Responding, Shidehara forbade such action: "It cannot be permitted that such protest of this incident influence the good offices of China in apprehending (*torishimari*) Communist Koreans"

25

(JFMA, A.6.1.5.6). In other words, Shidehara insisted that in this case, his subordinate look the other way while these Japanese subjects were mistreated. He did not, however, indicate any desire for policy change, despite the fact that Ishii and other Japanese consuls in Manchuria had repeatedly recommended that Japan's position be changed to permit Koreans to naturalize as Chinese. Rather, Shidehara seemed to endorse a shifting application of the Japanese position, encouraging Ishii to read between the lines the difference between Japanese intention (*honne*) and policy (*tatemae*).

This incident and the responses are examples of a pattern of conflicting Japanese actions and views concerning the presence of large numbers of Koreans in Manchuria and, by extension, concerning Korean subjects in the whole of the Japanese empire. In path-breaking analyses of European colonial societies, Ann Stoler (1989, 1992) has suggested the contours of analogous ambivalence on the part of ruling colonials toward populations that fell within what she has termed "contradictory colonial locations." Such marginal categories lay at the porous boundaries between colonial and colonized and were subject to "a frequently shifting set of criteria that allowed them privilege at certain historical moments and pointedly excluded them at others" (Stoler 1989, 154–155). Korean and Taiwanese people, while in the ranks of the colonized in their own societies, fell into grayer, often impermanent, categories when displaced to other realms of the Japanese empire.[1] What were the implications of such status for Korean people on the lower rungs of *Japanese* ruling society in Manchuria before 1931? Here, I will offer not an opposing but an alternative view to the current readings of the more dichotomous discourse of race emerging in pre-1945 Japan (Duus 1995; Weiner 1994, 1995). Just as the debate on the priorities of race and class continues today, I believe scholars of Japan have to bear in mind multiple discourses in the empire concerning "Japaneseness" and "Other." The situation of informal empire in Manchuria before 1931 provides a particularly rich site for investigation as a peripheral realm where Japanese colonial agents were subject to an extreme example of what Stoler terms "the allusive, incomplete nature of colonial knowledge" (Stoler 1992, 154). This essay will provide an overview of Japan's presence in Manchuria followed by sections analyzing three different views of Koreans: as "problems" or potential threats to the colonial order; as compatriots; and finally, as Japanese citizens who deserved the right to naturalize as Chinese citizens.

JAPANESE RIGHTS AND AGENTS
IN MANCHURIA, 1905–1931

As one of the spoils of the Sino-Japanese War, Japan joined the ranks of the Great Powers and won the privileges of extraterritoriality in China. Significantly, the Treaty of Shimonoseki even extended the joint system of informal empire in China by claiming foreign rights to navigate the Yangzi and to manufacture in treaty port cities (Beasley 1987, 60–68). Over the next few decades, but particularly with the Twenty-one Demands of 1915, Japan further enlarged the rights and privileges of imperialism in China and more specifically in Manchuria: despite continuing dispute, Japan insisted on its rights to consular police and stationed them in areas of Manchuria distant from the rail corridor; Japanese consuls retained rights of review and intervention into legal cases involving Japanese nationals in such areas; Japanese nationals came to hold complicated rights to lease land, run businesses, travel, and reside in areas outside the official concession areas of Manchuria.

Recent scholarship on treaty-port society in China "from the ground up" has begun to illuminate its diversity and lack of cohesion under any one central or national authority. Eileen P. Scully has described the futile efforts of American officialdom to impose law and order on Shanghai's "subterranean and illicit China market," composed of "renegade lawyers, notorious prostitutes, sharks, swindlers and gamblers" whose flourishing commercial activities were blocking the development of legitimate American trade (Scully 1995, 63–65). The Japanese Foreign Ministry maintained its largest consular force in the world to nominally manage Japanese communities in China's treaty port cities, but administrative authority was diffuse, and Foreign Ministry outposts often struggled with smaller budgets, less manpower, and more tenuous local connections than other Japanese (Peattie 1989; Brooks forthcoming). China under extraterritoriality was a borderlands society where competing jurisdictions of authority—Chinese government one among them—clashed, and power and wealth that were acquired both legitimately and illegitimately prevailed. Manchuria, where the Japanese presence was numerically greatest and most geographically extensive, epitomized these conditions.

In the aftermath of the Russo-Japanese War, Japan secured a Manchurian territorial base in the form of the leased territory of the Kantōshū, thirteen hundred square miles at the tip of southern Manchuria; railway rights in southern Manchuria; and the right to garrison the rail corridor between Port Arthur and Changchun. In 1909 Japan won similar rights along the Andong-Fengtian (Mukden) railway and corridor that linked the South Manchurian network to Korea. To administer these rights, a "four-headed" Japanese administration evolved that included the colonial government of the Kantōshū, the South Manchurian Railway, the Kantō (Kwantung) Army, and the Foreign Ministry's consular network. Many have pointed out that a fifth head should be included in this list: After the Japanese annexation of Korea in 1910, the colonial government of Korea (Chōsen Sōtokufu) was an important actor in Manchurian and Chinese affairs because of Korean emigration to the region as well as the Sino-Japanese disputes and complications along the Korean-Chinese border.[2] As I shall explain, the diversity of Japan's institutions and authorities in Manchuria, as well as its disparate categories of residents, were central factors in shaping colonial discourses that were "derived from fragmented knowledge as well as from competing hierarchies of credibility" (Stoler 1992, 153).

In the effort to better understand opposing views regarding "the Korean problem," this essay focuses on the statements and opinions of Japanese diplomats prior to the Manchurian Incident of 1931, when the Kantō Army moved to occupy Manchuria. The 1920s was a period of political and social change in Manchuria on a number of fronts, but perhaps the dominant tension involved the conflicting moves by Chinese and Japanese military men to consolidate control for their sides. Korean settlers in Manchuria were often caught in the middle and fell victims to escalating violence. The Foreign Ministry, as Beasley phrased it, had "a proprietorial interest in the treaty port system" (Beasley 1987, 197). For this reason and because of consular responsibilities as caretakers for the Korean communities in Manchuria, diplomats on the scene often found themselves at odds with the prevailing discourses concerning Koreans in Manchuria that served to strengthen Japan's justification for imperial expansion.

THE KOREAN PROBLEM

The period of the Japanese occupation of Korea witnessed an unprecedented diaspora of Koreans—to Manchuria, Japan proper, Sakhalin, the Siberian maritime provinces, and the north of China. By 1944 up to 11.6 percent of Koreans resided outside of Korea with approximately two million in China's northeast (Cumings 1981, 54). Unquestionably changes brought on by the Japanese colonial regime in Korea spurred on the increasing out-migration from rural villages. In 1931 the eminent Japanese social scientist Amano Motonosuke, famous for his village studies in China, analyzed the primary cause of Korean migration to be the impoverishment of farmers resulting from the introduction of capitalist practices, including laws enforcing ownership of land, registration of uncultivated or public terrain, and increasing concentration of ownership in the hands of large landlords and Japanese development companies such as the Oriental Development Company (quoted in Young 1932, 59–60). In the late 1920s, as Japan sought to close off the passage by ship from Pusan of poor Koreans seeking labor in the metropole, the Korean colonial government increasingly came to rely on northward migration to help solve socioeconomic distress, and Koreans from the south became more numerous in Manchuria (Usui 1984, 20).

This exodus of Koreans seeking opportunities in other realms of the Japanese empire was the root cause of the problems concerning Koreans discussed so widely by Japanese officials and the media. The catchphrases employed across the empire to express concerns regarding Koreans are striking for their uniformity, even if the "colonial lexicons were unevenly appropriated" by the empire's agents on the ground (Stoler 1992, 183).

During the nineteenth century Manchu restrictions on migration northward relaxed and Korean and Chinese migration into the Manchurian region increased. In the 1880s both the Korean and Chinese governments took measures to open up the border region on the Manchurian side to cultivation and settlement by Korean farmers forced to leave their villages because of increasing pressures on their land. Still, by 1904 the estimated Korean population in Manchuria was 78,000 (Kim 1992, 37).[3] Conservative Foreign Ministry estimates of the Korean population indicate: for 1912, 238,403; for 1920, 488,656; for 1925, 513,973; and for 1931, 629,000. The Foreign Ministry spokesman issuing these figures in 1932 added that they did not include large numbers of Koreans living in the interior; "one million at least" was his total figure for Koreans in Manchuria and Mongolia in 1931 (Young 1932, 253).

Up to half of the Korean population in Manchuria lived north of the Tumen River in the southeast corner of Jilin province, an area known as Jiandao (Kantō in Japanese, today known as Yanbian in Chinese). This borderlands region on the edges of China, Korea, and Russia was not considered part of the south Manchurian region, where after 1905 Japanese enjoyed a wider range of rights and privileges than in other areas of China proper. Nevertheless, as a place where up to 80 percent of the population was Korean, Japan claimed the right to station consular police in scattered outposts *(hashutsujo)* in the area to "protect" the community. These police numbered at least four hundred on the eve of the Manchurian Incident.

The "Jiandao problem" *(Kantō mondai)* was perhaps the most outstanding diplomatic issue between China and Japan until 1931. A series of Sino-Japanese treaties regarding Jiandao indicate the continuing controversy between both governments regarding the Koreans who lived there. In 1909, the Japanese seemed to concede limited Chinese jurisdiction over Korean residents; in 1915 the Twenty-one Demands reversed this and insisted on their status as Japanese with the full range of new rights and privileges then enumerated; and in 1925 the Mitsuya Agreement laid out conditions under which both Japanese and Chinese authorities would pursue and apprehend Korean partisans.

In a new study of the disputes over Jiandao and the instability of Japanese policy there, Li Sun-han (I Sunhan) has argued that understanding these conflicts can restore to us the significance of Korea in the dynamics of East Asian international relations in the period of the Japanese empire. Korea's importance as a nonstate actor while under Japanese occupation has been neglected because of fixed attention to the "state-to-state" actors of China and Japan (Li 1991, 1–3, 314–320). Moriyama Shigenori has argued that although in 1909 the Qing government (with international backing) forced Japan to acquiesce to a border agreement that placed Jiandao in China, this outcome strengthened Japanese resolves to obtain more legitimate control over Korea through annexation, which occurred in 1910 (Moriyama 1985, 69–94). Kitaoka Shin'ichi has outlined the post-1911 plans by the Colonial Bureau (Takushoku Kyoku) and South Manchurian Railway head Gotō Shimpei to create a Korean-Manchurian joint colony (Kitaoka 1978, 56–57, 115–117). Clearly Japanese designs on Manchuria cannot easily be separated from plans and policies for Korea and Korean emigrants throughout the prewar period. The territorial and administrative discourse about the "Korean problem" helped shape the evolving form of the Japanese empire itself: after 1931, Japanese military authorities finally chose to separate Manchukuo from Japan's colonial territories and administration (and the administrative threat, perhaps, of the Chōsen Sōtokufu) in the transition from treaty-port domination in Manchuria to Kantō Army rule through puppet government (Brooks forthcoming; Matsusaka 1996).

Especially after the March 1919 uprising in the Korean colony, official and popular parlance reflected a discourse of the ruler's fear of the colonized. The phrase that echoed from periphery to metropole was *futei Senjin,* translated as "recalcitrant Koreans" (Lee 1967) or "Korean malcontents" (Weiner 1994, 71–73). In the 1920s, successive meetings of Japanese consuls working in the Manchurian region *(ryōji kaigi)* focused on Korean problems, but the issues regarding *futei Senjin* were most prominent (JFMA, M 2.3.0.1–2). A 1924 report of the Korean military command categorized recalcitrant Koreans into five types: nationalists; Communists; professionals, that is, bandits or "horse thieves" who simply used the rhetoric of partisanship; fellow travelers; and "coerced" recalcitrants, that is, those who were forced to join because of threats to their families and livelihood from more revolutionary or criminal elements (Chōsen Shireibu 1924, 15–17). All these varieties of recalcitrant Koreans flourished primarily in the borderlands region of Manchuria.

On the popular level, a discourse concerning *futei Senjin* as "Koreans gone bad" was implicitly opposed to one about the good, poor, primarily agricultural Koreans in the empire. In 1920 a Japanese journalist blamed the Chōsen Sōtokufu for misleading poor Korean farmers into believing they could find a land of opportunity for wet-rice cultivation in Manchuria when in fact many were at the mercy of "crafty and unscrupulous" Chinese landlords, lacked capital to begin farms, and had no food or even warm clothes in the cold winters. Their impoverished circumstances led them to a "policy of desperation": falling in with others in plots against the Japanese authorities ("Senjin no Manshū ijū" 1920, 34–37). In 1919, however, domestic and colonial media attention focused on the threat of *futei Senjin* in the wake of the massive uprising against Japanese authorities in Korea, and the next several years featured stories of the Chōsen Sōtokufu's punitive raids (*tōbatsu*) across the border into the Jiandao region in pursuit of Korean partisans. In October 1919, after a motley band of Koreans and Chinese attacked a consulate branch office in the Manchurian town of Hunchun, killing one consular police officer and wounding others, the Sōtokufu sent larger numbers of troops northward to punish the offenders (*Gendaishi shiryō* 1972, 28:14–138). The resulting international furor over the expedition's violation of China's sovereign territory and its damages to Chinese life and property prompted more domestic claims regarding the threats of *futei Senjin* and the fact that among the Jiandao Koreans "the good people" (*ryōmin*) praised the actions of the Japanese soldiers and wished for them to stay (750).

Domestic Japanese citizens assimilated this discourse concerning recalcitrant Koreans with telling results in the wake of the September 1923 earthquake. Michael Weiner has also pointed to the complicity of prominent former Sōtokufu officials, including Home Ministers Mizuno Rentarō and Gotō Shimpei, who returned to duties in the metropole prior to the earthquake and helped disseminate false rumors of Korean sabotage in its aftermath (Weiner 1994, 85–86). Hysteria over reports in the media of the activities of *futei Senjin* motivated vigilante groups (*jikeidan*) in many parts of Japan to terrorize, beat, and kill Korean residents by the thousands. The media term for the campaigns, "Korean hunts" (*Senjin-gari*), was even reminiscent of those describing the expeditions of the Korean colonial government in Manchuria. In this way, an official discourse of fear and hatred, embodied in the government records about the "Korean problem" of *futei Senjin*, spread from the Korean colony, where discrimination against Koreans was strongest, to the popular language of people throughout the empire.

KOREANS AS COMPATRIOTS

While the 1920s witnessed an increasing discourse of fear and prejudice toward Koreans, there was no lessening in the competing Japanese discourse of inclusion. Even before annexation, a specific strand of pan-Asian thinking and scholarship asserted the common ancestry and many common features of Japanese and Koreans through examination of cultural attributes such as geographical place names, structural similarities of the two languages, and shared historical experiences. This type of view, for example, saw the annexation of Korea in 1910 as the return of a "branch family" to the "main family" (Kita 1910, 77–79; Duus 1995, 413–423). Such scholarly efforts in linguistics and classic textual study continued through the 1920s (Kanazawa 1929) and contributed to a popular Japanese discourse of cultural similarity regarding Koreans that held particular meaning in the context of Manchuria.

In Manchuria, the outstanding and widely recognized affinity of Korean and Japanese culture was wet-rice agriculture. The anthropologist Emiko Ohnuki-Tierney has studied the contemporary implications of rice agriculture for Japanese "self-identity," but its colonial-era identification with Korean culture as well may be powerfully suggestive of a more embracing "self-identity" (Ohnuki-Tierney 1993; also Duus 1995, 270–278). Japanese officials reported that 90 percent of Korean occupations in Manchuria were agricultural, and of these, 30 percent were in their field of special talent (*tokui*), wet-rice farming (Chōsen Sōtokufu Naimukyoku 1923, 123; 1927, 486): some 51,106 hectares in all of Manchuria in 1923 (Chōsen Sōtokufu Naimukyoku 1923, 140). Other sources cite a nearly threefold increase in rice production in Manchuria between 1915 and 1930 (Young 1932, 256). In 1921 a Fengtian consul general wrote:

> Wet-rice cultivation is a native-born skill for the Korean farmer. Their methods are natural and rudimentary either for large-scale or individual farming. They are satisfied to work every hectare, no matter how poor the land may seem. Moreover, in no time at all they transform even the vacant prairie lots onto which they move into rice paddies, reaping unimaginable harvests from such wild, abandoned, weed-infested land. (Akatsuka 1921, 241)

Japanese officials stressed that in the 1860s Korean settlers had first brought this unrivaled skill, which claimed unused land, to the north of China and documented the growth of rice paddies from that time (Chōsen Sōtokufu Naimukyoku 1927, 510–512). While Japanese writers often hoped for more Japanese immigration to expand wet-rice cultivation, it was recognized that almost all of this "Japanese" contribution to life in Manchuria was in Korean hands. In 1922 Hori Isamu, the head of the Fengtian branch of the Oriental Development Company, emphasized the future importance of Manchurian wet-rice cultivation to solve Japan's domestic shortage of rice production ("Manshū no suiden" 1922, 22–24). Indeed, by 1930 Japan imported about 50 percent of the rice grown in Manchuria (Young 1932, 256).

Chinese farmers were said to have welcomed Korean settlers for their wet-rice cultivating techniques until they, too, began to mimic this style of farming and sometimes demand the return of their land. In fact, Korean encroachment on these lands was often very complicated, especially the patterns of land-leasing from Chinese landlords. Korean settlers also built irrigation networks that deprived neighboring Chinese farmers of water, culminating in communal conflicts over land and water rights that grew worse after 1927 (Chōsen Sōtokufu Keimukyoku 1930, 157–227). The most notorious case was the Wanbaoshan Incident of the summer of 1931, which resulted in widespread rioting inside Korea against resident Chinese, causing injury, loss of life and property to that ethnic minority. Because only Chinese citizens could own land, a long-standing dispute between China and Japan over the rights of Korean settlers to naturalize simmered throughout the 1920s.

From at least the beginning of Japan's Korean protectorate the Japanese government began to make clear its position on Korean citizenship. In the wake of changes in Seoul, the Russian legation recalled one of its ethnic Korean officials who had served as official interpreter. This man owned land in the vicinity of the new Government General that was confiscated along with other Korean-held land by the Japanese army for its use. Russian officials protested this action and demanded the return of the land. In 1907, the acting consul general denied the request, insisting that "a Korean subject naturalized in any foreign state without permission of the Korean government is not recognized by the latter as a foreigner." The Russian consul-general persisted, insisting that the individual in question was born and grew up in Russia; his parents were naturalized. The Japanese response elaborated (JFMA, 8.3.8.7.19):

> [A] state has the perfect right of deciding whether or not its subjects shall lose their original nationality when they have acquired citizenship in a foreign country. It is true that no law or ordinance has yet been established in Korea regulating naturalization of the Korean subjects in other states, but it may be observed that the inherent authority of a government can in no wise be affected by non-existence of law or ordinance governing such matters. . . . As his parents' government's permission has neither been applied for or given, it naturally follows that they still remain Korean subjects so far as the authority of the Korean Government extends.

After annexation, officials extended the same logic to many cases that claimed ethnic Koreans as Japanese subjects, even if their parents or grandparents had left Korea during Yi-dynasty times. In criminal cases on Chinese soil, records demonstrate Japanese refusals to recognize even the official papers of ethnic Koreans claiming Chinese or Russian citizenship. In one case in Shanghai in 1932, Legation Minister Shigemitsu Mamoru himself laid out the complicated case for the Japanese citizenship of an ethnic Korean criminal with a provenance far removed from Korean soil (JFMA, Z 1.3.0.11). The individual in question was the radical Yun Bong-gil, who carried out the infamous assassination attempt of April 29, 1932, when a bomb exploded on the dais at a military review in Hongkew Park. Shigemitsu lost his leg in this incident. Yun, who was born in Jiandao, was executed by the Japanese military on December 19. Japanese consular officials, attempting to bring order to treaty-port society, could thus apply this official position to prevent Korean and Taiwanese suspects from claiming alternate nationalities, a major "weapon of resistance" to legal adjudication (Scully 1995, 77).

In other instances, however, Japanese privileges of extraterritoriality worked to protect Koreans engaged in illicit activities from prosecution under Chinese law. Chinese fears of the large numbers of Korean immigrants and of their involvement in smuggling and opium production and trafficking led them early on to protest that Korean immigrants were simply the "vanguard of Japanese penetration and absorption of Manchuria" (Young 1932, 259). In international meetings Chinese and Korean delegates protested that because Korean immigrants were regarded as Japanese citizens, their widespread presence invited Japanese intervention in China's hinterlands: "The charge is that wherever Koreans go, Japanese consular police follow them" (Condliffe 1930, 195). In memoirs of these years, one consul general remarked that "the opinion was that our economic development of Manchuria was to proceed with Koreans as the base" (Hayashi 1978, 82). Immigration from the metropole was insubstantial, but as Japanese subjects, often labeled "compatriots" (dōhō) in the press, Koreans were touted for proving Japan's stake in settling Manchuria. In 1928, although the Japanese (naichi) residents in Manchuria did not exceed two hundred thousand and many were in government service, in a speech before the Diet, Prime Minister Tanaka Giichi stated that "because we now have over one million Japanese subjects residing in Manchuria, we have important rights and interests in this region. . . . We are resolute to prevent any event which would hurt our important rights and interests" (translated in Kim 1992, 80). Clearly the rhetoric of inclusion served the purposes of Japanese expansionists.

Significant Korean involvement in the illicit economic penetration of Manchuria and China continued through the prewar period. Cultivation of opium poppies in Manchuria began as late as 1907, but the Chōsen Sōtokufu estimate for opium production in 1921 was 22,500 jin (Chōsen Sōtokufu Naimukyoku Shakaika 1923, 165) and "The special characteristics of Korean agriculture, wet-rice farming and cultivation of poppies, are more and more evident, and it is not too much to say that the market produce of these two great crops accounts for almost all of the Korean commercial production" (140). Through the late 1910s many Korean cultivators switched to raising poppies as a sole crop. During the harvest Korean laborers headed to the hills for seasonal wages, and in areas such as those near the Russian border or the railways, where the traffic in refined opium flourished, living standards rose and secondary businesses—tea houses, noodle shops (reimenya), inns, gambling and drinking establishments—sprang up. While on the Manchurian side Chinese bosses were involved in opium smuggling, across the Russian border thirty thousand Koreans were thought to be engaged in the opium business (Chōsen Sōtokufu Naimukyoku, 166–172). In 1923

Yamazaki Masao, a traveler to Harbin in northern Manchuria, was struck by the wealth, education, and Russian cultural attributes (even the offering of Russian tea with a lump of sugar) of Korean merchant families there who were engaged in the opium business. His shock at the loss of their Korean culture—some knew no Korean language and seemingly had no recollection of their homeland—echoed the concerns of Japanese proprietary claims to the "common culture" of Japan and Korea ("Senjin o chūshin" 1923, 33–36).

In such statements diverse Japanese voices indicated an embracing, adjunct role in the project of imperialism for Korean immigrants to Manchuria, welcoming their numbers and their cultural and economic influences. Koreans leaving their homeland, where the colonial ordinances were very restrictive, found advantages derived from Japan's official policies of inclusion. In the metropole, they had better access to higher education and jobs, and after 1925 they could even vote if they met residential and literacy requirements. In the 1930s some Koreans even achieved election to public office in Japan. In Manchuria before 1931, most of their advantages derived from extraterritoriality. The discourse of inclusion there was ambivalent and often instrumental. A South Manchurian Railway report of 1936 even admitted that, prior to the Manchurian Incident, claims to protection over Koreans had been a pretext for increasing Japan's police and military presence in Manchuria (Minami Manshū Tetsudō 1936, 257). In fact, Japanese protection and state services for Koreans were far from adequate. When it suited Japanese power-holders to categorize Koreans as citizens, they did, but the shifting boundary of that inclusiveness often placed Korean residents in Manchuria in grave danger.

DISSENTING VOICES: THE JAPANESE CONSULS IN MANCHURIA

Under the unequal-treaty system, the Japanese consuls in China took on expanded powers that reflected the privileged legal status of the Japanese nationals in his care. Consuls ran police forces *(Gaimushō keisatsu)*, legal courts, and jails and served as the top authority in the management of Japanese communities in concession areas. The consuls authorized the rules for the local Japanese Residents' Association (Nihonjinkai), which ran the settlement, and had final approval over any candidates slated for its elections. Consuls thus took on roles encompassing the duties of judge, sheriff, and mayor in these small boomtowns (Brooks forthcoming, chap. 3).

After the Russo-Japanese War, consuls in Manchuria were designated joint employees of the Chōsen Sōtokufu to undertake the care of resident Koreans, with some funds coming from that source (for 1923, see Chōsen Sōtokufu 1923, 868). Other employees of the Chōsen Sōtokufu were sometimes sent on assignments to the Japanese consulates in Manchuria to oversee Korean-related matters, but the Foreign Ministry's personnel were almost solely responsible for the affairs of resident Koreans in Manchuria. Korean residents in accessible areas were organized into Korean Residents' Associations *(Chōsenjinkai),* of which detailed records remain (Chōsen Sōtokufu Naimukyoku Shakaika 1923, 191–238; 1927, 641–656). Rapidly, consuls found themselves overwhelmed by the problems of this community, including the lack of funds for facilities and services; the presence of dissidents and organized anti-Japanese groups; issues over land rights; coordination of competing Japanese agencies; and whether or not Japan would allow the naturalization of Koreans in China. The records of their periodic meetings (seven times from 1917 to 1930) indicate that over time their paramount concerns were issues regarding Korean residents (JFMA, S 13.2.3.0–3).

Japanese Foreign Ministry officials reasoned that many issues regarding the protection of Koreans from Chinese authorities could be solved through naturalization. In 1913 Abe Moritarō, the head of the Political Bureau of the Foreign Ministry, submitted to his superiors an important plan urging moderation in China policy. In a section titled "The Problems of Koreans in Manchuria," he argued that Japanese authority over the Koreans in Manchuria should be relinquished to permit them to naturalize as Chinese (JFMA, 1.1.2.78). Abe's plan was not realized; in fact, he was soon assassinated by a fanatic youth who then committed ritual suicide by disemboweling himself over a spread-out map of China.

Despite such a climate of expansionism at home, until 1931 many Japanese consuls continued to argue that Koreans should be allowed to naturalize and lose their status as Japanese subjects. In 1923 Fengtian Consul General Akatsuka Shōsuke wrote (232):

> Viewed from the Japanese position, our population is now increasing at a rate that exceeds 100,000 per year. It's in fact a good trend for Korean people to move to the neighboring land of Manchuria. Moreover, it seems we have no reason to oppose their naturalization when it will give them benefits in such things as land ownership and rents. Right now in America there is a struggle over their denial of Japanese rights to naturalize. These facts should compel us to recognize that an enlightened policy would be to do what we can to aid our excess population to emigrate and naturalize.

A few months later, Fengtian Consul General Funatsu Tatsuichirō extended this argument, protesting the "discriminatory treatment" of Koreans as compared to *naichi* Japanese, who were allowed to lose their Japanese citizenship as they naturalized in different parts of the world (Chōsen Sōtokufu 1923, 737). Their situation was exactly the same as that of Japanese in

California who desired to naturalize and own property (745). He insisted that most Korean residents' motives for acquiring Chinese citizenship lay not in their antipathy to Japan but in the advantages for a stable livelihood that they could obtain (740). Besides, Funatsu insisted, even if Koreans naturalized as Chinese were involved in the subversive and criminal acts of *futei Senjin,* strong protest should be enough to motivate the Chinese authorities, who were obligated by treaty, to punish the offenders (737–738).

In fact, large numbers of Koreans, especially in the Jiandao region, had taken out Chinese citizenship papers. In 1923 the Chinese governor of Jilin province made known his support for a policy of naturalization, and the Japanese-language newspaper *Chōsen shimbun* anticipated that a November meeting of Manchurian consuls in Seoul would change Japanese policy to allow such naturalization, adding that many Koreans in Manchuria were already manipulating citizenship—sometimes Japanese and sometimes Chinese—to obtain their best advantage (*Chōsen shimbun* 1923, 11.15; JFMA, S 13.2.3.0–3). This ability of Korean residents in Manchuria to maximize "flexible citizenship" and subvert multiple national authorities resonates with contemporary global diasporic strategies (Ong 1993). Nevertheless, the 1923 meeting brought about no policy change, only the continuation of its uneven application.

In a 1923 article in *Chōsen oyobi Manshū*, Consul General Funatsu also challenged some common Japanese assumptions, beginning with numbers. Rather than the often quoted one million or one million twenty or thirty thousand resident Koreans, he insisted that there were only seven to eight hundred thousand, with nearly half in Jiandao. Most of them were poor farmers, extremely vulnerable to natural disasters and often squeezed by local Chinese elites. Funatsu stressed that "we cannot imagine how much they themselves fear *futei Senjin,*" isolated as they were from Japanese outposts and protection. The consuls' resources were inadequate, and Chinese authorities would not permit the addition of even one policeman to the consular force. The best hope for the future well-being of Korean residents lay in amicable Sino-Japanese relations and cooperation in attending to their needs and safety ("Manshū ni okeru Chōsenjin no genjō" 1923, 37–38).

Private consular documents indicate that after 1923, anti-Japanese, and increasingly Communist, insurgency among Korean residents became perceived as the greatest problem of Japanese administration in Manchuria. In addition, upheavals in China, the Chinese rights recovery movement, and the rise of the Guomindang from 1926 complicated and intensified the Manchurian situation. The Guomindang party of Chiang Kai-shek also sought allegiance with a significant number of noncommunist or cultural nationalist groups in Manchuria. There was even a Korean commander and fighting men among the ranks of the Guomindang expeditionary forces (JFMA, A 5.3.0.8), and consuls alleged that the Guomindang provided funds to pay the fees of Koreans taking out Chinese naturalization papers in Manchuria (JFMA, S 13.2.3.0–3).

Many of the specifics about Korean insurgency were never made public; as early as November 1924 *Chōsen oyobi Manshū* apologized for the censorship of two articles, "War in China and Korean Groups" and "The Current State of Korean Independence Groups and the Situation in China" (12). In 1928 the consuls agreed that the problem of secret Communist bands had "become concrete" *(gutaika)* after 1923. They also agreed to keep absolutely secret, so as "not to cause misunderstandings," a new plan to substitute some of the Kantō leased territory police force for the consular police.[4] In 1930 they deplored publicity in the Chinese press about the possible abolition of extraterritoriality and Japan's intransigence regarding Korean naturalization, because these trends exacerbated Chinese abuse of Korean settlers (JFMA, S 13.2.3.0–3).

Official Japanese efforts to keep the lid on information about insurgency contributed to the diffuse and blindly prejudicial fears of *futei Senjin* that spread among both Chinese and Japanese residents in Manchuria, or as Ann Stoler expresses it, to "blurring the boundaries between events 'witnessed' and those envisioned, between performed brutality and the potentiality for it" (Stoler 1992, 154). In other words, the harsh and violent actions of Chinese authorities in the Dunhua incident and the Korean domestic response to the Wanbaoshan Incident were examples of the escalating communal tension.

For Japanese imperialists on the eve of the Manchurian Incident, the beauty of their policy was their profit from seeding violence and fear between Chinese and Korean people (Kim and Wales 1941, 143–146). After 1927 violence and Chinese oppression of Korean settlers grew worse, in no small part due to Japanese encouragement of Chinese management of insurgency, embodied in the 1925 Mitsuya Agreement. Harassing even settled farmers, Chinese authorities closed *Chōsenjinkai* and Korean schools and revoked local registrations of alien Koreans (Chōsen Sōtokufu Naimukyoku 1930, 195–305). One consul, Morishima Morito, later stated that in this climate, Koreans came to welcome the Kantō Army occupation of 1931, believing that conditions for emigration and livelihood in Manchuria would vastly improve with the removal of Chinese authorities (IMTFE, 3037). Ironically, Japanese internationalists such as Foreign Minister Shidehara supported the policy of tolerance toward Chinese repression of Korean communities in Manchuria as the path of least resistance, to avoid the more "positive" policy of endorsing Japanese troop deployments (Li 1991). Shidehara's consuls in Manchuria, however, argued instead for radical reform to resolve the contradictions of the Korean residents' position.

In 1928 Fengtian Consul General Hayashi Kyūjirō began a campaign to alter Japanese jurisdictions in Manchuria to place all police and all responsibility for resident Korean affairs under a separate and enlarged budget, in the control of a high commissioner to be appointed from Foreign Ministry ranks (Hayashi 1978, 78–82; JFMA, S 1.5.3.0–1). At a time when public attention was focused on the murder of Zhang Zuolin by the Kantō Army and railway negotiations, Hayashi claimed that resolution of Korean problems in Manchuria was Japan's most urgent priority. Although Hayashi tacitly supported other consuls in 1928 and 1930 in urging metropolitan authorities to permit resident Koreans to naturalize as Chinese citizens, given the impossibility of that outcome, he moved more stridently to try to unify Japanese intent and policy toward Koreans. Hayashi stressed the importance of this issue to the internal stability of the Korean colony and demanded more facilities and funds for policing and welfare services for Korean residents (JFMA, S 13.2.3.0–3). If Japan were to regard Koreans as Japanese citizens, then adequate protection and resources had to follow.

One result of Hayashi's approach was like-minded Consul Ishii Itarō's 1930 appeal to Shidehara to take up the Dunhua arrests and protest, government-to-government, the maltreatment of Korean settlers in the hands of Chinese authorities. Another, however, was the increasing animosity of other Japanese authorities to Hayashi and consuls who supported his ideas. In June 1931 an extremely hostile interview with Hayashi was published ("Hōten no Hayashi" 1931, 11):

> REPORTER: There are increasing instances of problems of Chinese authorities oppressing or harassing Koreans in Manchuria. Isn't this very dangerous?
> HAYASHI: Dangerous? Isn't this inevitable because they are said to be Japanese citizens just like us? I treat Koreans as citizens of the empire in just the same way I treat Japanese people. The majority of problems of my job concern ordinary Korean people.

Hayashi's strategy of forcing Japanese, officials and populace, to live up to the meaning of the inclusive boundary of discourse and law that incorporated Koreans in Manchuria into the ranks of the colonizers bore no fruit before 1931 and may have hastened the occupation of Manchuria by further antagonizing army authorities. While the voices of Japanese consuls in Manchuria remained minority opinions informed by a differing fragment of colonial knowledge, a historical reconstruction of their concerns about Koreans in Manchuria helps focus the colonial discourse of inclusion with its many inconsistencies.

AFTER THE MANCHURIAN INCIDENT

On September 18, 1931, the Kantō Army began a series of military actions to effect the entire occupation of China's northeastern provinces. From the outset, notable resistance came from Japanese consuls in Manchuria, including Hayashi and Ishii. The immediate dispatch to Manchuria of four thousand troops under the Japanese high command in Korea was crucial to complete this daring endeavor. In the later evolution of the "colony" of Manchukuo, the dominant Kantō Army was able to gradually reduce and then eliminate other Japanese agencies, such as the Foreign Ministry and the South Manchurian Railway (Brooks forthcoming; Matsusaka 1996).

While many accounts of the Manchurian Incident stress its lack of bloodshed—the Chinese did not resist but turned to an appeal to the League of Nations—this was far from the case. In the wake of Japanese troop movements, Zhang Xueliang's troops fled from their northern encampments toward Fengtian and Kaiyuan, pillaging and murdering in the agricultural settlements of Koreans along the outskirts of the South Manchurian Railroad corridor. In the month following September 18, nineteen hundred resident Koreans were killed and forty-five hundred were reported missing, presumed dead. In October the Kantō Army denounced Zhang and his troops for slaughter of "our compatriot Koreans" (waga dōhō de aru Chōsen-jin) (Usui 1984, 30–31; Nakanishi 1931). Again, the rhetoric of inclusion served Japanese imperialist purposes, but the resident Koreans paid the price for its insincerity.

Despite Korean hopes, their location in the new colonial order remained contradictory. In 1932 a debate on the extent to which Japanese authorities would encourage Korean versus Japanese immigration to Manchuria was widely waged in the Japanese media. Former Consul General Hayashi Kyūjirō, among others, argued that standards of living in Manchuria were too low for Japanese immigrants but that Koreans had already proved their abilities to produce record amounts of rice (reprinted in Chōsen Sōtokufu Sōtokukan shingishitsu 1932). In their first plans, the Kantō Army indicated that an increased presence of Korean immigrants would be welcome, but in early 1932 at a major conference on immigration in Fengtian the opinion dominated that no resources should be diverted from the project of encouraging metropolitan Japanese immigration. Some even argued that Koreans should be "kicked out" to make room for Japanese immigrants (which did come to pass on a limited scale) (Kantōgun 1932; Kim 1992, 132–141). Japanese ambivalence toward the Koreans in Manchuria continued.

Nevertheless, Korean immigration continued, and the place of Koreans among the ranks of the colonizers in Manchuria became more tangible over time. After March 1932, Japan officially permitted the dual citizenship of Koreans as Japanese and Manchukuo subjects. The Chōsen Sōtokufu under Governor General Ugaki Kazushige from 1932 to 1937 continued to press for much-needed Korean emigration to Manchuria, which was achieved in a planned form from 1936 (Kim 1992). Koreans in Manchukuo were recognized as one of the five ethnic groups, along with Japanese, Manchus, Mongolians, and Han Chinese. Many came to serve in the Manchukuo government, and more than a thousand joined its army; eventually some received training in Manchukuo's officer academies (Eckert 1996, 29–31). Especially with the advent of war from 1937, well-to-do and professional Koreans willingly came in greater and greater numbers to Manchuria and occupied China for opportunities open to those in the ranks of the colonizers.

But while the colonial society of Manchuria under Japanese domination grew less fragmented and hierarchies of credibility less diverse after 1931, its essential nature did not change. The Japanese army's instrumental and strategic manipulation of metropolitan farming immigrants suggests that they, too, found themselves in the lower colonial ranks and subject to contradictory policies (Wilson 1995). Korean insurgents continued to flourish in Manchuria, aiding the Chinese Communist victory and the eventual triumph of communism in North Korea. Despite the Japanese rhetoric of cohesiveness, development, and harmony in Korea and Manchukuo, telltale shifting boundaries of colonial privilege were one sign of tenuous Japanese dominance.

In a similar fashion, the discourse of the "Korean problem" in the wider empire stabilized but did not go away. As Japan entered the 1930s, society's preoccupation with the ramifications of the colonial project were displaced by the more compelling and closer concerns of mobilization of the metropole for economic rehabilitation and further campaigns in China, and later, the Pacific War. As war expanded the empire, Japan's colonial citizens (Koreans, Taiwanese, even Okinawans) quietly found new opportunities in the wider empire as comparative "insiders," but the Japanese colonial authorities in their homelands grew harsher and more demanding. Still, as new subject peoples came under Japanese occupation, in China and elsewhere, they did not enjoy even the rhetoric of inclusion: they were never offered a chance at Japanese citizenship. Instead, as war heightened, in contrast to the draconian measures of assimilation for Koreans and Taiwanese citizens, other peoples were offered "independence" and pan-Asian brotherhood within the beneficent Greater East Asia Co-Prosperity Sphere. Such rhetorics of status both conceal and reveal much about Japanese methods of imperial control. From at least a legal standpoint, Koreans in the wider empire continued to be reckoned in the lower ranks of the Japanese colonizers. In fact, the contradictions of their location in the order of the colonial empire still constrained their actions and opportunities, reflecting a deeper Japanese dilemma of confusion and conflict between empire and nation.

NOTES

I wish to express appreciation to the Research Foundation of the City University of New York and a PSC-CUNY grant that funded the research for this essay.

1. Japanese authorities referred to Taiwanese subjects as *sekimin*, "registered people," distinguishing them as officially recorded Japanese citizens from other Chinese people. The Foreign Ministry archives contain numerous files on Taiwanese and Korean individuals and collective groups in many areas of the empire, demonstrating the watchfulness of Japanese authorities toward these subjects (JFMA, A 5.3.0.8).

2. After 1905, the Japanese resident general (precursor to the Sōtokufu) disputed the northern border of Korea and attempted to maintain an office north of the Tumen River in the Jiandao region, but Japan and China reached a settlement concerning the official border in 1909.

3. One should read statistics on the actual population of Koreans in Manchuria at a given time with caution, both for political reasons and because of the "incomplete nature of colonial knowledge," discussed in this essay. South Manchurian Railway statistics are higher (Young 1932, 251–254).

4. By 1929 Shidehara ordered the consular police into plain clothes and even had them destroy *meishi*, letterhead stationery, and signs over their "police boxes" that said "Gaimushō police," in an attempt to draw international attention away from their increasingly disputed status in China. In 1931 C. Walter Young deplored the fact that the differing Japanese military and police forces in Manchuria could not be distinguished by their uniforms (Brooks forthcoming, chap. 4).

REFERENCES

Akatsuka Shōsuke. 1921. "ZaiMan Senjin mondai." Reprinted in Kankoku Shiryō Kenkyūjo, *Chōsen tōji shisyō* 10:225–261. Sansei Bijutsu Insatsu, 1972.

Beasley, W. G. 1987. *Japanese Imperialism, 1894–1945.* New York: Oxford University Press.

Brooks, Barbara J. Forthcoming. *Japan's Imperial Diplomacy: Treaty Ports, Consuls, and War in China, 1895–1938.* Honolulu: University of Hawai'i Press.

Chōsen Shireibu. 1924. "Futei Senjin ni kansuru kisoteki kenkyū." Reprinted in *Chōsen mondai shiryō sōsho* 6, edited by Pak Kyon-sik. Sanichi Shobō, 1982.

Chōsen Sōtokufu. 1923. "ZaiManshū Chōsen kankei ryōjikan uchiai kaigi hōkoku." Reprinted in Kankoku Shiryō Kenkyūjo, *Chōsen tōji shiryō* 8:563–917. Sansei Bijutsu Insatsu.

Chōsen Sōtokufu Keimukyoku. 1930. "ZaiMan Senjin to Shina kansen." Seoul: Gyōsei Gakkai Insatsujo. Reprint, Seoul: Seishin Bunka Sha, 1974.

Chōsen Sōtokufu Naimukyoku Shakaika. 1923. *Manshū oyobi Shiberia chihō ni okeru Chosenjin jijō.* Seoul: Keijō Insatsusho.

———. 1927. *Manshū oyobi Shiberia chihō ni okeru Chōsenjin jijō.* Reprinted in Kankoku Shiryō Kenkyūjo *Chōsen tōji shiryō* 10:371–682. Sansei Bijutsu Insatsu, 1972.

Chōsen Sōtokufu Sōtokukan Shingishitsu. 1932. "Manshū imin ni kansuru kaku hōmen no iken shōroku." Pamphlet.

Condliffe, J. B., ed. 1930. *Problems of the Pacific 1929: Proceedings of the Third Conference of the Institute of Pacific Relations.* Chicago: University of Chicago Press.

Cumings, Bruce. 1981. *The Origins of the Korean War.* Princeton: Princeton University Press.

Duus, Peter. 1995. *The Abacus and the Sword: The Japanese Penetration of Korea, 1895–1910.* Berkeley: University of California Press.

Eckert, Carter J. 1996. "Total War, Industrialization and Social Change in Late Colonial Korea." In *The Japanese Wartime Empire, 1931–1945,* edited by Peter Duus, Ramon H. Myers, and Mark R. Peattie, 3–39. Princeton: Princeton University Press.

Gendaishi shiryō. 1972. Volume 28. Misuzu Shobō.

Hayashi Kyūjirō. 1978. *Manshū jihen to Hōten sōryōji.* Hara Shobō.

"Hōten no Hayashi Sōryōji o tazunete." 1931. *Chōsen oyobi Manshū* 6:11–12.

IMTFE (International Military Tribunal for the Far East). 1946–1948. Proceedings.

JFMA (Japanaese Foreign Ministry Archives).

Kanazawa Shōzaburō. 1929. *Nissen dōsoron.* Tōko Shoin.

Kantōgun Tōjibu Sangyō Shimon Iinkai. 1932. "Manshū imin shimon gijiroku." Reprinted in *Kindai minshū no kiroku—Manshū imin,* edited by Yamada Shōji. Shinjinbutsu Ōraisha, 1978.

Kida Teikichi. 1910. *Kankoku no heigō to kokushi.* Sanseidō.

Kim, Ki-hoon. 1992. "Japanese Policy for Korean Rural Immigration to Manchukuo, 1932–1945." Ph.D. diss., University of Hawai'i.

Kim San and Nym Wales. 1941. *Song of Ariran: The Life Story of a Korean Rebel.* Cornwall, New York: Cornwall Press.

Kitaoka Shin'ichi. 1978. *Nihon rikugun to tairiku seisaku 1906–1918.* Gannando.

Lee, Chong-Sik. 1967. *Counterinsurgency in Manchuria: The Japanese Experience 1931–1940.* Santa Monica: Rand Corporation.

Li, Sun-han. 1991. *Kindai Higashi Ajia no seiji rikigaku.* Kinshōsha.

"Manshū ni okeru Chōsenjin no genjō." 1923. *Chōsen oyobi Manshū* 12:37–38.

"Manshū no suiden keiei ni tsuite." 1922. *Chōsen oyobi Manshū* 5:22–24.

Matsusaka, Y. Tak. 1996. "Managing Occupied Manchuria, 1931–1934." In *The Japanese Wartime Empire, 1931–1945,* edited by Peter Duus, Ramon H. Myers, and Mark R. Peattie, 97–135. Princeton: Princeton University Press.

Minami Manshū Tetsudō Kabushiki Kaisha Chihōbu Nōmuka. 1936. "Zaiman Chōsenjin nōgyō mondai." In *Manshū nōgyō imin hōsaku,* 2.1, no. 8: *Ritsuan chōsa shorui,* edited by Minami Manshū Tetsudō Kabushiki Kaisha Keizai Chōsakai, 1937.

Moriyama Shigenori. 1985. "Nikkan heigō no kokusai kankei: Chōsen mondai to

Manshū mondai no renkan." In *Nihon gaikō no kiki ninshiki* 7, edited by Kindai Nihon Kenkyūkai. Yamakawa Shuppansha.

Nakanishi Inosuke. 1931. "Mugotari! Zaiman Chōsen dōhō." *Chūō kōron* 12:244–249.

Ohnuki-Tierney, Emiko. 1993. *Rice as Self: Japanese Identities through Time.* Princeton: Princeton University Press.

Ong, Aihwa. 1993. "On the Edge of Empires: Flexible Citizenship among Chinese in Diaspora." *Positions* 1.3:745–778.

Peattie, Mark R. 1989. "Japanese Treaty Port Settlements in China, 1895–1937." In *The Japanese Informal Empire in China, 1895–1937,* edited by Peter Duus, Ramon H. Myers, and Mark R. Peattie, 166–209. Princeton: Princeton University Press.

Scully, Eileen P. 1995. "Taking the Low Road to Sino-American Relations: 'Open Door' Expansionists and the Two China Markets." *Journal of American History* 82.1: 62–83.

"Senjin no Manshū ijū to sono taisaku." 1920. *Chōsen oyobi Manshū* 5:34–37.

"Senjin o chūshin to seru Harubin no kōsatsu." 1923. *Chōsen oyobi Manshū* 12: 33–36.

Stoler, Ann Laura. 1989. "Rethinking Colonial Categories: European Communities and the Boundaries of Rule." *Comparative Studies in Society and History* 31.1:134–161.

———. 1992. "'In Cold Blood': Hierarchies of Credibility and the Politics of Colonial Narratives." *Representations* 37 (winter):151–189.

Usui Katsumi. 1984. "Kindai Nihon to Chōsen, Chūgoku." In *"Chōsen mondai" konwakai* 26. Gakushū Kenkyū Shiriizu.

Weiner, Michael. 1994. *Race and Migration in Imperial Japan.* London: Routledge Press.

———. 1995. "Discourses of Race, Nation and Empire in Pre-1945 Japan." *Ethnic and Racial Studies* 18.3:433–456.

Wilson, Sandra. 1995. "The 'New Paradise': Japanese Emigration to Manchuria in the 1930s and 1940s." *International History Review* 17.2:249–286.

Young, C. Walter. 1932. "Korean Problems in Manchuria as Factors in the Sino-Japanese Dispute." *Supplementary Documents to the Report of the Commission of Inquiry.* Study No. 9. Geneva.

❧ 2 ❧

Integrating into Chinese Society: A Comparison of the Japanese Communities of Shanghai and Harbin

Joshua A. Fogel

In the late nineteenth and early twentieth centuries, Japanese began settling in what were to become famous as the two most "international" cities in East Asia, Shanghai and Harbin. The Japanese communities that formed in these multicultural metropolises varied widely as they faced different issues and developed within different contexts. Writing in 1933 and 1934, the renowned journalist Edgar Snow cut through the "internationalist" hyperbole and inadvertently shed light on the question of ethnic integration within Shanghai and Harbin.

> Harbin, once delightful, today notorious as a place of living death, the worst-governed city in Manchukuo.
>
> Probably in no other city of the world is life so precarious. Harbin residents, including the 100,000 White and Red Russians, who here bend to the law of the yellow man, risk their lives if they go unarmed anywhere, even in daylight. Holdups, robberies, murders, kidnappings are common occurrences. . . .
>
> Some of the worst criminals are White Russians. Destitute, broken in spirit, unwilling to return to Russia under the Bolsheviks, unable to earn a living in China *under the Japanese,* they turn to crime, nourished on a diet of drugs, which are sold openly in shops infesting the city. . . . In Harbin alone there are more than 2000 licensed shops for the sale of opium, heroin and morphine. (Snow 1934, 81, 84. Emphasis added.)

∿

Within Greater Shanghai dwell nearly 3,000,000 people. The vast majority is of course Chinese. The last censor's notes list 50 different foreign nationalities with a total of 48,000. . . . To find men of all creeds and colors is not so phenomenal perhaps; New York, Paris, Berlin and Vienna can point to a medley of races. But in Shanghai there is for the most part no mixture; that is the phenomenon. Here, generation after generation, the British have stayed British, the Americans have remained "100 percenters." In Paris the foreigner enjoys learning French; in Berlin he must acquire German; in New York the American dialect is considered essential. But in Shanghai he does not learn Chinese, although it is the language of the city's 3,000,000, and beyond them, of the hundreds of millions from whom he hopes, with a little surprise, to extract a few coppers. It is believed that the study of Chinese weakens the fiber of the mind, and the few foreigners who do master the language are pointed out as eccentrics; significant smiles are exchanged behind their backs. . . .

[I]n Shanghai [the foreigner] . . . is immune from all but his own consular jurisdiction. . . . Many believe that it is advisable to have as little contact with the Chinese as possible. (Snow 1933, 173–174; Takatsuna 1995, 98–99)

Both cities were hailed throughout the early decades of the twentieth century—and they have been so remembered in the memoir literature since—as the "Paris of the East," because of their "international" (read: European) flavor. As one Japanese journalist wrote in 1940: "Harbin! . . . International capital of northern Manchuria amid the swirling eddies of extravagant and romantic adventure, where past and future play a zigzagged symphony. . . . What a wonderful place" (Tachibana 1940, 264, 266). Where else in East Asia could one on a daily basis brush shoulders with so many foreigners, dine in foreign restaurants, and shop in foreign stores? In fact, Shanghai and Harbin were probably far more cosmopolitan than Paris at the time.

The central question I address here is how the Japanese fit into Shanghai and Harbin, if indeed they tried. What roles did they play in these international communities? How well integrated were they into their economic, social, political, and cultural life? In the period preceding the concerted military invasion of the 1930s, what role did these cities play for the Japanese? Edgar Snow's words offer a hint. Shanghai was a mosaic world of different ethnicities living side by side but having as little to do with one another as possible, while Harbin was a melting pot, more a city of pioneers whose residents, even the Chinese, were newcomers and mixed far more in good times and bad than in Shanghai. I begin with a look at the origins of the two Japanese communities, then looks at the sorts of occupations Japanese residents of Shanghai and Harbin undertook before examining the communal organization they established in China. I focus on the politics of the Japanese communities and their interactions with the surrounding Chinese and conclude by looking at their relations with the Japanese homeland.

ORIGINS OF THE TWO JAPANESE COMMUNITIES

The Japanese were the last of the foreign powers to become a major presence in China. By the time the first Japanese vessel of the modern era, the *Senzaimaru,* docked at the port of Shanghai in 1862 (nineteen years after it officially opened), Britain, the United States, Holland, and France were already established there (See Fogel 1994b, 79–94; Haruna 1987, 555–601; Wang 1989, 140–156; Satō 1984, 67–96; Qiao 1989, 43–52). Only seven Japanese had already settled in Shanghai when diplomatic ties were concluded in 1871, but after the creation of a Japanese consulate the next year, major Japanese companies began setting up branches there. Through the early Meiji era, the population grew slowly and became roughly two-thirds women, with the men in a variety of business concerns and the women largely in the prostitution trade. By 1890 the resident Japanese population had reached 644, and men now first outnumbered women (339 to 305). The population approached 1,000 on the eve of the first Sino-Japanese War. During the war the overwhelming majority of Japanese withdrew, but most returned following Japan's victory. The Treaty of Shimonoseki concluding that conflict provided that Japan could build factories on Chinese soil, and as a result Japanese became more deeply involved in the Chinese economy. In late 1904 the resident Japanese population surpassed 3,300 and continued to rise much more rapidly from 1905 (Zhu 1995, 401, 406; Takatsuna 1995, 119–121; Katō 1974, 316–317; Yonezawa 1938–1939). Throughout the Meiji years the great majority of Japanese in Shanghai came from Kyushu and western Honshu.

Immigration to Harbin followed a somewhat different course. Although Harbin was home to the earliest Japanese settlement in Manchuria, before it even existed Vladivostok served as a source of goods from abroad; it was also Russia's mirror on the Pacific. Vladivostok fell within the Maritime Province, originally part of Qing territory, but it was ceded to Russia in 1860. It was then little more than a fishing village, and the whole region, as one source puts it, had more animals than people.[1] By 1877 there were some 80 Japanese living in Vladivostok, most involved in the brothel business serving the many visiting sailors; several years later the 140–150 Japanese, all from Nagasaki, had several restaurants and several laundries there. By 1890 there were 392 Japanese in Vladivostok with a 3:2 female-to-male ratio, unlike most frontier settlements, which tend to be predominantly male, but intriguingly like the contemporaneous experience in Shanghai. On March 31, 1891, the Trans-Siberian Railway began construction, and Vladivostok was teeming with the businesses involved and the new construction on the docks. Among the laborers mobilized for the effort, some 500–600 Japanese were recruited from northern Kyushu villages. As the century came to a close, the Japanese population reached 1,000; communal institutions were beginning to emerge, but a preponderant involvement in prostitution remained (one source indicates that there were more than 200 young women working as prostitutes in Vladivostok in the mid-1880s) (Sugiyama 1985, 14–15, 18–24, 27–28).

As the Ussuri Line of the Trans-Siberian Railway, linking Vladivostok with Khabarovsk, neared completion in the fall of 1896, Russia and China signed a secret treaty allowing Russia to spread rail lines across Manchuria. This became the Chinese Eastern Railway (CER), and in the spring of 1897 a construction authority for the CER was established in Vladivostok. A base of operations close to a river was still needed for the transportation of materials, and to that end a sparsely populated site near the Sungari River was selected. The necessary materials were brought by sea from Europe to Vladivostok, then by rail to Khabarovsk, and finally down the Sungari by ship to this site. The first construction team of twenty men with a Cossack guard of fifty left Vladivostok in March 1898, arriving a month later at a site to be known as Staryi Kharbin (Old Harbin). They found there a small settlement of roughly twenty huts where the natives were producing low-grade alcohol and growing opium on the moist banks of the Sungari. They purchased it all and began the massive railway construction efforts that would eventually employ as many as two hundred thousand Chinese who migrated north for the work. The first project entailed building a station and narrow-gauge track from the wharf to the center of the former local settlement, and this transport route later became the main thoroughfare of Harbin, known as Kitaiskaia Ulitsa (Chinese Street) in Russian and Zhongyang dajie (Central Boulevard) in Chinese. In less than two decades, this avenue would become the heart of non-Chinese Harbin, lined with a wide assortment of shops selling the latest fashions and foods from around the world. Russian city planners dubbed the new site Posyolok Sungari (Sungari Settlement), but in a Japanese work introducing Manchuria published in 1904, it is referred to as Harbin, and thus the name must have come into popular usage within that six-year period. Always Kharbin in Russian and Ha-er-bin (Harbin) in Chinese, it was more often than not Harupin in Japanese writings of the late Meiji and Taishō years.[2]

In a 1932 essay the famous writer Yokomitsu Riichi recounted the story of the first Japanese, a young woman named Miyamoto Chiyo, who settled in Harbin (Yokomitsu 1932, 2–17). She had moved from her native Kumamoto to Vladivostok in 1888 at the age of eighteen with her younger brother, making her living there as an assistant to the only Russian doctor in the city. When the doctor moved to Harbin in 1898, she accompanied him.

Because of her close association with the Russians, by century's end she was placed in charge of all Japanese immigration matters. At the time of the Boxer Rebellion, Sino-Russian border tensions mounted; in July of 1900 the Russian Army routed or killed the entire Chinese population of Blagoveshchensk, some three thousand to four thousand persons. Many Japanese residents fled Harbin for Khabarovsk and elsewhere, as did many Chinese. Yokomitsu reported that only twenty-two of Harbin's Japanese residents remained during the mass withdrawal, but that by 1901 the Japanese population had rebounded to more than three hundred again. At that point Miyamoto could no longer handle all the paperwork by herself, and a Japanese residents association, the Sōkakai (Sungari Association), was formed, another indication that by 1901, at least, the toponym Harbin had not yet been firmly established. By late 1902 there were 514 Japanese out of a total population of roughly thirty thousand in Harbin, according to a Sōkakai survey; there were roughly seven thousand Japanese throughout Manchuria at this time. There was another mass withdrawal from Harbin and elsewhere in Manchuria to Japan in 1903–1904 on the eve of the Russo-Japanese War, though Harbin remained untouched by the fighting (Sugiyama 1985, 30–32, 49–50, 56–60).[3]

Thus, the Japanese population of Harbin, which only surpassed its prewar figure in late 1907 when it reached 627, was vastly inferior to the Shanghai figure, which was nearing six thousand at the same time. Japanese residents in Shanghai had already attained a more gender-balanced population and a more professionally balanced one as well by the turn of the century, but these processes would take much longer in Harbin. Despite these differences and the fact that the surrounding populations were ethnically dissimilar, the two communities began to produce interestingly similar patterns of settlement and communal institutions that offer us a handle for comparing their integration into the two larger communities.

OCCUPATIONAL INTEGRATION: STORES, SHOPS, BUSINESSES, AND OTHER LINES OF WORK

The most remarkable quality of the entire Japanese enterprise in Shanghai was how extrinsic it was to the city itself and how much life was fashioned to resemble home. From the second decade of the twentieth century, Japanese began informally referring to their adopted city as "Nagasaki ken, Shanhai shi." This offhand remark indicates the extent to which most Japanese lived in a Japanese style, as fish and vegetables arrived from Nagasaki on a daily basis and were sold in the local markets. "It was as if a corner of the Nagasaki market had moved," noted one Shanghai Japanese from Nagasaki; and, as if to second the point made by Edgar Snow: "Japanese residents in Shanghai lived there oblivious to the fact that they were in a foreign country" (Takat-suna 1995, 125). While the Japanese community of Shanghai was a distinct ethnic enclave, it nonetheless came to represent an economic entity worth dying to protect. "Nagasaki-Shanghai" finds a fascinating parallel in the following statement of the famous travel writer and novelist, Muramatsu Shōfū:

> The Japanese have no intention whatsoever of throwing away fifty years of work that have gone into the building of "Shanghai-Japan." The Yangzi trade runs annually to five or six hundred million yen and often more than seven. As Manchuria is Japan's lifeline, Yangzi trade is Japan's line of nourishment, and it will under no circumstances throw this away. There is no reason to relinquish such great interests even if it means fighting. We must come to the aid of the 30,000 [Japanese] residents of Shanghai. We cannot let them die before our very eyes. This is our responsibility both as a state and as a government.[4]

Although the Treaty of Shimonoseki enabled them to establish a concession area, the Japanese never staked that claim in Shanghai, as they did in Tianjin and Hangkou. The great majority remained in the International Settlement; of the 26,208 Japanese living in Shanghai in 1935, 19,651 (75 percent) resided in the International Settlement. Even before the first Sino-Japanese War, Japanese were settling in the Hongkou (Hongkew) quarter of the settlement, soon to become known informally as the "Japanese Concession" or "Japantown."[5]

The first Japanese to move to Shanghai were principally government officials and independent businessmen who ran their own shops usually in the service sector. There were as well a few who worked as servants in the homes of Westerners. Through the end of the nineteenth century, women outnumbered men by a large margin and most worked as prostitutes for foreigners or as entertainers employed by Japanese businessmen to establish foreign contacts. In 1885, there were more than twenty Japanese-owned brothels and "teahouses" in Shanghai. The larger Japanese concerns began to set up branches in the Meiji era—Mitsubishi in 1875, Mitsui Bussan in 1877, Yokohama Specie Bank in 1893—but they did not begin to exert a strong influence until after the Sino-Japanese War and especially after World War I (Zhu 1995, 406, 410; Takatsuna 1995, 120; Peattie 1989, 183).

Whereas the major Japanese banks set up branches along the Bund, mid-level stores and trading firms were located in the French concession. Smaller shops were closer to the area in which most Japanese lived in Hongkou, primarily along North Sichuan Road, Wenjianshi Road, and Wusong Road. A December 1927 survey noted that Japanese were 47 percent of the entire foreign population of Shanghai. Those who worked for the larger concerns and the major banks were dubbed the *kaisha-ha,* or company clique, whereas those who operated smaller businesses and stores in Hongkou or Zhabei were known as the *dochaku-ha,* or "native" clique. This distinction undoubtedly reflects the fact that the former group were rotated in and out of Shanghai on two- or three-year terms, while the latter more often than not had settled in Shanghai. Through the Taishō years, there were ten Japanese-run *ryokan,* some twenty Japanese *geshuku,* and twenty-four Japanese restaurants and brothels, many of these owned by migrants from Kyushu.

One-fourth of all Japanese in Shanghai were directly tied to the cotton textile industry, and many more did business with it. These companies grew in tandem with the development of Japanese capitalism. Through the Taishō years, Japan gradually replaced Germany and France in economic influence in Shanghai and by the end of the 1920s reached a par with the United States and Great Britain, reflected in the fact that it had the largest number of foreign banks in Shanghai. From 1912, with the establishment of the Republic, Japanese banks began making loans to China and gained a toehold in the Chinese financial world through investments in Chinese railways and the like. Indeed, as the Japanese presence in the Chinese economy grew stronger—according to a 1915 survey, for example, there were seventy-five Japanese companies in Shanghai worth more than 50,000 yen in capital—the Japanese there began to see it as an intrinsic and essential part of their world (Zhu 1995, 412–414; Duus 1989, 65–100; Katō 1974, 318–319; Takatsuna 1995, 121–125; see also Nakamura 1973, 91–96).

The large Japanese economic stake in the Shanghai market certainly helps to explain the willingness of local Japanese, as the citation from Muramatsu Shōfū indicates, to square off and confront the Chinese nose-to-nose. Excluding Manchuria, Shanghai accounted for one-half of Japan's trade with China; there were immense investments to protect in the textile industry and with the larger trading companies. These factors, of course, also played an important role in producing anti-imperialist Chinese nationalism, and they served as well to strengthen Japanese resolve to defend their assets (Banno 1989, 314–329; Jordan 1991).

Unlike Shanghai, where each ethnic group lived in a small universe unto itself and enjoyed extraterritoriality, Harbin remained in Russian hands, for all intents and purposes ruled as a fiefdom of the CER by its head, Dmitri Khorvat; and this in spite of the concessions won by Japan after victory in the war. Unlike Shanghai where a Japanese consulate was opened as early as 1872, Miyamoto Chiyo's work was not turned over to consular officials in Harbin until 1907. The new infusion of capital from Japan from 1907 helped revive Harbin's sluggish economy. That year marked the beginning of a sustained return of Japanese to the city following the withdrawal at the time of the Russo-Japanese War. Mitsubishi and Mitsui both opened branches in 1907 as well.

As early as 1905 there were five competing companies plying the sea lanes between Japanese ports and Vladivostok. In December of 1907 the Japanese population in Harbin reached 627, superseding its prewar figure. Even before the war, larger enterprises had been founded by Japanese in Harbin, such as Tokunaga Shōkai, Suzuki Nichi-Man Shōkai, and Moritomo Shōkai. A local survey of Japanese businesses in Vladivostok, for example, showed that there were thirty general stores, seventy-five laundries, thirty-six barbers, twenty-seven cobblers, thirty-six carpenters, and sixty-two families engaged in the *kashiseki,* or "rooms for rent" business, clearly a euphemism for houses of prostitution. World War I brought prosperity to Harbin, as trade exports rose dramatically and, for example, the number of oil refineries rose from seven to twenty. During the war years Japanese contacts throughout Siberia rose to make it second only to the United States for the volume of its trade with Japan.[6] Yet, even as the Japanese population of Harbin continued to grow and mature as a group during the Taishō years, and as fresh business opportunities emerged, the number of Japanese involved in one end or another of prostitution remained extraordinarily high.[7]

The Bolshevik Revolution caused a major shift in power relations within the city. Struggles within the CER between Khorvat and the railway workers were exacerbated when local Chinese authorities began to demand the recovery of full sovereignty over the region and the railroad. From this point forward, while Russian culture continued to exercise a profound impact on the non-Chinese quarters of the city, Russian control in Harbin began a slide from which it was never to recover. Even as the Russian presence in Harbin continued to grow, in fact explode with the influx of White Russian refugees after 1917, they no longer enjoyed tsarist support and many were reduced to poverty or worse. Harbin was still a city of pioneers—Chinese, Japanese, Russian, and others—a new city undergoing far more change and flux than Shanghai in these years.

Following the war, the joint powers invaded Siberia in an effort to defeat the Bolsheviks, but by the end of 1918 all of the other powers had withdrawn. Japanese forces stayed for more than four years, despite worries on the part of the local communities in Siberia and the Chinese northeast of exacerbated tensions with the Russians and Chinese. There were by now thousands of Japanese expatriates (and far more Koreans now under Japanese hegemony) scattered through the towns and cities of Northeast Asia and along the Trans-Siberian Railway. When the decision was reached for the Japanese troops to pull out, many protested vociferously through the local Japanese press against such a move for fear of Soviet reprisals, in part at least because the Japanese army and navy had been so closely associated with propping up petty White Russian dictators such as Grigorii Semyonov.[8]

Nonetheless, as the Russian emigré population tripled during the Russian civil war years to 124,000 by 1921, the Japanese population also rose 75 percent over the same period to 3,545, and by far the largest segment of the local population, the Chinese, rose from 170,000 in 1917 to more than 315,000 by early 1922. Despite nominal control of the city now in Chinese hands, each of the local ethnic groups basically managed its own affairs. Each created its own array of institutions to protect its constituent population. Unlike Shanghai, though, there was greater interaction among the various communities.

COMMUNAL ORGANIZATIONS AND THE JAPANESE RESIDENTS ASSOCIATION

Like many ethnic groups who have settled away from the familiar surroundings of home, the Japanese throughout continental Asia established a panoply of communal institutions to organize the local community, mobilize it when need be, and see to the everyday social, educational, economic, and religious needs of its people. In this regard the Harbin and Shanghai experiences were similar. Already in the 1870s, the Japanese consulate in Shanghai took the lead in establishing communal institutions, building a Japanese cemetery in 1873 that was placed in the hands of the local Higashi honganji (founded 1874) in 1877. Control over the cemetery land was later passed to the Japanese Residents Association (JRA), which was founded in 1907 in Shanghai. The Higashi honganji also led the way with the establishment of medical facilities and clinics; by late 1907 there were seven Japanese hospitals in Shanghai and a Japanese Medical Association of Shanghai (Shanhai Nihon Ikai) was founded in May 1902. In 1869, even before diplomatic relations were normalized, the Japanese government lent a hand in the creation of schools in Shanghai. As more schools emerged over the course of the 1870s, they exerted a major influence on the permanence of the local Japanese community. The first school for young women was built in 1876, at a time when there were only forty-five Japanese in the city. That year also witnessed the establishment of a Japanese foundling home in Shanghai (Zhu 1995, 421–422, 426–427; Katō 1974, 319–320).

The JRA of Shanghai (Shanhai Nihon Kyoryū Mindan) fell directly under the management of the consulate and hence the Gaimushō and exercised considerable local authority within the Japanese community, in large measure because the Japanese enjoyed extraterritoriality in China. It was joined by the Japanese Street Federation of Shanghai (Shanhai Nihonjin Kakuro Rengōkai) and the neighborhood associations *(chōnaikai)*, which served at various levels to both protect and mobilize the entire Japanese community. By supporting local institutions and by speaking on behalf of local Japanese interests, the JRA served to strengthen the internal cohesion of the local community. Soon after its founding, the elite stratum among the Japanese gained control over the JRA. Among their formal duties were maintaining the Japanese volunteer brigade with its responsibility for guarding the International Settlement, maintaining JRA-run schools, running the local cemetery, and seeing to the preservation of hygiene and the prevention of disease. Schools were its particular preserve, with more than 80 percent of the JRA budget devoted to education. In 1908 there were 225 Japanese children in these schools; by 1931 there were 3,345. Over the course of the Taishō years, this number surpassed 2,000, as the percentage of students in the total Japanese population also rose. This change reflected the greater number of entire family units living in Shanghai; earlier, Japanese men had frequently moved to Shanghai alone (Takatsuna 1995, 125–127; Zhu 1995, 428). Also, the Tō-A Dōbun Shoin (East Asian Common Culture Institute), a Japanese postsecondary institution of higher learning, graduated more than 3,600 students between 1900 and 1945 (see below).

The street and neighborhood associations became essential to the fabric of the local community. When the Twenty-one Demands were delivered to the Yuan Shikai government in 1915, anti-Japanese boycotts broke out across urban China. A large number of Japanese left for home, and this confrontation provided the opportunity for the formation of six neighborhood associations in Shanghai. Together they worked with the JRA and the consulate to protect local Japanese as well as to streamline the operations of local communal institutions. In 1917 six more neighborhood associations were set up. At the time of the May Thirtieth Incident (1925), they were mobilized to act as effective policing agencies. By the end of the period of Japanese residency in Shanghai, there were altogether forty such associations. The overarching organization that managed the many neighborhood groups was the Street Federation. Unlike the JRA, which was controlled by the *kaisha-ha,* the neighborhood and street associations were controlled by the *dochaku-ha,* reflecting the sentiments of the bulk of the local Japanese population.

These organizations reflect a sense of isolation, unease, perhaps even alienation among the Japanese, all of which influenced their degree of integration into the community of Shanghai. As a group they tended to reproduce as many of the institutions of home as they possibly could. In the face of Chinese nationalism directed against Japan, as was to occur so frequently during the period under study, they remained on the whole staunchly nationalistic themselves. At the time of the Northern Expedition in 1927, fear that the forces of Jiang Jieshi (Chiang Kai-shek) would do harm to Japanese interests inspired the formation of a Shanghai branch of the

Reserve Officers Association from among the JRA members with military experience. Indeed, these organizations sadly provided the organizational structure for the massacres of Chinese who were rounded up on the pretext of being "plainclothes guerrillas" at the time of the first Shanghai Incident in January 1932. As tensions grew through the late 1920s and 1930s and Shanghai continued to be a major anti-Japanese center, despite both Japanese and Guomindang massacres, the JRA simply grew more intransigent. It led the call to punish China and feverishly demanded that the Japanese army defend local interests (Takatsuna 1995, 127–131).[9]

The Harbin community, albeit smaller in numbers, produced an impressive array of communal institutions as well. Although Harbin generally followed Valdivostok's lead in most civil matters, Harbin had formed a residents association, the Sōkakai, as early as 1901; Vladivostok followed suit in March 1902 at a time when there were 2,875 Japanese in the city (and a total of 4,334 throughout Siberia and the Russian Far East). The mass evacuation of Japanese from the northeast over the next two years left few behind to run communal affairs. As Harbin's Japanese population began to return to prewar levels at the end of the first decade of the twentieth century, the first Japanese elementary school was opened, with all of four children, in 1909 in a room at the local Nishi honganji; it did not have its own building until June 1923, when an impressive structure built by the Residents Association and the South Manchurian Railway Company (SMR), which from 1920 assumed one-half of all educational costs for local Japanese, was completed. The first elementary school was called Momoyama; a second one was called Hanazono (Sugiyama 1985, 66–67, 78, 116–117; Gotō 1973, 68–82; Sugiyama 1979, 8).

Despite these separate communal institutions, the Harbin community achieved a much higher degree of integration than that of Shanghai. In Shanghai most Japanese lived in blissful ignorance of the surrounding Chinese populace, whereas in Harbin most Japanese learned Russian and many even took a stab at Chinese. Inasmuch as those who settled in Harbin planned to remain there for the duration, it was only natural that they master the language of the predominant groups in the city, much as Japanese learned English in the United States or Portuguese in Brazil. In September 1920 a Russo-Japanese School opened, the forerunner of the Harbin Academy, which became famous as a training institute in the Russian language. The first principal, Inoda Kōhai, was a former student of Futabatei Shimei from the Tokyo Foreign Language School. A Sino-Japanese Evening School for language training opened in early April 1923 with similar aims of fostering Sino-Japanese understanding and friendship. In addition, many Japanese who worked outside the home adopted Western styles of dress from the end of the Meiji period. In fact, Japanese in Vladivostok early on became tailors, producing Western-style men's and women's clothing initially for the local

Russian population. Fresh Japanese produce was imported from numerous Japanese ports throughout the northeast as far as the Blagoveshchensk region with Chinese merchants serving as intermediaries.

In the aftermath of World War I and the Bolshevik Revolution, Harbin became congested with countless new immigrants. The year 1919 was particularly difficult, with the Japanese military confiscating freight cars for their own use. That same year, though, the Japanese community founded the Harbin Commercial Exhibition Hall (Harubin Shōhin Chinretsukan) dedicated to stimulating Russo-Japanese trade and incidentally to calming Russo-Japanese tensions. The head was Mori Gyoin, who was to become a central figure in the local Japanese community for the next two decades. The Exhibition Hall began that year to publish a monthly magazine, each issue well over one hundred pages, featuring all manner of local news, commercial statistics, and a variety of human-interest stories, mostly from Harbin but with occasional reports from Vladivostok and elsewhere in the region. By October of 1921 the Japanese Chamber of Commerce of Harbin had 113 members (Sugiyama 1985, 93–95, 97, 106, 111, 113–114; *Harubin tsūshin,* March 17, 1923, 3; March 18, 1923, 2; Yamamoto 1932, 357).[10]

Despite these efforts at smoothing over the ethnic frictions in the city, visitors noted that Chinese, Japanese, and Russians each had their own interests to protect and their own self-defense mechanisms. When the Japanese army withdrew in 1922, many Japanese residents of Vladivostok decided it was no longer safe to live there, and they resettled in Harbin; others moved to the Korean city of Ch'ongjin to the south, but Harbiners did not move in any significant numbers. The decade from the evacuation in 1922 through the Manchurian Incident marked Harbin's Republican Chinese phase. The central government in Beijing and later in Nanjing was never strong enough to exercise control over Harbin, and thus the city fell under the sway of the massive Manchurian satrapy of warlord Zhang Zuolin, who turned affairs over to his underling, Zhang Huanxiang. The latter Zhang began a course of action to sinify Harbin that met with considerable friction with the leaders of the other ethnic communities (Higashi 1918, 189; Sugiyama 1985, 114–115).[11]

In both Shanghai and Harbin, Japanese newspapers abounded, reinforcing the sense of separate communities. In addition to journalists from all the major Japanese dailies and weeklies, Shanghai produced several of its own, such as *Shanhai nippō* (founded 1903), *Shanhai nichinichi shinbun* (founded 1914), *Shanhai mainichi shinbun* (founded 1918), and *Jiangnan zhengbao* (founded 1918), a Japanese-owned newspaper published in Chinese. Although serving a smaller community, Harbin produced even more, such as *Harubin nichinichi shinbun, Taihoku shinbun, Harubin tsūshin, Ro-A jihō, Hoku-Man denpō,* and *Teikoku tsūshin* (Ozaki 1990, 10; Yanagida 1986, 234).

POLITICS WITHIN THE JAPANESE COMMUNITIES

The one area of life in Shanghai that witnessed considerable Sino-Japanese integration was left-wing politics, and this in spite of the variety of local Japanese police forces in Shanghai, including an office of the Special Higher Police (Tokkō). As we have seen, the great majority of Japanese in Shanghai were at least as supportive of their government and military as their friends and relatives back home. What was the purpose, then, of so many policing agencies? In part, the police were there to protect against intrusions from the Chinese; but there were good reasons, as mainstream politics veered sharply to the right at home, to keep a close watch on the activities of some Japanese in Shanghai as well. I shall introduce three interrelated topics, in each of which a high degree of cooperation between Chinese and Japanese was achieved: Uchiyama Kanzō, the Tō-A Dōbun Shoin, and the Sorge-Ozaki spy ring.

Uchiyama Kanzō first arrived in Shanghai in 1913 and four years later opened the Uchiyama Shoten on North Sichuan Road. He eventually built the largest collection of Japanese books in China proper, catering to local Japanese as well as to Chinese who had studied in Japan. As his business grew, he converted the second story of the shop into a tatami room for meetings between Chinese and Japanese writers. In a short time, Uchiyama became a broker and his bookstore a salon for Sino-Japanese literary contacts. It was through him, for example, that Tanizakai Jun'ichirō met with such eminent Chinese writers as Tian Han, Guo Moruo, and Ouyang Yuqian in 1926. The strongest and most famous bond Uchiyama forged with a Chinese writer was with Lu Xun, who moved to Shanghai from Guangdong in October 1927. In March of 1930 Lu Xun, fearing arrest, hid in the Uchiyama Shoten for more than a month (Ozawa 1972, 83; Uchiyama 1961, 122; Ozaki 1990, 26–33; Fogel 1989, 575–602; Uchiyama 1979, 39; NHK 1986).

Uchiyama went out of his way to remain as apolitical as possible, although as Sino-Japanese tensions mounted, being apolitical meant being unwilling to accept the pronouncements of his own government and the local Residents Association toward China. It meant as well that he had to avoid the endemic struggles within the Chinese literary movement of the 1920s and 1930s. Without a doubt, the overwhelming political bent of his Chinese clientele was leftist, and many were or would soon become Communists. Under extremely politicized circumstances, being apolitical bordered on the impossible, but that was, nonetheless, Uchiyama's stance. Also, because he was in China and not in Japan, he was able to sell Japanese works, such as translations of the writings of Marx and Lenin, that by the 1930s would have been increasingly difficult, if not outright impossible, to put on sale back home. Uchiyama remained in China through the end of World War

II and until his death in 1959; he was posthumously lionized in the People's Republic as a *lao pengyou* (lit., old friend).

Another Japanese institution that bred radical activities and fostered close Sino-Japanese integration in Shanghai was the Tō-A Dōbun Shoin. A product of the imagination of the adventurer and reformer, Arao Kiyoshi, and the hard work of his disciple, Nezu Hajime, together with Konoe Atsumaro, it was founded in 1900 in Shanghai, ideally for both Japanese and Chinese students. The curriculum emphasized contemporary subject matter: business, political science, agriculture, and much Chinese-language training (Reynolds 1987, 1989). A number of students developed overwhelmingly strong sympathies for the Chinese labor movement over the course of the 1920s; some witnessed the May Thirtieth Incident, Chinese workers' strikes, or even activities of the young Chinese Communist Party (CCP). Several of the Japanese students abandoned their education altogether to participate in the Chinese revolutionary movement, while others were expelled for becoming too involved; in either case their language training served them well and set them off from most of their local countrymen, who had shown little or no interest in learning Chinese. Despite the fact that the Japanese policing agencies kept a close watch on their movements, many Japanese students (together with their Chinese classmates) became deeply involved in leftist and anti-imperialist actions. These activities intensified into the early 1930s, when, as Chalmers Johnson has noted, "what amounted to a Japanese cell of the Chinese Communist Youth League had been established" at the Tō-A Dōbun Shoin (Johnson 1990, 55).

In 1930 a number of Tō-A Dōbun Shoin students joined with a small group of Japanese and Chinese journalists and writers in Shanghai to form the China Problems Study Group. The group's recognized leader was a Chinese Communist activist and graduate of Kyoto University, Wang Xuewen. Wang had studied economics under Kawakami Hajime and lived in Japan for a total of fourteen years. Because of his experience and language talents, the CCP had assigned Wang the task of rallying "antiwar, anti-imperialist" Japanese in Shanghai to the Communist cause (Nishizato 1977, 12, 25, 48–49, 74, 89; Kawai 1979, 207–211, 259, 262, 320, 339, 341–343, 368–369; Peng 1988, 28–29).[12] Though Wang's connections to the CCP were unknown to his Japanese acquaintances, none would likely have been surprised or upset by the news. The group discussed such issues as the developing Communist movement, the nature of Chinese society, and other *au courant* themes of the day among leftists. In mid-October one CCP member named Yang Liuqing suggested that the group move beyond discussion and participate in direct action. Wang agreed. Then, on the suggestion of Kawai Teikichi, who would become more prominent in the 1930s, they renamed themselves the Nis-Shi Tōsō Dōmei, or Sino-Japanese Struggle Alliance

(Kawai 1979, 371–374, 377; Johnson 1990, 57; Kawai 1973, 12–13; Ozaki 1990, 126–129; Kawai 1975, 2).[13]

The first and most startling act of the Sino-Japanese Struggle Alliance was an antiwar action aimed at the Japanese Naval Landing Party in Shanghai. The large cement structure housing the latter was a daily, visible reminder that Japanese nationals and their property fell under Japanese military protection. In commemoration of the thirteenth anniversary of the Bolshevik Revolution, the young men of the Alliance printed posters and leaflets in both Chinese and Japanese opposing all hostilities between the two nations. On the evening of November 7, 1930, they used coal tar to scrawl in immense characters on the side of the Naval Landing Party building:

Down with Japanese Imperialism!
Join hands with the Chinese Soviets!
Turn your guns around and bring down the capitalist-landlord state!
Long live the Chinese Communist Party!
Long live the soldiers, workers, and peasants!

Needless to say, the press widely reported the event. A group of students within the Tō-A Dōbun Shoin joined the Alliance and went on strike in sympathy. Several students and Alliance members were arrested in what was exaggeratedly reported in the press as the "Japan Communist Party Incident." By early 1931, most of the students had been released from jail and expelled; Nishizato Tatsuo, a recent graduate of Tō-A Dōbun Shoin, was arrested as a ringleader in Tokyo by the Tokkō later in 1931 and was not released until December 1932 (Kawai 1973, 11; Johnson 1990, 57–58; Ozaki 1990, 130–135; Nishizato 1977, 100, 110–114).[14]

Another CCP order to Yang in October 1931 directed him to find Japanese in Shanghai to cooperate with the intelligence-gathering work of Richard Sorge, an operative for Red Army intelligence. Yang turned to Ozaki Hotsumi, a well-respected journalist, and to Kawai Teikichi, whom he knew through the Alliance. Ozaki and Kawai met for the first time at Yang's home. Inasmuch as the Sorge-Ozaki spy ring has been discussed at great length by many fine scholars, we shall elide discussion of it here (Johnson 1990; Deakin and Storry 1966; Prange 1984; Mader 1984).[15]

The politics of Harbin were altogether different from those of Shanghai. Before the Japanese military seizure in the early 1930s, the city was administered on a daily basis by representatives of the different constituent communities, including the majority Chinese population. Left-wing activists certainly resided in or passed through Harbin, but it never became home to any sustained political movement of the left. In fact, as Edgar Snow hinted, the drug trade was to become a kind of Russo-Japanese joint venture.

Indeed, it was on the extreme right wing of the political spectrum in Harbin that Japanese and Russians found some common ground. From the late 1920s, the city experienced a rash of kidnappings, usually backed by the more fanatic elements in the Guandong Army working together with Russians fascist elements, of wealthy Chinese and of Russian Jews for huge ransoms; the Semion Kaspé kidnapping case is only the most notorious and grisly of many (Stephan 1978; Vespa 1941, 78–80, 89, 196, 198–203, 205–218, 238–239, 253, 272).

Harbin also provided the setting for major political events that, unlike those in Shanghai, had little connection to China or Chinese politics. For Japanese residents of the city, the most dramatic event of the entire first half of the twentieth century was the assassination of Itō Hirobumi in October 1909 in front of the railway station. The assassin, a disgruntled Korean nationalist named An Chung-gŭn, was unhappy at Prince Itō's prominent role in the coming annexation of Korea. A memorial statue to Itō was soon erected before the train station, and this event became a defining moment for the local Japanese community, even those born well after the event. About the same time, the Japanese consul general in Harbin, Kawakami Toshihiko, was also shot by a Korean, but he survived the attack (*Manshū nichinichi shimbun,* December 26, 1909, 1; Yanagida 1986, 209–217).

There were certainly Japanese spies in and around Harbin, but, unlike Shanghai, most of them were working for the Japanese government. Harbin was home to a branch of the SMR devoted to Russia-watching. Russian-language experts were stationed there to observe local Soviet politics and, more importantly, Soviet troop movements across the border. The Tokumu Kikan was an imposing presence that occupied two-thirds of an entire city block. Two blocks away it had another, smaller office, across the street one way from the headquarters of the Kenpeitai, or Military Police, which occupied half a city block, and the other way from the Harbin Shinto Shrine. After the murder of Zhang Zuolin in June of 1928 by officers in the Guandong Army, the political climate in Harbin took a decidedly chilly turn. From a general ambiance of "confused freedom," as one memoirist put it, there was a precipitous slide into a more militarized atmosphere, especially following the Manchurian Incident and seizure of power by the Japanese authorities (Matani 1981, appended maps).

The Guandong Army marched into Harbin in February 1932, several months after the Manchurian Incident. In a well orchestrated welcome, Japanese lined the streets of the city to greet them. There were still only about thirty-six hundred Japanese living in Harbin, though as many as two hundred thousand were scattered through the many cities and towns of Manchuria. Less than one month later, on March 1, the puppet state of Manzhouguo (Manchukuo) came into existence, and the Japanese era in Harbin, the third regime in as many decades in this city of ceaseless transitions, officially took control. Six years later there were thirty-seven thousand Japanese residents, and their numbers continued to grow until the early 1940s. Under Japanese control, the Tokumu Kikan allegedly set up bureaus for the various ethnicities of the city and, for example, hired impoverished Cossack malcontents to keep a watch on the local Russian community. With the fox watching the chicken coop, this policy was guaranteed to make virtually everyone unhappy. As Edgar Snow noted at the time, the Japanese police then sold off contracts to run houses of prostitution and drug dens to local toughs and other unsavory elements in various sectors of the city, drawing off a percentage of the take for themselves. Many Japanese visitors to Harbin in the 1930s lamented the fact that there were whole illicit industries thriving in Harbin that would have been completely illegal in Japan (Sugiyama 1985, 136–137; Vespa 1941, 33–35, 51, 86).[16]

CONCLUSIONS: RELATIONS WITH THE HOMELAND

While Shanghai was a mosaic society, as intimated by Edgar Snow, in which the Japanese residents had little meaningful contact with the surrounding peoples, Harbin was more a multicultural melting pot in the sense of different ethnic groups coming together and giving up something of themselves as they attempted to create something new, though the incidence of marriage across racial lines remained low. No one ever dreamed or certainly ever espoused such a fate for the ethnic communities of Shanghai, least of all the Japanese there. Since there was no population "native" to Harbin, everyone was a pioneer and shared common difficulties in a way unimaginable in Shanghai.

Born in Harbin in 1928, Sugiyama Kimiko remembers being thoroughly confused in mid-August 1945 when she was warned by her uncle, an employee at the Japanese consulate, that she should leave Harbin for "home" immediately. Harbin *was* home. Her parents had met and married there in 1925 and had run an agricultural implements store there. They were all part of the pre-Manzhouguo generation who, she claims, lived amid other Asians who were their friends and neighbors. During the tension of the Manchurian Incident, a Chinese man helped her father; both men were so far from their native places that neither had a clear idea what a country or an ethnicity really was. One of her close friends was a Korean who, her mother told her, was a cousin of An Chung-gŭn. She, of course, knew she was Japanese, but the primary "ethnic" affiliation she felt was as a Harbiner; and for that reason she felt neither overly upset at Japan's loss in the war nor particularly threatened afterward. When they left Harbin, their Chinese friends threw them a party, in spite of her father's worry that showing such attention to a

Japanese family might be dangerous. Returning to Japan was a truly perplex-ing experience, because it was alien terrain. Yes, Japan had lost the war, Manzhouguo had dissolved, and Japanese had to withdraw to their "mother" country, but what, she still wondered, did any of that have to do with her (Sugiyama 1979, 3–6, 9, 12–13, 15–16, 18–19; see also Kaetsu 1971).

There are many similar stories for Harbin and elsewhere in Manchuria. I have seen nothing comparable for Shanghai or anywhere else in China proper. Perhaps many emigrants to the Northeast Asian continent had truly internalized the propaganda of the day. More likely, they looked at the opportunities a new life in Manchuria afforded them much in the same way Japanese immigrants to the United States felt in the same years, though the presence of Japanese governmental and military agencies was far greater in Manchuria, to be sure, and Japanese did not enjoy extraterritoriality in the United States. The Shanghai community, though larger than the Harbin one, was never as stable nor as permanently fixed in its new home. Aside from rare exceptions such as Uchiyama Kanzō and the radical students and activ-ists described above, Japanese residents of Shanghai had little contact with the local Chinese population. Japanese in Shanghai thus only rarely achieved, or even desired, any level of integration with the surrounding populace. Unlike in Harbin, it was not a desideratum. In addition, there was considerable interaction among the various Japanese communities of Man-churia—baseball games, newspaper coverage, and other informal, social contacts—though little of a similar nature with or within the communities of China proper. There were far more Japanese communities and residents associations in Manchuria than in China proper and far more Japanese consulates in Manchuria than there are now.

In one of the interesting ironies of Japanese foreign policy during the Manzhouguo era, the government moved to disband the Japanese residents associations in Manchuria in the mid-1930s, because they did not want the other nationalities in the new nation—who were all supposed to live in *gozoku kyōwa* (harmony of the five ethnic groups)—to think the Japanese were enjoying special privileges. A report from the Gaimushō of October 1937 lists eight residents associations that were dissolved in late September and early October; Harbin's was to be discontinued in November. Also, the Japanese in Manchuria would, perforce, abandon all claims to extraterritori-ality, for they were no longer living on Chinese or contested terrain but in Manzhouguo. All the residents associations were to be incorporated into the Kyōwakai, or Concordia Society, in many ways the ultimate tool of multicul-tural integration. In fact, it was the local Japanese military that feared the continued existence of the Harbin JRA would lead to "ethnic animosities" (*minzokuteki tairitsu*). After a diplomatic fury between Harbin and the Gaimushō from October 1937 through early 1938, the latter agreed to avoid the displeasure of the Manzhouguo government and disband all special organizations that seemed to offer Japanese any kind of distinctive favors. The Gaimushō specifically wanted to avoid the impression of "racial bias" and act in the spirit of *gozoku kyōwa* (Gaimushō Archives, file K3.2.2.1–32, reports of June 16, 1935, December 14, 1937, October 25, 1937, January 21, 1938, May 24, 1938, June 18, 1938, and August 17, 1938). By comparison, it is hard to imagine the Japanese community of Shanghai remaining in existence without the JRA.

How did Japanese at home see the communities of Japanese on the mainland? Both Harbin and Shanghai were dubbed by journalists and travelers as the "Paris of the East," and both cities were visualized as dens of iniquity. But, these competing images were as alluring to some as they were reprehensible to others. No one thought of the Japanese in Shanghai as pioneers, though that image frequently was used to describe Japanese who had settled in the Northeast. One report from Dalian (Dairen) that appeared in *Chūō kōron* in 1920 belied an image of Japanese that could apply to Harbin as well.

> Children raised here don't know of the mild Japanese weather nor of its graceful scenic beauty. . . . They see decadent Chinese lives. . . . They will probably grow up with irregularities and with unimaginably strange psyches. Soon after birth, they see two races and learn two languages and see clearly the unnaturalness wherein one of the races overcomes the other. We know the children here are not the Japanese who pull rickshas or work as coolies. . . . Children molded by such a life as this—Japanese without a home place. . . . Elementary school students draw Mount Fuji, which they have never seen, from their imagination and paint it red. How will they ever see it right with the bald mountains of Manchuria [about them]? (Kimura 1920, 73–74)[17]

NOTES

1. Sugiyama 1985, 11, citing an 1892 work by Kawakami Toshihiko, future consul of Harbin, *Urajiosutoku*.
2. The Chinese recently have come up with some far-fetched theories claiming that Harbin goes back to the late eleventh century, thereby predating the Russian settlement by many centuries. They have as yet presented little substantive evidence. See Clausen and Thøgersen 1995, 3–4, 12–16. On the early Harbin and the CER, see Quested 1982, 32, 100–101, 129–131; Koshizawa 1989, 13–24; Matani 1981, 1. There have been any number of theories about the meaning and origin of the name Harbin, none of them particularly persuasive. Five of these are summarized in Sugiyama 1985, 52–54. A Japanese guidebook of 1924 discusses three theories but declines to take a stand; see *Harubin no gainen* 1924, 1. The most recent theory, not cited in Sugiyama, is that of Guan Chenghe, in his *Haerbin kao;* he argues that it is from a Jurchen word meaning "honored" and that the city dates from 1097 (see Li 1980, 3).

3. On Harbin and the Russo-Japanese War, see Yanagida 1986, 97–130. Chiyo's sister Fuino gave birth to a daughter in September 1900, the first Japanese born in Harbin.

4. *Mato* (Demon Capital), published in 1923, as cited in Takatsuna 1995, 131. On Muramatsu's writings about China, see Otani 1989, 93–108; Fogel 1996, chap. 9.

5. These figures come from Katō 1974, 316; slightly lower figures for 1935 can be found in Takatsuna 1995, 121; slightly different figures as well can be found in Peattie 1989, 170. The overall population of Shanghai at this time was roughly 3.6 million, making the Japanese 0.7 percent of the total.

6. Higashi Kochiku 1918, 184–186; *Manshū nippō*, December 18, 1907, 1, article on the civil administration of Harbin and the CER authorities mentions the coming to Harbin of Mitsui; Sugiyama 1985, 64–68, 75–78, 90–92.

7. *Harubin tsūshin*, February 1, 1923, 3. This report contains a survey of the local population, breakdowns by the suburbs of Harbin, and a detailed occupational breakdown. By this time, the men outnumbered the women roughly five-to-four (Song 1995, 104–107). There is a fascinating breakdown of the businesses owned and operated by Russians in Harbin in *Urajio nippō*, August 10, 1922, 3. With the exception of the brothel business, Russians (in larger numbers, to be sure) were engaged in many of the same sorts of affairs in the city.

8. See the appeal (May 1, 1918) to the Japanese government signed by the heads of the Japanese Residents Asssociations of Vladivostok, Harbin, Iman, Nikolsk, and Spassk-Dal'nyi, cautioning the authorities on the use of military force in the region (reprinted in Shinobu 1951, 483–484; *Harubin shōhin chinretsukan shūhō* 2.17, July 23, 1924; *Manshū tokuhon*, 1935, 356–358; Hirayama 1932, 236–238; Kazama 1938, 254–255; *Harubin tsūshin*, March 6, 1923, 3).

9. Though little studied, the Shanghai "Incident" beginning in late January of 1932 left 6,080 Chinese dead, 2,000 wounded, and 10,400 missing; 814,084 suffered direct losses, and 80 percent of urban workers lost their jobs; 50 percent of all factories in Zhabei were destroyed, largely from aerial bombardment, and 1.2 million Chinese were made refugees. This was mostly the work of the Japanese military, but the neighborhood associations played roles in the killing and destruction, and all in five weeks' time. Small consolation that the Chinese won this battle, though that victory proved a great inspiration in the next and far greater Pyrrhic victory of the Chinese against Japan.

10. A June 1922 document marked "secret" in the Gaimushō Archives complained that Japanese in Manchuria had changed their clothing in accordance with the conditions of life and work in the region, which the author regarded as potentially deleterious to long-term planning, and the Japanese "treat locals like slaves." See Miyahara 1922.

11. Higashi Fumio (1940, 46) reported that relations between young Japanese

and young Russians were excellent, with some intermarriage, but this strikes me as somewhat exaggerated or propagandistic. His book was published in 1940. More typical was Yamamoto Sanehiko's comment (1932, 346): "Who must bear responsibility for the crime of turning Harbin into a street of flirtatiousness?" The White Russians, of course. "All their great pride for the glories of the tsarist era they now discard in the gutters of Harbin. They keep groups of degenerate women, and they have transformed it [Harbin] into a prominent boil on the face of the earth." Stunning comment, considering that it was the Japanese who pioneered the flesh trade in Harbin.

12. Wang left Shanghai abruptly in 1937 and fled to Yan'an, where he and Japanese Communist Nosaka Sanzō organized and lectured at the Japanese Peasants' and Workers' School for captured soldiers of the Japanese army. See Nakamura Shintarō 1975, 231–240.

13. As Nishizato (1977, 90) explains, they opted for the "Shi" of Shina in their title, rather than Chūgoku, despite claims that the former denigrated the Chinese, because the latter would be unfamiliar to most Japanese, and the Chinese in the group agreed. On "Shina" and "Chūgoku," see Fogel 1994a, 66–76.

14. Unlike other sources, which generally follow Kawai, Nishizato (1977, 92) claimed that the line "Long Live the Chinese Communist Party!" was not one of the slogans plastered on the wall, because it would have been contrary to the nature of their movement.

15. I have discussed Kawai Teikichi's scholarship on China as a genre of non-academic sinology in Fogel 1993, 259–265.

16. Vespa claims that in 1936 there were 172 brothels, 56 opium dens, and 194 licensed narcotics shops in Harbin alone, and that in Heilongjiang and Jilin provinces there were 550 licensed brothels with 70,000 Japanese girls servicing customers (1941, 102). The Harbin figures, although high, are considerably lower than Edgar Snow's, as noted at the beginning of this essay.

17. Perhaps even more disturbing is Kimura's depiction of the Chinese: "To sport with them or tyrannize them would be 'unfair,' indeed doubly or triply abominable. One just has to subjugate them. Tyranny will not do. Even if they plead to excess, there is no other way. They have no feelings and are spoiled. Chinese youths are raised laboring for ten years until they reach marriageable age; then they steal from the cash box—for 'independence.' This is because their minds are empty. They are born that way. I learned that there were such people" (88).

REFERENCES

Bay Area Jews from Harbin, Manchuria. Unpublished interviews. Transcripts held in the Judah Magnes Museum, Berkeley, California. In Russian and English.

Banno Junji. 1989. "Japanese Industrialists and Merchants and the Anti-Japanese Boycotts in China, 1919–1928." In *The Japanese Informal Empire in China, 1895–1937*, edited by Peter Duus, Ramon H. Myers, and Mark R. Peattie, 314–329. Princeton: Princeton University Press.

Clausen, Søren, and Stig Thøgersen, ed. and trans. 1995. *The Making of a Chinese City: History and Historiography in Harbin*. Armonk, New York: M. E. Sharpe.

Deakin, F. W., and G. R. Storry. 1966. *The Case of Richard Sorge*. London: Chatto & Windus.

Duus, Peter. 1989. "Zaikabō: Japanese Cotton Mills in China, 1895–1937." In *The Japanese Informal Empire in China, 1895–1937*, edited by Peter Duus, Ramon H. Myers, and Mark R. Peattie, 65–100. Princeton: Princeton University Press.

Fogel, Joshua A. 1989. "Japanese Literary Travelers in Prewar China." *Harvard Journal of Asiatic Studies* 49.2:575–602.

———. 1993. "Senzen Nihon no minkan Chūgokugaku." In *Ajia kara kanagaeru*, edited by Mizoguchi Yūzō, Hamashita Takeshi, Hiraishi Naoaki, and Miyajima Hiroshi, Vol. 1, *Kōsaku suru Ajia*, 253–272. Tokyo University Press.

———. 1994a. "The Sino-Japanese Controversy over *Shina* as a Toponym for China." In *The Cultural Dimension of Sino-Japanese Relations: Essays on the Nineteenth and Twentieth Centuries*, 66–76. Armonk, New York: M. E. Sharpe.

———. 1994b. "The Voyage of the *Senzaimaru* to Shanghai: Early Sino-Japanese Contacts in the Modern Era." In *The Cultural Dimension of Sino-Japanese Relations: Essays on the Nineteenth and Twentieth Centuries*, 79–94. Armonk, New York: M. E. Sharpe.

———. 1996. *The Literature of Travel in the Japanese Rediscovery of China, 1862–1945*. Stanford: Stanford University Press.

Gotō Shunkichi. 1973. "Harubin Nihon shōgakkō." In *Harubin no omoide*, edited by Gotō Shunkichi, 68–86. Kyoto: Kyōto Harubin Kai.

Harubin no Gainen. 1924. Harbin: Harubin Nihon Shōgyō Kaigijo.

Harubin Shōhin Chinretsukan Shūhō.

Harubin Tsūshin.

Haruna Akira. 1987. "1862 nen bakufu Senzaimaru no Shanhai haken." In *Nihon zenkindai no kokka to taigai kankei*, edited by Tanaka Takeo, 555–601. Yoshikawa Kōbunkan.

Higashi Fumio. 1940. *Chōsen Manshū Shina tairiku shisatsu ryokō annai*. Seikōkan.

Higashi Kochiku. 1918. "Urajio yori Harubin e." *Taiyō* 24.9:183–190.

Hirayama Yoshie. 1932. "Harupin kanraku shō." *Keizai ōrai* 7 (March):234–239.

Johnson, Chalmers. 1990. *An Instance of Treason: Ozaki Hotsumi and the Sorge Spy Ring*. Stanford: Stanford University Press.

Jordan, Donald A. 1991. *Chinese Boycotts versus Japanese Bombs: The Failure of China's "Revolutionary Diplomacy," 1931–1932.* Ann Arbor: University of Michigan Press.

Kaetsu Mikio. 1971. *Nanasen mei no Harupin dasshutsu.* Self-published.

Katō Yūzō. 1974. "Shanhai ryakushi." In *Shanhai jidai, jaanarisuto no kaisō* by Matsumoto Shigeharu, 1:310–325. Chūō Kōronsha.

Kawai Teikichi. 1973. *Aru kakumeika no kaisō.* Shin Jinbutsu Ōraisha.

———. 1975. *Zoruge jiken gokuchū ki.* Shin Jinbutsu Ōraisha.

———. 1979. *Harukanaru seinen no hibi ni, watakushi no hansei ki.* Tanizawa Shobō.

Kazama Seitarō. 1938. "Kokkyōno machi Harubin tayori." *Bungei shunjū* 16.9:252–255.

Kimura, Sōhachi. 1920. "Dairen ni te." *Chūō kōron* 35 (December):72–90.

Koshizawa Akira. 1989. *Harupin no toshi keikaku, 1898–1945.* Sōwasha.

Li Shuxia. 1980. *Haerbin lishi biannian (1896–1926).* Harbin: Difang Shi Yanjiusuo.

Mader, Julius. 1984. *Dr. Sorge-Report: Ein Dokumentarbericht über Kunderschafter des Friedens mit ausgewählten Artiklen von Richard Sorge.* Berlin: Militärverlag der Deutschen Demokratischen Republik.

Manshū Nippō.

Manshū nichinichi shinbun.

Manshū Tokuhon. 1935. Tō-A-keizei Chōsakyoku.

Matani Haruji. 1981. *Harubin no machi.* Self-published.

Miyahara Tamihei. 1922. "Man-Mō bunka senden kōenkai ni kansuru ken." Number four series, "Hōjin no zai-Man seikatsu." Gaimushō Archives, no. 2631. June 13.

Nakamura Fukuzō. 1973. "Taishō jidai no Harupin." In *Harubin no omoide,* edited by Gotō Shunkichi, 91–96. Kyoto: Kyoto Harubin Kai.

Nakamura Shintarō. 1975. *Son Bun kara Ozaki Hotsumi e.* Nit-Chū Shuppan.

NHK. 1986. "Dokyumento Shōwa." Pt. 2: "Shanhai kyōdō sokai."

Nishizato Tatsuo. 1977. *Kakumei no Shanhai de, aru Nihonjin Chūgoku kyōsantōin no kiroku.* Nit-Chū Shuppan.

Otani Ichirō. 1989. "Muramatsu Shōfū to Chūgoku: Den Kan to Muramatsu, Muramatsu no Chūgoku ni taisuru shisei nado o chūshin ni." *Hitotsubashi ronsō* 101.3:93–108.

Ozaki Hotsuki. 1990. *Shanhai 1930 nen.* Iwanami Shoten.

Ozawa Masamoto. 1972. *Uchiyama Kanzō den: Nit Chū yūkō ni tsukushita idai na shomin.* Banchō Shobō.

Peattie, Mark R. 1989. "Japanese Treaty Port Settlements in China, 1895–1937." In *The Japanese Informal Empire in China, 1895–1937,* edited by Peter Duus, Ramon H. Myers, and Mark R. Peattie, 116–209. Princeton: Princeton University Press.

Peng Hao. 1988. "Chuanhe Zhenji de zuji: Sanshi niandai Ribenren zai Shanghai de fanzhan huodong." *Zhongguo Zhong-Ri guanxi shi yanjiuhui huikan* 14:26–31.

Prange, Gordon. 1984. *Target Tokyo: The Story of the Sorge Spy Ring.* New York: McGraw-Hill.

Qiao Shuming. 1989. "Jinru Shanghai zujie de Ribenren." *Shanghai yanjiu luncong* 3:43–52.

Quested, R. K. I. 1982. *"Matey" Imperialists?: The Tsarist Russians in Manchuria, 1895–1917.* Hong Kong: University of Hong Kong.

Reynolds, Douglas R. 1987. "China Area Studies in Prewar China: Japan's Tōa Dōbun Shoin in Shanghai, 1900–1945." *Journal of Asian Studies* 45.5:945–970.

———. 1989. "Training Young China Hands: Tōa Dōbun Shoin and Its Precursors, 1886–1945." In *The Japanese Informal Empire in China, 1895–1937,* edited by Peter Duus, Ramon H. Myers, and Mark R. Peattie, 210–271. Princeton: Princeton University Press.

Satō Saburō. 1984. "Bunkyū ninen no okeru bakufu bōekisen Senzaimaru no Shanghai haken ni tsuite." In *Kindai Nit-Chū kōshō shi no kenkyū,* 67–96. Yoshikawa Kōbunkan.

Shinobu Seizaburō. 1951. *Taishō seiji shi,* vol. 2. Kawade Shobō.

Snow, Edgar. 1933. *Far Eastern Front.* New York: Harrison Smith & Robert Haas.

———. 1934. "Japan Builds a New Colony." *Saturday Evening Post* 206 (February 24):12–13, 80–81, 84–87.

Song Shisheng. 1995. "The Brothels of Harbin in the Old Society." In *The Making of a Chinese City: History and Historiography in Harbin,* edited and translated by Søren Clausen and Stig Thøgersen, 103–108. Armonk, New York: M. E. Sharpe.

Stephan, John. 1978. *The Russian Fascists: Tragedy and Farce in Exile, 1925–1945.* New York: Harper & Row.

Sugiyama, Kimiko. 1979. "Harubin no ki: watakushi ga doko de mita koto, kangaeta koto." *Manshū to Nihonjin* 7 (November):3–20.

———. 1985. *Harubin monogatari.* Hara Shobō.

Tachibana Sotoo. 1940. "Harubin no yūutsu." *Bungei shunjū* 18.8:264–288.

Takatsuna Hakubun. 1995. "Seiyōjin no Shanghai, Nihonjin no Shanghai." In *Shanghai shi, kyodai toshi no keisei to hitotbito no itonami,* edited by Takahashi Kōsuke and Furumaya Tadao, 97–132. Tōhō Shoten.

Uchiyama Kanzō. 1961. *Kakōroku.* Iwanami Shoten.

———. 1979. "Ro Jin sensei tsuioku." In *Ro Jin no omoide.* Shakai Shisōsha.

Urajio Nippō.

Vespa, Amleto. 1941. *Secret Agent of Japan.* Garden City: Garden City Publishing Company.

Wang Xiaoqui. 1989. "Mumo Ribenren zenyang kan Zhongguo: 1862 nian 'Qiansuiwan' Shanghai zhi xing yanjiu." *Ribenxue* 1:140–56.

Yamamoto Sanehiko. 1932. "Harubin." *Kaizō* 14 (October):336–371.

Yanagida Momotarō. 1986. *Harubin no zanshō.* Hara Shobō.

Yokomistu Riichi. 1932. "Rekishi (Harupin ki)." *Kaizō* 14 (October):2–17.

Yonezawa Hideo. 1938–1939. "Shanhai hōjin hatten shi." Tō-A keizai kenkyū, pt. 1, 22.3 (July 1938):394–408; pt. 2, 23.1 (January-February 1939): 112–126.

Zhu Yong. 1995. "Shanhai kyoryū Nihonjin shakai to Yokohama Kakyō shakai no hikaku kenkyū." In *Yokohama to Shanhai, kindai toshi keisei shi hikaku kenkyū.* Yokohama: Yokohama Kaikō Shiryō Fukyū Kyōkai, 399–430.

❯❯·3·❮❮

Space and Aesthetic Imagination in Some Taishō Writings

ELAINE GERBERT

In his article, "Disciplinizing Native Knowledge and Producing Place," Harry Harootunian discusses the ways in which urbanization and industrialization led some intellectuals to reinstate the importance of local place in the formation of Japanese identity. To affirm the common identity of all Japanese at a time when applications of instrumental reason together with capitalism, individualism, and competition were creating divisions between city and country, and social conflict and disharmony, Yanagita Kunio (1875–1962), for example, emphasized the "timeless history of folkic life," rooted in rural Japan, as the essential unifying reality transcending differences of social class and function. Local place, reduced to a site of economic production in the writings of socialist thinkers and, later, novelists of the proletarian literature movement, was visualized as the repository of ancestral spirit and, hence, as a place of worship by Yanagita and Origuchi Shinobu (1887–1953). Native place was reconstructed as the "locus of authentic identity," the basis of a common heritage shared by all Japanese.

Paul Anderer addresses the issue of cultural identity, space, and a sense of place from the perspective of Japanese literature in the introductory chapter of his book, *Other Worlds: Arishima Takeo and the Bounds of Modern Japanese Fiction*. In analyzing the uniqueness of Arishima's alien spatial imaginary, located in the region outside the known and culturally familiar "homeland" *(naichi)*, Anderer discusses the prevailing sense of specific geographic place and bounded space that has characterized Japanese literature from early times and that continues to characterize it in the present. This "prevailingly, place-haunted nature of Japanese fiction" (An-

70

derer 1984, 6) continued very much intact throughout the Taishō period, a time of great cultural ferment and literary influence from abroad. It was especially conspicuous in the "rise to dominance of *watakushi shōsetsu* or *shinkyō shōsetsu* (personal fiction)," the genre whose place-centered quality writer and critic Kume Masao (1891–1952) underlined in a famous statement in which he likened the *shishōsetsu* to the *furusato* (country home) of Japanese literature (Kume 1973, 57).

This essay aims at furthering this discussion by exploring other visualizations of cultural space in Taishō literature. Whereas Arishima and writers cited by Anderer looked to spaces beyond the familiar bounded space of the *naichi* in their encounters with foreign culture,[1] Uno Kōji (1891–1961), Satō Haruo (1892–1964), and Tanizaki Jun'ichirō (1886–1965), three authors closely associated with the flourishing of cosmopolitan modernist literature during Taishō, used bounded, enclosed spaces to facilitate a meeting with and an assimilation of that which was strange and unfamiliar (i.e., Western culture). Circumscribed spaces in the early works of these writers offer not so much opportunities for rediscovering familiar traditions as opportunities for discovering and experiencing new perceptions fed by foreign culture. Circumscribed space functions as an *enabling* factor in the pursuit of literary fantasy inspired by the exotic, foreign Other.

The spatial imaginary in writings by Satō and Uno published after Taishō changes dramatically and, significantly, in a way that resonates with Yanagita Kunio's emphasis on local place and the continuity of communal consciousness. In their later works, the enclosed spaces of earlier literary experimentations disappear, as these writers write about life experienced in specific geographic and historic locations. In Uno's writing the rediscovery of the open space of the Yamato countryside is accompanied by a renewed interest in communitarian bounds transcending class differences, and in a kind of "spontaneous, unreflective, and collective" (Harootunian 1990, 106) behavior predating rational applications of instrumental reason of the kind associated with the modern nation state. Satō's writing points to a rediscovery of ethnic and historical identity situated in actual geographic spaces.

Akutagawa Ryūnosuke (1892–1927), reputed for his knowledge of Western literature, and Kobayashi Takiji (1903–1933), a leading representative of the proletarian literature movement, are two among other writers who should not be omitted in this discussion, were it only for the at times sharp contrast they provide in their treatment of space, which by itself affords a more insightful view of the aesthetics of Uno, Satō, and Tanizaki, and of the cultural and political history of Taishō.

The idea that alien culture should be received in special, circumscribed spaces, insulated from the rest of the society, was familiar enough by Taishō. Examples of this tendency to quarter foreign culture in a way that made it available on a *selective*, manageable basis, were seen in the erection of the

Rokumeikan (Deer Cry Pavilion), where the Japanese elite socialized with Europeans at exclusive Western-style parties in the 1880s, and later, the Denkikan (Electricity Hall), which opened in Asakusa in 1903 to introduce the urban populace to Western culture through the medium of motion pictures.

Special places, separated from society at large, were also created to provide writers and artists the sanctuaries they needed for their cosmopolitan experimentations. One such place was the Western-style Kikufuji Hotel in the Hongō district of Tokyo, which gave those who rented its rooms a haven in which to escape from family and the pressures of concomitant responsibility into an atmosphere where inspiration, fed by foreign literature, art, and philosophy, could flourish. Stressing their feelings of kinship with Western culture, its lodgers (including many well-known writers, scholars, and artists)[2] called their retreat "la Maison Vauquer," after the boarding-house in the novels of Balzac, which housed a similarly eclectic group of men and women. Similarly, the insulated Corbusier-style house from which Uno Chiyo (1897–1996) operated her stylish magazine company might also be viewed as an exotic hideaway in the middle of Tokyo. Separated enclosures such as these were sites of liminal spheres in which the creation and enjoyment of Western-inspired aesthetic games (asobi) could be pursued in the midst of a utilitarian society that remained basically hostile to such forms of personal self-gratification.

For other writers, a rented room in an inn or an annex with a poetic name inscribed over the threshold (a talisman marking the separation of the liminal sphere from the mundane world without) became the enclosed space wherein artistic imagination might turn inward. Tanizaki is known to have "included a hidden staircase and a secret window in an upstairs room of the house he designed for himself" (Chambers 1994, 3). And that secret window gave him a secret vantage point from which he could "gaze into his garden and watch the goings-on in his private paradise" (Chambers 1994, 3). Akutagawa sought a more communal sort of sequestration when, with his writer friends Kume Masao, Kikuchi Kan (1888–1948), Uno Kōji, Hirotsu Kazuo (1891–1968), and others, he retreated to a seaside villa on the Shōnan shore for summer months of reading, writing, and conversation.

More important than these secluded spots in which writers indulged their taste for foreign culture, however, were the enclosed spaces that functioned as metaphors for the introspective, artistic imagination in their stories.

During the more Westernized phases of their careers, Uno and Satō positioned their alter egos and characters in spaces cut off and protected from the concourse of business as usual in the everyday world. In those isolated enclaves, the characters—artists or men with an artistic bent—indulged themselves in foreign literature and art. The success that Uno and

Satō enjoyed in developing the thematic of the separate space may be regarded as a sign of the degree to which the search for a kind of privacy in which to engage foreign culture on one's own terms resonated with readers at the time. This topos of the enclosed space also suggests a disinterest in social issues that characterizes *junbungaku* (pure literature) of the Taishō period and dramatically underlines the retreat from any attempt to create a literature that addressed national concerns.[3]

I should like to call attention especially to the way in which the privatization of fantasy in an enclosed space was linked to unusual visual perceptions stimulated by ocular technology during Taishō. The play of light, particularly the artificial Western-type illumination, combined with leisure, and a certain regressive posture vis-ň-vis the world (a recumbent position, perhaps, or a reversion to childlike behaviors) abetted the spinning of private fantasies in the works of Uno, Satō, and Tanizaki. And as if to underline the decidedly nonutilitarian bent of their imaginative escapades in an "ever more mechanistic society," these writers often referred to their enclosed spaces, sheltered from the gaze of the world, as "fairylands," and to their writings, as "fairy tales."

The search for an enclosed space was a dominant recurring theme in Uno's early writings. He devoted himself to writing about the rooms in which he wrote and turned the tension between the inner and the outer, the private world of fantasy and pleasure and the public world of the censorious Other, into a personal myth that stoked his imagination and animated his writing.

Uno's protagonist in "Yaneura no hōgakushi" ("The Law Student in the Garret," 1918), for example, reads European literature in a dark attic, which serves as both a fictional setting and a symbol for the solitary, bookish life he leads. Its enclosed space lifts him high above the ground below and offers a view of the sky, disconnected from the earth (real life). Within its protective walls, he enjoys, from a safe secure distance, the delights of exotic foreign literature (mostly Russian translated into English).

Uno's "Yume miru heya" ("The Dream Room," 1922) is a story about the writer's room in a cheap lodging house near Ueno Park. The first-person narrator sets about detailing its interior, lavishing the kind of attention on its dimensions and arrangement that other writers might devote to their love affairs. The narrator recounts in detail the measures he takes to protect himself from the intrusive gaze of others. Holed up in his rented room, in which he has taken refuge from members of his household, he frets about being seen if people in the adjacent guest room should suddenly open the dividing *fusuma*. He forestalls this eventuality by piling up bookcases against the *fusuma* to deny other renters access to the drying platform on the roof outside his room, a hard-to-reach spot anyway (one has to place a stool under the window and then bend over to crawl through the window "like a fly"). Having ensured himself of the solitude he needs to daydream, he proceeds to maximize the room's efficacy as a "dream weaving place" *(yumeoriba)* by hanging his favorite pictures on the walls. Daydreaming is further enhanced by the horizontal position he assumes, lying in his futon, which he has spread on the floor in the middle of the room.

In the uninterrupted quiet of this private enclosure, eidetic memories of other places he has lived in come alive. Sheltered from direct exposure to the glare of sunlight, he luxuriates in the dim shadows and travels in memory back to the rooms of his childhood. He dwells on the time when he sought the protection of the even closer space of a closet in a dark house in a sunless alley in the *shitamachi* (old plebeian, commercial district) of Osaka. He recalls happy hours spent alone in its hot stuffy confines, where he once indulged in daydreams stimulated by slides projected in a magic-lantern box—childhood correlatives of dreams now generated by the adult in his "dream weaving" sanctuary.

The psychological interiority that marks much Taishō literature[4] finds an objective correlative in the private room that calls forth memories of the magic-lantern box. Containing within itself the slides that create the illusions of fairyland, the magic-lantern box seems to symbolize the self-contained imagination itself.

For the dreamer, secrecy is essential to the enjoyment of the imaginary world. He mentions the popularity of the magic lantern in the days "when neighborhood children would often invite each other at night to look at glass slides and have magic-lantern parties." Although he was sometimes invited to other children's homes to look at their slides, he never showed his to anyone.

> In fact, I was afraid that the other children would see my slides when I looked at them at home, and so I always went into a closet to view them. (I viewed them alone, and enjoyed them by myself.) Since the season for magic-lantern viewing happened to be summer, the air in the closet was as steamy as the inside of a kettle, and as I crouched in the closet, hunched over the small tin box, completely engrossed in my slides, my body from my stomach to my chest gradually became so hot from the heat of the lamp inside the box that I was soon drenched in sweat. How I loved the happy feeling of secrecy I experienced in that narrow closet filled with the strange smells of unidentified objects as I viewed my slides! (Uno 1968, 3:277)

The integrating power of the room not only joins the dreams of the present to those of childhood. In its completely private space, freed from the tyranny of the gaze of the Other, he can both look and objectify the viewed self according to the dictates of a peculiar, private fancy. In the liminal state stimulated by the dream room, he is free to become an extension of that which he loves best: the room and the magic lantern. He lies down under the square skylight, looks up at its tall funnel-shaped window that "seems like a telescope," and imagines that *he* is a magic lantern placed face up toward the night sky.

> I looked at the sky for over an hour. Was it evening or night? I had heard that it was a time of year when one could see the stars best. In my telescope, in place of the glass at the end, there seemed to be a quartz lens; in the deep navy blue sky, demarcated by the rim of the lens, stars blue green, red, large, small, far, and near, shone with a clear brilliance. It was strange and the longer I looked the stranger it seemed. It was like a toy I had when I was a child. I tried turning off the lights and shifting my position. I then saw different stars. At one time I imagined the whole of that perfectly square four-and-a-half mat room and that skylight thrust upward at the very center; I felt just as if I were in a magic-lantern box placed facing the sky. It seemed as though the interior of the room—myself, the bookcases, the futon, the photos on the wall—had become one picture, projected onto the night sky, through the lens of that skylight. (Uno 1968, 3:301)

He creates an entire world in the protected space of the dimly illumined room. Beginning with a photo of the geisha Yumeko, whom he loves, then of the town of Suwa, where she lives, and finally of the mountains of Shinano, where Suwa lies, he projects the negative of each onto the wall, burns it into bromide paper (a procedure that, he says, follows the principle of the magic lantern), and pastes the resultant image on the wall of the "dream weaving room."

Play with his imagination (not the faculty that *forms* images but, as Bachelard explains it, the faculty that *deforms* what we perceive, freeing us from immediate reality by *changing* it [Bachelard 1988, 1]) delights not in the exact replica but in the image that is *almost like* but different from the reality recalled. An image that moves him deeply is the photograph of a profile of a face in Francis Thompson's "French Portraits," which looks astonishingly like that of the geisha Yumeko in Suwa. (No matter that it is the face of the French Symbolist poet Ferdinand Severain.) His home-manufactured ontic illusions are far more amusing than the prepackaged dreams sold in the movie houses of Asakusa.

In Satō Haruo's stories, enclosed spaces such as the strange cottage occupied by the Andalusian dog in *Supein no inu no ie* (*The House of a Spanish Dog*, 1916) or the Metropole Hotel room in which artists create an ideal town in *Utsukushii machi* (*Beautiful Town*, 1919) provide arenas for the play of fantasy. Satō, who was an accomplished painter and was (like Tanizaki Jun'ichiro) involved in writing scenarios and play scripts for the nascent film industry, often explored connections between seeing and imagining. Many of his protagonists are artists. The painter in *Supein inu no ie* is led by his dog Fraté to a wondrous cottage in a magic wood. Peering into the enclosed confines of the cottage through a window (as through the aperture of a diorama), the artist witnesses a fantastic happening as the big black Spanish dog within turns into a man in a black suit.

Satō's ocular play, like Uno's, was often mediated by vision-altering technologies and unusual lighting conditions. His neurasthenic artist protagonist, who lives apart from society, passes idle days in the sequestered space of a country cottage (*Den'en no yūutsu* [*Gloom in the Country*], 1918) and gives himself over to the passive reception of arresting visual illusions that float before the eye. A "dome-shaped frame" for viewing is provided by the "branches of the pines and the branches of the cherries in his garden," which "poked out from the sides and mingled to create a vaulted space" (Satō 1993, 57). A distant hill, seen from the porch of the country cottage, appears as a distant world, "more dreamy than real, more real than a dream," that changes shape daily, depending on the light, the weather, and "the shading of the rain." At times it becomes "blurry" as if viewed "through frosted glass." The hill suddenly becomes magically alive when the severely nearsighted narrator puts on his glasses, which he had been neglecting to wear.

> After watching for a time, it seemed as though the boundary between the purple and the green on the hillside was swelling upward on its own, and the purple area was spontaneously inching outward. Staring so hard that the space between his eyebrows ached, he saw there a tiny, tiny midget who, stooping and squirming, was hard at work harvesting those green areas. Between the rows of seedling trees the farmer was growing some crop. To his eyes, though, it appeared not that a crop was being harvested but that the purple areas were swelling.
>
> He gazed into the mysterious depths revealed by his glasses; it was like watching a fairy at work in fairyland. Inspired with a feeling of transcendence for this little hill, he stared unblinking with a sense of yearning, like a child looking through a kaleidoscope (Satō 1993, 60).

A state of mental passivity is invoked numerous times in this mood piece in which habitual conceptual controls that govern the eye's relationship to the world are suspended and the narrator experiences with amazement images received by the "innocent" eye.

A Western hotel room provides the enclosed space where ocular play takes place in *Utsukushii machi*, in which bright electric lamps stimulate the imagination of an artist and his friends who create a miniature utopian town from paper and bits of glass. The magical effect of the artificial light is further enhanced by the images of the tiny electric lights in the paper houses, reflecting off the surfaces of ponds and streams fashioned from mirrors. Satō's artists work with happy, childlike absorption as they design their model town. Their pursuit of fantasy is guided by a foreigner; the artist who organizes the project to create a miniature "beautiful town" is a Eurasian named Theodore Brentano.[5] Satō's protagonist comments: "He [Brentano] was addicted to this serious pastime and enthusiastic as a child. As each house was finished we examined it too with the joy of children" (Satō 1996, 24).

The influence of Western artistic culture, and explicit references to Western literature, infuse works by these writers. The long passage in "Yume miru heya" about the protagonist's fascination with his magic lantern may recall the episode of the magic lantern in Marcel Proust's *Remembrance of Things Past*. The cottage in *Supein inu no ie* contains early twentieth-century German Biedermeier furniture (Kawamoto 1990, 15), books with German titles, and a heliochrome seapiece. Satō's *Den'en no yūutsu*—also titled *Yameru sōbi (The Sick Rose)* after a poem by William Blake—is prefaced with a quotation from Edgar Allen Poe and is redolent with an atmosphere of European fin de siècle melancholy.

The themes of fairy lands, fairy tales, and dreams intersect with perceptual distortions and illusions in the writings of Uno and Satō. Both men were writing at a time when everyday visual experiences included the still relatively novel phenomena of electric light and neon light, and dreamlike enchantments projected on movie screens. Their writings reflect some of the ways in which the relationship between the eye and the imagination was altered by new forms of lighting and by the new cinematic representations of movement and time.

In "Shimon" ("The Fingerprint," 1918) the blown-up image of a fingerprint in the American gangster movie *Gun Moll Rosario* sets into motion a detective story in which the sleuth, a Japanese who has returned to Japan after many years abroad, pursues the fingerprint's image into the celluloid world of film and loses his way back to the "real" world. For R., led by clues in the film to a "ghost house" in Nagasaki,[6] enclosed space takes on a nightmarish Poe-like quality when a secret underground chamber, complete with human skeleton and blood dripping from a ceiling, is discovered in the house.

We may pause here to consider the phenomenology of movie viewing and its relationship to mesmerization in a given kind of space. The spectator finds himself or herself in a passive, fixed position in a dark room, where space is defamiliarized, anonymous, and populated by strangers (Barth 1989, 346). His or her nervous system is stimulated by the light that strikes the photoreceptors of the eye, and attention is glued to representations composed of dancing light particles projected as a cone of light on the artificially illumined, *framed* space of the rectangular screen. Film theorists analyzing the psychological effects of film viewing have suggested that such experiences are regressive in nature and return the viewer to a state approximate to that of early childhood, in which the viewing subject "suffers from limited mobility and becomes dependent on hypertrophied visual experience, which produces a superreal sense of reality that cannot be tested" (Jay 1993, 475). In the inactive state induced by the darkness and the stationary positioning of the body and the head, the normal sense of self in space is suspended, and in the hypnotic state produced by the illumined image upon the screen, critical analytic activity is temporarily suspended.

The regressive effects of cinematic hypnosis are treated ironically in Tanizaki's *Chijin no ai* (Love of a Fool, 1924; translated as *Naomi*), in which private fantasies pursued in Western houses appear as analogues for a creeping moral rot invading the body of Japan. The child in the man that asserts itself through artistic play in Satō's *Utsukushii machi* expresses itself in a far more boisterous mode in the hands of Tanizaki, who parodies the enthrall-ment that the celluloid images of the West exercise upon Japanese viewers. In his "fairy-tale house," a semi-Westernized *bunka jūtaku* (cultured residence) near the tracks of the National Electric Line on the outskirts of Tokyo,[7] a staid Japanese engineer pursues fantasies inspired by American films with childlike abandon. The foreign fantasy-producing technology of *katsudō shashin* (moving pictures) exerts a corrosive effect upon the lives of Jōji and his protégée Naomi, who, shut off from society, play wild games of dress-up and make-believe in the "absurdly large atelier" of their cheap house (Tanizaki 1985, 16). These games are inspired by the photos of Western film stars whose photos cover the walls of the "theater-like atelier."

> Apparently she [Naomi] studied the actresses' movements when we went to the movies, because she was very good at imitating them. In an instant she could capture the mood and idiosyncrasies of an actress. Pickford laughs like this, she'd say, Pina Menicheli moves her eyes like this; Geraldine Farrar does her hair up this way. Loosening her hair, she'd push it into this shape and that. (Tanizaki 1985, 36)

The interior of their "shoddy Western-style house" is the stage upon which the drama of Jōji's enslavement to his infatuation for a vulgar young woman with Western-like features unfolds.[8] Jōji's eventual moral and spiritual reduction is foreshadowed in the games that he plays with Naomi:

> Wearing slippers on her bare feet and an unlined flannel summer kimono, Naomi would stamp time as she sang the songs she'd learned. Sometimes she'd play tag or blindman's bluff with me. Racing around the atelier, she jumped over the table, crawled under the sofa, and

knocked over the chairs. And when that wasn't enough, she ran up the stairs and scurried back and forth like a mouse on our theater box of a landing. Once I played horse and crawled around the room with her on my back.

"Giddup, giddap" she cried. For reins, she made me hold a towel in my mouth. (Tanizaki 1985, 21)

At story's end, Jōji is persuaded by Naomi to move into an even larger Western-style house, previously occupied by a Swiss family, located in the foreign enclave of Honmoku in Yokohama. We can imagine how his search for a "private enclosed space" in which to play out his Western fantasy will end in his total destruction as a man.

Space in the imaginary landscape may be defined not only as enclosed from the rush of the workaday world, that is, horizontally, but may be also defined along a vertical axis. Uno's protagonists occupy rooms on upper floors that position them to look out across the city and down on the life below. The experience of space in his writing is ascensional in *Yamagoi* (*Love of Mountains*, 1923), in harmony with the light, airy quality of his whimsical prose.[9] The writer-dreamer travels in a train up into mountain country. His inn is located on a hill at the foot of a mountain behind the town. He climbs a staircase to reach his room on the third floor of this inn, looking down upon Suwa and the lake. He ascends a mountain path and gazes down at the valley below. From his elevated perspectives, human figures below appear small and doll-like. At times his perspective is further empowered by the binoculars through which he gazes at the town below. The height of the view brings clarity, places him nearer the heavens, and creates a sense of the cosmic in a natural setting of mountains and woods. The clear vista he enjoys from the exceptionally wide window of his inn room is in keeping with the basically rationalistic, critical, and satirical stance he assumes as a writer in this novella.

In contrast, Tanizaki's imagination, particularly in the novels written after his move to the Kansai after the earthquake of 1923, moves earthward, down toward subterranean forces that operate beneath rational consciousness. This terrestrial orientation entails digging backward in time, to childhood, to memories of the figure of the mother. It includes memories of close enclosures, such as the dark interior of a ricksha, which he shared with his mother on a rainy night. The images are not primarily visual, but auditory, olfactory, and kinesthetic.

The total darkness within the hood would be heavy with the smell of the oil in the fabric, the fragrance of the oil in my mother's hair, and the sweet, cloying odor of her clothing. As I breathed in these scents and listened to the rain drumming intermittently on the hood, the images and the voices of the actors I had seen on the stage that day, the sounds of the chanters and the stage musicians would be revived once again in this world of darkness. (Itō 1991, 19)

Memory moves *backward* and *downward,* toward darkness and shadows. Ken Itō points out how the "redolent atmosphere of the covered rickshaw" and "the sensual presence of the mother" fuses with the fantasy worlds of the kabuki theater and the *shitamachi* (Itō 1991, 19). Tanizaki's *shitamachi* setting is the *down* town, the "lower city" of dark, narrow alleyways and the arcane customs of the once lowly *chōnin.* His excavations into the subconscious ultimately yield a focus upon the *lower* regions of the body—fixations upon feet, bodily odors, and the like—secrets emanating from and surrounding the (mother's) body.

The fusion of darkness, the past, and mysterious sexuality runs throughout Tanizaki's novels set in the Kansai region and written after his move to Osaka. This "rediscovery" of the shadows in which he shields himself from the shrill electric light of the modern present is articulated most eloquently in the famous essay "In'ei raisan" ("In Praise of Shadows," 1933–1934).[10]

The dynamic of the relationship between framed enclosures and aesthetic concern assumes a different form in the work of Akutagawa. While Akutagawa did not work the search for a sequestered space as a thematic into his stories, he exercised his penchant for "fantasy" by imposing strictly defined frameworks on his short, carefully crafted stories. Set in "distant time" eras, his stories are locked in neat, cleverly constructed narratives that freeze them in their remoteness from the present. Every detail of their construction is carefully calculated to serve a specific purpose in conveying the nuances of the moral characters of his dramatis personae and the subtlest shades of authorial irony. His narratives are filigreed cages in which fictional men and women are captured in minutely detailed tableaux.

As might be expected, a very different orientation toward space is found in the stories of writers associated with the proletarian literature movement. In place of a sought-after secrecy in which to nurture the imagination, proletarian writers tried to bring public witness to bear upon verifiable facts of objective reality, and space is handled accordingly. Far from seeking to enclose space to better pursue a private fantasy, these writers publicize space, open and expose it to the eyes of the world.

Space in the proletarian writings is a site of exploitation and resistance, an arena where competing forces clash. The competition may be viewed in terms of competing national interests, as in Kobayashi Takiji's *Kani kōsen* (*The Cannery Boat,* 1929), where the sea is objectified as a good that Japanese capitalists compete against Russians to claim. Or it may be cast in terms of class struggle on a local scale, as in Tokunaga Sunao's *Taiyō no nai machi* (The Sunless Street, 1929), in which a ravine located between two bluffs in Koishikawa ward in Tokyo becomes the place where warfare between workers of a printing house and its owner is played out.

In *Kani kōsen* the enclosed space of the ship's hold is a putrid iron hole into which a group of seamen is forced by an exploitive capitalist state. One seaman in the hold had previously been trapped in another insalubrious enclosure, symbolizing the oppressive stranglehold of the imperial state on the individual: a mine, in which a fellow worker had been sealed alive. There is little dialectic between an inner consciousness and an outer world in these writings. Kobayashi is not interested in the individual psyches of the men. For most of the proletarian writers, individuals were but members of groups and as such, representatives of the all-important categories of class.

Tanizaki's aestheticization of shadows lying in the dark, recessed spaces of a past imaginary occurred at a time when numerous intellectuals who had at one time devoted themselves to the study of Western thought, literature, and art were looking to native traditions for spiritual strength and rhetorical inspirations with which to resist the modern materialistic, technological culture sweeping in from the West.[11]

Other writers' disaffection from modernism led to other kinds of reconfigurations of space in their writings. Lacking perhaps the extraordinary creative drive of Tanizaki, who not only continued writing novels but created some of his masterpieces during the 1930s, Satō gave up his Western-style novelistic experimentations centered upon futurism (*Nonshalan kiroku* [The Nonchalant Records], 1929) and psychoanalysis (*Kōseiki* [Regeneration], 1930), turned away from stories about artistic fantasies set in enclosed spaces, and began writing biographies of famous Japanese figures of the past. His new settings were spread over a wide geographic area as he reexamined the lives of the thirteenth-century essayist Kamo no Chōmei (*Kamo no Chōmei*, 1935) and the medieval religious leader Hōnen (*Kikusui monogatari* [*Tale of the Chrysanthemum Spring*], 1936), and looked to the bay waters of sixteenth-century Nagasaki in his biographical novel about a samurai warrior who fought against the Portuguese (*Arima Harunobu*, 1942), and to the seas of Southeast Asia in his biography of a sixteenth-century samurai who battled Western colonial powers for trading rights (*Yamada Nagamasa*, 1942).[12]

Satō also evoked the traditional Japanese landscape through his recollections of the poetic wanderings of Saigyō and Bashō in his essay "Fūryūron" ("On Elegance," 1924), in which he turned to medieval Japanese aesthetics, centered on the concept of nothingness (*mu*), for a source of authentic Japanese thought and feeling in the modern world. His conceptualization of *fūryū* was broadly spatial in its essence, as he insisted upon the location of the human not outside but *in* nature and underlined the minuteness of the individual placed within the vastness of the cosmos.

The Japanese landscape also came to the fore in the debates about the *shishōsetsu*, which began in earnest shortly after the 1923 earthquake. At a time when European literary trends such as surrealism, dada, and futurism had grown increasingly bewildering and alien, and older writers who had established their reputations earlier in the Taishō period were feeling increasingly marginalized by the proletarian literary movement, the *shishōsetsu*, firmly grounded in the Japanese soil, offered the attractions of intimacy and immediate intelligibility.

Filled with images of sensate life as personally experienced by the author-narrator, the *shishōsetsu* was a genre characterized by a search for "real" experience in a "real" place. This place-centered orientation was expressed in a keen awareness of the rhythms of the natural life surrounding the author-protagonist and in the narrator's recollected memory of childhood days in the *furusato* (old home village). In the literature of personal reminiscence, *furusato* came to figure not only as an actual setting but, by extension, as a trope for nature, childhood, and the secure simplicity of a vanished communal life that writers constructed in their poetic rituals of nostalgia.

Discussion of the *shishōsetsu* was grounded in terms of a familiar spatial terrain, through metaphors such as the *hondō* (main road) of prose literature *(sanbun geijutsu no hondō)* and the *furusato* of the Japanese spirit.[13] The space of the *shishōsetsu* may have been enclosed, but if so, it was an encompassing that spoke not only of the exclusive privacy of an individual fantasy but also of the protectiveness of tradition and communality. Its dwelling space was the "house of tatami-mat rooms, *shoji* and attached gardens."[14]

A turn to the open, geographic spaces of the Japanese countryside can also be found in the later novels of Uno. The turning point in Uno's reinterpretation of the semiotic of enclosed space is dramatized in "Kareki no aru fūkei" ("Landscape with Dead Trees," 1933), a story about a painting by an Osaka artist[15] who had traveled to Europe, expecting to find inspiration and spiritual freedom in European space, only to find instead incomprehension and an emptiness that was as imprisoning as the confinement he had sought to escape by leaving Japan. After returning to Japan, disappointed by his inability to "understand" the spirit behind European art, the painter Koizumi Kensaku began to paint a series of haunting, enigmatic landscapes that seemed to express the anguish of spiritual displacement in a modern industrial Japan.

In the story, space, tightly enclosed within a picture frame, is relentlessly and tortuously interrogated in the painter's famous masterpiece, *Landscape with Dead Trees of 1930*. The artist's studio, no longer an enclosed, protected space in which the imagination is set free to roam, is a psychological prison. A new thematic of confinement, suffocation, and death is expressed novelistically through the metaphor of the mask, which describes his inability to show his true feelings to the world, and through a studied description of his last great landscape painting.

Landscape with Dead Trees *by Koide Narashige, 1887–1931.* (Modern Japanese Painting, an Art in Transition. *Kodansha International, 1967, 97.)*

Koizumi is depicted as a sickly, morose man, whose fatigue with the meaningless rituals of daily social existence is synthesized in the disgust he feels about having to produce paintings of French dolls for his practical, efficient wife to sell. His character is conveyed through the comments of his painting associates, who attempt to analyze and find the "real" Koizumi behind the different faces of an emotionally distant man who has returned to Japan from an artistic sojourn in France "changed" in ways that they cannot fathom.

Uno leads the reader into the hermetically sealed world of Koizumi's painting of an eerie landscape viewed from the window of his studio in Ashiya looking toward the wires over the Hanshin Railroad tracks (Miyagawa 1967, 97). A feeling of tension, oppression, and gloom fills the composition in which space is severely circumscribed. The picture plane is divided in half. On top, a blue sky with clouds is traversed horizontally by two sets of high-power wires rendered in heavy black lines extending from one end of the picture frame to the other. The imposing black form of a steel pylon cuts the painting in two vertically. The lower half of the picture frame is dominated by long dark tree trunks lying on the ground in a jumble of exaggerated curvilinear shapes that cast black shadows upon the earth. Their lifeless forms "almost resemble human bodies" (Miyagawa 1967, 97). Their heavy horizontal disposition repeats the pattern of horizontal lines created by the electric wires in the top half of the picture plane. The oppressive weight of horizontal lines is further emphasized by a line of low, dark barrack-like buildings that reaches across the midsection of the painting.

A disturbing hallucinatory sense of spatial and spiritual displacement is created through the black figure of a man seated on the topmost electric wire immediately to the right of the pylon.[16] The human, misplaced and set upon the high power line, has no natural place in the landscape, which has been cut up and wasted by industrial activity. At the story's end it seems that the only escape for the artist is through death: when Koizumi's body is discovered on his studio couch, sunshine floods the room and he smiles peacefully.

Uno's story implies a rejection of the modern, which he views with an irony that matches that of Koizumi's painting. Its title is a line from Bashō, and in the painting, the "crow perched on a withered limb" *(kareeda ni karasu ga tomarikeri)* is replaced by the figure of a man on a deadly wire; the bare branch *(kareeda)* gives way to dead trees *(kareki)* lying on the earth devastated by technological "progress."

Following the publication of "Kareki no aru fūkei" in the 1933 New Year's issue of *Chūō kōron,* Uno, who had been forced by illness to stop writing for seven years, was warmly embraced by the *bundan* (literary establishment). Critics celebrated his return to the *hondō* of literature with a story whose treatment of cultural conflict seemed to address a matter of concern to many.[17]

Uno thereafter devoted himself to writing about the lives of Japanese whose "ordinariness" echoed the "ordinariness" of the "ordinary and abiding people" *(jōmin)* representing the continuous social order of cohesiveness and solidarity that Yanagita Kunio believed he had found in the villages of Japan.[18] Uno peopled his "chronicle novels" *(keifu shōsetsu)* with farmers, small businessmen, shopkeepers, and small-town civil employees—working folk who had their feet firmly planted on the ground and who were part of a nexus of a continuing human community.[19] As he left the narrowly enclosed spaces of private idiosyncratic desire and fantasy, a widening of perspectives accompanied his return to the Japanese countryside as he chronicled the lives of the "little people" *(shōmin)* from a distance, recording their struggles and hardships, but also including wry observations on their foibles. A relaxed, warm, at times genial view of the doings of ordinary *(ippanteki na)* Japanese comes to the fore. As one reads these later novels about families (including branches of Uno's own extended family) that span several generations and make their lives over a wide geographic area, images of the broad flat plains of the Kansai region outside Osaka come to the fore.

Space expands in these later narratives, in which people move from one Japanese city to another in the course of their lives as they take different jobs, marry, raise families, grow old, and die. Occasionally among the folk whose lives Uno narrates are some seemingly ordinary characters who do rather unordinary things, which he records in a flat, nonjudgmental manner. Class differences are deemphasized in "Karada no aki" ("Autumn of the Body," 1941), in which the businessman Ishizō, who is middle-class and university-educated, befriends a local junkman, who in turn takes under his wing a landowner who has lost his farm and taken to drink. The subject of "Kanwa kyūdai" ("To Return to the Subject," 1937) is a Hokkaido postman who walks ten miles a day to carry a newspaper to an isolated farmhouse because he prefers the ritual of the daily fireside chat with the farmer to the rational, time-efficient alternative of delivering the paper three times a week. Such stories may be said to display the kind of "spontaneous, unreflective, and collective" behavior that Yanagita sought to document in his ethnographic writings (Harootunian 1990, 106).

References to countryside, *furusato,* and the common folk did not evoke images of comfort and nostalgia in the writings of the proletarian novelists. In works such as Kobayashi Takiji's *Fuzai jinushi* (*The Absentee Landlord,* 1929), the *furusato* is a denatured place where intimacy between land owner and land is erased in a capitalist economy in which land and peasants are but material and tools used for the production of wealth. For these writers, rural tradition and art for art's sake alike are associated with a system of economic exploitation that literature must expose.

For proletarian writers, ready to absorb a less complex kind of literature based on a political ideology, coming to grips with Western culture required not privacy for the individual but commitment in a politicized sphere. Given the nature of that ideology, the larger that space, the more meaningful and persuasive those literary endeavors could be. Forging connections between socialism in Japan and socialism in other parts of the world could but strengthen their vision, based on a Marxist understanding of history that held no room for sentimentalized notions of Japanese traditions and Japanese identities rooted in the countryside. Space, whether that of a room or a landscape, was invariably a site upon which contesting forces in a historical dialectic played themselves out.

Nor was there a journey "back to Japan" *(Nihon e no kaiki)* for Akutagawa. Subtitled "a novel without a plot" *(hanashi rashii hanashi no nai shōsetsu),* his 1927 "Shinkirō" ("Mirage") lacked the carefully plotted, rational structure with which Akutagawa was associated. As if to underline the absence of a comprehensive idea that organizes its elements into a meaningful pattern, the story is divided into two halves: a sunlit day and a black night. Like the positive and negative images of a silent film that offers images of sea and shore, expanses of sand, a flat blue sea, and a huge empty sky stretch out interminably into the distance in the daylight. In the absence of boundaries, objects, because they appear so fortuitous, take on a lurid superphysical vividness. The deep black ruts running diagonally across the sand are oppressive, and even portentous, precisely because they are so unexpected and senseless: "traces of a divine genius, originating from an unknown spot and ending nowhere. . . ."

At night the region of the unknown becomes greater, as the narrator's awareness of the sea, a vaster and more primitive world, is awakened through the sound of its incessant roar. The physical eye of daylight, deluded by mirages, gives way to the inner eye at night. Memory and dream open wider the horizons of awareness but also increase the chance of illusion and chaos. The subconscious is likened to the sand in which the objects lay buried; consciousness to the light of a match that haphazardly illuminates a circle of sand in the dark, underlining the profound unknowability of the surrounding world.

If "Shinkirō" offers a vision of incomprehensible space, enclosed space becomes the site of madness in *Haguruma (Cogwheels,* 1927). Mysterious telephone calls, rustling and scratching sounds outside the door, and whispering voices and hallucinations torment the narrator, housed in a hotel room, like chimerical signs of a pursuing vengeance. On the brink of madness, he is unable to reveal his condition to his family, for to do so would result in his confinement to a cell in an insane asylum. When the tension of being shut up in his room with his inner demons becomes unbearable, he rushes to the lobby, back into the arms of society, but the relief he finds is short-lived, for the people outside are, literally and figuratively, foreigners, with whom communication is impossible. Before long, the space outside the room becomes equally threatening as signs telling of immanent disaster start to multiply. For Akutagawa, who had restricted his imaginary space to the delimited settings of his well-defined plots, there was no way back to the space of the *hondō.*[20]

NOTES

I wish to thank Dr. J. Thomas Rimer for the valuable comments he made on an earlier version of this essay.

1. Writers cited for their "explorations of new and alien territory," "beyond the homeland's borders," are the Meiji political novelists; Mori Ōgai ("Maihime"); Natsume Sōseki ("Rondon tō"); Yokomitsu Riichi *(Shanghai);* Mishima Yukio; Endō Shūsaku *(The Samurai);* and Abe Kōbō (Anderer 1984, 9).
2. Residents included, at one time or another, the writers Tanizaki Jun'ichirō, Ishikawa Jun, Hirotsu Kazuo, Uno Kōji, Uno Chiyo, Miyamoto Yuriko,

Sakaguchi Ango, Masamune Hakuchō, and Naoki Sanjūgo; the artist Take-hisa Yumeji, whose drawings and paintings of the sad-eyed woman, "Yumeji," were among the most popular art objects of the day; the anarchist radical Ōsugi Sakae and his wife, Itō Noe; and several Russian students of Asian studies. The boarders and the lively social life that took place in the hotel are described in a book written by its proprietress, Kondō Tomie, *Hongō Kikufuji Hoteru* (1983).

3. Roy Starrs discusses this issue in his article in this volume.

4. This is a theme developed by J. Thomas Rimer in his introduction to *The Sick Rose, A Pastoral Elegy* (1994). This interiority, and its attendant daydreaming and idleness found in stories by Uno and Satō, may be viewed as a negative reaction to a society that had grown increasingly impersonal and mercantilistic. Christopher Dodd, for example, interprets Satō's retreat into aesthetic concerns as a criticism of Taishō society (Dodd 1994).

5. Brentano is the surname of the German Romantic poet Clemans Brentano (1778–1842), known for success with fairy-tale motifs. Satō was well ac-quainted with the work of Clemens Brentano and wrote about him in his 1919 essay, "The Art, That Is the Person" (Geijutsu sunawachi ningen). Given his penchant for literary games, this coincidence in nomenclature would seem to have been rather intentional.

6. The non-Japanese-style buildings in which fantasy is pursued are fre-quently located in the foreign enclaves of Japanese cities. *Utsukushii machi* takes place in the foreign quarter of Tsukiji in Tokyo. Kaname in Tanizaki's *Tade kuu mushi* (1929, translated as *Some Prefer Nettles*) finds relaxation in the Western quarter of Yokohama. Other sites for fantasy are fairy-tale-like settings of uncertain location, for example, *Supein inu no ie,* and foreign settings, for example, Satō's Chinese mystery story "Jōkaisen no kidan" (1925, translated as *The Bridal Fan*) is set in a haunted house in a seaside city on Formosa.

7. Tanizaki's positioning the *bunka jūtaku* alongside the tracks of the national railroad is surely ironic. The electric train was frequently regarded as a symbol of modernity, often for its more negative aspects. Philosopher Watsuji Tetsurō (1889–1960), for example, likened the train to "a 'wild boar' rampaging through the fields, out of step with traditional civilized society" (Najita 1988, 749). Naomi's slovenliness, wastefulness, and impetu-osity recall another phrase used by Watsuji in his critique of the material-istic civilization of the Americans, which had led them to lose their souls and return "to the life of the 'birds and beasts'" (745).

8. The figure of a man who is possessed by an impulse to remake a woman after his obsessive vision and who carries out his project in the privacy of an enclosed space appears in many of Tanizaki's best-known stories, from the jejune "Shisei" ("The Tattooer," 1910), in which a master tattooer fixes the image of a spider on the back of a beautiful girl, to the late *Kagi (The Key,* 1956), in which a professor turns his bedroom into a studio for taking pornographic pictures of his drugged, naked wife. *Naomi* is reminiscent of

Somerset Maugham's novel, *Of Human Bondage*, in which a cultured, refined man loses his head over a coarse-grained woman who brings about his ruin.

9. For a translation of *Yamagoi*, see Uno 1997.

10. Tanizaki Jun'ichirō's reorientation toward the past and the places of traditional Japan, following his move to the Kansai, is discussed in Keene 1984; Edward Seidensticker's introduction to his translation of *Tade kuu mushi*, tr. *Some Prefer Nettles* (1955); Itō 1991; and Gessel 1993.

11. The philosopher Kuki Shūzō (1888–1941), for example, looked back to the Tokugawa-period aesthetic of *iki* and grounded his notion of the essence of the Japanese character in this concept. See Pincus 1993.

12. Satō's broadened geographical perspectives were also due ultimately to the fact that he actually did travel far and wide on the Asian continent and in the Pacific as a correspondent attached to the Imperial Army as it moved through China and then on to Malaysia and Indonesia. Earlier, as a young man, he had traveled to Formosa and Amoy.

13. The term "main road of prose literature, its essence" *(sanbun geijutsu no hondō, shinzui)* appeared in part 1 of Kume Masao's "Watakushi shōsetsu to shinkyō shōsetsu," and the phrase, "the *furusato* of the novel," in part 2. The essay first appeared in *Bungei kōza* in February 1925.

14. As Isoda Kōichi points out in the essay, "Jūkyo kankaku no deirenma" ("The Dilemma of Domestic Sensibilities," 1983), the *shishōsetsu* is a genre that "prevents the invasion of the 'modern' by completely rejecting it" (Isoda 1995, 53).

15. The story of Koizumi Kensaku is based on the life of the artist Koide Narashige (1887–1931). For a discussion of this artist, see McCallum 1987, 86–90.

16. The man on the black wire is wearing the same sort of hat that had appeared in Koide's earlier self-consciously rendered *Self-Portrait Wearing Hat* (1924), in which the artist was depicted standing in the center of his studio (McCallum 1987, fig. 50).

17. The autobiographical content of "Ko no raireki" ("The Life Story of a Child," 1933) and "Hitosamazama" ("Various Folk," 1933) was further evidence for some critics to see Uno's resumption of writing as a return to the *hondō*. Even "Kareki no aru fūkei" was read as a thinly veiled *shishōsetsu*.

18. In his focus on these alternative images of modernity, Uno's "rediscovery" of the lives of the little folk recalls Yanagida Kunio's earlier writings on the "abiding folk" *(jōmin)* and their communitarian style of living, in which individuals are bound together through their relationship to the land and its tutelary *kami*. For discussions, see Harootunian 1990, 99–113; Najita 1988, 750–752.

19. Ara Masahito says that in writing "chronicle novels" *(keifu shōsetsu)* about distant members of his extended family, Uno defined the outer limits of the *shishōsetsu* (Ara 1953, 316–317).

20. Akutagawa's attempted journey into the interior of the self was aborted

forever on a sultry day in July 1927 in the annex of his main house, where he committed suicide.

REFERENCES

Akutagawa Ryūnosuke. 1987. *Akutagawa Ryūnosuke zenshū*, vol. 6. Chikuma Shobō.

Anderer, Paul. 1984. *Other Worlds: Arishima Takeo and the Bounds of Modern Japanese Fiction*. New York: Columbia University Press.

Ara Masahito. 1953. "Kisei sakka Uno Kōji." In *Gendai bungaku sōsetsu II, Taishō Shōwa sakka*, edited by Nishio Minoru and Kondō Tadayoshi. Gakudōsha.

Bachelard, Gaston. 1988. *Air and Dreams, An Essay on the Imagination of Movement*, translated by Edith R. Farrell and C. Frederick Farrell. Dallas: Dallas Institute Publications.

Barth, Roland. 1989. *The Rustle of Language*, translated by Richard Howard. Berkeley: University of California Press.

Chambers, Anthony Hood. 1994. *The Secret Window. Ideal Worlds in Tanizaki's Fiction*. Council on East Asian Studies, Harvard University. Cambridge: Harvard University Press.

Dodd, Stephen. 1994. "Fantasies, Fairies, and Electric Dreams: Satō Haruo's Critique of Taishō." *Monumenta Nipponica* 49.3:287–314.

Gessel, Van C. 1993. *Three Modern Novelists: Soseki, Tanizaki, Kawabata*. Tokyo: Kodansha International.

Harootunian, Harry. 1990. "Disciplinizing Native Knowledge and Producing Place: Yanagita Kunio, Origuchi Shinobu, Takata Yasuma." In *Culture and Identity: Japanese Intellectuals during the Interwar Years*, edited by J. Thomas Rimer. Princeton: Princeton University Press.

Isoda Kōichi. 1995. "The Dilemma of Domestic Sensibilities," translated by Alan Tansman. *Journal of Japanese Studies* 21.1:49–63.

Itō, Ken K. 1991. *Visions of Desire: Tanizaki's Fictional Worlds*. Stanford: Stanford University Press.

Jay, Martin. 1993. *Downcast Eyes: The Denigration of Vision in Twentieth Century French Thought*. Berkeley: University of California Press.

Kawamoto Saburō. 1990. *Taishō gen'ei*. Shinchōsha.

Keene, Donald. 1984. *Dawn to the West: Japanese Literature of the Modern Era Fiction*, vol. 1. New York: Holt, Rinehart, Winston.

Kobayashi Takiji. 1973. *The Factory Ship, and The Absentee Landlord*, translated by Frank Motofuji. Seattle: University of Washington Press.

Kondō Tomie. 1983. *Hongō Kikufuji Hoteru*. Chūō Kōron.

Kume Masao. 1973. "Watakushi shōsetsu to shinkyō shosetsu no mondai." *Kindai bungaku hyōron taikei*, vol. 6. Kadogawa Shoten.

McCallum, Donald F. 1987. "Three Taishō Artists: Yorozu Tetsugorō, Koide

Narashige, and Kishida Ryūsei." In *Paris in Japan, the Japanese Encounter with European Painting*, edited by Shūji Takashina and J. Thomas Rimer with Gerald D. Bolas. St. Louis: Washington University.

Miyagawa Torao. 1967. *Modern Japanese Painting: An Art in Transition*, translated by Toshizō Imai. Kodansha International.

Najita, Tetsuo. 1988. "Japanese Revolt against the West: Political and Cultural Criticism in the Twentieth Century." In *The Cambridge History of Japan*, vol. 6, edited by Peter Duus. Cambridge: Cambridge University Press.

Pincus, Leslie. 1993. "In a Labyrinth of Western Desire: Kuki Shūzō and the Discovery of Japanese Being." In *Japan in the World*, edited by Masao Miyoshi and H. D. Harootunian. Durham: Duke University Press.

Satō, Haruo. 1993. *The Sick Rose, a Pastoral Elegy*, translated by Frank Tenny. Honolulu: University of Hawai'i Press.

————. 1996. "Beautiful Town." In *Beautiful Town: Stories and Essays by Satō Haruo*, translated by Frank Tenny. Honolulu: University of Hawai'i Press.

Takeuchi Yoshio. 1971. *Karei naru shōgai*. Sekai Shoin.

Tanizaki Jun'ichirō. 1977. *In Praise of Shadows*, translated by Thomas J. Harper and Edward G. Seidensticker. New Haven, Connecticut: Leete's Island Books.

————. 1985. *Naomi*, translated by Anthony H. Chambers. New York: Alfred A. Knopf.

Uno Kōji. 1968. *Uno Kōji zenshū*, vols. 1 and 3. Chūō Kōronsha.

————. 1997. *Love of Mountains*, translated by Elaine Gerbert. Honolulu: University of Hawai'i Press.

❧ 4 ❧

The City and the Countryside: Competing Taishō "Modernities" on Gender

MARIKO ASANO TAMANOI

Although the notion of modern(ity) always resists a single definition, few would deny that the notion emerged with the rise of the nation-state. Indeed, a "modern nation-state" is almost an oxymoron, as a nation-state is always modern.[1] The rise of a nation-state also constitutes a process in which the idea of a nation and that of a "culture" merge. Hence, "the articulation of a unified Japanese ethnos with the 'nation' to produce 'Japanese culture' is entirely *modern*" (Ivy 1995, 4, emphasis in original; see also Sakai 1991). Such an imaginary Japanese nation-culture, however, could be discursively constructed by suppressing its internal differences. Various parts of an entire nation-state could be used as the markers of national differentiation (of, here, Japan) from another nation-state, each serving as a metonym for the whole. Those parts themselves, however, are not given their own autonomous statuses.

In this essay, I should like to focus on one such "spatial" part of Japan, that is, the countryside, and its place in the question of "Japanese" modernity in the early twentieth century. What I would like to explore is the notion of modernity that might have emerged in the countryside, and if such a notion ever existed, how it competed with the notion of modernity in the conceptual opposite of the countryside, the city. I must point out here that time (i.e., the time arrow in modernization process) almost always prevails over space in the study of modernity. In the words of Foucault, for example, time is "richness, fecundity, life, dialectic," while space is treated as "the dead, the fixed, the undialectical, the immobile" (Foucault 1980, 70; see also de Certeau 1984, 95; Fabian 1983; Soja 1989; Rosaldo 1989, 103).[2] Even when one tries to relate modernity to a part of the nation-state, one commonly does so to an "urban" area. Referring to Euro-American modernism after 1848, geographer David Harvey argues that it "was very much an urban phenomenon" and "existed in a restless but intricate relationship with the experience of explosive urban growth, strong rural-to-urban migration, industrialization, mechanization, massive re-orderings of built environments, and politically based urban movements . . ." (Harvey 1989, 25). Furthermore, this urban modernity is almost always "Western." We tend to create "unified readings [of the modern] out of local Euro-American practice" and allow "those to overpower interpretations elsewhere" (Rofel 1992, 93). For many scholars of the Taishō era (1912–1926), then, the combination of urban energies and rising capitalism is modern; the brightness of the city hardly reached the countryside, where farmers were left to themselves without electricity; the countryside was largely a remnant of modernity, or even premodern.[3]

However, another name for premodern is the "traditional." In other words, one could argue that the modern refers to the process in which a national history is situated against the background of the nation's "tradition." While the "tradition" is the invented one, such a history always appears as "progressive," and therefore "modern," history (see Ivy 1995, 5).[4] It is thus an entirely modern activity to imagine a national community by utilizing the traditional, which one could envision temporarily (the past as tradition), spatially (the countryside as the traditional), or the combination of both. In the early twentieth-century Japan, then, it was the countryside that offered this tradition. I have discussed elsewhere the role of Japanese folklore studies/native ethnology *(Nihon minzokugaku)* in the 1930s and 1940s in "Japanese" modernity, that is, the active collection of rural customs and lore by native ethnologists as a modern/scientific activity, which contributed to the formation of a Japanese nation-state (Tamanoi 1996). We must note, however, that such a process of creating Japanese modernity effectively erased the voices of the Japanese residing in the countryside; they were spoken for by folklorists, anthropologists, and government bureaucrats, but they themselves rarely spoke. Consequently, they remained "traditional," as they were not given an opportunities to write their own history.

Kären Wigen, however, depicts Shimoina a rural region in southern Nagano prefecture at the turn of the century, in the following way:

> Fueled by strong markets for timber and silk, the county's population had grown nearly 30 percent since the turn of the century, and the net value of local goods and services had grown even faster; most residents now had access to schools, banks, electricity, and improved roads or cableways. (Wigen 1995, 222)

Indeed, contrary to the widely shared image of the Japanese countryside as "premodern" and "traditional," it had been increasingly incorporated into the national polity since the 1870s (Gluck 1985, 37). Taking the region of Shimoina as an example, it was designated as a meaningful unit in the new administrative hierarchy in the early Meiji period (1868–1912); it also was granted electoral representation in Nagano prefecture; Shimoina county's citizens secured development funds from prefectural and national coffers, and, at the same time, the government raised the land tax to finance the nation's industrialization and imperial expansion (Wigen 1995, 11). Thus, as Shimoina had been incorporated into the centralized state and the global market by 1920, this rural region too became modern. Shimoina's modernity was a rather precarious one; as this region increasingly depended upon a single, distant commodity market for silk, its economy eventually declined by the late 1930s. This, however, does not mean that we could ignore its rural modernity.

I have so far briefly described the material or institutional modernity of a rural region. Did those residing in the countryside think and, therefore, write that they were modern? In 1928, a man named Suzuki Saburō, who lived somewhere in the Japanese countryside, sent a letter to the journal *Ie no hikari* (The Light of the Home).[5] In it, he wrote:

> I occasionally meet a woman who cuts her hair very short and makes up her face with rouge, lipstick, and an eyebrow pencil. But when I scrutinize her clothes, I find them not matching her hair style and makeup. She seems to be satisfied with herself only because she can catch the attention of others. I find her modern [*modan*], but my feeling toward her is that of contempt. She lacks something to be truly modern [*modan*]. (*Ie no hikari*, October 1928, 144)

Suzuki Saburō did on more than one occasion meet a woman "who cut her hair very short and makes up her face with rouge, lipstick, and an eyebrow pencil." He described her in the image of the urban Modern Girl, "a glittering, decadent, middle-class consumer who, through her clothing, smoking, and drinking, flaunt[ed] tradition" in the Taishō era (Silverberg 1991, 239). Hence, he uses the term *modan* (modern) to describe this woman, who might have moved to the city and occasionally came home to her village or, even without moving to the city, might have been influenced by the image of the urban Modern Girl. What is interesting is that a man, most probably a farmer, dissatisfied with modernity originating in the city, was actively searching for the "truly modern" woman in the midst of the Japanese countryside.

In this essay, I shall center my argument on the issue of gender in investigating rural modernity in early twentieth-century Japan. Although gender is a relational concept, and considering it "requires that all domains be examined for the relational structures they embody" (Bestor 1985, 284), gender here is a somewhat unidirectional concept. I shall explore the notion of modernity among rural men as they describe their ideal relationship to rural women. This is because I hardly found women's written narratives in the discursive space of the village newspapers, which I shall discuss shortly. I also feel that the rural women's sense of modernity should be another topic in itself.[6] In what follows, I shall first introduce the reader to a particular rural region of Ueda, about one hundred kilometers north of Shimoina, in Nagano prefecture. After briefly discussing the socioeconomic conditions of the area during the Taishō period, I shall search for the notion of modernity in a variety of articles published in village newspapers. I shall then relate this notion to the issue of gender, that is, the ideals of gender relationship held by those men who resided in this region in the early twentieth century.

TAISHŌ MODERNITY AND DEMOCRACY IN RURAL NAGANO

In the early 1990s, I visited Ueda Hakubutsukan (Ueda History Museum), located on the compound of the Ueda Castle Park. Ueda, which became an administrative city in 1919, first developed as a castle town in the sixteenth century. Since then it has served as a commercial center, being surrounded by numerous villages, many of which now have been incorporated into the city itself. At the museum, I found piles of old newspapers published in the thirty villages surrounding Ueda during the 1920s and 1930s. Generically called *sonpō* or *jihō*, these are the newspapers published by a group of local youth, called *seinenkai* or *seinendan,* in each village.[7] Table 1 lists the titles of these newspapers, most of which are the village names themselves, and the dates of their first publication.[8]

By the end of the 1940s, all of these groups of local youth had stopped publication of their village newspapers, owing to the scarcity of the paper and the increasing ideological control by the government during the war.[9] In one small column at the bottom of the last page of *Urazato sonpō,* published in 1922, one finds the following editorial statement.

> You may contribute an article on any topic to this village newspaper, not only on local politics and economy but on your inner thoughts. The deadline is the fifteenth of every month. Please keep and file all the newspapers delivered to you, as such a file will constitute the important history of our village. (*Urazato sonpō,* March 15, 1922)

If history is "one of the most important signs of modern" (Dirks 1990, 25), writing for, reading, and preserving these village newspapers surely consti-

TABLE 1

Jihō *and* Sonpō *in Ueda and Vicinity*

Initial Publication	Titles
1919	*Shiojiri* and *Ebōshi no hana* (later called *Motohara*)
1921	*Aoki* and *Urazato*
1923	*Takeishi, Toyotomi, Kanagawa,* and *Nishi Shioda*
1924	*Nishiuchi, Naka Shioda, Muroga, Osa-mura, Kano, Yazu Izumida, Shiokawa,* and *Kamishina*
1925	*Fujiyama, Higashi Shioda, Kawabe, Yoda-mura,* and *Wada*
1926	*Agata-mura* and *Bessho*
1927	*Tonoshiro* and *Shigeno*
1928	*Nagase, Daimon,* and *Maruko*
1929	*Nagakubo*

Source: This table is based on information from the Ueda History Museum. Kano Masanao has published a similar table (Kano 1973, 98–99).

tutes a most important sign of the modern. It is in the discursive space of these village newspapers published between 1919 and 1930 that I attempted to explore the notion of rural modernity.[10] Before discussing the notion of rural modernity, however, I must briefly situate these village newspapers in the larger historical background of the 1920s, which later historians often describe as the period of *nōson hihei,* that is, the deterioration or ruination of rural conditions.

In her article "The Transformation of Rural Society, 1900–1950" (1988), historian Ann Waswo brilliantly captures the moments of change in rural Japan in the Taishō period. With the sudden end to the post–World War I economic boom, crop prices began to fall in 1920 and fluctuated unpredictably at lower levels for the next several years (1988, 583). On the other hand, local tax burdens continued to increase. This economic shock particularly affected farmers of middling and lower status. This was more so in Nagano prefecture than in other prefectures, in which the majority of farmers depended on sericulture for cash income.[11] Because of the gradual decline in the price of raw silk, farmers' incomes declined accordingly. The culmination of this process was the world depression, which hit Japan in the late 1920s and early 1930s. The price of silk cocoons "dropped by forty-seven percent between September 1929 and September 1930," leaving in distress the roughly two million farm households engaging in agriculture throughout rural Japan (Waswo 1988, 596). Rice prices also fell sharply. The indebtedness of farm households increased markedly. In addition, the return of thousands of unemployed workers from the city to the countryside made economic conditions worse.

This deterioration of rural conditions also invited the state to penetrate further into the countryside, a process that already had begun in the late nineteenth century with the state's reforms of land tax and local administration. The state tightened its grip on the countryside by issuing a series of laws in order to increase agricultural output at the turn of the century. The state also assaulted vestiges of village autonomy by encouraging farmers to participate in the Local Improvement Movement (Chihō Kairyō Undō). The state began to control those local autonomous organizations by placing them under national organizations. Furthermore, facing the increasing number of tenant disputes, the state attempted to suppress the so-called dangerous thought of socialism, communism, and anarchism among village youth, while recognizing the "alternatives" that they could employ in order to solve their grievances.[12] Waswo, however, argues that the state's penetration encouraged not only "centrifugal" forces within the village that increasingly mobilized farmers for national goals but also "centripetal" forces, which created the desire for communal autonomy among farmers (Waswo 1988, 557–558).

What was the nature of the local youth groups that published the newspapers? According to Waswo, a local youth group was the product of both "centrifugal" and "centripetal" forces. That is, "the young men's group" (*wakamonogumi*), which had existed in each rural community during the Tokugawa period (1600–1867), began to be revived in the mid-1890s by farmers themselves. Their functions related to everyday life, such as "patrol duty to protect the community from fire or theft, labor services on communal land, and participation in festivals at the local shrine." From 1905 onward, the Home Ministry, working in concert with the Ministry of Education, tried to mobilize the young men's groups in local improvement causes. The Home Ministry also gave, in Waswo's words, "a new, more modern name" to the young men's group, *seinenkai* or *seinendan*, a local youth group or corps (573).

Although Waswo argues that membership became almost standardized throughout Japan by 1915, beginning when a young man finished elementary school and ending when he reached the age of twenty (574), the membership of local youth groups in villages in the vicinity of Ueda deviated from this norm. For example, the members of a local youth group of the village of Urazato were village male residents between the ages of fifteen and thirty. In 1922, there were 484 such members, 162 of whom resided outside the village and were not active members (*Urazato sonpō*, August 15, 1922). This does not mean that all 322 of them were actively involved in the publication of the village newspapers. In reality, the members had to pay a variety of fees to become active members of the group; for example, twenty-five yen for joining or leaving the group, thirty yen for attending its once-a-year general meeting, fifty yen for attending a five-day lecture series, and eighty yen for joining sports clubs (*Urazato sonpō*, February 15, 1923). Those who could pay these fees were largely middling farmers, that is, landowning farmers or large-scale tenant farmers. They were thus situated, according to historian Suzuki Masayuki, one rank below the rank of "local government officials, teachers, Shinto priests, and Buddhist monks" (Suzuki 1977, 19).

As exposure to education must have varied almost directly with economic status, the active members of the local youth groups were also more educated than others, many of whom were graduates of second-class agricultural schools. They were the ones who actively used the reading and writing skills that they acquired in the Meiji compulsory educational system. They were also the ones who were significantly influenced by what the state described as "dangerous thought." In all thirty of these villages, the active members of the local youth groups built village libraries in the early 1920s, purchased Marxian literature, and invited urban-based intellectuals as guest speakers (see also Kano 1973, 129; Nakamura 1978, 214, 217). The village newspapers periodically published lists of the books purchased by the libraries. One such list includes *Marukusu zenshū* (The Complete Works by Marx), *Shakai shisō-shi kenkyū* (The Study of Social Intellectual History) by Kawai Eijirō, and *Shakai kaizō no genri* (The Principles of Social Reconstruction) by John Russell, along with dozens of literary works by such writers as Arishima Takeo and Mushakōji Saneatsu (*Urazato sonpō*, May 10, 1926). The term "Marukusu bo'oi" (Marx boy), whether used in a positive or negative sense, also appeared occasionally in the village newspapers. Furthermore, historian Aoki Keiichirō (1964) reports the existence among farmers in Nagano of numerous study groups that read *Kaizō* (Reconstruction), a popular journal of urban liberalism, and other proletarian literature in the 1920s and 1930s (see also Suzuki 1977, 7; Nakamura 1978, 217). Taking the village of Urazato as an example, then, only about sixty men were actively involved in the publication of the village newspapers, soliciting articles from other residents, editing them, contributing articles themselves, and distributing newspapers (*Urazato sonpō*, February 1, 1922). It was they who took the initiative in publishing their own newspapers. Many of them were eager to learn leftist thought in order to "reconstruct the countryside" (*nōson kaizō*); yet, they were cognizant of their positions as national subjects of modern Japan.

What were the main purposes of publishing village newspapers? The inaugural issue of *Ebōshi no hana,* published on May 1, 1919, succinctly summarizes them.[13] The first was to publish all information regarding the self-government (*jichi*) of the village; this, however, included information coming from the state, for example, the dates of examinations for military conscription and the payment of national and local taxes. The second was to provide discursive space for all the village residents to exchange freely their own uncensored views. But the other purpose stated in the same issue contradicts the second goal: to prevent "dangerous thought" among the village youth and make them most useful for the construction and expansion

Illustration of a woman. (Urazato sonpō, May 15, 1922.)

of the nation-state of Japan. In other words, we can recognize here both "centrifugal" and "centripetal" forces within the countryside.

Did the village newspapers offer this opportunity to exchange opinions freely to rural women? *Urazato sonpō* published on May 15, 1922, an interesting illustration that is relevant to my inquiry. It shows a naked woman from her waist up, with a long, black, and somewhat curly hair, holding a pen. Does this represent the desire of the members of the local youth group for women to contribute their writings to the village newspapers? Indeed, in *Urazato sonpō* published in 1932, I found the following article.

> I lament over the fact that no woman has ever contributed even a single article so far this year to this village newspaper. How should we interpret this reality? Women should not forget this kind of important means of letting their thoughts publicly known. I really would like to know the world of women. (*Urazato sonpō*, May 1, 1932)

It is not, however, that rural women did not read, nor write for, the village newspapers. Another article published in 1923 reads:

> When we offered a class on ethics [to the members of the youth group] on one icy cold night, we saw two women listening to the

lecture intently outside the classroom's window. We were so moved by their eagerness to learn that we immediately sent a letter of invitation [for the next class on ethics] to the women alumni. (*Urazato sonpō*, March 15, 1923)

The article does not say women alumni of which school; it may be the elementary school, which, by 1923, offered six years of compulsory education to both boys and girls. Indeed, though only very sporadically, one finds articles by women in the village newspapers.[14] However, almost all of these articles seem to have been chosen specifically by the editors for publication in accord with their own thoughts. It is for this reason that I have focused on the rural men's notion of modernity in the area of gender relationships in this essay.

RURAL MODERNITY AND GENDER IN NAGANO

How and what, then, did these men write about gender? They almost always wrote about this particular topic in its relation to "culture" *(bunka)*, or more specifically, "genuine culture" *(makoto no bunka)*.[15] Some scholars observe in the Taishō period what they do not see in the previous Meiji period, namely, the emergence of the notion of culture (Minami 1965; Harootunian 1974a, 1974b; Roden 1990). Thus, historian Minami Hiroshi even argues that the Japanese term for culture, *bunka*, is itself a product of the Taishō period. These scholars, however, largely refer to the city. Since the writers of the village newspapers use "genuine culture" as something superior to (urban) culture, I first must discuss the connotations of the term *culture* as it is discussed by these scholars. Donald Roden, for example, characterizes Victorian England, postbellum America, Wilhelmian Germany, and Meiji Japan as civilizations of character (1990). Civilization refers to "a basically material realm that embraced the institutions of state and technology of the machine age." Culture, on the other hand, refers to "a basically spiritual realm that embraced literature and the arts." Culture "springs from the inner spirit of every person" and is "indistinguishable from personality or the qualities of being over doing, feeling over accomplishment, and madness over reason" (Roden 1990, 40).

Under the slogan of "civilization and enlightenment" *(bunmei kaika)*, the Meiji oligarchs introduced Western institutions and technologies, which made it possible for Japan to construct a modern nation-state and develop capitalism. Those who supported civilization were men whose character was molded in schools to be masculine, nationalistic, and self-sacrificial. These men in turn were supported by women whose character was modest, chaste, and submissive and whose duties were to "devote themselves to the home, as 'good wives and wise mothers'" (Roden 1990, 41). The Meiji men, however, built civilization by sacrificing the "cultural life" *(bunka seikatsu)* of each individual man and woman. Minami characterizes the Taishō era as one in which an individual Japanese restored his or her "cultural life" largely through the so-called cultural industries *(bunka sangyō),* that is, the new mechanisms of communication such as radio, the photograph, and the phonograph (1965). One's "cultural life," then, sprang not so much from one's character as from one's natural and often nonrational personality. Thus, even the clear division of labor by gender became blurred in the Taishō period; there emerged masculine women, independent and self-confident, as well as feminine men, dependent, fragile, and indecisive.

The writers of the village newspaper articles, however, argued that the Japanese countryside had never observed the emergence of civilization in the first place. They argued instead that civilization had always been the product of the city, but that it had penetrated the countryside and eroded its economic foundations. One contributor thus wrote in 1924 that farmers no longer drank clean water from the nearby brook but drank "soda" brought from the city, which was a sign of civilization in the countryside (*Urazato sonpō,* March 15, 1924). In describing the middling farmers' notion of culture, I must stress here the significance of the Great Kantō Earthquake, which hit the Tokyo metropolitan area and killed more than a hundred thousand urban residents in 1923. It is not that these farmers embraced a rosy image of the city before 1923. Their attitudes toward the city and its civilization before 1923 can best be described as ambivalent. For example, about six months before the Great Kantō Earthquake, a young male resident of Urazato contributed to his village newspaper an article titled "For My Friends" in which he wrote:

> These days, many village youth are talking about "the city." The term seems to carry a sweet charm. The shadow of smoke covering the sky; the clamoring sound of engines; the horde of urban laborers; the trains; and the busy tempo of life of the urbanites. How such atmosphere of the city has seized the hearts of the village youth! I think it is by all means possible that they, bored with the monotonous life of the countryside, will run for the city. The city is so stimulating like strong wine! (*Urazato sonpō,* February 15, 1923)

The author, though ultimately criticizing those who left for the city, here attempts to understand the urban charm captivating the minds of many local youth.

Another contributor, also writing before the Great Kantō Earthquake, argued: "We should not prevent the local youth from leaving for the city as long as they do so with firm decisions in accord with their own ideal future visions. Nor can we stop those impoverished tenant farmers from leaving for the city as long as they aim to improve their economic lots" (*Urazato sonpō*, May 15, 1922). What mattered to these writers, however, was their perceived reality in which "the countryside was left alone with its twelfth- or thirteenth-century customs while the city was monopolizing the civilization of the new age" (*Urazato sonpō*, April 15, 1922). In other words, at least before 1923, these writers' attitudes toward urban civilization were ambivalent, as they criticized and envied it at the same time.

These articles published before the earthquake are silent on the problem of rural women leaving for the city. Although many village newspapers offer statistical data on the numbers of local men residing outside their natal villages, they are conspicuously silent on the numbers of local women residing outside their natal villages. However, the majority of the Modern Girls, whose true identity behind the glittering urban consumer image was the female wage worker (Silverberg 1991; see also Oshima 1982), did move from the countryside to the city in order to assist their families at home.[16] For example, in 1917, 176 men and 160 women left Motohara; in 1921, 104 men and 188 women left (*Ebōshi no hana*, November 10, 1922). These figures do not tell us the migrants' destinations. These numbers may thus include women who moved to another village upon their marriage. However, the number of women who moved into Motohara in 1921 was only 66. Thus the figures of 160 and 188 women who left the village in 1917 and 1921 do at least indicate the migration of significant numbers of women to the city every year. Indeed, even a year after the Great Kantō Earthquake, 206 men and 232 women left Motohara (*Ebōshi no hana*, April 5, 1924). Not until much later, around 1929 and 1930, did the rate of migration from this village to the city begin to decrease, the reasons being not so much the earthquake as "the poverty which spread by then into the city itself" (Kano 1973, 105). One must wait, however, until the postearthquake period in order to read criticism of rural women leaving for the city. Before discussing this, I shall first return to the postearthquake discourses on culture.

Indeed, culture is repeatedly mentioned in the village newspapers after the Great Kantō Earthquake. Such culture should be simultaneously "rural" (*nōson bunka*), "regional" (*chihō bunka*), "genuine" (*makoto no bunka*), and "modern" (*kindaiteki bunka*). Such culture could be constructed only in the countryside by the rural population. This "rural" and "genuine" culture, then, is quite different from the "urban" culture of the same period, which was "indistinguishable from personality or the qualities of being over doing, feeling over accomplishment, and madness over reason" (Roden 1990, 40). Further, although I find commonalties between "rural/genuine" culture and the Meiji urban civilization, these writers of the village newspapers presented their culture as the complete antithesis of urban and material-based civilization. When urban culture is mentioned in the discursive space of the village newspapers, it is specifically marked as the "so-called" (*iwayuru*) or "mundane" *(futsū no)* culture. The local youth group of the village of Urazato, for example, in 1924 invited a speaker whom they called "a critic of civilization" *(bunmei hihyōka),* who apparently gave a public speech on the decline of Roman civilization and the turmoil (in World War I) of Western civilization *(Urazato sonpō,* March 15, 1924). Of course, the rural youth did know very well that they could construct genuine culture only when they could improve the rural economy. Hence, the three terms, *nōson shinkō* (the improvement of rural economy), *nōson kaizō* (the reconstruction of rural life), and *nōson bunka* (the rural culture) almost always appear together; and it is in such spaces of the village newspapers that the middling farmers presented their views on gender.

I shall cite here two village newspaper articles on gender relationships. Although they seem to send two very different messages, they in fact present similar views. Both were written by the chief editors of the *Urazato sonpō* in 1924.

> Until today, Japanese society always has been a male-centered society *(danshi no shakai).* It was Japanese men's will and knowledge that created every institution and system of this society and it was their power that improved them. Rural Japan in particular has been so far a patriarchal world, where there has been no opportunity for women to use their will and knowledge. Now that Japanese are suffocated in this male-oriented society, I must ask the following questions. Does this signify the limit of men's knowledge and power? Does the present ruination of the countryside mean the ruination of rural men's knowledge and power? If so, we desperately need the great power of rural women, which has long been forgotten, for the development of our society and the reconstruction of rural Japan. . . . Indeed, the recent activities of the Urazato women's association surprise us all. They have had a series of classes in order to improve home economy *(kasei)* and female morality *(futoku).* They have already had ten classes about dyeing and weaving. When we reflect on this awakening consciousness of rural women, we envisage a bright future for this village. Recently, the village government appointed the leaders of the women's association to be the leaders of "the movement for improving the quality of everyday life" *(seikatsu kaizen undō).* These women will thus make efforts for the self-government of our village along with men. They already have presented very logical opinions at the meetings, about which we men have hardly thought. While the ruination of the countryside has been discussed loudly throughout Japan, the awakening consciousness of these women gives us a hope. Today, when the civilization supported by men does not have a way out, these rural women suggest a future path for us to take to improve our society *(Urazato sonpō,* February 15, 1924).

The other presents the following view on gender:

> Men and women are and should be inherently different. Modern civilization, however, is about to lose sight of this important difference. Essentially speaking *(honshitsuteki ni)*, women do not need suffrage. We must regard it simply as a means to rescue women out of their present misery. . . . As long as modern civilization progresses, we shall never be able to save the Japanese countryside. We can rescue the countryside in a society of culture *(bunka no shakai)*, which can be constructed only after the fall of civilization (*Urazato sonpō*, February 15, 1924).

This author endorses the innate difference between genders. He then claims that "modern civilization" (not urban culture) is "about to lose sight of this important difference." He also argues that women's participation in politics will not save women. After men rescue women from their present misery, however, the author seems to demand that women contribute to the construction of a "society of culture." The earlier quotation sounds much more liberal; yet, what the author observes in his village is far from the emergence of masculine women but of women who still firmly know their own, gender-specific, duties. This author, too, asks women to play a certain role for the self-government of the village. The key issue connecting these two quotations is "the movement for improving the quality of everyday life" *(seikatsu kaizen undō).*

In *Urazato sonpō*, the term *seikatsu kaizen* appears for the first time in 1922 (*Urazato sonpō*, June 15, 1922), although another article, published in 1923, claims that the movement was already discussed in Urazato in the late Tokugawa period (*Urazato sonpō*, May 15, 1923). From June of 1922, *Urazato sonpō* repeatedly published articles, slogans, and lists of what to do in this particular movement to remind the reader of the importance of *seikatsu kaizen*. This was also the case with other village newspapers. For example, *Motohara jihō* in 1925 published a list of those tasks, which urged rural women to (1) use time in the most effective way; (2) curtail unnecessary costs in their everyday lives; (3) save money for the education of their children; (4) buy daily necessities with cash, not on credit; (5) use public markets; (6) use simple makeup; (7) wear simple clothes; (8) respect work, do side jobs *(fukugyō)*, and utilize scraps *(haibutsu riyō)*; (9) curtail unnecessary costs of weddings; (10) respect the Shinto-style wedding ceremony; and, lastly, (11) reserve one day a month as a day of women's volunteer work (*Motohara jihō*, June 15, 1925). This list specifically asked women to improve rural life.

Of course, men were also supposed to participate in this movement. They were to refrain from drinking and smoking, practices regarded as destroying the body, brain, and family life of each individual (*Urazato sonpō*, April 15, 1922; December 15, 1924). They also were not to visit pleasure quarters frequently (*Urazato sonpō*, September 15, 1922; June 15, 1924). But the same articles that indicate the negative nature of these practices also indicate that these have been "public secrets" (*kōzen no himitsu*) and "the practices which we have tolerated" and which will continue to be tolerated (*ōme ni mitekita mono*). In other words, while both men and women were supposed to participate in this movement, it was largely women who were asked to carry out the bulk of the tasks for *seikatsu kaizen*.

Those women who were seriously involved in the movement for *seikatsu kaizen* were also described as the opposite, or rather the transcendent, of the urban Modern Girl. Such women should not have left for the city in the first place. Thus one author wrote:

> Why, Ms. N, do you have to transmogrify yourself with such heavy makeup every morning? . . . When you walk carrying a big bag on the glittering city streets at night, you really look like a monkey. . . . Ms. N, I secretly adored you when you were here [in this village] working so diligently picking mulberry leaves, wearing a white cotton apron. Don't you know that the sweat on your forehead sparkled in the sun? A woman's beauty shines only when she works in the countryside. (*Kamishina jihō*, January 15, 1925)

Ms. N (we do not know whether she was real or imaginary) moved to the city, became the Modern Girl, and lost her beauty in the eyes of this author. For him, a woman who diligently worked in the countryside was the only woman who could create genuine culture. Returning to the quotation I cited earlier from the journal *Ie no hikari*, we could argue here that the author distinguished between "the so-called Modern Girl" and "the truly modern girl," because the former was the product of urban and so-called culture and the latter the product of rural and genuine culture.

Ms. N may have physically moved to the city and become the Modern Girl. But the Modern Girl seems to have been also present in the countryside because of the urbanization of the rural area. Thus, one author described "contemporary [rural] women" as "snakes" and argued that "they are not genuine women. Their bodies may be those of women, but their souls are certainly not." This precluded the possibility of "genuine love" (*makoto no ren'ai*) in the countryside (*Urazato sonpō*, May 15, 1923).[17] Another wrote disapprovingly about the village girls who used parasols to protect their skin from the sunlight and demanded the elderly take care of farming (*Kamishina jihō*, January 15, 1925). Another lamented the recent phenomenon wherein rural women preferred men of blue-whitish skin color and slender arms; some women described such men as "high collar" (*hai kara*), meaning "modern," but they were in fact fond of half-sick men *(han byōnin)* *(Ebōshi no hana,* March 20, 1922). As for the activities of village women's associations, one author disapproved that the members invited a woman suffragist but approved their meetings for *seikatsu kaizen (Motohara jihō,* June 15, 1924).

The "truly modern" woman, however, was not the "traditional" woman of the feudal period. She could "wear pretty clothes and put on makeup if not excessively heavy." If she did not do any of these, it meant she was "accepting the stereotypical idea of the farmer's being stupid" *(Shiojiri jihō,* September 11, 1919). She should not be the kind of a woman who "won't read books once she is married and who won't search for beauty and truth." The "traditional" woman was surrounded by a "traditional" husband and parents-in-law who, even if she tried to search for beauty and truth, would suppress her desire. Such a woman "won't bring a spring breeze to her family" *(Kangawa jihō,* May 1, 1925). A "truly modern" woman "dances to the tunes of Western music" and yet "takes care of her family, believes in Shintoism, worships her ancestors, and won't ask money for this-or-that gadget" *(Ebōshi no hana,* February 15, 1923).[18] The "truly modern" woman is also "scientific"; she would accept the knowlege of "eugenics" when choosing her marriage partner *(Kamishina jihō,* June 15, 1926) and appreciate any lecture on "hygiene, food and nutrition, and scientific child-rearing practices" *(Ebōshi no hana,* February 15, 1924). Furthermore, the "truly modern" woman is not the Meiji woman either, who devoted herself to the home. The beauty of the "truly modern" woman comes from the fact that she physically works and sweats in the healthy and wholesome environment of the countryside. The "truly modern" woman thus needs "day-care facilities." A village assemblyman in Urazato argued in 1925 that there were 686 babies and toddlers in his village and that they would deprive their mothers and siblings of their labor because of the lack of day-care facilities. He therefore contended that day-care facilities should make it possible for "truly modern" women to work and produce more *(Urazato sonpō,* November 10, 1925).

In the village newspapers, then, the figure of a "truly modern" woman in the "genuinely cultural" countryside finally emerges, and we can capture the sense of modernity for the middling and educated farmers who wrote to these papers. Their sense of modernity certainly competed with urban modernity. Or I must argue that it even transcended urban modernity, which these middling farmers regarded as the product of material civilization. They then invited rural women to work along with them in order to realize the self-government of the village and construct what they called a genuine rural culture. Still, these middling farmers clearly preserved their patriarchal power over rural women. Acknowledging the "essential" difference between men and women, they rejected the possibility for rural women to participate in politics. What they asked of women instead was to shoulder the major responsibility for the *seikatsu kaizen* movement. Maruoka Hideko, who conducted extensive research on the working conditions of farming women in the 1920s and 1930s, demonstrated that they suffered from extreme fatigue as a result of excessive work and undernourishment under the patriarchal family system in the countryside (1937). Without questioning the nature of rural women's labor, the middling farmers in the vicinity of Ueda asked women to produce, save more, and improve the rural economy. Of course, women must have accepted, perhaps selectively, those modern elements discussed in the village newspapers. They must have welcomed village day-care facilities to the extent that those facilities eased their labor. But we also must note that the village assemblyman of Urazato regarded the day-care facilities as a means to increase the productivity of women and even children (i.e., the toddlers' siblings). As the village newspapers contained hardly any voices of rural women, I must conclude that rural modernity was strictly a male and a patriarchal version of modernity.

Furthermore, rural modernity did not resist the state's power. Some historians may argue here that those farmers influenced by leftist thought did challenge state power, at least until the late 1920s, when tenant militancy began to subside (see Waswo 1988, 584). Indeed, these mainline historians distinguish between the farmers of the 1910s and early 1920s and those of the late 1920s and 1930s.[19] According to them, the former were largely tenants and "revolutionary," while the latter were more conservative, holding the views of *nōhonshugi*, that is, antiurban, anticapitalist, and profarming agrarianism. The mainline historians thus trace the transformation from "democracy" to "fascism" in the Japanese countryside, claiming that it corresponds to the changing ideologies of the farmers.

In my reading of the village newspapers, however, I see more of the coexistence of both types of discourse throughout the 1920s and 1930s.[20] *Seikatsu kaizen* was thus a mixture of both "revolutionary" and "agrarianist" discourses and a product of "centrifugal" and "centripetal" forces within the village. While the local youth promoted it for the goal of self-government, the state actively promoted it from the beginning of the twentieth century under various slogans, such as *chihō kairyō undō* (local improvement movements), *seikatsu kaizen undō*, *keizai kōsei* (economic regeneration), and *jiriki kōsei* (self-regeneration). By appealing to the "traditional" sense of frugality and diligence among the rural population, especially among women (from the early 1920s onward), the state aimed at improving the rural economy, while being dependent on it for tax revenues and human resources. What is important for my argument is that this "traditional" sense of frugality and diligence became an important part of the sense of modernity among the middling farmers, which they then pressed upon rural women.

CONCLUSION

David Harvey interprets the mid-nineteenth century as a watershed in the history of Western modernism when the optimism brought by the notion of universal rationality began to be shaken. This important transition cannot be explained without taking into consideration the massive transformation of material foundations in the mid-nineteenth century, which greatly affected Europeans' sense of space and time. The construction of railroads, the invention of the radio, telegraph, bicycle, automobile, airplane, cinema, and photography, the technical and organizational innovations in production, the emergence of corporate forms of organization and distribution, and the massive investment in the conquest of colonial space all radically transformed Europeans' sense of space. Harvey thus argues: "En route, the world's spaces were deterritorialized, stripped of their preceding significations, and then reterritorialized according to the convenience of colonial and imperial administration" (Harvey 1989, 264).

What interests Harvey, however, is the counterforces sweeping throughout Europe against the expansion, and therefore the growing abstraction, of space. Scholars of Western modernism express this dialectic in terms of the tension between universalism, internationalism, or imperialism on the one hand and particularism, nationalism, or exceptionalism on the other (see, for example, Kern 1983; Schorske 1981). The same tension could also be expressed in terms of the dialectic between Becoming (the annihilation of space by time) and Being (the spatialization of time), as Harvey did, or, more simply, between space and place. The search for a place, then, signifies the return to the original or the authentic location, the location from which the conquest of space began. Hence, one common explanation given to the growth of Nazism in Germany is the Nazis' wish to search for a place for the Aryan race, which was depicted predominantly as rural. When the countryside became "subsidiary, and knew that it was subsidiary" in mid-nineteenth century Europe (Williams 1973, 243), it began to carry the potential of becoming the metonym for the entire nation-state.

I have not dealt here with such a process in which rural modernity became the metonym for "Japanese" modernity. I must argue, however, that the sense of rural modernity shared among middling farmers carried with it the potential to become "Japanese" modernity, as they imagined the countryside to be the place of the origins of authentic Japan. Rural modernity certainly competed with urban modernity, at least during the Taishō period. The middling farmers in the vicinity of Ueda created a rural modernity through their resistance to the penetration of urban modernity into the countryside. Though benefiting from various elements of urban modernity, especially the so-called cultural industries (in which I certainly include the printing of village newspapers as a means of mass communication), these middling farmers created their own version of modernity, rejecting urban material civilization and the "so-called" culture that blurred gender distinctions.

However, their sense of modernity was a male and patriarchal modernity, in which rural women were asked to labor to fulfill patriarchal goals, that is, to create a genuine rural culture. In such a culture, rural women were asked not to participate in politics; rather, they were to play a very specific role to "improve the quality of everyday life." Meanwhile, Japan began active imperial expansion in the 1930s. Harvey argues, quite correctly, that modernity carries with it the potential for "creative destruction and destructive creation" (Harvey 1989, 17). Rural modernity in Japan was created by those farmers who sought to destroy urban modernity in order to realize a profarming nation-state. When the state began actively to co-opt this rural modernity into the greater Japanese modernity to fulfill imperial desires, these farmers increasingly left for the battlefields in Asia. In the end, they could not fulfill their patriarchal wish but left women in the countryside to meet the ever increasing state demand to produce both material and human resources.

NOTES

1. James Faubion argues that modernity is "multidimensional. Opinions on which of its dimensions are more definitive, which are less, significantly differ. Opinions on when, and where, and with whom the modern era might begin accordingly differ as well" (1988, 365).

2. Foucault's criticism can also be applied to the two "modern" academic disciplines of anthropology and history. James Fernandez argues that anthropology has "the problem of metonymic representation," that is, "one place, which is simply a part of a much larger place [where an anthropologist engages in his or her field research] . . . comes to stand for a whole place" (1988, 2). Similarly, Kären Wigen argues: "History 'takes place' in a spatial as well as temporal dimension"; and yet, historians often forget that places are "historically constituted" (1995, 268).

3. According to Katō Shūichi, one of the historians who represent this view of the Japanese countryside, the rural Japanese in the 1920s were the most vulnerable to economic depression and were also quite alien to urban modernity, which was characterized by the spread of mass media and mass education and the potential of mass participation in politics. Instead, the rural Japanese cherished the "traditional" values of loyalty and the obedience of the lower to the higher. The rural Japanese thus developed an inferiority complex vis-ň-vis urban elites. The only place they could try their luck was the Imperial Army. The complex of the rural Japanese was "finally to find its outlet in ugly uniforms and hysterical outbursts of anti-intellectualism" (1974, 229).

4. Are the *Kojiki* and *Nihon shoki*, written narratives of "Japanese" history compiled in the eighth century, not modern? To answer this question, I

refer to Prasenjit Duara's discussion on the nation-state and modernity. In his *Rescuing History from the Nation: Questioning Narratives of Modern China* (1995), Duara challenges the interpretation of national conscious-ness as a radically novel/modern mode of consciousness; while the system of nation-states is new, political self-consciousness and representations of community as a social totality are not new, especially in such places as China, India, and Japan. I largely agree with Duara, but I also argue that the combination of a novel institutional arrangement of the world system and "national" consciousness (of not only the aristocrat but the majority of Japanese owing to the development of what Benedict Anderson called "print capitalism") is new. For this reason, I still argue that a progressive national history is modern.

5. The national headquarters of the agricultural cooperatives (Sangyō Kumiai Chūōkai) first published *Ie no hikari* in 1925. It has been distributed from that time to this day to subscribers through the local branches of agricul-tural cooperatives in rural Japan.

6. For rural women's sense of modernity, see Itagaki Kuniko's two important works (1978, 1992). Based on her reading of *The Light of the Home*, published from 1925 until 1945, she argues that the everyday life of rural women was "modernized" to a significant extent, as they came to learn hygienic practices, scientific methods of rearing children, rational utiliza-tion of time and resources, and so forth. I am grateful for Professor Sheldon Garon, who drew my attention to Itagaki's important works.

7. There are two excellent secondary sources about these village newspapers. One is Kano 1973. Chapter 2, "Seinendan undō no shisō" (pp. 56–154), is especially useful. The other is Nakamura 1978, 197–262.

8. Owing to the limited period of time of my field research, I read only several village newspapers, that is, *Urazato sonpō, Eboshi no hana* (later called *Motohara jihō*), *Kamishina jihō, Shiojiri jihō,* and *Kangawa jihō.* For the present study, I focused on *Urazato sonpō* and referred to the other village newspapers when necessary.

9. Some village newspapers, notably *Urazato sonpō,* became *kōhō* between 1940 and 1942, which printed only the central government's notifications for the local residents. *Kōhō* were thus no longer village newspapers but the central government's newspapers.

10. For the purpose of my argument, I take this time bracket (1919–1930) very loosely and often go beyond 1930. Local youth groups in most of these thirty villages resumed publication of their village newspapers in the early 1950s after the war. The village newspapers eventually disappeared by the early 1960s. For the past ten years or so, groups of local historians in the Ueda region have been attempting to publish them in the form of *fukkokuban,* reprints of ceased titles of the village newspapers.

11. In Ueda and its rural vicinity, the ratio of mulberry fields (for silkworms) to total agricultural land was 50.3 percent in 1925. The ratio of income from sericulture to total income in the same year was 67.0 percent (Kano 1973, 102).

12. Those measures included the Tenancy Conciliation Law of 1924; the Regulations for the Establishment of Owner-Cultivators of 1926; and the revision of the Industrial Cooperative Law of 1900 (see Waswo 1988, 588).

13. The name of this particular *sonpō* means "the flowers in the mountain of Ebōshi," the mountain located in the village of Motohara.

14. For example, there is an article titled "A Young Woman's Cry," published in *Ebōshi no hana*, in 1921 by a woman who identified herself as M.Y. (*Ebōshi no hana*, March 5, 1921). Much later, I spotted another article by a woman who used only her first name, Keiko, as her pen name (*Urazato sonpō*, October 25, 1933). Both articles present a rather conservative view of rural women. Using a horticultural metaphor for the nation of Japan, both M.Y. and Keiko argue that rural women should be proud of themselves as they nurture the roots of plants that blossom in the city. Keiko then writes, "It is now time for us to gain and use knowledge for not only consumption but production. Those tasks that are suitable for women, such as tending vegetable and fruit gardens, taking care of domestic animals, or growing plants and flowers, are accumulating in front of our eyes."

15. The quotation marks around "culture" (and later "civilization") are meant to indicate the historical specificities of the discursive constructions of these particular terms. I shall, however, generally not use quotation marks around these terms for the rest of this essay.

16. Using the results of *Shokugyō fujin ni kansuru chōsa* (Research on Working Women), published by the Tokyo Social Affairs Bureau in 1924, historian Margit Nagy maintains that, of the 3.5 million women in the labor force in the mid-Taishō era, "[n]early three-quarters of these employed women (2.6 million) were classified as manual workers, while the remaining one-fourth engaged in intellectual or mental work" (1991, 202). The image of the Modern Girl emphasizes her identity not only as a consumer but as a middle-class professional. Both Silverberg (1991) and Nagy, however, emphasize her identity as a producer, who often worked in poor conditions and thus could be politically active in the labor movement.

17. As a rebuttal to this article, a letter sent by an anonymous woman appeared in *Urazato sonpō* a month later. In the letter, she laments the weakness of the male author, who could not see "women" but "snakes." She then argues, "We women have respected you men. Indeed, your physical strength, knowledge, and will are all far superior to those of ours. You men are always 'senior' to women. The flower of culture is the product of the efforts of both men and women, but I believe it is largely men who constructed it. . . . Please, you should be stronger and wiser. While you see us as snakes, your soul remains impure. Even if we women are snakes, do not be afraid of us like frogs. You should be generous enough to teach us women."

18. In 1925, members of a young unmarried women's association of the village of Urazato were reported to have traveled to Karuizawa, where they visited a Western-style hotel and were invited by the hotel staff for hot chocolate. Rural modernity thus had significant Western elements in it (*Urazato sonpō*, October 10, 1925).

19. For the controversy between the mainline and the revisionist camp (in which I place myself), see Waswo (1988, 555–559). As exemplary works of the mainline historians, Waswo cites Moore 1967, 291–313, and Maruyama 1969, chap. 2.
20. For example, a man named Kitagawa Tarokichi argued in *Kangawa jihō*, July 1, 1927, that farmers should construct a "classless society" *(mukaikyū no shakai)*. However, such a society is not socialist or communist. He thus argues that: "Those of you who work like horses under the golden civilization of the city, you were once our brothers who had lived in this countryside but moved to the city, weren't you? Please return to our village as soon as possible. After you return, let's build our community together and let's work for ourselves. We do not hate capitalists, but we do hate capitalism. We do not admire such cultures as that of Russia, which was created by a proletarian dictatorship. We want a classless society in which everyone works not for money, but for life!"

REFERENCES

Anderson, Benedict. 1991. *Imagined Communities: Reflections on the Origins and Spread of Nationalism.* London: Verso.

Aoki Keiichirō. 1964. *Nagano-ken shakai undō-shi.* Gan'nan-dō.

Bestor, Theodore C. 1985. "Gendered Domains: A Commentary on Research in Japanese Studies." *Journal of Japanese Studies* 11.1:283–287.

De Certeau, Michel. 1984. *The Practice of Everyday Life.* Berkeley: University of California Press.

Dirks, Nicholas B. 1990. "History as a Sign of the Modern." *Public Culture* 2.2:25–32.

Duara, Prasenjit. 1995. *Rescuing History from the Nation: Questioning Narratives of Modern China.* Chicago: University of Chicago Press.

Fabian, Johannes. 1983. *Time and the Other.* New York: Columbia University Press.

Faubion, James. 1988. "Possible Modernities." *Cultural Anthropology* 3.4:365–378.

Fernandez, James W. 1988. "Andalusia on Our Minds: Two Contrasting Places in Spain As Seen in a Vernacular Poetic Dual of the Late 19th Century." *Cultural Anthropology* 3.1:21–35.

Foucault, Michel. 1980. "Questions of Geography." In *Power/Knowledge,* edited by Collin Gordon, 63–77. New York: Pantheon Books.

Gluck, Carol. 1985. *Japan's Modern Myths: Ideology in the Late Meiji Period.* Princeton: Princeton University Press.

Harootunian, Harry D. 1974a. "Between Politics and Culture: Authority and the Ambiguities of Intellectual Choice in Imperial Japan." In *Japan in Crisis: Essays on Taishō Democracy,* edited by Bernard S. Silberman and H. D. Harootunian, 110–155. Princeton: Princeton University Press.

———. 1974b. "Introduction: A Sense of an Ending and the Problem of Taishō." In *Japan in Crisis: Essays on Taishō Democracy,* edited by Bernard S. Silberman and H. D. Harootunian, 3–28. Princeton: Princeton University Press.

Harvey, David. 1989. *The Condition of Postmodernity.* Oxford: Basil Blackwell.

Itagaki Kuniko. 1978. "'Ie no hikari' ni miru nōson fujin: 1925–1945." In *On'na tachi no kindai,* edited by Kindai Joseishi Kenkyūkai, 309–336. Kashiwa Shobō.

———. 1992. *Shōwa senzen, senchūki no nōson seikatsu: zasshi ie no hikari ni miru.* Mitsumine Shobō.

Ivy, Marilyn. 1995. *Discourses of the Vanishing: Modernity, Phantasm, Japan.* Chicago: University of Chicago Press.

Kanō Masanao. 1973. *Taishō democrashii no teiryū: dozoku-teki seishin e no kaiki.* NHK Books.

Katō, Shūichi. 1974. "Taishō Democracy as the Pre-Stage for Japanese Militarism." In *Japan in Crisis: Essays on Taishō Democracy,* edited by Bernard S. Silberman and H. D. Harootunian, 217–236. Princeton: Princeton University Press.

Kern, Stephen. 1983. *The Culture of Time and Space, 1880–1918.* Cambridge: Harvard University Press.

Maruoka Hideko. 1937. *Nihon nōson fujin mondai: atarashiki shuppatsu.* Yakumo Shoten.

Maruyama, Masao. 1969. *Thought and Behaviour in Modern Japanese Politics.* Enl. ed. London: Oxford University Press.

Minami Hiroshi, ed. 1965. *Taishō bunka.* Keisō Shobō.

Moore, Barrington, Jr. 1967. *Social Origins of Dictatorship and Democracy: Lord and Peasant in the Making of the Modern World.* Boston: Beacon Press.

Nagy, Margit. 1991. "Middle-Class Working Women During the Interwar Years." In *Recreating Japanese Women, 1600–1945,* edited by Gail L. Bernstein, 199–216. Berkeley: University of California Press.

Nakamura Masanori. 1978. "Keizai kōsei undō to nōson tōgō: Nagano-ken Chiisagata-gun Urazato-mura no baai." In *Fuashizumu-ki no kokka to shakai.* Vol. 1, *Shōwa kyōkō,* edited by Tokyo Daigaku Shakai Kagaku Kenkyū-sho, 197–262. University of Tokyo Press.

Ōshima Eiko. 1982. "Ryō-taisen-kan no josei rōdō." In *Nihon josei-shi,* edited by Josei-shi Sōgō Kenkyū-kai, 5:1–38. University of Tokyo Press.

Roden, Donald. 1990. "Taishō Culture and the Problem of Gender Ambivalence." In *Culture and Identity: Japanese Intellectuals during the Interwar Years,* edited by J. Thomas Rimer, 37–55. Princeton: Princeton University Press.

Rofel, Lisa. 1992. "Rethinking Modernity: Space and Factory Discipline in China." *Cultural Anthropology* 7.1:93–114.

Rosaldo, Renato. 1989. *Culture and Truth.* Boston: Beacon Press.

Sakai, Naoki. 1991. *Voices of the Past: The Status of Language in Eighteenth-Century Japanese Discourse.* Ithaca: Cornell University Press.

Schorske, Carl. 1981. *Fin-de-siecle Vienna: Politics and Culture.* New York: Vintage Books.

Silverberg, Miriam. 1991. "The Modern Girl as Militant." In *Recreating Japanese Women, 1600–1945,* edited by Gail L. Bernstein, 239–266. Berkeley: University of California Press.

Soja, Edward W. 1989. *Postmodern Geographies: The Reassertion of Space in Critical Social Theory.* London: Verso.

Suzuki Masayuki. 1977. "Taishō-ki nōmin seiji shisō no ichi-sokumen, I." *Nihonshi kenkyū* 173:1–26.

Tamanoi, Mariko Asano. 1996. "Gender, Nationalism, and Japanese Native Ethnology." *Positions* 4.1:59–86.

Waswo, Ann. 1988. "The Transformation of Rural Society, 1900–1950." In *The Cambridge History of Modern Japan,* Vol. 6, *The Twentieth Century,* edited by Peter Duus, 541–603. Cambridge: Cambridge University Press

Wigen, Kären. 1995. *The Making of a Japanese Periphery, 1750–1920.* Berkeley: University of California Press.

Williams, Raymond. 1973. *The Country and the City.* New York: Oxford University Press.

❦ 5 ❧

Naturalizing Nationhood: Ideology and Practice in Early Twentieth-Century Japan

JULIA ADENEY THOMAS

Modern nationhood has been portrayed as profoundly unnatural. Whether analyzed by Hegel or Maruyama Masao, Benedict Anderson or Ernst Gellner, the creation of modern nationhood has been deemed an artificial act. Neither the natural bonds of kinship nor rootedness in the soil impelled its creation; rather, the impetus behind nationhood has been ascribed to the working out of the Hegelian Ideal in History, to invention (*sakui*) in Maruyama's theory, to exile and hybridity in Anderson's, or to a particular type of industrial culture in Gellner's. The nation (as opposed to the state) in these analyses emerged in the nineteenth century not as an evolutionary outgrowth of the past but as a form of discontinuity—a new relationship with time and space, with fellow citizens, and with nature itself, an overcoming of nature's dictates in favor of those of human beings.

But not all twentieth-century nations have celebrated conscious self-creation, nor have they embraced the existential responsibilities inherent in such an identity. In the early decades of the twentieth century, many nations, including Japan, sought to reinscribe the nation as natural. Nature and nationhood became so closely bound that this process of restructuring national identity might be described with equal justice as nationalizing nature and as naturalizing nationhood. In Japan, immemorial tradition was evoked in support of this newly constructed identity, but, as I will argue, the naturalized nationhood of the Taishō period is more correctly understood as a reaction against Meiji conceptions of nature and the form of semimodernity they represented. I shall analyze the category of nature as precisely as space permits in order, first, to suggest the way Japan's naturalization of nationhood circumscribed legitimate political discourse, augmenting oligarchic power, and, second, to place Japan's engagement with modernity in a global perspective beyond the dichotomy of East and West.

As is often the case with developing ideologies, the first formulations of Japan's new naturalized nationhood appeared in a piecemeal but concrete fashion. Elements of the new vision emerged through governmental policies directed at land use and religious shrines, government-sponsored textbook depictions of community, and governmental economic exhortations. Together, these documents laid the literal and figurative groundwork for the new relationship between Japan and nature. This relationship would be fully systematized only later during the war years when paeans to the coalescent intimacy between Japan and nature ring forth in works such as *Kokutai no hongi* and texts by Kyoto School philosophers like Watsuji Tetsurō (1889–1960). Although the earlier documents are diverse, the concept of nature *(shizen)*[1] that emerges is anything but diffuse. In other words, while ideological production was piecemeal in the early decades of the century, the cumulative definition was coherent. Indeed, through these documents, the concept acquires precise material referents and theoretical parameters. It is possible, in fact, to understand the power and distinctiveness of this new approach to nature both as the concrete lived experience of Taishō villagers and as an abstract formulation.

Turning first to the new ways nature was experienced, let us imagine a village scene during the early decades of the twentieth century when the population was still predominately rural.

In those years, a schoolboy might have sat disconsolately on the stump of a venerable old tree that used to shade his village's shrine. The tree has been cut and sold for lumber as part of the central government's "one shrine per village" consolidation policy. On this imaginary afternoon, however, what worries the boy is not the desacramentalization of the old shrine ground where he played in early childhood but rather the tediousness of his ethics textbook proclaiming him and his school fellows to be children of the paternal emperor.[2] The boy's more immediate father, a local farmer, stands gossiping with his friend, and this lengthy conversation also makes the boy impatient. His father reiterates his long-standing complaint about the Hōtoku (Repayment of Virtue) Society, which had been a locally controlled rural economic improvement society until 1906, when the Ministry of Home Affairs took charge. The farmer's frugality no longer repays his own ancestors' sacrifices but is instead directed by and toward Tokyo. "It's not the same anymore," grumbles the boy's father. "We'll soon be calling it the Hōtoku Naimushō (Home Ministry Repayment) Society," he says, repeating the worn-out joke that has been making the rounds. The boy, fidgeting on his tree stump, is subject to the new national articulation of nature that places him in a landscape centered on Tokyo and in a genealogical relationship to that new imperial center through his multiple fathers.

In this scene, nature oscillates between physical and conceptual dimensions; it enters the religious, educational, and economic discourses of the nation. Despite this superficial multiplicity, nature is beginning to achieve a systematicity rare for a concept that usually frustrates with its fecundity of meaning.[3] In every instance, nature adopts a national guise shorn of both localism and universality. It refers neither to local communities and flora, fauna, and environment nor to universal human nature and the cosmos. Even more precisely, it adopts the meaning of human, particularly Japanese, cultural genealogy. In other words, this nature stands not opposed to culture but allied with a particular culture, that of Japan. Further, this acculturated, genealogized nature, contrary to normal modes of historical and sexual genetic transference, is assumed to reproduce itself in nearly exact replica, with variation kept to a minimum.[4] Nothing is lost or gained in the timeless passage of generations. In short, there emerges a definition of nature that is extremely nationalistic, constrained, and static. Let us turn to the question of how and why this concept mutated in this particular way as Japan confronted modernity.

OVERCOMING SOCIAL DARWINISM

The creation of a system of thought, the coordination of practice in many arenas, is sometimes attributable to the active design of a single person or group. In early twentieth-century Japan, however, there was no mastermind reconstructing nature for national purposes. Although an appeal to "the State" as the agent of this design may be justified with regard to certain policies, the conclusion that government officials implemented a predetermined view of nature does not seem warranted, given the length of time involved (about thirty years), the sheer variety of practices effected, and the vacillation apparent even where matters were in government hands, such as with educational policy. I would argue instead that the coordination of practice and ideology extended beyond state policy and achieved its systematicity not through positive design, but through adverse reaction to a precise and potent idea of nature that mid-Meiji Japan had thoroughly embraced: social Darwinism. The specificity and breadth of social Darwinism's challenge configured the seemingly coordinated response of early twentieth-century Japanese involved in defining and exploiting nature.

Much research has been done to illuminate exactly what forms of "Western learning" were being introduced to Meiji Japan. We now are cognizant that, adventurous and expansive as Meiji readers were, they encountered not Western culture per se, as earlier scholarship sometimes implied, but the particular Western culture of the mid and late nineteenth century (Kinmonth 1981; Westney 1987). Nevertheless, it is still difficult to grasp the tremendous power of the concept of social evolution, particularly as expressed by Herbert Spencer. Not only was Spencer one of the most imposing intellectual figures of his generation, but his concepts were perhaps the West's primary intellectual export in the late nineteenth century.[5] Between 1877 and 1890, at least thirty-two translations of Spencer's works were published in Japan; Spencer was, in fact, predominant among Western social and political theorists translated into Japanese (Nagai 1954, 55). His ideas were further bolstered in Japan by works of European, particularly German, and American proponents of social Darwinism.

So overwhelming was the Spencerian influence that his name was reverentially evoked both by advocates of democracy such as Baba Tatsui (1850–1888)[6] and by advocates of imperial oligarchy such as Katō Hiroyuki (1836–1916).[7] Socialists as well found inspiration in Spencer, as a respectful death notice in the December 27, 1903, issue of *Heimin shinbun* demonstrates. Social Darwinism crept into educational theory as Japanese children were taught to see the different peoples of the world climbing the trail of progress with Europeans and Asians on top moving down through Arabs to Africans and aborigines (Yamazumi 1970, 21).[8] Tokutomi Sohō (Ichirō) (1863–1957) used Spencerian educational theory to promote moral training in *Shin Nihon no Seinen* (*Youth of the New Japan*, 1886), Spencerian historical theory in *Shōrai no Nihon* (*The Future Japan*, 1886), and the theory of the "survival of the fittest" (*yūshō reppai*) to exhort young men to economic enterprise. University professors, both imported and native, and public lecturers extolled social and natural evolution much to the frustration of Christian missionaries and their supporters.[9] Periodicals such as *Tōyō gakugei zasshi* and *Gakugei shirin* were crammed with articles demonstrating the extraordinary interest in evolution which, as Watanabe Masao and Ose Yōko point out, "was discussed mainly on the ground of social science rather than natural science" (Watanabe and Ose 1968–1969, 141). Most famously, Japan's envoy to Britain, Mori Arinori (1847–1889), approached the great Spencer himself for comment on the Meiji Constitution (Peel 1972, 253–257). To an extraordinary extent, Meiji Japan refocused its understanding of society and politics through the lens of Spencer's evolutionary sociology.

Social Darwinism's influence in Japan as elsewhere was the result in part of its usefulness to so many sides in so many questions. Since Spencer's views shifted in the course of his lifetime from utopian socialism to rigid conservatism, they were convenient for political quotation by opposing sides, though volatile in their ideological consequences. Nevertheless, evolutionary nature could not be all things to all people despite its many political variations. Most importantly, nature in this form was not diametrically opposed to historical change, but partook of history at its very essence. Nature became a historical phenomenon in itself and a historical force working through human beings. The corollary of this recombinant naturalized history was that, to varying degrees, human beings as individuals, nations, and a species were not entirely masters of their own fates. Fortunately, this natural fate tended toward the good in general if not in particular instances. Progress toward a good society might creep at a snail's pace through centuries of brutal misery and competition or it might be realized more immediately depending on how nature's political message was read, but progress would somehow be realized. In other words, nature in the last instance was moral.

Despite resistance to social Darwinism in some quarters, it offered a beguiling certainty, a definite historical narrative, and the imprimatur of science. It was, for a while, the highest expression of truth: progressive, Western, scientific. Although it challenged the traditional Neo-Confucian view that nature offered an unchanging copybook of the proper hierarchy from Heaven to Earth, social Darwinism supported belief in a natural morality apparent in the fabric of social interaction rather than a system of ethics and laws created through human endeavor. It further supported a general sense that the elite were there by desert rather than design. In its naturalized politics, social Darwinism discounted the unnatural politics of social contract, conscious idealism, and revolution that marked early modern nationalism in many parts of the globe. Along with renaturalizing politics, it also renaturalized culture and capitalist economic practices. In other words, it is possible to argue that in engaging social Darwinism—already intent on displacing contingent or consciously created history—Japan cannot be said to have engaged fully modernity in the sense described by many theorists of nationalism.

Japanese enthusiasm for social Darwinism peaked in the early 1880s. By the turn of the century, however, the fervor had died. The theory met with severe criticism in Japan on four counts: its tendentious universality, its problematic ethics, its focus on material progress, and its stress on individual competition required to fuel that material progress.

Social Darwinism functioned universally but not universally at the same rate. Its Japanese and Western advocates tended to place Japan on the evolutionary ladder below the more "advanced races." The feeling voiced by Herbert Spencer in his condescending remarks on the Meiji Constitution to one of its drafters, Kaneko Kentarō (1853–1942), was that six to eight generations would need to elapse before Japan attained the social foundation necessary for representative government. Spencer also warned that Japan must "keep other races at arm's length as much as possible" in order to achieve this advance (Peel 1972, 257). By 1893, Tokutomi Sohō, among others, reacted with disgust against this threatening presumption of naturally determined Western hegemony. From his former acceptance of Spencer, particularly Spencer's view that developed industrial societies were necessarily pacifist, Tokutomi moved to embrace a militarily assertive Japan. The victory over China, he said, showed that Japanese, too, had a "character suitable for great achievements in the world" (Beasley 1987, 31). A decade later, Japan's victory in the Russo-Japanese War dramatically overturned the international model of nations arrayed in strict, unchanging order on the evolutionary ladder.

The post-Meiji generation and even the Meiji generation turned away from the thesis of social evolution as a moral basis for society. Katō Hiroyuki had been concerned with the ethical problems of *shinkaron* (evolutionary theory) even when he trumpeted his embrace of the concept in 1881 (Katō 1984, 416). The promise of future social good achieved through years of misery and strife was insufficient to him if not immoral. After 1905, Katō expressed his increasingly keen doubts about social evolution's ethical ramifications in a series of lengthy publications, including *Shizenkai no mujun to shinka* (*The Contradictions of the Natural World and Progress*, 1906), *Shizen to rinri* (*Nature and Ethics*, 1912), and *Jinsei no shizen to gohō no zento* (*Human Nature and the Future Prospects of Our Country*, 1916). Katō gradually gutted the workings of social evolution by promoting a guiding elite to ameliorate social dislocation and maintain social morality in the present.

Those few who continued to support social Darwinism lost their optimistic assessment of the future to which it pointed. In 1912, physiologist Oka Asajirō (1868–1944) made the case for Darwinian struggle only as a grim alternative to complete destruction. Human beings struggled for survival against a recalcitrant nature that responded to economic development with floods and polluted rivers, with tuberculosis in "quiet revenge" against modern medicine, and with increasing strains in the social system as gaps between rich and poor widened. And yet, as Oka warned, "international competition was so cut-throat that to stop material progress would invite conquest and suffering worse even than 'nature's revenge'" (Stone 1975, 405). After the turn of the century, nature's promise seemed double-edged to many Japanese.

Nature as social evolution and its associated ideas had been imported as the epitome of contemporary Western thought, but by the early twentieth century this concept assumed a pessimistic hue, assuring neither a good society nor immediate progress. Ideologically, its combination of universalism and racial hierarchy undercut Japanese national identity and government authority; practically, its emphasis on material wealth for competitive individuals contributed to social disturbance. If this is the concept of nature that early twentieth-century Japanese were rejecting—and it is certainly possible to sympathize with their response—the question becomes what alternative natural matrix did they create for the Japanese polity? For most Japanese did not reject nature outright; instead, they redefined it. Since it is impossible here to trace this effort in all arenas, I have chosen to examine three different but powerful formulations in Shinto practices, economic exhortations, and ethics education.

SHINTO'S NATIONAL NATURE

During the Meiji period, Shinto went through so many contortions that even calling it a "religion" touches on its disputed basic character. For a brief period within the initial government structure, Shinto was established as the state faith and given precedence over other religions. By 1872, however, it was dislodged from this privileged position because of objections by Buddhists and Christians, and because the varying practices designated "Shinto" provided little coherent support for government policy. After a lull, Shinto, around 1905, was adapted as a nonreligious state ideology, a unique, patriotic practice wherein former priests became bureaucratic overseers of national ritual. In this way, rites encouraging national unity could be imposed on all people regardless of their professed beliefs. In the words of Mizuno Rentarō, minister of home affairs, in May 1918, the "shrines are the unique institutions of our nation. They are the essence of our national organization. They are inseparably related to the state" (Holtom 1922, 42). This unprecedented use of Shinto as national patriotic essence required a complete systemization and centralization of haphazard shrines, amorphous doctrines, and rites expressing local custom (Hardacre 1989, 9–13).

This effort to nationalize Shinto had direct bearing on Japan's understanding of nature since traditionally Shinto—if it is permissible to use this anachronistic term for the variety of practices and beliefs before Meiji (Hardacre 1989, 18–19)—had supported various ideas of nature and protected many natural sites. The simplicity of Shinto rites suggested spontaneous or natural reverence, the aversion to doctrine a natural faith, its wooded shrines and delight in waterfalls and other phenomena a deep appreciation for physical nature, and its rites of family continuity a sacerdotal view of kinship and ancestral lineage. Ideologically and practically, Shinto in its new national role sloughed off some of these natures, especially the focus on nature as sacred space, the physicality and rooted locality of places and things. As Shinto was nationalized, emphasis fell increasingly on sanctifying the family as the most fundamental natural and national unit.

D. C. Holtom, a scholar and contemporary observer of the new state Shinto, describes this reformulation of nature as the devaluation of *tennen sūhai* (worship of physical nature) in favor of *sosen sūhai* (worship of ancestors or human genealogical nature). Holtom notes "a marked tendency on the part of the modern directors of thought in Japan, in religious, educational and political spheres alike, to emphasize the latter element as the more characteristic Japanese expression" (Holtom 1922, 5). It is difficult to ignore the ideological utility of such a preference. An emphasis on ancestor worship disengaged ritual practice from particular places and, literally, mobilized it. Statements such as those in the 1914 government-issued prayers (*norito*) clearly equating family ancestors with *kami* (deities) and enfolding these *kami* within the Imperial household, were possible only if the particular, the local, the familial could be made national and imperial. The ancestral dead attained a convenient metaphorical quality, permitting analogy between the honor due to grandfather and that due to Imperial Deities. On the other hand, the neighborhood shrine's tree, no matter how stately, retained a concreteness that hindered the play of tropes through which it could be linked with Tokyo. The migratory dead achieved precedence over the stationary, local, rooted, living emblems of former practices.

The de-emphasis on spatial nature also created a logic whereby Shinto could be transposed and imposed on colonial possessions. By 1937, for instance, there were 368 Shinto shrines in Korea, mostly dedicated to Amaterasu (Hardacre 1989, 95). Had nature's sacredness not been abstracted from the soil, it would have moved less easily as national boundaries expanded. Of equal importance was the fact that while the genealogized, abstract quality of nature could move beyond the home islands, the reverse trajectory was impeded by lack of genetic connection. In 1906, for instance, the annual meeting of Shinto priests considered enshrining in Yasukuni Jinja the Koreans who fell in the Russo-Japanese War and decided to restrict that privilege to "real" Japanese born of Japanese parents (Hardacre 1989, 95). This conception of natural connection prevented non-Japanese from claiming kinship.

Without this distinction between ancestral divinities, who were metaphoricized and mobile, and the rooted divinities of place, the government's controversial policy of shrine mergers would have met with even more severe difficulties than it did. Reaching its height between 1906 and 1912, the *isson issha* goal of one shrine per administrative village was intended, according to authorities, to lift the financial burden of supporting so many small shrines and to increase popular reverence by replacing shabby places of worship (sometimes used to store night soil, as one outraged official explained) with more awe-inspiring ones.

In practice, this policy meant that tutelary shrines in the old customary villages (*buraku, ōaza*) were rent asunder. The physical aspect of the shrine was destroyed: the old shrine torn down, the trees sold for lumber, the fauna dispersed, the land plowed under or, in town, commercialized.[10] The other less concrete aspect of the shrine, the *shintai*, or *kami*-body in which the *kami* inhered, was carried by villagers, sometimes in great state, to the receiving shrine. Although, according to Wilbur Fridell, this policy primarily took the form of suggestions rather than formal directives from the central government, it was enormously successful. Between 1903 and 1920, no less than 52 percent of the small ungraded shrines and 13 percent of village shrines were merged (Fridell 1973, 19–20; Hardacre 1989, 98).

Needless to say, the *isson issha* policy did not find favor with communities that had for centuries expressed their fellowship through worship and festivals at their local shrines. Absurd situations developed. In one case, villagers had to travel by foot nearly twenty-five miles to the shrine housing their "local" deity (Fridell 1973, 85; Yanagita 1957, 294). In at least in one case, the men who bore the sad burden of the *shintai* away to its new resting place died unnatural, sudden deaths (Hardacre 1989, 99). Local dissatisfaction with the policy resulted in its uneven application throughout the country.

Nationally, resistance to shrine mergers was articulated on the basis of both biology and folk custom. In 1911, Minakata Kumagusu (1867–1941), the flamboyant microbiologist who traveled with an Italian circus in South America and published articles on algae in the famed British journal *Nature*, teamed up with folklorist and government official Yanagita Kunio (1875–1962) to petition for an end to the mergers. Minakata's vision of the ecological role played by shrines is particularly interesting for the way in which physical and conceptual natures are intertwined. Combining concern for local customs with concern for local flora and fauna, he suggests that local shrines are integral to all life. Without shrine trees to nest in, swallows and other birds can no longer keep the insect population in check. Growing insect populations destroy crops or force farmers to spend money for commercial insecticides, costing more and diminishing self-reliance within the village. Fresh water supplies, protected since shrines are often built near springs, are also threatened. According to Minakata, all things from rare fungi to fish to human hopes and ideals are endangered without shrines (Minakata 1971, 477–590; Tsurumi 1977). The natural community promoted by Minakata, and with even greater emphasis on human customs by Yanagita, is local, physical, and fecund in contrast to the apotheosized community of the ancestral dead abstracted to a national level.[11] Although resistance to the shrine merger policy ultimately led to its cancellation, the concept of nature promulgated by those opposing the policy remained marginalized.

The transformation of nature through State Shinto may be expressed as a series of ironies. Nature in the small shrine sanctuaries all over the country was destroyed for the sake of naturalizing the nation. Traditional natural communities were reconfigured into artificial townships in order to support a newly naturalized center. Government policy rationalized shrine lands and trees, placing the formerly sacred on the market as commodities, in order to create mystical underpinnings for the nation. What had been chaotic, customary, and fertile became organized, bureaucratized, and restrained. The celebration of life became remembrance of the dead. To understand this transformation simply as ironic, however, misses the intensity of the conflict between radically different concepts of nature. There was no one "nature" being manipulated by authorities to produce paradox but several natures in contention. Central authorities responded to the challenge of universalism represented by social Darwinism by delimiting and redefining nature as an abstract and unifying principle resonant with the mystical imperial center. "Nature" in this version was equated with national culture. Resisting that centralized, abstracted version of nature, Minakata and Yanagita found a mystical resonance in local folk custom, insisting that nature was physical, fecund, and consonant with particular popular cultures.

ECONOMIZING NATURE

Analyzing this domestic debate as being among natures that on all sides retain something of the mystical has important ramifications for our understanding of Japan's new conceptualization of nature in relation to economic practice. One prominent model of the uses of nature in modern political thought takes sacral nature to be a form of false ideology always at odds with rationalizing modes of production. Terry Eagleton, for instance, argues that capitalistic societies

> still feel the need to legitimate their activities at the altar of transcendental values, not least religious ones, while steadily undermining the credibility of those doctrines by their own ruthlessly rationalizing practices. The "base" of modern capitalism is thus to some extent always at odds with its "superstructure." A social order for which truth means pragmatic calculation continues to cling to eternal verities; a form of life which in dominating Nature expels all mystery from the world still ritually invokes the sacred. (Eagleton 1991, 155)

This model neatly encapsulates a powerful position in the analysis of Western cultures whereby highly efficient individual exploitation of natural resources is celebrated as divinely sanctioned.[12] Nature is thus mere resource to entrepreneurs while it is the sign of manifest destiny and divine blessing to the nation. Tension develops between the "base," an infinite nature prone before the grasping hands of economic "man,"[13] and the "superstructure," the national ideology of an untouchable, sanctified Truth of divine creation. This tension becomes particularly extreme when environmental limits are reached.

While nature became a national ideology in Taishō Japan, its conceptual uses were not entirely at odds with its practical exploitation as in the case described above. This is not to say that capitalistic pragmatism never impinged on local and national mysticism or there was no falsity in the

Japanese national mythos. Rationalizing the exploitation of resources and rationalizing national ideology, in part through such capitalist practices as commodifiying old shrines, were most definitely part of early twentieth-century Japan. However, the central government's ideological pronouncements and the practices it encouraged on the land partook of the same circumscribed, cautionary view of nature and the possibilities of exploiting it. Even among social Darwinists in Japan, the productive capacities of physical nature were never entirely trusted to underwrite social progress. Physical nature was never proclaimed infinite; neither individuals nor companies had license to ravish "her" solely for their own benefit. Instead, slender resources had to be cherished for national benefit.

Where hopes were greatest for wealth from nature, as with ventures in Hokkaido or the Ashio Copper Mine in Tochigi prefecture, there was disappointment. Hokkaido did not prosper as expected and remained an impoverished backwater until the 1930s. While by 1900 the Ashio Mine was producing 50 percent of Japan's copper, and copper was Japan's third most important export behind silk and tea, the scandalous pollution it created chastened official hopes of nature's bounty (Notehelfer 1984; Strong 1977; Pyle 1975). Even where nature was cooperative, the means of exploiting it were suspect in the early twentieth century. As Tetsuo Najita argues, there was "a deeply felt concern regarding the aggressive pulls of technology [because] culture was not in ideological control of technology" (Najita 1988, 409). To suggest that nature as physical resource might provide infinite possibilities was to suggest that it might slip beyond the control of culture—a Frankensteinian nightmare to be avoided.

Edicts promulgated during the century's early decades reiterate the theme not of nature's economic possibilities but of its limits. For instance, the Boshin Rescript of 1908 on Thrift and Diligence urges hard work and frugality on peasants and workers who are "to inure themselves to arduous toil without yielding to any degree of indulgence." If they restrain their desires, promises the rescript, "the growing prosperity of Our Empire is assured" (*Japan Year Book* 1911, 496). These injunctions have as their immediate aim labor unrest, widespread unemployment, and the 1908 run on the banks, but in broader terms they also insist that natural resources are finite and individual engagement with them should benefit the nation. In other words, the rescript suggests a view of nature's beneficence far more pessimistic than that of laissez-faire capitalists or social Darwinians.

This pessimism was shared by the Local Improvement Movement (Chihō Kairyō Undō) inaugurated in 1909 by officials at the Ministry of Home Affairs to implement the Rescript on Thrift and Diligence. Great emphasis was placed on respect for superiors, including village headmen and landlords. Their slogan, "Accept your lot humbly and defer to superiors" (*bundo suijō*), is the antithesis of social Darwinian promise of social and economic gain for the strong and active. For officials of the Local Improvement Movement, the farmer's engagement with nature must promise no individual social advancement.

Demographics further conspired to certify this view of physical limits. While the Bureau of Shrines composed prayers for large families with many sons for the army, the Japanese population jumped from around forty million in 1890 to sixty-four million in 1930, excluding overseas territories (Hunter 1984, 258). The limits of the land were strongly felt and strongly argued in international disputes.

In Japan, both practically and ideologically, the biology and geography of the physical world were made over to national purposes rather than local and individual ones. Economic practices exploiting nature and ideological practices nationalizing nature were not greatly at odds because there was no sharp contrast between a raw individual energy creating a progressive history through natural exploitation and a transcendent, eternally stable natural sanction for nationhood. Unlike America and other Western nations where nature remained tangible, for Japanese nationalism, the definition of nature as physical resource became secondary to a more abstract, acculturated concept of nature. The material natural world might be limited and unpromising, but the genealogized natural nation was far more expansive, requiring colonization and emigration.

THE NATURAL NATIONAL FAMILY

While shrine policies constructed an abstract, apotheosized nature and economic exhortations represented physical nature as limited in abundance and limiting in the opportunities it offered for individual advancement, educational policy defined nature as national family. Analogies between filial piety and patriotic imperial loyalty had been common, of course, before the twentieth century, but after 1900, and particularly by 1910, the kinship relationship between families, villages, and the Imperial Household was transformed from analogy to actuality. As one historian writes, "The nation was not *like* a family, it *was* a family by virtue of the fact that the distant ancestors of ordinary Japanese households were offshoots of the main imperial line" (Fridell 1979, 829). Ethics textbooks consciously promoted this ideological transformation of Japan from historical nation into the natural nation of *kazoku-kokka* (family-state).

In response to the variety of privately produced interpretations of the 1890 Imperial Rescript on Education, the National Diet in 1897 decided that ethics textbooks should be produced by the government. Their ruling created a Ministry of Education committee, chaired by Katō Hiroyuki, with instructions to compile an official ethics series for school use. The initial set of textbooks was completed in 1903, and, as historian Ishida Takeshi points out, it was not particularly concerned with nature as family (Ishida 1954, 8). Indeed, these volumes retained a certain progressive emphasis, no doubt in part because Katō had not yet entirely shaken his social Darwinian rhetoric.[14] Only after the Russo-Japanese War and the social disturbances that followed were these ethics primers transformed into hard-hitting boosters of patriotism and sacrifice for the national family.

By 1910, a new, more nationalistic series of ethics textbooks had been completed by a committee chaired this time by staunch conservative Hozumi Yatsuka, dean of the Tokyo Imperial University Law School. The transformation in the nature of the nation is evident when these two series are compared. As historian of education Karasawa Tomitarō observes:

> In the 1910 revision, the modern ethics of the 1903 texts were eliminated, and in their place a feudal family ethic was stressed. All lessons such as "Others' Freedoms," "Social Progress," and "Rivalry" were removed, and new lessons like "Ise Shrine," "The Founding of the Nation," "The National Essence (*kokutai*)," "Guard the Prosperity of the Imperial Throne," . . . and "The Dying Instructions of our Imperial Ancestors" were added in their place. (Karasawa 1960, 286; quoted in Fridell 1979, 827)

In other words, the new books eliminated lessons echoing social Darwinian ideas of social progress and competition (rivalry). In their place were put not only the nationalistic lessons suggested by the titles above but also an emphasis on the fatherly beneficence of the emperor, for whom all Japanese should be willing to die.

The fusion of filial piety and national loyalty expressed in the phrase *chūkō no taigi* (the great principle of loyalty and filial piety) resounded in these school texts. Ninth graders were told:

> It is only natural for children to love and respect their parents, and the great loyalty–filial piety principle springs from this natural feeling. . . . Our country is based on the family system. The whole country is one great family, and the Imperial House is the Head Family (*sōka*). It is with the feeling of filial love and respect for parents that we Japanese people express our reverence toward the Throne of unbroken imperial line. (Miyata 1959, 499)

Like an algebraic proof, the passage neatly establishes the equivalence of family, village, and nation.

Promoting a national family, however, did more than simply pull the periphery into the center to form an organized organic whole. The *kazoku-kokka* was also a statement about the way nature could replace history as the guarantor of authentic culture. While Darwinian social progress treated human cultures as stages in a naturalized history, Japan's naturalized nation insisted on a culture tangential to quotidian time even while resting on the most quotidian of groups, the family. The eternal naturalness of the Japanese nation authenticated a culture that could not be transformed by pedestrian changes in daily life; yet, paradoxically, it was represented in the daily activities of each Japanese person. The ninth-grade ethics text cited above admonishes pupils that, "the state *(kokka)* exists independently forever, but the individual only for a time, and compared with the state his life is very brief. It is only natural that the people must conform to the purposes of the eternal state, and give no heed to personal interests" (Miyata 1959, 494). According to this view, nature as family, nation, and culture was divorced from common life and almost from life itself. As the naturalized nation transcended the mundane, it took nature with it, leaving the quotidian as a form of half-life, a prelude to individual death and national eternity.

Because Japan became at once both natural and transcendent, its national nature was distinguishable from the social Darwinian version with its focus on nontranscendent biological struggle *and* from narratives that saw national history as antinatural, the transcendence of nations and humanity above nature. As with the nationalized nature of Shinto and of economic exhortations, the nationalized nature of ethics primers absorbed the concrete local world of daily life within the excess of a timeless national nature where death and abundance cohered.

The "natures" created in opposition to social evolution and in support of the state were compatible and mutually supportive, even though they were initially produced with specific reference to religion, economics, and education. Abstract, apotheosized, limited in its tangible benefits but infinite through the imperial line, nature in this new form became almost identical with the Japanese nation. Consequently, other peoples, cultures, and places became less natural, and alternative domestic versions of nature, such as those voiced by Minakata and Yanagita with their emphasis on the local and the physical, were overwhelmed.

CONCLUSION

One of the most tantalizing questions concerning the Taishō period is how the state was able to assimilate so much political and cultural production seemingly at odds with it. Advances in technology, urbanization, colonization, and participation in international markets, social trends, and wars might have destabilized Meiji power structures and opened the way to greater democracy and a more independent civil society, but they did not. Instead, Japan failed to follow either modernization theory's trajectory toward liberalism or the Marxist thrust toward revolution; its confrontation with modernity led to a stronger, nondemocratic imperial state presiding over modernity's material bounty. I have argued here that taking the politicality of "nature" seriously provides a new tool for understanding how this Japanese state emerged triumphant, hushing possible dissent.

In particular, analyzing the naturalization of nationhood in early twentieth-century Japan reveals how the givens of the situation were redefined in ways detrimental to dissonant views and even to political discussion. When the boundaries of the nation—and ultimately of national culture—were made coterminous with the form of nature described above, disagreeing became an act of perversion in its root sense: an abomination of nature. One was either natural and, therefore, what one said and did was in harmony with Japanese culture, or one was unnatural, at odds with the national body and, not being part of that body, ultimately invisible and inaudible. Almost any Japanese person's particular commitments could be assimilated to the naturalized nation because that person's natural identity was seen to trump his or her conscious choices. In other words, although conflicting interests and social visions were seen as unnatural, the individual Japanese was always naturally part of the state and could be assimilated on that basis despite "unnatural" ideas. Only in very extreme cases, such as that of village headman Tanaka Shōzō (1841–1913), who fought against the Ashio copper mine's pollution and ended up without position, family, and home, or that of the radicals executed after the 1910 High Treason Incident, was social and natural identity completely annihilated rather than absorbed and muffled.

Although confronting the hegemonic power of this naturalized nationalism was extremely difficult, one method was to attempt to define nature in alternative ways. Minakata and Yanagita promoted this avenue of resistance by investing local custom with a naturalness preceding that of the nation. Another potent means of leveraging local nature against the naturalized nation was through environmental struggles. As historian Kano Masanao argues, the fight against pollution in the late Meiji and Taishō periods was one of the strongest available tools for battering oligarchic power not just on the question of industrial policy but on the whole relationship between the people and their government (Kano 1971, 334). However, these challenges were not successful in redefining nature for the nation either as local custom or as an independent environmental realm. In the end, the rhetoric of Japan's unique natural polity continued to boost national morale and assimilate dissent throughout the war years.

For "nature" to have been ideologized in this way underscores the need for historians to examine such seemingly innocuous and apolitical terms for their political potency. Nature is neither a neutral concept nor one always at the disposal of conservative forces as Maruyama claims (Maruyama 1974, 228). Instead, it requires precise analysis because, however defined, nature molds our sense of what is given about ourselves and our societies and the extent to which these can be changed. Sometimes this is indeed conservative, but other times it offers a challenge to the status quo. Nature is not one thing only. Taishō Japan did not choose "nature" as such against the onslaught of Western culture; instead it crafted a particular nature in response to one of many natures—social Darwinism—that happened to be ascendant at the time Japan sought knowledge of the West. From this particular international engagement and the particular domestic debates it spawned, there emerged a form of naturalized nationhood that refused to recognize the independence of either individuals or their physical environment.

NOTES

1. *Shizen* did not become the standard term for nature until about 1890. Before that time, many terms were in use. See Yanabu 1977, 32–34; Minamoto 1974, 42–55.
2. Tsukamoto Seiji, chief of the Bureau of Shrines in the Ministry of Home Affairs, gave a speech in 1918 that rationalized the mergers on the grounds that the miserable little shrines had grown weedy and disreputable and had become playgrounds for children (Fridell 1973, 17).
3. For instance, John Stuart Mill's essay, "Nature," discusses many meanings for nature before dismissing it as a useless concept for moral and political philosophy.
4. The analogy to asexual reproduction could be expanded into a discussion of the relationship between gender and nature. Although there is no space here to do more than make passing reference to this issue, the nationalized nature of early twentieth-century Japan, to the extent that it can be categorized in gender terms, seems to be either asexual or male. Opposing concepts of nature, which again I only touch on here, adopted sexual and feminine guises in some cases.
5. Contemporary lack of respect for Spencer's theories and dismay over sociobiology jointly constrain our ability to see these theories in the context of their day. For an excellent discussion of Spencer's position in nineteenth-century thought, see Richards 1987, 295–330.
6. Baba translated the first chapter of Spencer's *First Principles* in Baba 1884 and advocated Spencerian ideas in Baba 1879a and 1879b. He used Spencer in direct response to Katō Hiroyuki's attacks on the people's rights movement, as expressed in Baba 1976 and Baba 1927.
7. Katō declared his conversion to evolutionary theory in *Jinken shinsetsu* [1882] (A New Theory of Human Rights) (Katō 1984).
8. Herbert Spencer's *Education: Intellectual, Moral, and Physical* (1861) was translated into Japanese in 1880.
9. *Rikugō zasshi*, a Christian publication, consistently criticized such advocacy. See, for instance, their response to Edward S. Morse's public lectures on evolution ("Lecture" 1882, 35–41).

10. Wilbur Fridell discusses some instances of resistance where the old shrine was registered as private property but maintained as a shrine.
11. State Shinto's emphasis on death is worth noting. Although government-prescribed rituals, such as 1914 prayers for the annual Harvest Festival, seek abundance for everyone from "the Imperial Princes and their off-spring to the people of the land," government bureaucrats in Tokyo only begrudgingly countenanced the traditional shrine rites concerned with pregnancy and birth. The establishment of Yasukuni Shrine and its prefectural branches further deflected Shinto rites from life to death.
12. Perhaps the most famous formulation of this position is in Lynn White's attack on Christianity's supposed sanction of environmental destruction. See White 1967.
13. See Kolodny 1975 for a discussion of nature and gendered terms.
14. Postwar scholars of the history of education defend this first government-produced ethics series as quite modern. See Miyata 1959; Karasawa 1960; Fridell 1979.

REFERENCES

Akira Nagazumi. 1983. "The Diffusion of the Idea of Social Darwinism in East and Southeast Asia." *Historia Scientiarum* 24:1–18.

Anderson, Benedict. 1983. 1991. *Imagined Communities: Reflections on the Origin and Spread of Nationalism.* New York: Verso.

———. 1994. "Exodus." *Critical Inquiry* 20.2:314–327.

Baba Tatsui. 1879a. "Heikin ryoku no setsu." *Kyōson zasshi* 14 (March). Reprinted in *Ōi Kentarō, Ueki Emori, Baba Tatsui, Ono Azusa shū.* Vol. 12. *Meiji bungaku zenshū.* Edited by Ienaga Saburō. Chikuma Shobō, 1973.

———. 1879b. "Shinka bunri no niryoku." *Kyōson zasshi* 42 (October 23); 46 (November 19). Reprinted in *Ōi Kentarō, Ueki Emori, Baba Tatsui, Ono Azusa shū.* Vol. 12. *Meiji bungaku zenshū.* Edited by Ienaga Saburō. Chikuma Shobō, 1973.

———. 1884. "Supensaru shi tetsugaku ron." *Kokyū sōdan* 1 (January 9, 1884).

———. 1927. *Tenpu jinkenron.* Reprinted in *Jiyū minkenron.* Vol. 5. *Meiji bunka zenshū.* Edited by Yoshino Sakuzō. Nihon Hyōronsha.

———. 1976. "Homi Katō Hiroyuki kun *Jinken Shinsetsu.*" Reprinted in *Meiji shisōshū.* Vol. 30. *Nihon shisō taikei.* Edited by Matsumoto Sannosuke. Chikuma Shobō.

Beasley, W. G. 1987. *Japanese Imperialism, 1894–1945.* Oxford: Clarendon Press.

Eagleton, Terry. 1991. *Ideology: An Introduction.* New York: Verso.

Fridell, Wilbur M. 1973. *Japanese Shrine Mergers, 1906–1912.* Sophia University Press.

———. 1979. "Government Ethics Textbooks in Late Meiji Japan." *Journal of Japanese Studies* 29.4:823–833.

Hardacre, Helen. 1989. *Shintō and the State: 1868–1988*. Princeton: Princeton University Press.

Harootunian, Harry D., and Tetsuo Najita. 1988. "Japanese Revolt against the West: Political and Cultural Criticism in the Twentieth Century." In *The Cambridge History of Japan*, vol. 6, edited by Peter Duus, 711–774. Cambridge: Cambridge University Press.

Hegel, Georg Wilhelm Friedrich. 1956. *The Philosophy of History*. New York: Dover Publications.

Holtom, D. C. 1922. "The Political Philosophy of Modern Shinto: A Study of the State Religion of Japan." *Transactions of the Asiatic Society of Japan* 49, pt. 2.

Hunter, Janet E. 1984. *Concise Dictionary of Japanese History*. Berkeley: University of California Press.

Ishida Takeshi. 1954. *Meiji seiji shisōshi kenkyū*. Miraisha.

Japan Year Book. 1911.

Kano Masanao. 1971. "Shakai mondai no hassei to shoki shakaishugi." In *Kindai nihon seiji shisō shi*, vol. 1, edited by Hashikawa Bunsō and Matsumoto Sannosuke. Yūhikaku.

Karasawa Tomitaro. 1960. *Kyōkasho no rekishi*. Sōbunsha.

Katō Hiroyuki. [1882] 1984. *Jinken shinsetsu*. Republished in *Nishi Amane, Katō Hiroyuki*, edited by Uete Michiari. Chūō Kōron Sha.

———. 1906. *Shizenkai no mujun to shinka*. Kanekōdō Shoseki.

———. 1912. *Shizen to rinri*. Shūeisha.

———. 1916. *Jinsei no shizen to gohō no zento*. Shūeisha.

Kinmonth, Earl. 1981. *The Self-Made Man in Meiji Japanese Thought: From Samurai to Salary Man*. Berkeley: University of California Press.

Kolodny, Annette. 1975. *The Lay of the Land: Metaphor as Experience in American Life and Letters*. Chapel Hill: University of North Carolina Press.

"The Lecture by Mr. Morse." 1882. *Rikugō zasshi* 3.26:35–41.

Maruyama Masao. 1974. *Studies in the Intellectual History of Tokugawa Japan*, translated by Mikiso Hane. Princeton: Princeton University Press.

Mill, John Stuart. 1958. "Nature." In *Nature and the Utility of Religion*. New York: Bobbs-Merrill.

Minakata Kumakusu. 1971. *Minakata Kumakusu zenshū*. Vol. 7, 477–590. Heibonsha.

Minamoto Ryōen. 1974. "Komento." In *Shizen no shisō*. Kenkyūsha.

Miyata Takeo, ed. 1959. *Dōtoku kyōiku shiryō shūsei*. Vol. 1. Daiichi Hōki.

Mori Ichiō. 1971. "Kyōkasho ni arawareta 'shinkaron' no henka ni tsuite." *Kagakushi kenkyū* 10.100:229–232.

"Mr. Herbert Spencer." 1903. *Heimin shimbun* 27 (December 1).

Nagai Michio. 1954. "Herbert Spencer in Meiji Japan." *The Far Eastern Quarterly* 14.1:55–64.

Najita, Tetsuo. 1988. "On Culture and Technology in Postmodern Japan." *South Atlantic Quarterly.* Special Issue: *Postmodernism and Japan* 87.3:401–418.

Notehelfer, F. G. 1984. "Between Tradition and Modernity: Labor and the Ashio Copper Mine." *Monumenta Nipponica* 39.1:11–24.

Oka Asajirō. "Jinrui no seifuku ni taisuru shizen no fukushū." *Chūō kōron* 27.1:13–20.

Peel, J.D.Y., ed. 1972. *Herbert Spencer: On Social Evolution.* Chicago: University of Chicago Press.

Pyle, Kenneth. 1975. "Symposium: The Ashio Copper Mine Pollution Incident." *Journal of Japanese Studies* 1.2:347–407.

Richards, Robert J. 1987. *Darwin and the Emergence of Evolutionary Theories of Mind and Behavior.* Chicago: University of Chicago Press.

Stone, Alan. 1975. "The Japanese Muckrakers." *Journal of Japanese Studies* 1.2:385–407.

Strong, Kenneth. 1977. *Ox Against the Storm: A Biography of Tanaka Shōzō, Japan's Conservationist Pioneer.* Vancouver: University of British Columbia Press.

Tsurumi Kazuko. 1977. "Social Price of Pollution in Japan and the Role of Folk Beliefs." Paper delivered at Princeton University, March 8, 1977, and published in Series A-30, Institute of International Relations.

Watanabe Masao and Ose Yoko. 1968–1969. "General Academic Trend [*sic*] and the Evolution Theory in Late Nineteenth-Century Japan: A Statistical Analysis of the Contemporary Periodicals." *Japanese Studies in the History of Science* 7-8:129–142.

Westney, Eleanor. 1987. *Imitation and Innovation: The Transfer of Western Organization Patterns to Meiji Japan.* Cambridge: Harvard University Press.

White, Lynn, Jr. 1967. "The Historical Roots of Our Ecological Crisis." *Science* 155.3767 (March 10):1203–1207.

Yamazumi Masami. 1970. *Kyōkasho.* Iwanami Shoten.

Yanabu Akira. 1977. *Honyaku no shisō: "shizen" to "nature."* Heibonsha.

Yanagita Kunio. 1957. *Japanese Manners and Customs in the Meiji Era,* translated by Charles S. Terry. Ōbunsha.

❧ 6 ❧

Asano Wasaburō and Japanese Spiritualism in Early Twentieth-Century Japan

HELEN HARDACRE

Nineteenth-century spiritualism from the West was a subject of great interest in early twentieth-century Japan. Situated on a border between mass culture and the more rarefied pursuits of Westernized, bourgeois salon culture, Japanese spiritualism represented, in part, the importation of Western cultural fads for seances, telekinesis, clairvoyance, and hypnosis. As such, it was romantic and escapist in a larger cultural context of empire, industrialization, and the expansion of state powers. Like its American and British counterparts, Japanese spiritualism adopted a general orientation of universalism, based on the idea that all humanity is united by possessing an eternal, undying soul, each of which is both unique and part of a universal community of souls, which it will rejoin upon the body's death. This universalist emphasis was counterposed to nationalism, and spiritualists by and large eschewed nationalism in favor of ideas about universal solidarity.

Among the many Japanese intellectuals who dabbled in spiritualism, Asano Wasaburō (1874–1937) stands out, not merely as a representative of the several cultural currents to be seen in Japanese spiritualism, but because he was responsible for a remarkable rapprochement between the spiritualism of bourgeois salons and Japan's indigenous shamanic tradition.[1] Through his involvement in the new religious movement Ōmotokyō (founded 1892), he conferred intellectual respectability upon this small and otherwise still unknown religion based on the shamanic experience of its founder, Deguchi Nao (1837–1918). Using the purchase of a nationally circulating, Osaka-based newspaper to promote the group, Asano used his literary skills and contacts with intellectuals and military officers to catapult Ōmotokyō to national prominence. During his involvement with Ōmotokyō, Asano propounded an emperor-centered nationalism unusual in the spiritualism to be seen outside the religion. The sudden expansion of national media attention to Ōmotokyō was coordinated with a proselytization campaign on university campuses and military installations, spearheaded by Ōmotokyō's highly charismatic cofounder, Deguchi Onisaburō (1871–1948), proclaiming an imminent apocalypse. State alarm at this sudden expansion of Ōmotokyō and at its uncanny ability, like the Pied Piper, to "beguile" highly educated Japanese youth contributed to the state suppression of the religion in 1921. Following this experience, Asano left the religion and returned to Tokyo, where he promoted spiritualism, now shorn of Ōmotokyō influence, among the new middle class. He traveled and lectured widely in spiritualist circles in Japan, journeying also to the United States and Britain to lecture on Japanese spiritualism. After his departure from Ōmotokyō, Asano no longer preached nationalism, turning instead to universalism.

Weaving in and out of indigenous religious practice, importing Western ideas and spiritualist practices, Asano's career reveals a wider current of interest in the occult in early twentieth-century Japan. Though such occultism was itself a minor theme in contemporary cultural life, its retreat from nationalism, imperialism, and state bureaucratism had broader affiliations with liberalism and internationalism. Japanese spiritualism in the first three decades of this century illustrates the development of popular religious pursuits severed from folk culture, local communal organization, and historical religious tradition, as well as the growth of a globalized—and privatized—consumerism in popular religious life. This essay examines the career of Asano Wasaburō in order to illuminate the broader cultural significance of spiritualism in early twentieth-century Japan.

INTRODUCTION

Nineteenth-century spiritualism in the West began with the 1848 "Rochester Rappings" of the Fox sisters in upstate New York. Anticipated by romanticism and sentimentalism in popular culture, spiritualism had its center in a yearning to communicate with the dead, whose spirits were caused, by mediums, to manifest themselves in seemingly infinite ways: rappings, speaking through a medium, automatic writing, spirit photographs, and wraithlike appearances in seances. Spiritualists exalted in emotional expression, even while proclaiming the harmony of science with the spiritual. After the first rappings, "spirit circles" were formed in every major American city, developing in Britain as well. Associated with liberal, progressive causes such as women's rights and the abolition of slavery, spiritualism took root in the salon culture of the northeast United States and in London, manifesting itself in utopian communities such as those founded by Robert Owen and attracting support from otherwise highly respected academics, though their colleagues found them something of an embarrassment (Ellwood 1988).[2]

Growing out of spiritualism, the Theosophical Society was founded in 1875, with Helena P. Blavatsky at its head.[3] The Society for Psychical Research was founded in London in 1882, and the Society's American Branch was founded in 1884 by William James. The development of hypnosis by Anton Mesmer encouraged spiritualists to adopt the technique enthusiastically. The 1893 World Parliament of Religion brought representatives of Asian religions to Chicago and heightened interest in Buddhism and Hinduism (especially Vedanta). Ideas and techniques from these traditions soon began to appear in the spiritualist repertory. Spiritualism's ideas about the universal truth of the eternal existence of the soul resonated harmoniously with the relativism of emerging anthropological and psychological theories of religion, and among these, William James' *Varieties of Religious Experience* (1902) and James George Frazer's *The Golden Bough* (1890) were especially influential, being widely read by a popular readership as well as in the universities.[4]

These same patterns found an echo in Japan. Spiritualists were hosted by salons, influenced utopian communities, and found academic support. Dedicated to popularizing the study of philosophy, Inoue Enryo (1858–1919), founder of the Tetsugakukan (later Tetsugakukan University, thereafter called Tōyō University), wrote prolifically on spiritualism, partly on the basis of extended field research (traveling to no fewer than 215 sites in Japan). He assembled a number of influential academics and intellectuals to join him in a group he founded in 1886, the Society for Research on the Mysterious (Fushigi Kenkyūkai): among the founding members were Miyake Setsurei (1860–1945), Tsubouchi Shōyō (1859–1935), and physicist Tanakadate Aikitsu (1856–1952). The group studied Japanese ghosts, foxes, badgers, Tengu,[5] dog-spirit owing,[6] physiognomy, and prophecy. They discovered Japanese examples of a new type of spirit manifestation documented in Western spiritualist circles: *kokkuri-san*, people who could emit threads and viscous matter called—originally by Western spiritualists—"ectoplasm" from their hands. Inoue delivered a series of lectures on *kokkuri-san* and other occult phenomena at the Tetsugakukan from 1893 to 1894 called "The Study of Ghosts" (*yokaigaku*).[7]

The universities were host to (and validators of) psychic experiments. Besides Inoue, Fukurai Tomokichi (1869–1952), an assistant professor in psychology at the Tokyo Imperial University and translator of William James, was another notable example of "psychical research" in the academy. Frequently undertaking joint research with Kyoto University professor Imamura Shinkichi, Fukurai performed a number of highly publicized "experiments" on female clairvoyants in 1911, assembling a large audience of distinguished academics to witness and confirm the psychic abilities of women like Nagao Ikuko (1871–1911) and Mifune Chizuko (1886–1911) to read what had been written on paper, then sealed in lead containers. The women themselves were without education, and hence half of the amazement came from their ability to make out difficult characters in compound form, to say nothing of having to see through lead. These experiments sometimes went wrong, however, and when it was revealed that one of the professors had switched containers and led to Mifune's public humiliation, she took her own life. The university eventually came to take a dim view of such psychic displays, especially when Mifune's suicide proved their ability to bring the institution into disrepute. Fukurai was forced out of his post in 1913, later becoming head of Kōyasan University and founder of the Japan Institute of Psychical Research (Nihon Shinri Kenkyūkai) in 1929. He continued to write widely on psychic phenomena (Minami 1992, 608–612; Oishi 1989, 663–664; Nakayama 1965, 245, 305–306).

Hypnotism was a subject of great interest in late Meiji culture. Based only on the works collected in the Maruzen Meiji microfilm collection, about eighty works containing the word "hypnotism" (saimin, saimin jutsu) in the title were published between 1904 and 1912. There were at least eight national societies for research on hypnosis, such as the Imperial Society for the Study of Hypnotism (Teikoku Saimin Gakkai) and the Japan Society for Hypnosis Philosophy (Nihon Saimin Tetsugakkai). The titles of some such societies indicate their dedication to the practice as well as the academic study of hypnotism, such as the Japanese Society for the Practice of Hypnotism (Dai Nihon saimin jutsu kyōkai), which was the most active of the national hypnotism societies in publishing, producing fourteen works in this period. Besides the national societies, there were regional and city-based associations publishing works on hypnotism, as well as therapeutic institutions offering psychological treatment based on hypnotism and training in hypnosis technique, such as the Hokuetsu Psychological Clinic (Hokuetsu Shinri Ryōin) and the Tokyo Hypnosis School (Tokyo Saimin Gakuin). Some societies publishing works on hypnosis were dedicated to other techniques on the fringes of occultism, such as physiognomy, as in the case of the Physiognomy Society (Seisō Gakkai). Other such societies adopted titles suggesting a broader interest in spiritualism: Academy for the Study of the Spirit (Seishin Kenkyūkai), Japan Society of the Mind (Nihon Shinsōkai), and the Spiritual Science Institute (Seishin Kagakusha). Publications on hypnotism varied widely in their content, including such subjects as: manuals on medical therapies involving hypnotism, hypnotism at a distance from the subject, hypnotizing animals, magic and hypnotism, educational uses of hypnotism, hypnotism and clairvoyance, records of hypnosis experiments, hypnotic communications, hypnosis and direct encounter with gods and buddhas.

The development from early Meiji of a vocabulary for discussing the spiritual life (discussed in greater detail below) assisted in spiritualism's spread: seishin, seishinshugi, shinrei, shinrei sekai, and related terms had a variety of exponents with various emphases. The derivation of these terms through translation of Western terms facilitated thinking about the spirit in a context free of nationalist, chauvinistic rhetoric. The example of Kiyozawa Manshi's (1863–1903) *seishinshugi* shows that it was quite possible to interpret the "spirit" in a Buddhist sectarian framework,[8] while the attempts of Tsunajima Ryōsen (1873–1907) (Tsunajima 1976, 12–16) to "see God" show how a mysticism quite congruent with spiritualism could be given a Christian framing. Whereas these two thinkers emphasized self-cultivation and intense contemplation of deity, the stress of Asano and other "spiritual researchers" fell on the soul and upon techniques for communicating with spirits of the dead, to operate on inanimate objects in "experiments," and the like. These several orientations were similarly free from connection with nationalist rhetoric. Their universalism was distinguished from the orientation of those like Uchimura Kanzō, who were preoccupied with reconciling religion and national identity. Spiritualists' universalism was a retreat from an increasingly oppressive state. Spiritualism of the early twentieth century can be seen as escapist, shunning engagement and confrontation with the state, retreating into privatized religious activities. The taint of escapist dilettantism was usefully obscured by the pseudoscientific trappings of "experimentation," mostly focusing on women or the lower social orders.

The "salon culture" seen in the early decades of this century provided the display space for spiritualists and many other newly emerging, Western-influenced phenomena. The salon hosted by Soma Kokkō and her husband Aizō, owners of the Nakamuraya coffee house chain headquartered first in Hongō and later in Shinjuku, is a good example of a general orientation, though it was not directly involved in spiritualism. Liberal and internationalist in outlook, the Nakamuraya salon received Uchimura Kanzō, Indian independence activists, and White Russians in flight from the revolution in their homeland. The Indian connection resulted in the introduction of "curry rice," now ubiquitous, as well as significant artistic patronage, displaying paintings and sculpture by Russian artists as well as assisting younger Japanese artists working in Western styles and media. Salon life offered a space (made possible by Westernized domestic architecture, which included parlors, on the assumption that people would sit on chairs) in which to enact Westernized, bourgeois forms of sociability, especially the ideal of companionate marriage, as educated women attended with their husbands and were expected to interact with other couples.[9]

The development of new terms for discussing spirits, the soul, and the spiritual life formed an important part of Japanese spiritualism's cultural foundations. Changes in usage reflected such contemporary events as the death of large numbers in the Russo-Japanese War and a growing attraction to Western spiritualism. The term *shinrei*, written with the character for a god *(kami)* and the character for a spirit, in the sense of a ghost or the soul of a deceased human or animal, is characteristic of the early Meiji period, but it disappeared from book titles by the early 1890s. It was superseded by a homonym that retained the second character but substituted the character for "heart-mind" (*kokoro*) for the first. This new term *shinrei* differed from its predecessor in usage, frequently referring to Western spiritualist ideas and to hypnosis, clairvoyance, and telekinesis. It was usually divorced from the indigenous shamanic tradition. It was associated with ideas of the universality of the soul and an imagined community of souls after death, sometimes transcending national boundaries. The new *shinrei* came into prominence in the early years of the twentieth century, with the publication of numerous works adopting it in their titles from around 1904.

An examination of works on the spirit, "the spiritual," or "spiritual life" using this later term *shinrei*, published from around 1904 to the end of the Meiji period, reveals several clear trends. The first is that several religious traditions, including Christianity and such Shinto sects as Shinshūkyō and Taiseikyō, took an interest in "the spiritual" and authored books locating their own doctrines in relation to it. Numerous works offered instruction on "spiritual cultivation" (*seishin shūyō*), frequently promoting it as a support for "morality education" (*shūshin kyōiku*), which was a subject of public school curricula in these years. Other works offered therapeutic regimens drawing on the spirit, such as *Experimental Spiritual Therapy (Jikken seishin ryōhō)* and *Spiritual Techniques of Breathing (Seishinteki kokyūhō)*. Some works on the spirit reflect an interest in hypnotism, such as *Spiritual Phenomena in Hypnotism (Saimin jutsu ni okeru seishin no genshō)*, while others showed an interest in techniques for manipulating spirits for effect, such as *The Magic of Astounding Spirits, Mysteries of Manipulating Spirits (Kyōiteki dai majutsu ichimei seishinsayō dai fushigi)*. Many sought a rapprochement with science, such as *Spiritual Physics (Seishin butsurigaku)*.

The question of spiritualism's relation to science was highly problematic for intellectuals attracted to spiritualism, both in the West and in Japan. If it could not be established that spiritualism was not disproved by science, then intellectuals would be forced to admit that they were involving themselves in something "unscientific," "superstitious," or "irrational." They could not make such an admission and expect to remain in university appointments or in positions of intellectual leadership. Their understanding of the meaning of being "modern" human beings and their understanding of a proper, modern nation were based on a personal and a national commitment to "rationality," with science as its principal arbiter. Therefore, it was imperative that spiritualism be reconciled with science. Hence, salon demonstrations adopting the model of scientific experimentation were meant to validate not only telekinesis, hypnotism, and the rest but also the claim of these intellectuals to modernity as they understood it. Rationality was primary among the characteristics they identified with the modern, but secondary characteristics were also validated in the process, such as companionate marriage and a commitment to internationalism.

In the case of Japanese intellectuals, apparently ephemeral aspects of the setting such as Western-style houses, chairs, the adoption of Western dress, and the participation of women in the company of their husbands carried a highly charged, politicized meaning in the context, given that Japan had for decades been debating the possibility of being at one and the same time "modern" and unqualifiedly "Japanese." Since the traditionalist side in this longer debate regularly argued that ethnic identity was threatened by any adoption of things associated with the West, those who enthusiastically appropriated Western styles of architecture, dress, social relations, and spirituality were taking a political position in doing so. This entailed risks, including the risk of being labeled unpatriotic, a stooge, or fifth column for those imagined conspirators who would take over Japan's intellectual and spiritual heritage from inside. Intellectuals who became associated with spiritualism actually risked estrangement from both sides because of the inherent tension between spiritualism and rationalism. Japanese intellectuals involved in spiritualism were thus objects of suspicion both from Westernizers and traditionalists, especially in a climate of enthusiasm for war.

One of the most striking trends in publications on the spirit is a clear connection, after the Russo-Japanese War, to the spirits of the war dead and to the cultivation of a military spirit. Works in this category include the 1911 publications *Spiritual Education: Memorials to the Dead of the Russo-Japanese War (Seishin kyōiku Nichi-ro senshi byōbotsusha tsuitō kinenshi)* and *Soldiers' Spiritual Education and the Home (Seishinteki guntai kyōiku to katei)*. These works and others like them adopted a more nationalistic tone than other kinds of spiritualist writing and reflected a desire to go beyond "cultivation" of the spirit to more structured training that could be called "education." In the background was a vague desire to contact the spirits of those who died in war. This phenomenon of spiritualism's popularity rising in relation to war has been well studied for Britain and Europe, and it is widely recognized that World War I triggered a great interest in seances in which participants hoped to contact those who had fallen in battle. In this case, Japan's experience of the same kind, following the Russo-Japanese War, preceded the European example.

ASANO WASABURŌ: EARLY LIFE, EDUCATION, MARRIAGE, AND CAREER

Born the third son of an Ibaraki family of physicians, Asano had little to say about his early life other than to stress its ordinariness and lack of any remarkable quality. He studied English and American literature at Tokyo

Imperial University from 1896, graduating in 1899. Lafcadio Hearn impressed the young Asano as a brilliant lecturer and as a mysterious figure with an intense, penetrating gaze. Hearn had lost sight in one eye, which appeared cloudy and did not move in synchrony with the other. Asano immersed himself in Shakespeare, Dickens, and Washington Irving, and he wrote a novel himself in 1898 which was highly praised in the Akamon literary circle, *Fubuki* (Blowing Snow). In the same year he won a prize for a short story in English in a competition organized by Hearn.

In 1899 Asano took a post lecturing on English literature at an academy in Yokosuka for prospective naval officers (Kaigun Kikan Gakkō). An active scholar, writer, and translator, he contributed to the journals *Shinsei* (later *Shinchō*) and *Teikoku bungaku,* as well as translating Shakespeare, and, over an eight-year period, he authored a history of English literature of more than one thousand pages.[10] In 1900 he married Azumi Takeko, whose father was a naval officer, as was Asano's elder brother Masayasu, who was an artillery instructor. Asano and Takeko had three sons (a daughter was born while they were in Ayabe), and they went out *en famille* every Sunday for picnics, hiking, or ocean swimming, the perfect, new-style bourgeois couple. Thus, from his university graduation through his thirties, Asano pursued an active academic career, established a solid scholarly reputation, enjoyed a happy marriage, and was very attached to his children, all in all, a situation many would have envied.

As a young man, Asano was aware of contemporary interest in spiritualism, especially hypnosis, but he made no connection at the time between it and any aspect of Japan's historical religious traditions. He was first introduced to hypnosis by a naval officer, a colleague who frequently hypnotized his own wife, daughter, and maids, inviting his friends to witness his technique. Asano speaks of these displays as "experiments" *(jikken).* In one example, the officer hypnotized one maid and sent a second on a shopping expedition. He interrogated the maid under hypnosis about the route taken, the precise purchases, and so on. The audience found when the other maid returned that everything was exactly as the hypnotized maid had said (Minami 1992, 102–103).

These episodes reveal the desire to provide "scientific" buttressing for middle-class forays into the occult world. To speak of such a display as an "experiment," to invite an "objective" audience to witness the event in all details, and then to confirm the result, allowed the participants to think of their activities as a kind of scientific investigation. This enabled them to think of their involvement in spiritualism as something confirming their rationality and modernity, rather than as something calling those characteristics into question. Their most intense specularity was usually directed to women of a lower social ranking, who, as females and as social "others," were appropriate objects for a masculinist, "rational" gaze.

Asano's descriptions of these "experiments" reveal his awareness also of the popular-psychological interpretations made of them: the unconscious *(senzai ishiki)*, the split personality *(nijū jinkaku)*, personality change *(jinkaku henkan)*, and so on. He writes that he had many doubts about the explanations for hypnosis, which neither convinced him nor satisfied him that even the most skilled practitioners were any the wiser for their mastery of the technique. He soon lost interest.

Asano's first intense experience of religion came at the age of forty-two, right on schedule by folk traditions, which anticipate that that age will be a time of great misfortune or change *(yakudoshi)* in the male life cycle. Every morning around ten, Asano's third son, Saburo, would begin to run a fever, which mysteriously disappeared at dusk. After six months and a parade of physicians, Takeko confessed to her husband that she had consulted a healer, a woman her hairdresser had told her about, wife of a naval factory worker. Asano's reaction was humiliation that his family should have been brought in contact with what he had always considered a "completely different world," but he agreed to investigate the woman's credentials.

Ishii Fuyu told Takeko that she had the power to see into Saburo's body and that he had a small tumor, which, with the help of the gods, could be cured. She predicted a complete recovery on November 4, 1915. Asano performed a variety of "experiments" on Ishii and found that she was able, for example, to divine precisely how much money was in his wallet and perform other feats of clairvoyance. Asano found these powers impossible to ignore, added to which, his son was cured on exactly the predicted day. Nevertheless, while Ishii's technique was accurate, she could not satisfy Asano's curiosity about why it worked, nor did she seem to have any greater insight into the workings of the universe, for all her powers. Not only that, he found his notion of a "proper" religionist violated by Ishii's rough speech and her gluttonous predilection to eat huge amounts of food, four or five times what a "normal" person would consume (Minami 1992, 105–112).

DECISION TO JOIN ŌMOTOKYŌ

Visiting Ishii in late 1915, Asano met there a former colleague, still a naval officer, Iimori Masayoshi. Iimori, formerly a Christian, was one of a number of Taishō military personnel and intellectuals recruited by the new religion Ōmotokyō (Yasamaru 1973, 2:435). On this occasion Iimori was wearing a sash reading "Spirit Army" *(Shinreigun)* (Minami 1992, 113). The Spirit Army was a peripatetic proselytizing corps formed by Ōmotokyō in 1914, representing the religion's first attempt to evangelize throughout the country systematically, an early move to expand the group's rural, peasant following to the cities, there to include intellectuals and members of the middle class (Deguchi 1970, 91).

Iimori, accompanied by the founder's third daughter, Fukushima Hisako, worked tirelessly to recruit Asano to Ōmotokyō, persuading him to visit Ayabe in early 1916. There Asano was greatly impressed with Nao, the philosophy she was elaborating in her writings called the *Ofudesaki* (not yet published in toto), and her millennial prophecies. By comparison with her forceful and unadorned theology of an eternal god, put down by evil competitors but destined to assume control of the universe after a mighty apocalypse, the philosophy of China, the West, and the Bible seemed to Asano hopelessly artificial, childish, and worthless. When Nao gave Asano a lock of her hair, calling it the symbol of the god Ushitora Konjin, Asano began to think of leaving his academic post and moving to Ayabe (Minami 1992, 120–129).

In late April, 1916, Asano summoned the cofounder Onisaburō for personal instruction in Yokosuka. On each of three consecutive nights, Asano assembled seven or eight of his colleagues to hear Deguchi lecture, and Asano confessed himself amazed at Deguchi's ability to answer all his queries. Deguchi stressed particularly the eternal existence of the soul and its individual guardian spirit *(shugojin),* and he offered to perform the rite *chinkon kishin* to give Asano indisputable proof.

Chinkon is a rite deriving from Shinto, having the meaning of pacifying the spirit, usually meaning the spirit of a deity. In Ōmotokyō's usage, however, it was employed to calm one's own mind and spirit, to contact the spirit world, including the dead and one's own guardian spirit. Sometimes it was used in an individualized manner, like a form of meditation. More often, however, it was employed in a dual-role framework, in which one person takes the role of a spirit medium, while a second interrogated the first in trance. This second person, the shamanic interlocutor, is called a *saniwa.*

On the second night, Deguchi asked Asano to take the *saniwa* role, and, quite unexpectedly, Asano succeeded in putting a younger colleague into a trance, interrogating the spirit thus embodied, with Deguchi coaching Asano on what to say. On another occasion, Deguchi showed Asano his power to levitate. During a trip to a nearby shrine, Asano found a stone with a hole in it, which could be blown like a flute, for use in *chinkon kishin.* In trance it was revealed that the deity Kozakura Hime had bestowed this flute on Asano as a sign of his destiny to be a *saniwa.* Later, knowing nothing of these events, Takeko went into a trance and became possessed by the same deity, who turned out to be her guardian spirit. In this instant, Asano felt that he could see through his karmic destiny, realizing for the first time why he had been led to Yokosuka, to the naval school, and to marry this woman. She and he were not, as he had thought, an ordinary couple bound by nothing more substantial than social convention, but, instead, their union was ordained and blessed by a deity (Minami 1992, 128–141).

Deguchi's visit left Asano feeling, he wrote, like a man in the sixteenth century, declaring that the earth is round, knowing that others would find his new discoveries about the spirit world irrational and bizarre. As if to confirm this insight, the naval school began to warn Asano about holding frequent seances, but a handful of students followed him, and one young colleague even took up residence with Asano to practice *chinkon kishin* full time, much to the alarm of the young man's wife and parents. Asano persisted, accumulating experience as a *saniwa*, holding seances in which spirits of the dead spoke through a medium, and generally becoming increasingly involved with Ōmotokyō. Takeko developed the "divine eye," clairvoyant ability to see at a great distance, and eventually both of them became able to see into the earth, the ocean, and the interior of the body (Minami 1992, 147–170).

On a three-week trip to Ayabe in July and August, 1916, Asano consulted with Nao daily and read the *Ofudesaki*. Nao evidently hoped that Asano would assist her in publishing the work. Asano also went on pilgrimage to two islands in the Japan Sea believed in Ōmotokyō to be the dwellings of deities. Returning to Yokosuka, Asano resigned from his post, sold all the family's possessions, and moved to Ayabe in December 1916 (Minami 1992, 170–191),[11] but not before he published the reasons for his decision in the journal *Jinbun* (October 1, 1916). Anesaki Masaharu, founder of the Department of Religious Studies at Tokyo Imperial University, responded with a critique, saying that Asano lacked critical judgment in evaluating Ōmotokyō so highly.

ASANO WASABURŌ IN ŌMOTOKYŌ

Asano had seen effective religious rites and pseudoreligious techniques before, in his acquaintance with hypnosis and healing, but whereas that experience had left him unsatisfied for lack of connection to a more comprehensive religious world view, Ōmotokyō seemed to speak to all his reservations. It offered the basic elements that Asano's Western training had led him to expect: creation mythology, prophecy, soteriology, and eschatology. He was reassured also that while its founder, leaders, and followers may have lacked formal education and were peasant rustics, they were austere in their personal habits, eating little and paying scant attention to their attire, and severe—even ascetic—in enduring hours of seated rites that were initially torture to those, like Asano, brought up to sit on chairs.

From another perspective, Asano and Ōmotokyō had much to offer to each other. Asano was a great catch for a religion seeking to expand to the cities and the middle class. As an intellectual, Asano's membership alone was good advertising for Ōmotokyō, but added to that were his considerable literary skills and social contacts. He was accustomed to writing by the ream, and he was already well published in a variety of influential journals. The prospect of capturing such a man and turning his talents to the purpose of promoting the religion through the print media was highly attractive, as was the prospect that his affiliation could lead to more extensive contacts in the Navy. On the face of it, Ōmotokyō's attraction for Asano is more difficult to explain, but his early training under Hearn, well known for his interest in all things mystic and occult, as well as the timing of Asano's first contact with the religion probably played an important role. The cure of his son immediately beforehand by a healer probably left him more receptive to religion than at any prior time. Also, he records that he was considering writing about "spiritual phenomena," because this was one of the few topics not yet appropriated by literary writers like himself (Minami 1992, 115). In other words, he thought the general topic of the spiritual might provide a niche in which he could distinguish himself. At forty-two, that is, he had led a successful career, but he probably could also see that his prospects were not unlimited. The realization that, say, he would never rise to head his school, never receive "the call" to return to Tokyo Imperial University, never achieve the fame of the Tokyo intellectuals, nor rise through the naval ranks so esteemed in Yokosuka may have made Ōmotokyō unexpectedly attractive. In addition to his affection for its founder, the religion probably appeared to Asano as a small pond in which he could be a very big fish indeed, a stage from which to launch a public presence in a new way, in which he would not have to compete with so many others to make a mark. He could successfully "recreate" himself at mid-life.

In 1916 the religion expanded rapidly, driven by its first nationwide proselytization campaign. The religion was directed at this time by a leadership council living communally at Ayabe, with as many as eighty-nine leaders and their families in residence, taking all meals together. Large bands of proselytizers were sent out to preach on the streets, an uncommon sight because women as well as men were preachers, and the men wore their hair long and unbound, in imitation of Onisaburō. In 1916 alone, thirty-seven new branches were established throughout Japan. Asano joined the top echelons of this leadership council to systematize the doctrinal content of proselytization. Unlike the other leaders, who had mainly risen through the ranks by success in organizing local branches or in proselytization, however, Asano received special deference because of his intellectual background, apparently reporting directly to Nao until her death in 1918 (Ōmoto Nana-jūnenshi Hensankai 1964, 1:339 ff., 344–345).[12]

Over the years of Asano's connection with Ōmotokyō (1916–1925), important changes occurred in the religion. In 1916 it changed its name to Kōdō Ōmoto, "Imperial Way Ōmoto," signaling increasingly nationalist, imperialist rhetoric. Onisaburō's radicalism was revealed in his advocacy of a Taishō Restoration. He criticized the government for aping the West, relying on money rather than spirit, for failing to make the country self-sufficient, and—most frightening to the state—for taxation. Taxation of all kinds should be abolished, Onisaburō proclaimed, as a first step in creating an earthly paradise (Deguchi 1917). Asano and Onisaburō worked together in formulating the paired ideas of Ōmoto as an "Imperial Way" and as leader of a "Taishō Restoration." Both rested on an emperor-centered nationalism. In the years 1917 to 1921, Ōmoto publications promoted the idea that Ōmotokyō possessed "a divine law of governing the world" *(tenka o tōji suru shimpō shinsoku),* an attempt at symbolic alliance with the imperial house. In the desired restoration, all land, assets, and industries were to be "returned" to the emperor, who would rule directly. Asano wrote that Nao's prophesied "world renovation" would result in a unification of imperial rites and rule *(saisei itchi).* This concentration of all authority in the emperor would enable Japan to fulfill its mission of governing the world, based on the spiritual power of Ōmotokyō (Ōmoto 1964, 358, 364–371; Ikeda 1982–1985, 2:137–189). In 1917 the journal *Shinreikai* commenced publication, with Asano at its head, mostly proclaiming Nao's prophecies of millennium. That same year saw the publication of the book *Ōmoto shin'yu,* outlining the religion's entire belief system on the basis of Nao's *Ofudesaki,* published for the first time in *Shinreikai.* From 1918, *Shinreikai* began to predict a world war pitting Japan against the rest of the world, which Japan was destined to lose. After Nao died in 1918, a rift between Asano and Onisaburō became apparent. While Nao's daughter Sumiko had been designated the spiritual successor, her husband Onisaburō began assuming actual control of the organization. Although his ascension was not uncontested, his personal charisma and vision for rapid expansion swept other contenders away. Thus, while no clear distinction of rank had separated Asano and Onisaburō during Nao's lifetime, Asano's continued link with the religion after 1918 depended upon his allegiance (and subordination) to Onisaburō (Deguchi 1970, 93–97; Yasumaru 1973, 435–436; Ōmoto 1964, 351, 355, 397, 401–403).

In 1919 Ōmotokyō established a second headquarters in the city of Kameoka through the purchase of the site of the former Kameyama Castle. In the following year, Ōmotokyō purchased the Osaka newspaper *Taishō nichi nichi shinbun,* which at the time had a circulation of 480,000. Asano was the paper's president, and it was the first national daily to be run by a religion. The plan was to use the paper as the main forum for spreading Ōmotokyō's beliefs and prophecies. However, the paper was in deep trouble from the commencement of Ōmotokyō control, and in only three months it lost 200,000 subscriptions. The paper's reporters were effectively shut out of all official news sources, because of the widespread sense that operating a newspaper was not a properly religious activity, and because all the other newspapers opposed Ōmotokyō control (Deguchi 1970, 98–100).

Asano was instrumental in recruiting navy personnel to Ōmotokyō, starting with his brother Masayasu, and including such high-ranking officers as Akiyama Saneyuki (1866–1918), a distinguished strategist of the Russo-Japanese War. Each such contact had the potential to multiply through the influence of officers on their subordinates. Support groups were formed from Ōmoto converts serving on particular naval vessels (Ōmoto 1964, 360, 401).

The newspaper and journal edited by Asano made Ōmotokyō's thought known all over the country. Both were distributed gratis to all public schools, to many businesses, and to military installations. Ōmotokyō's prophecies of imminent millennium added fuel to a spreading sense of social disorder, occasioned by the political agitation of socialists and labor unions, the Rice Riots, and revolutionary expectations stemming from the Russian Revolution.[13] Ōmotokyō lost no time in claiming that these events, along with a disastrous outbreak of Spanish influenza, had been foretold in the *Ofudesaki*, predicting that 1921 would bring a "rain of fire," natural disasters, widespread death of the population, world war, and that Japan would be brought to the brink of destruction. In the end, Mount Fuji would erupt, and the whole country would be sucked down a gigantic ocean whirlpool (Yasumaru 1973, 435–437; Ōmoto 1964, 373–401).

To understand the state's alarm at the publication of these ideas, it is important to bear in mind that high-ranking naval officers were joining the religion, raising the specter that the military could be infiltrated with millenarian expectations and antistate prophecy. Contemporary newspaper accounts make clear that this possibility was in the air, along with similarly unpalatable prospects. State alarm at Ōmotokyō's sudden increase of activity and membership rested in no small part upon the belief that even a small number of elite members from the professions and the military exerted a disproportionate influence, their membership alone providing sufficient warrant to the less educated that the religion was a force for good in society. Thus, the mainline newspapers expressed great alarm when it was reported several times that students of prefectural middle schools in Ishikawa, from the Shiba Middle School in Tokyo, and no fewer than two hundred students from Keio University were running off to Ayabe without permission, wearing their hair long in imitation of Onisaburō, or giving up their studies to evangelize for the religion. Asano was frequently singled out as the one most responsible for increasing intellectual followers of the religion, even accusing him of manipulating Onisaburō.[14] It was also alarming that Ōmotokyō was able to raise large sums of money from contributions, and police officials repeatedly complained that millennial prophecies were a threat to the social order and that they were hamstrung by the constitutional protection of religious freedom. All the while, however, Ōmotokyō's publications were heavily censored (*Shimbun shūroku Taishōki* 8:197–198, 303).

Inevitably, the axe fell, and in 1921 Asano and Onisaburō were convicted of lèse-majesté and violation of the Newspaper Law. The former charge stemmed from several items of Nao's mythology about Ushitora Konjin that were seen to impugn the imperial dignity. The latter charge held, as above, that millennial prophecy was a threat to the social order. Both were convicted, but the verdicts were eventually thrown out, and the two were pardoned in a general amnesty following the death of the Taishō emperor (Ishida 1955, 436–441; Matsumoto 1989, 163).

ASANO THE INDEPENDENT SPIRITUALIST

Like Ōmotokyō's other intellectual members, Asano began to distance himself from the religion after the first suppression. With the newspaper effectively defunct, he remained as editor of the journal *Shinreikai,* but it was clear that Nao's writings could no longer be published. Added to that, Onisaburō began to compose his own work of divine inspiration in 1921, *Reikai monogatari,* making it obvious that he planned entirely to supersede Nao (to whom Asano had originally been most directly attached). In the face of these restricting circumstances, Asano tried to steer an autonomous course by using *Shinreikai* to establish the scientific basis for spiritual phenomena in general, including, but not limited to, those seen in Ōmotokyō. In this attempt, however, he could not avoid making Ōmotokyō subordinate to, a local, contingent manifestation of, the universal scientific laws he took to underwrite it. Inevitably, then, he gradually parted company with the religion and moved back to Tokyo for good in 1925 (Matsumoto 1989, 163–168).

Asano had already begun to establish a base in the capital, founding the Society for Scientific Research on Spiritual Phenomena (Shinrei Kagaku Kenkyūkai) in 1922. His cofounders numbered some of the same kind of intellectuals he had earlier converted to Ōmotokyō, minus the military contingent: Eki Makoto (1858–1925), founder of Chūō University and head of the Tokyo Bar Association, and Miyazaki Tōten (1871–1922).[15] The society was a small-scale, elite salon, carrying a hefty five-yen membership fee and undoubtedly recruiting on the basis of social status, by introduction only (Matsumoto 1989, 163–168; Minami 1992, 603).

In the 1924 issue of *Shinreikai,* Asano presented the case of Osanami Toshie, which became widely known. Osanami was a healer who was also able to create "spirit paintings" and to write while in trance, though she had no education and seemed to have subnormal intelligence where ordinary affairs were concerned, behaving like a child of five when not in trance. Asano reverted to his earlier technique of persuasion by presenting "experiments" to establish that thoroughly rational people like judges and newspaper reporters were utterly amazed, but completely convinced, by Osanami's feats. He further buttressed his experimental data by recording that the writings of H. P. Blavatsky contained many similar miracles (Minami 1992, 213–235).

Asano kept abreast of developments in spiritualist circles in the West, transmitting these through the journal. He serialized the works of Arthur Conan Doyle and took a great interest in Oscar Wilde. In 1928 he attended the third World Council of Spiritualists in London, where he met Doyle and lectured on Japanese spiritualism. On the return trip, he lectured also in Moscow, Dalien, Harbin, and the United States (Ōmoto 1964, 1:682–685; Matsumoto 1989, 187–193).

Returning from this journey in late 1928, Asano gave a series of public lectures on spiritualism, establishing the scientific basis of the soul's existence, the workings of hypnotism, and cataloging the history of nineteenth- and early twentieth-century spiritualism. He began with the "rappings" of the Fox sisters in 1848, continuing up through contemporary manifestations he had witnessed on his foreign travels, including automatic writing, "spirit photographs," and telekinesis, in a record of more than six hundred pages.[16] After his second son, Shinkichi, died, both Asano and his wife began to receive spirit messages from him; Asano also lectured widely on this phenomenon.

In May 1929, Asano discovered Kamei Saburō (dates unknown), whom Asano came to believe was the only one adept at telekinesis in Japan. Asano took Kamei on numerous lecture and demonstration tours to spiritualist circles in Tokyo, Yokohama, Karuizawa, Nagoya, and Osaka. He had his own lectures on these occasions, as well as Kamei's demonstrations, recorded on gramophone records, sold for five yen. One of these included a seance in which an Indian moghul spoke. Kamei could perform Houdini-like escapes from ropes, make a glass of water pass through a table, make crockery levitate, see into closed, wooden boxes, perform spirit rappings, make objects fly, and make multiple musical instruments play simultaneously, without touching them. The meetings at which he performed were conducted like salons, attended by a small number of professional and upper-middle-class men, whose wives also frequently were present. The framework in which Asano always introduced the demonstrations was the scientific experiment on some spiritual phenomenon already validated in the West, with the evening's events to reveal the first and only known Japanese example (Minami 1992, 463–518).

Thus, Asano's public career assumed its final form as a publicist of spiritual phenomena from all over the world, linking these to what he believed were universal, scientific laws about the existence of souls and their manifold possibilities for manifesting themselves in the human world. He transmitted the latest Western developments in spiritualism, its universalism heavily influenced by Theosophy's claims of a universal fraternity of the spirit. Asano could "consume" from a globalized spiritualist menu, the ideas of which were in turn commodified and circulated through elite salons and the press industries of mass culture, as the example of one of his seances being recorded in the women's magazine *Shufu no tomo* (May 1936), shows.

Asano and others like him helped develop the character of one sector of modern religious life, embedded in bourgeois culture, thoroughly conversant with and participating in a globalized market of religious ideas and associated practices, like seances, and as increasingly privatized, making no claims of relevance to the state, the national educational curricula, nor, indeed, to anything beyond the individual and small circles of the like-minded. Spiritualism in the cities floated above the folk tradition, drawing upon it in some cases (though not always aware of doing so), more informed on Western trends than on indigenous tradition. Spiritualism was one variety of religious life that could be consumed without reference to traditional modes of religious affiliation and without reference to those factors otherwise largely determining religious affiliations before the twentieth century: kinship, community of residence, and status in that community. New religious movements of the period tended to be much more connected with these factors, and while offering some potential for commodification and consumption, they did not yet participate nearly so freely in the internationally circulating stock of religious ideas and practices. With the exception of the small number of intellectuals they attracted, they were mainly populated by the lower middle ranks of society at that time, at least in the case of the urban groups.

Spiritualism in the West has been linked to the decline of religion's roles in the public sphere, due to the growing prestige of science, and also to the many deaths occasioned by modern warfare, especially World War I. Unable any longer to believe in Christianity's mythology of redemption in the face of Darwinism and general scientific progress, accompanied by a confidence that science eventually would prove able to explain everything, and stimulated by romanticism and a general sentimentalization of culture, facilitating the desire to communicate with the dead, the interpretation goes, many intellectuals took up the fad for spiritualism. For many, this amounted to no more than fleeting participation in parlor seances; for others, it proved a lasting preoccupation (Oppenheim 1985; Cerullo 1982). This general line of analysis may prove applicable to Japan, as well, but with one crucial difference.

Not all Japanese participants in spiritualism turned their backs on indigenous religious tradition, rejecting it in favor of spiritualism's pseudo-science. Raised in the True Pure Land sect of Buddhism, Inoue Enryo, to be sure, was very well educated in Japanese religious thought, as well as Western philosophy. But there were surely many others who, like Asano Wasaburō, simply never encountered religion in their formal education, had little contact with Buddhism or Shinto outside of formalistic participation in funerals and memorial services, and who were not so much turning their backs on this aspect of Japanese history and culture as they were totally uninformed about it, as Asano was prior to his conversion to Ōmotokyō. Thomas Rimer has shown how university education encouraged young men to seek their intellectual guides from among the luminaries of German philosophical tradition, trying to confirm the uniqueness of the personal self, leaving them conspicuously alienated from Japanese tradition (Rimer 1990, 3–6). Asano's education, centered on Britain and the United States, his translation skills, and experience with Ōmotokyō left him superbly prepared to create a bridge between Western spiritualism and urban middle-class Japanese salon society. But like the intellectuals Rimer describes, Asano was also alienated from Japanese tradition. Asano was originally receptive to Ōmotokyō in no small part because of his complete ignorance of the entire history of Japanese popular religion. Perhaps his generation of Japanese intellectuals was one of the first to be so innocent, the first to be so separated from this aspect of his heritage as he matured. It may be because of this that his ideas about modernity and rationality proved to be so fragile, scarcely capable of surviving an encounter with spiritualism or a mass religious movement influenced by it, like Ōmotokyō, as the defensive posture adopted by him and other Japanese spiritualists in their attempt to reconcile spiritualism with science shows.

NOTES

1. The details of Asano's life appear in several primary and secondary sources. Asano wrote of his early life, up through his 1916 decision to join Ōmotokyō, in a work called "Shutsuro," reprinted in Minami 1992, 93–211. In the same volume, Asano's works from 1925 and later are also reprinted (213–235, 463–518). A substantial collection of Asano's later works on spiritualism is available in Asano 1985. A recent biography of Asano is Matsumoto 1989. A useful essay placing Asano in the context of early twentieth-century spiritualism is Nishiyama 1990, 69–111. Asano's major works on English and American literature are listed in note 10.

2. For analysis of various historical approaches to spiritualism, see Galbreath 1983, 11–37.

3. Blavatsky's close colleague Henry S. Olcott visited Japan from February 9 to May 28, 1889, but it appears that this visit did not immediately result in the founding of a Japanese branch of the Theosophical Society; see Olcott 1935.

4. For a cultural history of British spiritualism, see Oppenheim 1985 and Cerullo 1982. On William James' extensive interest in spiritualism, see

Myers 1986, 10, 370–372, 381–382. Sōseki and Anesaki Masaharu (founder of the Department of Religious Studies at Tokyo Imperial University) were important conduits for introducing James' work in both psychological and religious forms into Japan, as was Fukurai Tomokichi (see below), translator of James; see Okura 1989 and Stone 1990, 232n20.

5. An imaginary being having human form, with wings, a red face, and a great, pendulous nose, thought to have extraordinary strength and magical powers.

6. A type of witchcraft based on the notion that some individuals are able to send spirit helpers (the spirits of magical dogs) to attack their enemies; this ability is believed to be inherited, leading to interdiction on marriage with "dog-owning" families.

7. See Miyata 1990, 44–53. Inoue's lectures on the study of ghosts can be consulted in Inoue 1896.

8. On Kiyozawa's understanding of *seishinshugi*, see Yoshida 1992, 254 ff.

9. Both Kokkō and Aizō had received baptism under the influence of Nikolai (Jovan Demitrovich Kasatskin, 1836–1912), who brought the Greek Orthodox tradition to Japan in 1861, but they were also deeply attached to the Jodo school of Japanese Buddhism. Kokkō was fluent in Russian, and the salon hosted regular meetings for the study of the Russian language as well as the country's art and literature. The couple were much attracted to Uchimura Kanzō, who was a regular visitor and who is said to have persuaded them to resist the temptation to sell liquor in the coffee shop. Kokkō and Aizō supported the development of Western theater in Japan and were particular patrons of the actress Matsui Sumako. They received the Indian poet Tagore, as well as the Bengali activist for Indian independence, Rasvihari Bose, whom their daughter Toshiko married. See Nakamuraya 1968. The couple's diaries may be consulted in Soma 1956 and Soma and Soma 1952.

10. The following are some of Asano's most important early publications: Asano 1903, 1906, 1907, and 1908.

11. Meshima was understood to be the dwelling of Ushitora Konjin, and Oshima was taken to be the palace of five Dragon Kings.

12. Because of the belief that Onisaburō was an incarnation of the goddess Hitsujisaru Konjin, he was in the habit of wearing his hair long and wearing women's clothing. This belief developed in combination with the idea that Nao represented an incarnation of a male god, Ushitora Konjin. See Hardacre 1994, 215–239.

13. Asano's various activities in Ōmotokyō have been fictionalized by novelist Takashi Kazumi in Takashi 1993, first published in 1977. In that work he appears as Nakamura Tetsuo.

14. See *Shimbun shūroku Taishōki*, 8:110; *Yomiuri shimbun*, March 23, 1920, 8:224; *Tokyo nichi nichi shimbun*, June 16, 1920, 8:238; *Yomiuri shimbun*, June 30, 1920, 8:245; *Yomiuri shimbun*, July 4, 1920, 9:62; *Yorozuchōhō*, February 19, 1921.

15. Other members of the society were Taniguchi Masaharu (1893–1985), like Asano, formerly an Ōmotokyō member, who later founded the new religion

Seichō no Ie; attorney Hanai Takuzō (1868–1931), who had represented the religion in the 1921 suppression; botanist Matsumura Shōnen; Sano Shizuo; Sugiyama Yoshio; and Muto Inajirō.
16. These lectures were collected in Asano 1985, vol. 6.

REFERENCES

Asano Wasaburō. 1903. *Eibun hyōshaku*. Jinbunsha.

———. 1906. *Eikoku bungakushi*. Jinbunsha.

———. 1907. *Eibungakushi*. Dai Nihon tosho.

———. 1908. *Beikoku bungakushi*. Dai Nihon tosho.

———. 1985. *Asano Wasaburō chōsakushū*. 6 vols. Reprint, Chōbunsha.

Cerullo, John J. 1982. *The Secularization of the Soul, Psychical Research in Modern Britain*. Philadelphia: Institute for the Study of Human Issues.

Deguchi Eiji. 1970. *Ōmotokyō jiken*. San'ichi Shobō.

Deguchi Onisaburō. 1917. "Taishō ishin ni tsuite." *Shinreikai*, February. Reprinted in *Deguchi Onisaburō chōsakushū*. 5 vols. Edited by Yasumaru Yoshio, 2:155–179. Yomiuri Shimbunsha, 1973.

Ellwood, Robert. 1988. "Occult Movements in America." In *Encyclopedia of the American Religious Experience*, 2:711–722. New York: Charles Scribner's Sons.

Galbreath, Robert. 1983. "Explaining Modern Occultism." In *The Occult in America: New Historical Perspectives*, edited by Howard Kerr and Charles L. Crow. Urbana: University of Illinois Press.

Hardacre, Helen. 1994. "Gender and the Millennium in Ōmoto Kyōdan: The Limits of Religious Innovation." In *Innovation in Religious Traditions*, edited by Michael Williams, Collett Cox, and Martin Jaffee. The Hague: Mouton de Gruyter.

Ikeda Akira, ed. 1982–1985. *Ōmoto shiryō shūsei*. 3 vols. San'ichi Shobō.

Inoue Enryo. 1896. *Yokaigaku kōgi*. 2 vols. Tetsugakkan.

Ishida Bunshirō. 1955. *Taishō daijikenshi*. Senseisha.

"Kujō Takeko fujin to kataru reikai no zadankai." 1936. *Shufu no tomo* (May):170–185.

Matsumoto Ken'ichi. 1989. *Kami no wana: Asano Wasaburō: Kindai chisei no higeki*. Shinchōsha.

Minami Hiroshi, ed. 1992. *Meishin, uranai, shinrei genshō*, vol. 19. Kindai shomin seikatsushi. San'ichi Shobō.

Miyata Noboru. 1990. *Yokai no minzokugaku*. Iwanami Shoten.

Myers, Gerald E. 1986. *William James, His Life and Thought*. New Haven: Yale University Press.

Nakamuraya, ed. 1968. *Soma Aizō, Kokkō no ayumi*. Nakamuraya.

Nakayama Yasumasa, ed. 1965. *Meiji hennenshi*. 15 vols. Saisei Keizaigakusha.

Nishiyama Shigeru. 1990. "Reijutsu-kei shinshūkyō no taitō to futatsu no kindaika." In *Kindaika to shūkyō būmu*, edited by Kokugakuin Daigaku Nihon Bunka Kenkyūjo. Dōbōsha.

Oishi Ryūichi. 1989. *Zenkoku reinō, shinreika meikan.* Taka Shobō.

Okura Shūzo. 1989. *Natsume Sōseki: Wiriamu Jemuzu juyō no shūhen.* Yūseidō.

Olcott, Henry S. 1935. *Old Diary Leaves.* 6 vols. Adyar, India: Theosophical Publishing House.

Ōmoto Nanajūnenshi Hensankai. 1964. *Ōmoto nanajūnenshi.* Kameoka: Tenseisha.

Oppenheim, Janet. 1985. *The Other World, Spiritualism in England (1850–1914).* Cambridge: Cambridge University Press.

Rimer, Thomas. 1990. "Introduction." In *Culture and Identity: Japanese Intellectuals During the Interwar Years.* Princeton: Princeton University Press.

Shimbun shūroku Taishōki.

Soma Aizō and Soma Kokkō. 1952. *Bansō.* Dainihon Insatsu K. K.

Soma Kokkō. 1956. *Tekisuiroku.* Dainihon Insatsu K. K.

Stone, Jackie. 1990. "A Vast and Grave Task: Interwar Buddhist Studies as an Expression of Japan's Envisioned Global Role." In *Culture and Identity: Japanese Intellectuals During the Interwar Years,* edited by Thomas Rimer. Princeton: Princeton University Press.

Takahashi Kazumi. 1977, 1993. *Jashūmon.* Asahi Shimbunsha.

Tsunajima Ryōsen. 1905, 1976. "Yo ga kenshin no jikken." In *Gendai Nihon bungaku taikei.* Chikuma Shobō.

Yasumaru Yoshio, ed. 1973. *Deguchi Onisaburō chosakushū.* 5 vols. Yomiuri Shimbunsha.

Yoshida Kyūichi. 1992. *Nihon kindai Bukkyōshi kenkyū.* Kawashima Shoten.

⇒ II ⇐

Cosmopolitanism and National Identity

❧ 7 ❧

Becoming Japanese: Imperial Expansion and Identity Crises in the Early Twentieth Century

TESSA MORRIS-SUZUKI

At the end of the twentieth century—when some eighty million "guest workers" inhabit the margins of the international order—images of belonging, nationality, and identity shift and blur in disconcerting ways. In Japan (to take one small example) the sociologist Katō Hidetoshi warns that increasing immigration challenges the very "core" (*shutai*) of Japan, and calls for the development of a "New National Learning" (*Shin-Kokugaku*) to counter this challenge (Katō 1995). It is easy to imagine that there was once a simpler time, when the boundaries of citizenship were certain and national "cores" clearly defined. But to assume a simpler past is to forget how much the structures and imagery of citizenship were born not just from the rise of the nation-state but also from the experience of imperialism.

The recent urge to pin down the nation's "core"—to define "what is Japan"—raises echoes of the prewar quest of scholars like Kita Sadakichi, who in 1918 launched the new journal *Minzoku to rekishi (Ethnos and History)* by posing the question "who are the Japanese people?"[1] (Kita 1918; compare Umehara 1990, Sakaiya 1993). It was a question that was to obsess Kita for the next decade and one to which he repeatedly returned, producing ever more complex and detailed answers. His fullest statement on the subject, published in 1929, summarized mythical accounts of Japanese origins contained in ancient chronicles like the *Kojiki* and *Nihon shoki* but rejected a literal belief in these stories. "In recent times," Kita wrote,

> examinations have been undertaken from an archaeological perspective of the remains left by ancient inhabitants of our country, and from

an anthropological perspective of skeletal remains, and these researches, which endeavor to clarify the ethnic identity of our people—the one in terms of cultural heritage and the other in terms of
skeletal measurement—have together achieved great progress. As a
result, very many issues which previously could not be learned from
the ancient myths have now become clear. (Kita [1929] 1978,
224–225)

On the basis of this scientific study, Kita could confidently refute the mythical vision of the Japanese as racially pure descendants of divine ancestors:

[f]rom the first, we Japanese people have not been a homogeneous
ethnic group *(tanjun naru minzoku)*. Rather, many people of different
lineages have lived together in this archipelago for long periods of
time, and in the process have intermarried, adopted one anothers'
customs, merged their languages and eventually forgotten where they
came from. Thus an entirely united Japanese ethnic group has come
to be created. (Kita [1929] 1978, 213–214)

What is intriguing about Kita's approach is the way in which he combines this self-consciously "modern" and scientific rejection of racial homogeneity with impassioned support for Japanese imperialism. His logic runs
counter, in other words, to a common assumption that prewar imperialist
ideology can be equated with a belief in Shinto mythology and in Japanese
racial purity (See Yoshino 1992, 26). Even some of the best postwar critiques
of notions of "ethnic homogeneity" have implied that prewar thought was
founded on a conflation of "race, tribe, clan, ethnic group and nation" and
that recognition of Japan's diverse racial origins is essentially a post-1945
phenomenon (for example, Ubukata 1979, 27–28). But, as recent work by
Yoon Keun-Cha, Kevin Doak, and Oguma Eiji suggests, Kita Sadakichi was
just one of a number of prominent early twentieth-century scholars whose
writings suggest a more complex relationship between citizenship, national
identity, and imperialism (see the chapter by Doak in this volume; also Yoon
1994; Oguma 1995).

In this essay I will use one example from Japan's early twentieth-century
colonialism as a means of exploring these complexities and of drawing out
their implications for contemporary visions of the meaning of "being" or
"becoming" Japanese. In particular, I shall address five points that seem
central to an understanding of early twentieth-century issues of imperialism
and identity. The first point concerns the relationship between "nationality,"
a legal status embodied in passports, population registers, and the like, and
"national identity," a sense of belonging created imaginatively in the writings
of political theorists, historians, novelists, poets, and so forth. Recent debates
on "national identity," focusing on the imagined quality of nationhood, some-

times underestimate the very real force contained in the instruments of official "nationality." Here I will explore the continuing and complex inter-relationship between official definitions of "Japanese" status and the imagined sense of national community. Second, in examining this relationship, I want to emphasize the "modern" nature of much Taishō-period rhetoric about national identity. As we have seen from the example of Kita Sadakichi, and as I shall argue more fully below, debate about the unique characteristics of the Japanese was not so much a retreat into traditionalism as a response to the modern problems of colonialism: a response that relied heavily on imported sciences of biology, archaeology, and anthropology.

Third, I will suggest that, because they attempted to juggle two essentially contradictory principles—the principle of the nation-state on the one hand and the principle of colonialism on the other—official definitions of nationality and national identity in the Taishō period were almost inevitably fraught with insoluble paradoxes. One of the most important of these paradoxes (fourth) was that the colonial order needed to produce both similarity and difference in its subjects. Rather than defining colonial policy simply as "assimilationist" or simply as "discriminatory," I want to show how much assimilation and discrimination, Japanization and exoticization, were different sides of the same colonial coin. Last, it is important to emphasize that these complex issues of nationality and national identity were issues both for colonizer and for colonized. Even the smallest and most vulnerable indigenous communities were not just passive victims of state policy but shaped their own identity within the framework of empire, often participating with surprising vigor in colonial debates.

THE DILEMMAS OF CITIZENSHIP

Prewar debates about Japanese ethnicity are worth reexamining because they point not just to specifically Japanese dilemmas of identity but to wider paradoxes in the concepts of nationality and citizenship. The modern nation-state, in theory, draws a sharp line around the community of its members. While pre-Meiji thought had been dominated by the vision of *tenka* (the world under heaven)—where each individual life was embedded in a social hierarchy whose outer limits were only dimly perceived—the new vision of *kokka* (the state) brought with it a sense of unequivocal common membership of a single body politic. From the beginning, however, "citizenship" was an iridescent concept whose various interwoven meanings often pulled in opposite directions.

On the one hand, the idea of citizenship was based on a set of ideas about individual rights and freedoms that emerged from the European Enlightenment and the French Revolution. On the other, it also implied that these rights and freedoms were acquired through membership in a "national community." Nineteenth- and early twentieth-century European thought, by and large, accepted that the world was naturally divided into such identifiable communities, held together by "a common consciousness based upon race, language, traditions, or analogous ties and interests" (Royal Institute of International Affairs 1937, 308). Each national community, besides, was not a world unto itself, but was part of a competing system of rival nations, always vulnerable to threats from others. So the status of citizen was inextricably bound up with the obligation to defend the nation—that is, the willingness to die (or at least to kill) for one's country.

In the early Meiji period, until the passing of the first Japanese citizenship law in 1899, the status of "being Japanese" was legally defined through enrollment in the family registration *(koseki)* system. This system had been established in 1872 as a prelude to the introduction of military conscription, and its structure and meaning continued to be closely associated with military service until the end of the Pacific War. As one 1930s theorist put it, status in the *koseki* system "is primarily determined by whether or not one has a duty of military service, and the duty of military service is primarily determined by whether or not one possesses the spirit of a Japanese subject *(Nihon shinmin taru no seishin)*" (Satomi 1939, 308). In Japan as elsewhere, the link between citizenship, military service, and an amorphous "national spirit" had two important consequences.

First, it meant that citizenship was qualified by gender: women, who were not expected to kill for their country (and who presumably lacked the full "spirit of a Japanese subject"), had limited rights to acquire and pass on membership in the national community. Second, formal nationality became inextricably entangled with *kokumin seishin*—that sense of solidarity and group loyalty that was assumed to spring from shared customs, language, and ethnicity. Since Japan has never been culturally homogeneous, this relationship was a troubling one. While some minority groups were from the very first included in the family registration system (one example being the Korean community of Naeshirogawa in Southern Kyushu, who had maintained their own language and customs since the early seventeenth century), the inclusion of the multicultural settler population of the Ogasawara (Bonin) Islands was the subject of heated debates (Ubukata 1992, 28; Arima 1990). Another anomaly was the Ryūkyū Archipelago, which was annexed by Japan in 1879: its inhabitants did not become liable for conscription until 1898 and did not receive the franchise until 1911.

The vision of a naturally ordained world of competing nations produced further paradoxes. The logical extension of the idea of citizenship to the realm of international politics pointed inexorably toward the concept of self-determination—the right not just of the people to membership in the state but of peoples to equal membership in the international community. At the same time, though, the success of the nation in the eternal Darwinian struggle between national communities was demonstrated precisely by its expansion and its absorption of other communities. So a web of conditions and compromises circumscribed international acceptance of the principle of self-determination in the post–World War I era. The "self" that was to do the determining had, for one thing, to be of a certain size—ideally big enough to sustain a modern industrialized society (Sureda 1973, 32). Even more importantly, just as full-fledged citizenship was restricted to the adult and autonomous individual (and bestowed only in a more limited form on women, children and the insane), so self-determination was reserved for communities that (it was felt) were sufficiently civilized to face "the strenuous conditions of the modern world" (Sureda 1973, 24). Other societies were to remain colonies or become mandated territories under the control of the major powers, who would guide them toward maturity. This in turn, of course, implied that there was some objective and recognizable standard of "civilization" that could be divorced from the particular culture of the colonizing power: in other words, that it was possible for colonialism to "civilize" the colonies without depriving them of the very cultural identity on which their claim to self-determination rested. In Japan after 1899 the tension between the theoretical equality of citizenship and the practical inequalities of the colonial order was embodied in the distinction between *kokuseki* (formal citizenship), which was applied to the colonies as well as to "Japan proper," and *koseki* (family registration), which was governed by separate systems in different parts of the empire.

Citizenship in the colonial world, then, was torn by contradictory impulses. The ruling state's urge to exalt and spread the values of its own "civilization" contended with its desire to maintain the differences that justified unequal access to power. The representation of strength through images of a united colonial citizenry conflicted with the symbolic value of ethnic and cultural diversity as an emblem of imperial might. The homogenizing force of civilizing missions coexisted with the creation of new settler cultures, uncomfortably suspended between mother country and colonial territory. Empires were full of overlapping, jostling, discordant "imagined communities," within which both colonizers and colonized struggled to visualize coherent identities. Colonial citizenship was therefore almost inevitably hedged around by a byzantine mass of qualifications, so that (as one study of the British Empire bluntly put it) "in conferring political rights the state may discriminate between various classes of subjects, and in many parts of the Empire it does in fact discriminate, particularly on racial and economic grounds" (Royal Institute of International Affairs 1937, 309).

In the Japanese empire, this problem had a particular salience for two reasons. First, the nature of the modern Japanese state, and the circumstances of its creation, produced a vision of citizenship in which the sense of individual autonomy and rights was relatively tenuous and the emphasis on duty (particularly on the duty to defend the nation) relatively strong. Second, apart from Russia, Japan was the only major power to create a large and long-lasting contiguous empire: an empire that stretched geographically outward from the "mother country," rather than being strung in far-flung constellations across the face of the earth. Japan colonized the regions with which it had the deepest and most ancient cultural ties. Japanese colonization, therefore, evoked no allusions to "empires on which the sun never set," but instead provoked an almost obsessive concern with similarity and difference: a passion both for detailing the links that bound colonizer to colonized and for assiduously tending the frontiers that kept them apart. The intellectual legacy of this ambivalence survives to the present day.

"NATIVES" AND NATIONALS: THE CASE OF KARAFUTO

We can catch some glimpses of these tensions of identity by looking at the small and relatively neglected example of the indigenous people of southern Sakhalin (Karafuto). (For studies of Karafuto, see Hora 1956; Stephan 1971; Tanaka and Dahinien 1978; Karafuto Ainu Kenkyūkai 1992; Akizuki 1994; Howell 1995; Grant 1995.) The modern Japanese state has always been unsure of its own northern boundaries. In the late eighteenth and early nineteenth centuries, "Ezo" (the area comprising modern Hokkaido and the dimly perceived regions of Sakhalin and the Kurile Islands beyond) both was and was not part of Japan; today, control of the southern Kurile Islands is still in dispute, and the official position of the Japanese government is that sovereignty over Southern Sakhalin has not been determined under international law. Although Japan does not actively pursue a claim to its old colony of Karafuto, many contemporary Japanese maps still show two northern frontiers—one following the Sōya Straits between Hokkaido and Sakhalin, and the other running through the middle of Sakhalin.

During its colonization of Hokkaido in the second half of the nineteenth century, Japan rejected the U.S. option of treating indigenous societies as (theoretically) separate "dependent nations" and instead pursued an energetic policy of assimilation (Morris-Suzuki 1994). Ainu were included in the family registration system from 1872 but were distinguished from the rest of the population by the memorably equivocal term "former native" (*kyū-dojin*) and were not liable for conscription until 1889 (1898 in the most "remote" areas) (Satō 1988, 154–155). Further north, the status of the indigenous people became even more uncertain. Both Russian and Japanese colonizers repeatedly used particular indigenous groups to support territorial claims to Sakhalin—the first pointing to the presence of "our Tungus," the second to the presence of "Japanese Ainu" (Ivanov, Smolyak, and Levin

1964, 762; "Karafuto wa Nihon no mono de aru," appendix to Nishijima 1941; see also Akizuki 1994). But the 1875 Treaty of St. Petersburg, which gave Sakhalin to Russia in return for Japanese control of the Kurile Archipelago, denied indigenous citizenship: "the natives of Karafuto [Southern Sakhalin] and the Kurile Islands have permanent residence in these places but have no rights as subjects of the present ruling powers" (quoted in Karafuto Chō 1973, 1:28).

This left the indigenous population as trophies to be passed from one power to another as territory changed hands: the Ainu inhabitants of Sakhalin—who numbered about two thousand and many of whom had worked for years in Japanese-run fisheries—would automatically become Russian unless they left their homes and moved to Japan, while the small Ainu and Aleut population of the northern Kurile islands—many of whom spoke Russian and had been converted to Orthodox Christianity—would automatically become Japanese unless they moved to Russia. Since Japan desperately needed labor for the development of Hokkaido, 841 Sakhalin Ainu eventually chose or were persuaded to move to Japan. At least 84 indigenous inhabitants of the Northern Kuriles were also relocated to Kamchatka (Shubin 1992). In both cases, the move proved disastrous. Huddled into large settlements for the first times in their lives, many succumbed to infectious diseases. Of the Sakhalin Ainu, who were resettled in the village of Tsuishikari near Sapporo, almost half died from cholera and other epidemics (Karafuto Ainu Kenkyūkai 1992).

In 1905, at the end of the Russo-Japanese War, Japan regained control of the southern half of Sakhalin, which now became the colony of Karafuto. But, dazzled by a vision of the natural wealth and unturned soil of "rich Karafuto," the new rulers seem temporarily to have forgotten the existence of an indigenous population. The Treaty of Portsmouth, marking the end of the war, made no reference to the remaining Ainu population, nor to the five hundred or so other indigenous inhabitants, most of whom belonged to the Uilta and Nivkh language groups. No provisions were made to give them Japanese citizenship, and they remained theoretically Russian until the time of the Russian revolution, after which they lapsed into a sort of civic limbo—a state of affairs that the eminent Japanese legal expert Yamada Saburō described as an "unerasable disgrace" (Yamada 1933, 19). In 1925, after a brief Japanese foray into the northern half of Sakhalin, the Russian authorities decreed that all inhabitants of Southern Sakhalin who wished to retain Russian (now Soviet) citizenship must register with the local consulate. It is very unlikely that any of the indigenous people of Southern Sakhalin were aware of this decree. Certainly, none registered; as a result, they were left without any formally defined citizenship (Morimoto 1930).

This oversight was symptomatic of a wider official uninterest in indigenous society (Fujii 1938). Half-hearted efforts were made to encourage the development "native fisheries"—run by Japanese managers but employing Ainu[2]—and to set up "native schools" in Ainu villages; but even here at least part of the initiative seems to have come from the Ainu themselves rather than from the colonial authorities (see, for example, Kasai 1927, 68). In the early stages, the only project that the authorities pursued with real vigor was a scheme to persuade the indigenous people to move from their small scattered settlements into larger villages, where they could be more easily assimilated, educated, and controlled (Karafuto Chō 1973, 2:1692). The Ainu population was gradually shifted into ten "designated hamlets" *(shitei buraku)*—five each on the west and the east coasts of the colony—and in 1927 the settlement of Otasu, on a sandbank in the Poronai River, was chosen as the site for a village to house the Nivkh and Uilta populations, as well as a small number of indigenous people from other language groups.

Meanwhile, however, six years after Japan had gained control of the region, the colonial government had begun to feel the need for a more coherent "native policy" and commissioned two Japanese experts to conduct surveys of the indigenous islanders. The famous ethnographer and archaeologist Torii Ryūzō studied the customs and beliefs of all the colony's indigenous groups, while linguist Nakanome Akira focused mainly on the Tungusic language of the people, whom he called the "Orok" (but who are now

The village of Otasu in the early 1930s. (Changing Japan as Seen Through the Camera. *Asahi Shimbun, 1933, 261.*)

normally known as the Uilta) (*Karafuto nichinichi shimbun,* August 14, 1912; reprinted in Utari Kyōkai 1989, 783).

Nakanome's published reports convey a particularly sharp sense of colonial paradoxes. They were, in some ways, pioneering works. Nakanome had no phrase books or grammars to guide him in learning the Uilta language, and he studied by spending several summers in a Uilta village in the northern part of the colony. His efforts to unravel the mysteries of Uilta linguistics were constantly undermined by his hosts' disinclination to spend hours repeating basic words and phrases to him (Nakanome 1917, 45–46). All the same, he did manage to obtain some grasp of grammar and pronunciation, and to make more general observations about the lives of the all indigenous people of the region, including Nivkh and Ainu-speaking as well as Uilta-speaking communities. He recorded myths, provided a rough account of social structures and religious beliefs, and noted that the Uilta "think that their country is their own, and that it is an independent country" (Nakanome 1917, 31).

Nakanome, however, saw his role as being to prescribe as well as to describe: to define the position that the indigenous people of Sakhalin should occupy in the colonial order. At one level, his prescription was straightforward. Japanization was to be achieved through social Darwinism. The "natives," he wrote, should be exposed to Japanese culture so that "the weak will die and the strong become civilized" (Nakanome 1918, 101). This could best be achieved by face-to-face contact. People from "Japan proper" *(naichi)* should be encouraged to visit, or better still to settle in, native villages; representatives of indigenous communities were to be taken on tours of the colonial capital, Toyohara, where they could marvel at such symbols of superiority as trains and electric lighting (Nakanome 1918, 103); employment in Japanese-owned fisheries was to be used as a way of teaching diligence and the Japanese language; for (as Nakanome put it) when Uilta and Nivkh worked alongside members of their own community, they had "no opportunity to forget their native language" (Nakanome 1918, 105).

In this sense, Nakanome's vision was of an assimilating mission that would obliterate all differences between colonizer and colonized. But at another level he also recognized that the indigenous people of Karafuto were not simply destined to become "Japanese" but were to be a particular sort of "Japanese," filling a specific niche in the colonial order. Their value, in his eyes, was that they were adapted to the extreme climate of the far north, which many Japanese settlers found unbearable. The function of "native education," therefore, was "nothing other than to turn them into permanently resident laborers *(eijūteki rōdōsha)*" (Nakanome 1918, 107).

The implications of this were spelled out in Nakanome's detailed proposals for the education of the Uilta and Nivkh communities. Here, the emphasis on language training was carefully circumscribed. Indigenous children were to be taught to speak Japanese, since this was necessary for their future role as laborers, but not to read or write. Indeed Nakanome bitterly criticized the Ainu "native schools," where children learned Chinese characters and where there were even proposals to allow them to study alongside "more highly civilized children from Japan proper" (Nakanome 1918, 118). A more appropriate language-teaching style, he suggested, would be the Berlitz direct method, which would avoid the need for textbooks. As well as spoken Japanese, the children should be taught ethics, simple arithmetic, and singing (the last because it would help to improve their language skills). This was to be the sum total of their academic curriculum. Afternoons should be devoted to practical handicrafts such as metalworking, leatherworking, and carpentry for boys and sewing and embroidery for girls, activities that might help to turn them into "people of economic worth to the state" (Nakanome 1918, 108, 114–116).

Nakanome's ideas seem to have had a real effect on colonial policy. Segregated education for Ainu children was maintained until the early 1930s, and the first and only school for other indigenous children, opened in the settlement of Otasu in April 1930, proclaimed its mission as being to "foster sentiments of nationality *(kokuminteki jōsō)*," "impart vocational training," "nurture a spirit of cooperation," and "develop a spirit of diligent labor" (Shisuka Dojin Jimusho 1935, 31). It is instructive to compare these aims with the official guidelines for education in the colony as a whole, which similarly emphasized the fostering of patriotism, productive skills, cooperation, and diligence but included an extra clause on the need to create "autonomous citizens" *(jichiteki jūmin)* (Karafuto Chō 1973, 2:1482). Although reading and writing were included (and at least one pupil was later to remember the special delight he had felt in learning to link the sounds of Japanese to the written word), study focused on Japanese language, ethics, arithmetic, and singing, and large periods of time were devoted to practical handicrafts (See Tanaka and Dahinien 1978, 35). In the school building, half of which served as a house for the teachers, Kawamura Hideya and his wife Nao, the blackboard was inscribed with basic words and numerals in Uilta and Japanese. Lessons (all of which were conducted in Japanese) emphasized stories from Shinto mythology and the heroic moments of Japanese history, and the class received several visits from military officers who gave glowing accounts of Japanese military victories (Vishinevskii 1994, 126–127).

A description of the school in 1941 suggests how close its results were to Nakanome's aim. To the outside observer, its classes seemed to have done little to change the pupils' basic "ways of thinking about things," but graduates from the school were "said to be outstanding" when they worked together as seasonal laborers. The children's knowledge of patriotic and military songs was particularly noteworthy, and their drawings and paintings, on the eve of Pearl Harbor, evoked a peculiar mixture of emotions. They were "pictures of soldiers, pictures of war, and pictures of battleships . . . but is the mentality here the same as that of Japanese children? What we see here, to be sure, is their world—blue seas glittering with ice, seals, reindeer—all drawn energetically and with a strange nostalgia. Seeing those pictures, the lives of their ancestors seemed to float before my eyes. . ." (Kasai 1941, 106–107).

Patriotism and a strange nostalgia. These, indeed, are threads that run intertwined through all the short history of Japanese Karafuto. Occasionally the nostalgia reflected a real interest in indigenous culture. The headmaster of Otasu School, Kawamura Hideya—who was genuinely liked by many of his pupils—spent much of his time in the colony recording indigenous languages and traditions. Seeing himself perhaps as the hapless instrument of social Darwinism, he seems to have mourned the passing of indigenous culture even as he systematically eradicated it (See, for example, Kawamura 1937; Kawamura 1938, 69–70; Vishinevskii 1994, 127). But there was also a sense in which colonial rule needed difference as much as it needed uniformity. Difference was important not only because it made people easier to exploit but also for symbolic reasons. In a curious sense, the very success of assimilation policies was best demonstrated by applying them to people who were visibly different. Cultural hybridity was, as Homi Bhabha observes, at the heart of the colonial experience (Bhabha 1994). So the indigenous people of Karafuto, while being gradually deprived of the basis of their social autonomy, were also exposed to a steady stream of anthropologists, tourists, and photographers coming to marvel at the exotic customs of this corner of "far northern Japan." Even Nakanome Akira's prescriptions for assimilation included the recommendation that "ethics" lessons should include the teaching of traditional legends and botanical knowledge. And when Crown Prince Hirohito visited the colony in the summer of 1925, he did not see its native inhabitants working in the fisheries or tilling the fields that they were being encouraged to farm, but was greeted instead with displays of traditional Ainu music and Uilta reindeer herding (Karafuto Chō 1973, 2:1701).

This two-way pull between the polar forces of assimilation and difference seemed to increase as time went on. In Karafuto, the rise of militarism and nationalism and the eventual elevation of the island from colonial status to part of "Japan proper" in 1943 were accompanied by the growth of a particular sort of local settler patriotism: a distincitve *tōmin seishin* (islander character) which struggled to make itself heard above the wider background echoes of *kokumin seishin* (national character) (Kawabe 1942, 18–22). The rise of settler patriotism may have done very little to improve the actual social position of the indigenous people, but it did increase the use of indigenous motifs for symbolic purposes. Perhaps the most striking examples of this were the East Asia Northern Region Development Exhibition of 1939, held in Karafuto to mark the tenth anniversary of the colony's Central

Research Institute, and the Karafuto: Guardian of the Northern Gate Exhibition, staged by the island's colonial government in Tokyo in 1940 as part of the nation's "2,600th anniversary" celebrations. The Northern Region exhibition included displays of indigenous arts and crafts, while the Tokyo exhibition included a life-sized panorama of the village of Otasu, where visitors could see waxwork models of the settlement's Nivkh and Uilta people engaged in traditional fishing and herding activities, while listening to recordings of the village children singing Japanese patriotic songs (Karafuto Chūō Shikenjo 1942; "Hokumon no mamori" 1940, 75).

The colonial equivocation between assimilation and discrimination was reproduced in the government's failure to explicitly to define the indigenous people as Japanese and its decision to place them in the distinct category of "natives" *(dojin)*. As a result of this policy, the indigenous people of Karafuto came to occupy what can be seen as the outermost, and most ambivalent, position within the many concentric circles of colonial citizenship. The inner circle, with the fullest measure of citizenship, was occupied by the "Japanese proper" *(naichijin)*[3] although with qualifications separating out groups like the former natives *(kyū-dojin)*. Next came the colonial subjects of Korea and Taiwan, who were Japanese citizens from the point of view of international law, but were enrolled in "external family registers" *(gaichi koseki)*, had neither the right of parliamentary representation nor (until the final stages of the Pacific War) the duty of military service, and were generally educated separately from Japanese settlers. The "Karafuto Natives" *(Karafuto dojin,* significantly without the preface "former") had no family registers at all but were enrolled in a "Native List" *(dojin meibo)*. This not only excluded them from conscription but also meant that they were not covered by the provisions of Japanese criminal and civil law, which made it virtually impossible for them to acquire property or run their own businesses. The convoluted set of distinctions was further complicated by the fact that most of the surviving Ainu who had been resettled after the Treaty of St. Petersburg eventually returned to Karafuto, retaining their distinct status as Japanese "Former Natives."

The way in which the colonial system juggled notions of similarity and difference created profound dilemmas of identity both for the indigenous people themselves and for their Japanese colonizers. In many indigenous communities there was clearly a strong sense of being heir to distinct and special traditions. Nakanome himself observed that the Uilta-speaking population, in the early years of colonial rule, considered themselves "an independent people, not recognizing that they are blessed with imperial favors as subjects of the territory of the Japanese empire," and described the prominent Nivkh elder Bōkon as being full of *aizokushin*—"love for his tribe," the ethnic equivalent of *aikokushin* or patriotism (Nakanome 1918, 62; 1917, 73).

But as colonization ate away at the basis of traditional existence—confiscating hunting grounds, cutting down forests, polluting rivers—it became increasingly obvious that survival would depend on access to the full rights of citizenship. For the small indigenous communities of the north, the prospects of obtaining internationally recognized political autonomy were negligible, and the best defense against annihilation lay in "becoming Japanese." To "become Japanese," in this context, clearly meant above all to be treated as equal members of the empire, without necessarily implying the renunciation of a distinct history. The delicately balanced relationship between nationality, equality, and identity is well illustrated by a remarkable petition composed by Kaizawa Hisanosuke, a thirty-eight-year-old Ainu villager from Biratori in Hokkaido. The document, addressed to the local government, demanded the right for Ainu, Uilta, and Nivkh representatives to attend the 1926 Congress of Asian Peoples (Ajia Minzoku Taikai), sponsored by the Japanese government and held in Nagasaki. Kaizawa wrote as "a member of the Japanese ethnic group and a member of the people of the world," but went on to state that

> all humans are under the control of god, and restoring the world of god can only mean that all the humans of the world should stand in an equal line. Since this is so, can such a Congress exclude us Ainu, Orochon (i.e., Uilta) and Gilyak (i.e., Nivkh)? As a member of the Ainu people, I want to watch very closely to see what is the real meaning of this Congress, and I have my own ideas of proposals which should be placed before the Congress. (*Hokkai Taimusu*, July 26, 1926; reprinted in Utari Kyōkai 1989, 865)

In Karafuto, a rising tide of indigenous demands for full citizenship was inseparably linked to a campaign for equal rights and greater economic autonomy, particularly for direct control of the "native fisheries." During the late 1920s the colonial government was repeatedly presented with petitions calling for the removal of Japanese "overseers" from the fisheries. When colonial critics countered that the "natives," who were not covered by civil law, were incompetent to manage their own affairs, the issue expanded into a wider claim for citizenship. In 1930, for example, the minister for colonial development, on an official tour of Karafuto, was met at Tarandomari Station by a delegation of Ainu, including what the press termed "modern Ainu" dressed in their best kimonos, and presented with a petition demanding: "1. That Japanese administration should be extended to the Ainu people; 2. that Ainu should be given civil rights (*kōminken*)[4]; 3. that the Tarankotan fishery, which is designated as a 'native fishery', should be placed under direct native management" (*Karafuto nichinichi shimbun*, August 17, 1930; reprinted in Utari Kyōkai 1989, 883).

It is important not to oversimplify here. Indigenous interpretations of "becoming Japanese" varied according to generation, circumstances, and individual personalities and often had cultural as well as political connotations. Education in the "native schools" inevitably influenced the pupils' sense of social identity, and the exposure of indigenous traditions to the exoticizing glare of colonial curiosity had the power to crystalize them into unfamiliar forms, alienating them from their living owners. Dahinien Gendānu, who was later to become an activist for Uilta rights and the preservation of Uilta traditions, recalled the pride that he felt in his newly acquired Japanese name—Kitagawa Gentarō. And, although he happily spoke his own language in the indigenous space of Otasu village, he still, years later, remembered the shame he had experienced when his mother spoke to him in Uilta in the Japanese public space of Shisuka (the town nearest to Otasu) (Tanaka and Dahinien 1978, 43–44). The colonial image of the imperial patriot in fancy dress was a cartoon image masking people who, in many cases, felt a profound ambiguity about their own identity and a profound desire not to have a resolution to that ambiguity imposed on them by others. Postcolonial enthusiasm for the cultural potential of hybridity should not be allowed to conceal the pain from which it was conceived.

Despite these dilemmas of identity, there is in almost every indigenous call for citizenship a common theme: a vision of "becoming Japanese" as being a matter not of homogeneity but precisely of autonomy—the right to control resources, the right to be taken seriously, the right to be left alone. We can hear its echoes even in the strangely moving (and ignored) appeal addressed to the colonial government in the early 1930s by the village elder Jonburainu, speaking on behalf the Uilta and Nivkh communities of Otasu. The text, in halting Japanese, was composed with the help of students from the newly established local native school (it was not for nothing that Nakanome Akira had warned against teaching indigenous people to write): "For the natives of Otasu . . . there is no firewood for homes or logs to build houses, so we've got to ask for help. The Japanese living back of the Shimkuki River cut them down to their stumps, every year two miles long by a mile wide. That's why we've got to ask for help. We want to become Japanese quickly, so please help us" (quoted in Tanaka and Dahinien 1978, 61).

The authorities' response did little to resolve the ambiguities of indigenous identity. In 1932, at the height of the patriotic excitement induced by the "Manchurian incident," the colonial government extended full Japanese citizenship to all Karafuto Ainu but not to other indigenous groups. This hesitant response was presented as the correction of anomaly—the fact that some Karafuto Ainu held citizenship while others did not—and the exclusion of non-Ainu was justified by unelaborated references to their "way of life." But the ambiguities of citizenship allowed the meaning of the gift to be displaced in the very moment of giving. Ainu groups clearly had fought

The effects of logging in Sakhalin. (Changing Japan as Seen Through the Camera. *Asahi Shimbun, 1933, 264.*)

for citizenship as a means of obtaining dignity, equal education, and economic autonomy; but the colonial press, celebrating the extension of citizenship to the Ainu, interpreted it not as a recognition of civil rights but rather as "giving the Ainu their long hoped-for opportunity to serve in the armed forces" (*Karafuto nichinichi shimbun,* December 14, 1932; reprinted in Utari Kyōkai 1989, 898).

TORII RYŪZŌ, KITA SADAKICHI, AND THE NATURE OF THE JAPANESE

Torii Ryūzō, though commissioned at the same time as Nakanome Akira to study the indigenous people of Karafuto, set about the task in a quite different way. His published reports contain no prescriptions for colonial policy but are simply meticulous ethnographic accounts of the origins, language, customs, and religion of the region's native peoples. Torii spent ten days in the summer of 1911 traveling by canoe up the Poronai River, stopping here and there to study the Uilta and Nivkh settlements along its banks, and then went south to conduct surveys of the colony's Ainu villages (Torii 1976a, 267–272). The result was a series of detailed accounts of the physiognomy, language, diet, housing, hairstyles, rituals, and religious practices of the indigenous population of Karafuto. Torii was particularly zealous in pointing out connections between the cultures of the region and Japanese language and traditions. He noted, for example, that the Uilta ate raw fish like the Japanese and built storehouses that resembled the treasure houses of ancient Japanese shrines, and he argued that this group might be the people referred to in the earliest Japanese chronicles as the *mishihase* or *shukushin* (Torii 1976b, 400–404).

Torii's researches in Karafuto were just part of a much larger and more ambitious project in which he tried, through the study of ethnography and prehistory, to bring order to the vexed question of national identity. His work for the Karafuto government was only one of several similar requests from colonial administrations: the colonial authorities in Seoul also invited him to survey Korean archaeological sites, and the authorities in Taiwan to study the island's indigenous people. During the Japanese intervention in Siberia following the Russian Revolution, he enlisted the help of the expeditionary forces to travel to northern Sakhalin and Eastern Siberia, where he collected a rich store of ethnographic data (Shiratori and Yawata 1978, 302–313). Out of all this, Torii wove an image of the nation's ethnic origins that was most fully elaborated in his 1925 classic study, *Yūshi izen no Nihon* (Prehistoric Japan).

The originality of this vision lay in its emphasis on Japan's racial diversity. Scholars in Japan already were debating whether the Japanese were a racially pure group, or whether they originated from an intermingling of a primordial stone-age population (Ainu according to some, non-Ainu according to others) with later Bronze-Age migrants (See Mizuno 1960, 33–39). Torii, however, was much more adventurous. At a time when Japan was confronted with the political realities of an ethnically diverse empire, he painted a picture of a prehistoric Japanese population drawn from all corners of imperial territory and beyond. In this way, while writers like Nakanome spelled out detailed suggestions for colonial policy, Torii contributed to the wider intellectual framework rationalizing the perplexing crosscurrents of ethnicity in the colonial world.

Torii once likened his technique to that of a chemist separating elements from one another in a test tube. The task of the ethnographer, he argued, was to define the physical and mental characteristics of each race (*jinshu*) or ethnic group (*minzoku*). But in advanced nations like Japan this task was almost impossible, because society had been exposed to so many different influences in the course of its history (Torii 1975, 471–480). So he embarked on the painstaking process of analyzing this complex whole, little by little separating out its component parts so that the entire formula that constituted "the Japanese" could be revealed. The main elements in this mixture were the Ainu, who were the earliest inhabitants of Japan; the "Japanese proper" (*koyū no Nihonjin*), an Altaic group whom Torii saw as having migrated to Japan in the Stone and Bronze Ages via the Korean peninsula; a southern Negrito group, who reached Japan via Indonesia; a separate bronze-using group, who originated in Indochina; and the Korean and Chinese immigrants who had been assimilated into the Japanese population in the Nara and Heian periods (Torii 1976b, 381–390). More peripheral influences—perhaps we might call them "trace elements"—included societies like the Uilta, whom Torii saw as having both remote ancestral ties with the "Japanese proper" and long historical contacts with the Japanese state.

The most interesting aspect of this analysis is that, despite his emphasis on diversity, Torii still singled out one racial group as the "Japanese proper": depicted not just as the largest component part but in a sense as the trunk onto which all the minor branches are grafted. The choice of this name gives the whole structure a curiously two-edged character. It allows Torii at once to acknowledge the complexity of the modern Japanese ethnos and to reaffirm the continuous centrality of a single ethnic group, the "Japanese proper," repeatedly referred to as "our ancestors" (e.g., Torii 1976b, 190, 381). So, although Torii clearly saw the prehistoric Ainu as having intermarried with, and in part been absorbed into, the Japanese race, he nonetheless writes that "to begin with, Japan was inhabited by the Ainu, and then later our ancestors migrated into the country"; and although Indochinese are part of the ethnic mixture that becomes the modern Japanese, they are still seen as arriving in Japan bearing techniques that "we Japanese did not know of before" (Torii 1976c, 541; Torii 1976b, 389). This sense of ethnic interaction, not as a random process of mixing but as an ordered pulling-in toward the center, is heightened by the focal position assigned to the emperor:

> the Japanese are not a single ethnic group, but as we have seen a complex of many peoples has created this island empire. However, throughout this time one imperial family with a single lineage has continuously existed. This is truly something unique in the world. It is because numerous ethnic groups have formed Japan with this imperial house at its center that today the mingling of many distinct ways of thought has produced an interesting national character. (Torii 1976b, 390)

In this scheme of things it is important to notice the interplay of the notions of race and ethnicity. Torii himself often used the two terms interchangeably, but his account of the Japanese past depicts many different biological races (Ainu, negritos, Northeast Asian "Japanese proper," etc.) being merged into a single cultural ethnos. In one of Torii's rare excursions into the field of contemporary ethnic politics, he deployed this distinction, with dexterous subtlety, to condemn the views of those who called for

Korean self-determination. The Koreans, as close relatives of the original "Japanese proper," were not, he argued, a separate race from the Japanese and were therefore not entitled to self-determination. On the other hand, the fact that they had a different culture merely provided the grounds for arguing the importance of imperial policies of assimilation (Torii 1976d, 538–539).

Torii's ethnographic perspective, in other words, was molded by the practical opportunities for fieldwork that colonial rule opened up. These opportunities enabled him to collect a superb mass of ethnographic detail, but they also produced a world view that, in a sense, projected the colonial order back onto the past. Japanese ethnicity, like colonial Japanese citizenship, consisted of concentric circles of inclusion. The "Japanese proper," in this scheme of things, play the part of prehistoric *naichijin*, forever assimilating surrounding ethnic groups without losing their own identity. In this way the diversity of the Japanese could be acknowledged without its disturbing the author's, or the reader's, sense of belonging to the still center that absorbs and domesticates difference. Koreans, Ainu, and others could be claimed as part of us without our having to see ourselves as part of them.

Torii Ryūzō's ideas made an immensely important contribution to the intensifying Taishō debate over questions of ethnic identity. Although ideas of racial purity did not disappear, and were to resurface with renewed force in the 1930s, the twin concepts of racial diversity and cultural homogenization had great appeal in the Taishō context and were enthusiastically adopted and developed by other writers (See Yoon 1994, 65–69). Besides Torii himself, the most prominent example was probably the historian Kita Sadakichi. Kita's approach to problems of Japanese ethnicity was in many ways close to Torii's, although Kita was a more enthusiastic popularizer and was always more willing than Torii to draw explicit lessons from prehistory for Japan's imperial present. In answering his own question—"who are the Japanese people?"—Kita recognized that it was necessary to distinguish between two sorts of Japanese citizens. In a broad sense, Japanese imperial subjects included "the descendants of Chinese migrants to Taiwan, and the natives *(seiban)* who live in the Taiwanese mountains, as well as the Koreans—that is, people of the former country of Korea which was recently united to Japan—and also the small numbers of Ainu, Oroks (i.e., Uilta), and Gilyaks (i.e., Nivkh) who live in Hokkaido and Karafuto" (Kita 1921, 119). All of these, however, could be distinguished from the Japanese (or Yamato) ethnic group *(Yamato minzoku)*, the people who had lived "since ancient times in what is today called *naichi:* that is, in Honshu, Shikoku and Kyushu" (Kita 1921, 118).

Like Torii Ryūzō, Kita saw the *Yamato minzoku* as having been created through the intermingling of people from many different origins. As Oguma Eiji has pointed out, his emphasis on ethnic heterogeneity was part of a conscious struggle against the evils of racial and social discrimination; yet ultimately it came to serve the cause of Japanese imperial expansion and assimilationism (Oguma 1995, 119–135). Japan, Kita argued, had originally been inhabited by a variety of races, including ancestors of the present-day Ainu. These races had been subjugated and molded into a single ethnicity by a group of Bronze-Age newcomers who included the ancestors of the Japanese emperors, and who were seen, in a somewhat ill-defined way, as being ancient relatives of the Koreans. This, however, was not the end of the process of ethnic assimilation. Later migrants from Korea and China had also been absorbed into the *Yamato minzoku,* as had the Ainu inhabitants of northern Honshu. Kita disagreed with Torii Ryūzō about the inclusion of a Southeast Asian negrito strain in Japan's ethnic origins but agreed with him in seeing the imperial family as the cornerstone holding together the complex edifice of Japanese ethnicity: the "strongest bond" uniting the *Yamato minzoku* was the presence of "a single imperial line existing from time immemorial" (Kita 1918, 1).

But ethnic unity was a result of Darwinian competition as much as of imperial integration: "the customs and languages of the various elements that make up the Japanese ethnic group have not all been preserved in their original ratios. The superior assimilates the inferior, and the inferior is absorbed by the superior" (Kita [1929] 1978, 214). Thus the celebration of racial purity could be silenced by the claim that Japanese culture was unrivaled precisely because it had been forged by this multicultural process of natural selection; at the same time, the outer circles of imperial subjects—the still unassimilated Ainu, Koreans, Taiwanese, Uilta, Nivkh, and others—could be defined as incomplete Japanese, whose destiny was "little by little, as history has demonstrated, to be totally melted into the single Japanese *minzoku*" (Kita [1929] 1978, 315).

The image of Japan as melting pot, however, raised a new question: how could one recognize the point at which other identities had dissolved into Japaneseness? How, in short, did one become Japanese? The answer to this was not straightforward. Speaking the right language was not enough, for (as Kita pointed out) many Ainu of the younger generation spoke better "standard" Japanese than their contemporaries in the remoter regions of "Japan proper." Many, too, had adopted Japanese customs; indeed the use of customs as a defining feature of ethnic identity was problematic, since regional cultural difference abounded in Japan. The biological boundaries of race were also hazy, because Japanese blood flowed in Ainu veins just as Ainu blood flowed in Japanese veins. In the end, there remained only one impermeable dividing line: "As long as they themselves are conscious of being Ainu, they cannot be regarded as being one with the Japanese ethnic group" (Kita [1929] 1978, 212). In other words, the Ainu, like other members of the outer circles of imperial subjects, had not taken the final step that had marked the assimilation of others before them—they had not "forgotten where they came from" (Kita [1929] 1978, 227).

Out of the struggle with the irreconcilable paradoxes of nationalism and colonialism, nationality and citizenship, ethnocentrism and empire building, there thus arose an image of national identity as a projection of the nation back upon the past. Japan, in this scheme of things, came to be seen as an expanding circle, forever absorbing and consuming difference; "Japanese-ness" was the acknowledgment of this single history—the adoption of a common pool of forebears as "our ancestors"; and assimilation became a matter of amnesia. In this sense, racial diversity was accommodated at the cost of insistence on a single ethnicity. So the historical structures devised by prominent intellectuals to deal with the issues of ethnic diversity and assimilation were framed in a language that excluded the equation of "becoming Japanese" with the acquiring of civil rights and foreclosed the possibility of identifying oneself simultaneously as a member of "the Ainu people," "the Japanese ethnic group," and "the people of the world."

POSTCOLONIAL EPILOGUE

The paradoxes of colonial citizenship, and the theories designed to deal with them, had an influence that lasted far beyond the Pacific War. After Japan's defeat, virtually the entire Ainu population of Karafuto was evacuated to Japan, where they began the task of building a new life in a strange land (NHK 1992). The other indigenous groups—despite their status as "natives," which officially excluded them from conscription—were drafted to carry out transport and espionage activities for the Japanese armed forces in the closing stages of the war. But when, in August 1945, they sought evacuation to Japan, they discovered that the letter of the law had suddenly been reapplied: lacking Japanese family registrations, they were not eligible for places on the evacuation boats. Most of the young men from the Uilta and Nivkh populations were rounded up by the incoming Soviet troops, accused of war crimes because of their "espionage" activities, and sent to labor camps, where about fifty of them died (Tanaka and Dahinien 1978; Tanaka 1993). During the 1950s a small number of survivors and their families were granted resettlement in Japan on the grounds that, as ex-imperial subjects, they were "Japanese in the broad sense of the word" (kōgi no Nihonjin) and should be granted registration on the same basis as "Japanese of Japanese ethnicity" (Nihon minzoku taru Nihonjin) (Choe 1975, 153).

The paradoxes of citizenship and ethnicity therefore still survive, and forgotten origins reappear in new forms to haunt the memories of the next generation. So one of the most thoroughly assimilated of the former Karafuto Ainu can find himself confronted, in the 1990s, by an adult son who knows nothing but Japanese language, life, and education and still asks him "am I Japanese?" (NHK 1992). The prewar intellectual struggles to resolve these dilemmas, too, have continued to shape the language of identity. Although postwar theories have seldom emphasized the central role of the imperial family in the formation of Japaneseness, the image of diverse branches grafted onto a central stock has remained entrenched. Torii Ryūzō's writings exerted a palpable influence over later ethnographers such as Nishimura Shinji and, in the postwar period, Mizuno Yū, in whose works the place of "Japanese proper" was occupied by a neolithic group termed "proto-Japanese" *(gen-Nihonjin)*, "the original basic race of our ethnic group" (Mizuno 1960, 342; Ōbayashi 1991).

From the late 1960s onward, Japan recovered its role as a leading regional power, albeit an economic power, and once again cast a spotlight on the dilemmas of citizenship and identity. Now, however, the issue was not simply the national status of forcibly colonized peoples but of overseas workers who have arrived in Japan voluntarily and in growing numbers. Katō Hidetoshi, echoing Kita Sadakichi's prewar reflections of "Japaneseness," draws comfort from Japan's long history of ethnic assimilation and suggests that these "New Japanese" must be absorbed by developing a "new National learning" that will apply the wisdom of "our ancestors" *(warera no senzo)* and "our ancient sages" *(warera no sengaku)* (Katō 1995, 163).

One purpose of this essay, however, has been to suggest that similar approaches in the past have merely tightened the knot of the irreconcilable contradictions within the modern notions of nationality and citizenship. Today, as populations grow more mobile and the function of the nation-state itself is steadily transformed, it is surely time to turn to the task of unpicking those inherent contradictions: decoupling the entitlement to basic human rights from membership in the nation-state and membership in the nation-state from the vision of an ethnically determined "national spirit." This is not a challenge that Japan alone faces but one that all contemporary nation-states confront in varying ways. At the core of this process lies a rethinking of history, which may free the past from the long shadow cast by the nation-state, making it possible for people to share a common citizenship without necessarily acknowledging the same single engrafted family tree as "our ancestors." To meet the challenges of the future, in other words, it may first be necessary to give those many groups who form (and have always formed) "the Japanese" a choice of pasts.

NOTES

The research on which this essay is based received the support of the Toyota Foundation. I am particularly grateful to Prof. Tanaka Ryō, Mr. Hanazaki Kōhei, Prof. Akizuki Toshiyuki, and Mr. Ishihara Makoto for their advice and assistance in finding the material on which the study is based.

1. Literally, "What is the Japanese Ethnos?" (*Yamato minzoku wa nani zo*). It is interesting that Kita uses the characters "Nihon" but the *furigana* "Yamato."
2. As David Howell notes, in the early stages, it was often difficult to persuade Ainu to work in these fisheries, because their peak season coincided with the months when Ainu families were busy with farming and hunting activities. In 1910, according to a newspaper report, only two of the designated "Ainu fisheries" actually employed Ainu (Howell 1995, 171).
3. The term *naichi* (literally, inland) is somewhat problematic. In official and legal terms, *naichi* included the four main islands of the Japan and the smaller surrounding islands (including Okinawa prefecture). Karafuto was also included after 1943. In popular usage, however, *naichi* excluded Karafuto and Okinawa.
4. The term *kōminken* often refers specifically to voting rights in local elections, but it is unclear from the context of this petition whether the word is being used in that sense here.

REFERENCES

Akizuki Toshiyuki. 1994. *Nichirō kankei to Saharintō*. Chikuma Shobō.

Arima Midori. 1990. "An Ethnographic and Historical Study of Ogasawara/the Bonin Islands, Japan." Ph.D. diss., Stanford University.

Bhabha, Homi. 1994. *The Location of Culture*. London: Routledge.

Choe Chan-Fa. 1975. *Kokuseki to jinken*. Sakai Shoten.

Fujii Naomasa. 1938. "Mushi sareta dojin taisaku." *Karafuto* 12.11:68–71.

Grant, Bruce. 1995. *In the Soviet House of Culture: A Century of Perestroikas*. Princeton: Princeton University Press.

"Hokumon no mamori Karafuto tenrankai." 1940. *Karafuto jihō* 33:69–77.

Hora Tomio. 1956. *Karafuto shi kenkyū*. Shinjusha.

Howell, David. 1995. *Capitalism from Within: Economy, State and Society in a Japanese Fishery*. Berkeley: University of California Press.

Ivanov, S. V., A. V. Smolyak, and M. G. Levin. 1964. "The Oroks." In *The Peoples of Siberia*, edited by M. G. Levin and L. P. Potapov, 761–766. Chicago: University of Chicago Press.

Karafuto Ainu Shi Kenkyākai, ed. 1992. *Tsuishikari ni ishibumi*. Sapporo: Hokkaido Shuppan Kikaku Sentā.

Karafuto Chō, ed. 1973. *Karafuto Chō shisei sanjūnen shi*. 2 vols. 1936. Reprint, Hara Shobō.

Karafuto Chūō Shikenjo. 1942. *Sōritsu jūnen kinenshū*. Toyohara. Karafuto Chūō Shikenjo.

Kasai Takechiyo. 1927. "Karafuto dojin kenkyū shiryō." Mimeographed report.

Kasai Takeshi. 1941. "Otasu no dojintachi." *Karafuto* 13.10:104–107.

Katō Hidetoshi. 1995. "Shin 'ijin' kō." *Chūō kōron* (February):144–164.

Kawabe Katsushi. 1942. "Atarashiki hoppō seikatsu." *Karafuto* 14.6:18–22.

Kawamura Hideya. 1937. "Orokko, Giriyāku no seikatsu to fūzoku." *Karafuto Chōhō* 6:155–165.

———. 1938. "Karafuto ken shikan." Pt. 2. *Karafuto chōhō* 19:53–75.

Kita Sadakichi. 1918. "'Minzoku to rekishi' hakkan shuisho." *Minzoku to rekishi* 1.1:1–8.

———. 1921. "Nihon minzoku no seiritsu." Pt. 1. *Minzoku to rekishi* 5.2:117–140.

———. [1929] 1978. "Nihon minzokushi gaisetsu." In *Nihon minzoku bunka taikei 5: Kita Sadakichi*, edited by M. Ueda, 211–316. Reprint, Kodansha.

Mizuno Yū. 1960. *Nihon minzoku no genryū.* Yūzankaku.

Morimoto Setsuo. 1930. "Karafuto ni okeru dojin no kokuseki ni tsuite." In *Hakubutsukan kyōiku*, edited by Karafuto Chō Hakubutsukan, 14–17. Toyohara: Karafuto Chō Hakubutsukan.

Morris-Suzuki, Tessa. 1994. "Collective Memory, Collective Forgetting: Indigenous People and the Nation State in Japan and Australia." *Meanjin* 53.4:597–612.

Nakanome Akira. 1917. *Karafuto no hanashi.* Sanseidō.

———. 1918. *Dojin kyōka ron.* Iwanami Shoten.

NHK Hokkaido. 1992. *Wakasakanai: Yakusoku no mura.* Documentary film broadcast on October 29.

Nishijima Sadaki. 1977. *Karafuto no rekishi.* 1941. Reprint, Kokusho Kankōkai.

Ōbayashi Taryō. 1991. "An Ethnological Study of Japan's Ethnic Culture: A Historical Survey." *Acta Asiatica* 61:1–23.

Oguma Eiji. 1995. *Tan'itsu minzoku shinwa no kigen.* Shinyōsha.

Royal Institute of International Affairs. 1937. *The British Empire.* Oxford: Oxford University Press.

Sakaiya Taiichi. 1993. *What is Japan?* Kodansha International.

Satō Bunmei. 1988. *Koseki uragaeshikō.* Meiseki Shoten.

Satomi Kishio. 1939. *Nihon seiji no kokutaiteki kōzō.* Nihon Hyōronsha.

Shiratori Yoshirō and Yawata Ichirō. 1978. *Nihon minzoku bunka taikei 9: Shiratori Kurakichi, Torii Ryūzō.* Kodansha.

Shisuka Dojin Jimusho. 1935. Orokko sono ta dojin no kyōiku. Hisuka: Shisuka Dojin Jimusho.

Shubin, V. O. 1992. "Zhizn 'Kuril'tsev' na Kamchatke v 1877–1888 godax." *Kraevedecheskii Byulleten* (Yuzhno-Sakhalinsk) 3.4:37–52.

Stephan, John. 1971. *Sakhalin: A History.* Oxford: Clarendon Press.

Sureda, A. Rigo. 1973. *The Evolution of the Right to Self-Determination: A Study of United Nations Practice.* Leiden: A. W. Sijthoff.

Tanaka, Ryō. 1993. *Saharin hokui gojūdo sen.* Kusa no Ne Shuppankai.

Tanaka Ryō and Dahinien Gendānu. 1978. *Gendānu: Aru hoppō shōsū minzoku no dorama.* Gendaishi Shuppankai.

Torii Ryūzō. 1975. "Jinrui no kenkyū wa ika naru hōhō ni yorubeki ya." In *Torii Ryūzō zenshū.* Vol. 1, 471–480. 1910. Reprint, Asahi Shimbunsha.

————. 1976a. "Aru rōgakuto no shuki: Kōkogaku to tomo ni rokujūnen." In *Torii Ryūzō zenshū.* Vol. 12, 137–343. 1953. Reprint, Asahi Shimbunsha.

————. 1976b. "Yūshi izen no Nihon." In *Torii Ryūzō zenshū.* Vol. 8, 167–405. 1925. Reprint, Asahi Shimbunsha.

————. 1976c. "Yūshi izen no Nikkan kankei." In *Torii Ryūzō zenshū.* Vol. 12, 539–541. 1920. Reprint, Asahi Shimbunsha.

————. 1976d. "Nikkanjin wa 'dogen' nari." In *Torii Ryūzō zenshū.* Vol. 12, 538. 1920. Reprint, Asahi Shimbunsha.

Ubukata Naokichi. 1979. "Tan'itsu minzoku kokka no shisō to kinō: Nihon no baai." *Shisō* 656 (February): 23–37.

Umehara Takeshi. 1990. *Nihon to wa nani ka.* NHK Books.

Utari Kyōkai, ed. 1989. *Ainu shi.* Vol. 4, pt. 2. Sapporo: Hokkaido Utari Kyōkai.

Vishnevskii, Nikolai. 1994. *Otasu.* Yuzhno-Sakhalinsk: Dal'nevostochnoe Knizhnoe Izdatel'stvo.

Yamada Saburō. 1933. "Pōtsumasu jōyaku daijōjō to Karafuto dojin no kokuseki mondai." *Hōgaku Kyōkai gojūshūnen kinen ronshū.* Vol. 1, 3–34. Hōgaku Kyōkai.

Yoon Keun-Cha. 1994. *Minzoku gensō no satetsu: Nihonjin no jikozō.* Iwanami Shoten.

Yoshino Kosaku. 1992. *Cultural Nationalism in Contemporary Japan: A Sociological Enquiry.* London: Routledge.

⇛ 8 ⇚

Culture, Ethnicity, and the State in Early Twentieth-Century Japan

KEVIN M. DOAK

Some sense of ethnic Japanese identity may be projected retroactively through Japanese history to the murky ancient beginning, but for the modern sense of the ethnic nation in Japan we need look no further back than the late nineteenth and early twentieth century. Here one finds the emergence of a very specific use of ethnicity, along with a new term, *minzoku* (the ethnic nation), to redefine national membership in the context of the modern political state (Yoon 1993, 16–19). This newly formulated sense of ethnic national identity carried with it a complex assortment of political values that drew from and subsequently helped inform attitudes toward racism, fascism, populism, and even democracy. To understand the fragility and nature of debates on democracy in early twentieth-century Japan, we need to gain a better understanding of how positive appraisals of ethnic national identity in Japan were reinforced not only by beliefs in racial superiority and chauvinistic nationalism but also by a sense of popular disenfranchisement and mass movements. Given the complexity in how ethnic national identity emerged in modern Japan, it will not suffice to offer generalizations that simply equate ethnic identity with the Meiji state nor with a belief in racial homogeneity, since the actual use of this new concept of ethnic identity reveals a remarkable degree of flexibility and change in practice and in political value. Until we come to better terms with how this new, and largely twentieth-century, concept of ethnic nationality developed in relationship to the Meiji state, we will fail to grasp important aspects of democracy and democratic theory in prewar Japan.

On the eve of the twentieth century, representations of national identity in Japan were turning from an emphasis on the recently constructed Meiji state to a naturalized version of the ethnic nation built around cultural and populist motifs. One early attempt to redefine the Meiji concept of national identity is evident in the 1899 Nationality Law and the Law for the Protection of Former Hokkaido Aborigines. Here we already find some of the earliest references to a concept of the ethnic nation emerging in reference to Hokkaido and the Ainu people. There was nothing unique about Japanese encounters with ethnic minorities. A transformation of national identity along ethnic lines was, in fact, beginning to spread across the globe in the early twentieth century, and many nations were grappling with ways of establishing national identity in the context of reassertions of ethnic identity. The timing and form of the debate on ethnic national identity in Japan reminds us how broader historical events influenced public discourse in Japan, just as that discourse reinterpreted the significance of events at home and abroad.

This growing ethnic national consciousness in early twentieth-century Japan can best be explained as a process that superimposed domestic anxieties on international trends in race and racial studies. The final decade of the nineteenth century witnessed a nearly universal obsession with the racial struggle that Ludwig Gumplowicz had outlined in *Der Rassenkampf (The Race Conflict)* as early as 1883. Heightened concerns over worldwide racial competition as the determining force in world politics loomed as one of the manifestations of a fin de siècle anxiety that was truly global in character, spilling beyond the border of Europe into East Asia. In China, even before the turn of the century, Zhang Binglin had developed a global view of politics that was premised on a belief in an inevitable war between the White and Yellow races (Chow 1994). Gumplowicz found fertile ground in Japan, as well, thanks in no small part to educator and journalist Takayama Chogyū, who predicted that the twentieth century would merely be a continuation of "the 600 year old racial war (*jinshu kyōsō*) between the Aryan race and the Turanian race" (Takayama [1900] 1930, 5:313). Chogyū's thought frequently mingled race and nation, as his concerns were as political as they were biological. Chogyū's suggestion that the betrayal of Turkey, the "Asia of Europe," at the Congress of Berlin in 1878 had simply caused the conflict between the races to move further east, to become the "Far Eastern problem," is at first rather perplexing. But when seen in the context not only of the 1897 war between Greece and Turkey but also the earlier 1875–1878 Russo-Turkish War, Russia's role in the Triple Intervention, and growing competition between Russia and Japan over Korea, one gets a better sense of what it meant for Chogyū to declare Turkey "the Asia of Europe."

Race alone was not a sufficient response in the harsh realities of international competition: a specific nation had to lead, and Chogyū believed that leading nation had to be Japan. The "Turanian race," like all races, was composed of what Chogyū called (in German) *Naturvölker (shizen minzoku)* and *Kulturvölker* (*jinbun minzoku*), the former indicating backward nations still mired in a state of nature and the latter representing modern nations that had left the stage of nature and constructed a particular national culture and a state (Takayama [1898] 1930, 5:20–22). Chogyū drew from such different thinkers as Henry George and Max Müller to conclude that the state cannot be reduced to the territory it holds but must include infrastructure and productive facilities, which the government is merely entrusted to manage. In essence, Chogyū employed a distinction (although one he did not always employ consistently) between a broader concept of the nation founded in the people that historically preceded the state and the state as a construct of, and managing agency for, the people. Culture, state, and the people were, however, closely connected for, as Chogyū argued, "generally, the development of culture requires the establishment of a state, and the establishment of a state requires a sovereign people and a definite territory" (Takayama [1898] 1930, 5:33). And since the "Turanian race" only had one *Kulturvölk*, equipped with a powerful state to defend it, all Asians (especially Koreans) should rely on Japan in what Chogyū could already see as the impending war with Russia.

THE ORIGINS OF THE ETHNIC NATIONALIST CHALLENGE, 1900–1914

As I noted above, the formation of ethnic national discourse in modern Japan interwove issues concerning the race, culture, the nation, and the state in a complex manner, and the precise conditions of its formation still elude complete understanding. Western theories on race and the state were not the only factors mobilizing this concern with ethnicity in Japan. By 1900 there was a broadly shared discourse on ethnic national identity throughout East Asia that was both a response to developments in Western social and political theory and a reflection of the specific conditions in each particular country. This discourse eventually would claim a common "East Asian" component that drew on elements of a shared modern political vocabulary and some overlapping concerns with national viability in the face of encroachments by Western imperial powers. Japanese, Chinese, and Koreans who wrote about ethnic nationality were often reading each others' writings, although they retained considerable autonomy over how they interpreted and applied what they read in their own national contexts.

One of the earliest incarnations of this East Asian discourse on national identity may be found in the Chinese-language *Yi shu hui pien*, a "monthly magazine of translated political works," that was published in Tokyo by Sakazaki Sakan.[1] The magazine's August 1901 issue opened with a translation of "Book One: The Nation" from Columbia University professor John

W. Burgess' *Political Science and Comparative Constitutional Law*. Burgess began his discussion of the nation by declaring that "primarily and properly the word nation is a term of ethnology, and the concept expressed by it is an ethnologic concept" (Burgess 1893, 1). Burgess' concept of the ethnic nation was well translated into Chinese as *minzu* (J: *minzoku*), as was his qualification that "I do not include common descent and sameness of race as qualities necessary to national existence" (Burgess 1893, 2; *Yi shu hui pien*, August 1901, 2–3). But his insistence on "how very important it is to distinguish clearly the nation, both in word and idea, from the state" was either lost on his translators, or more likely, intentionally omitted from the Chinese translation, which merely noted that the nation is not always necessary in constructing the state (Burgess 1893, 4; *Yi shu hui pien*, August 1901, 4).[2]

In China, of course, the revolutionists who sought to overthrow the Manchu Qing dynasty had every reason to ignore Burgess' distinction between the ethnic nation and the state, as they believed that modern China ought to be a single Han ethnic nation-state. By defining the vast majority of Chinese as belonging to one, single ethnic nation, Sun Yat-sen could mobilize this concept of the ethnic nation as early as 1904 to differentiate the Chinese from Western peoples (Luo 1971, 105–106). The interconnectedness of the discourse on ethnic nationalism in East Asia is further supported by the work of An Ch'ang-ho who founded the Taesong School in Korea in 1907 and encouraged young Korean nationalists to read Liang Qichao's writings. An's Korean nationalists were impressed by Liang's distinction between historical and nonhistorical ethnic nations (Allen 1990, 789), a distinction that recalls Takayama's *Naturvölker* and *Kulturvölker*.

In Japan, however, where the question of state formation was more settled than it was in Korea and where, unlike China, there was no history of ethnic minority rule, this dialogue on the ethnic nation and the political state was reshaped to fit Japan's own historical and social conditions. In Japan, nation followed state: that is to say, ethnic nationalism's focus on the "people" as the source of national legitimacy developed in the context of a growing popular antagonism toward an already existing Meiji state, rather than as a condition for building a modern nation-state. A strong sense of antagonism between the state and the people was already palpable in the 1905 Hibiya Riots. Certainly, the executions that followed the High Treason Incident of 1910 did little to assuage fears of populists and socialists that the Meiji state was little interested in serving the interests of the Japanese people. And while the chilling effects of the executions of Kōtoku Shūsui and his alleged coconspirators would hold socialist populism at bay for a while, the lessons of the Hibiya Riots provided an example of how populism might be directed against the state. But if the High Treason case could be used to label attacks on the state as extremist and unpatriotic, the same strategy would not succeed with the mass rallies held to "protect constitutional government" that broke out in late 1912 and early 1913.

To recognize the partisan bickering among political elites within the movement to protect constitutional government in no way undermines the broader sense of nationalism that was unleashed by the movement. All nationalist movements are inevitably the result of elite attempts to represent the nation. What is more important is how this crisis of constitutional government that occurred simultaneously with the beginning of the Taishō period employed metaphors for national identity that eventually transcended the elite partisan debates that had sparked the crisis.

A good example is Katō Hiroyuki's desperate attempt to save the work of the Meiji state builders in his defense of state sovereignty. Katō tried to walk a narrow line between Minobe Tatsukichi's suggestion that the people were central to the modern constitutional state *(kunmin dōchi)* and the insistence of Hozumi Yatsuka and Uesugi Shinkichi that Japan's sovereignty rested in its unique national tradition of the "emperor" *(tennō)*. Katō rejected both theories for failing to appreciate fully how universal natural science supported the legitimacy of the Japanese state. That is, Minobe's popular sovereignty failed because it relied on an old, indigenous term *(kunmin dōchi)* that was not in keeping with the origins of the modern Japanese state that Katō knew was based in Western theories of monarchical governments. Similarly, Hozumi and Uesugi went too far, Katō argued, in suggesting that Japan's monarchy was unique, when in fact it was in keeping with the universal principles of "natural science" (Katō [1913] 1990, 630, 632, 633, 644). Katō rejected the idea that the people are natural and the state artificial, maintaining that the reverse is true. The state is natural, he insisted, since it accords well with "natural science" (Katō never really specifies what "natural science" means, beyond the common legal principles Japan shared with Western states); and the people are not a natural or organic body, since the modern political concept of the people is the *kokumin*, the recently constructed concept of the nation that, according to Katō, is not based on an exclusive ethnic identity (Katō [1913] 1990, 647).

To understand what was at stake in this constitutional debate, especially for the later development of ethnic nationalism, it might be helpful to view the debate through Stanley Payne's typology of the political right in prewar Germany. Payne has identified two major rightist movements in prewar Germany (in addition to fascism): conservative authoritarians and the radical right (Payne 1980, 3–21). Katō best fits the category of conservative authoritarian in that he sought to reinforce the traditional social hierarchy, avoid the uncertainties of populism, and shore up the monarchy through traditional Meiji legal principles. His rejection of Hozumi and Uesugi's revision of the Japanese monarchy also suggests some of the differences posed by the radical right, who also used traditional principles but were more reactionary in their ideal form on monarchy. And just as the radical right in Germany drew closer to the military than the conservative authoritarians, Uesugi and Hozumi's legal theories found more favor than Katō's among Japanese militarists during the 1930s.[3] As a conservative authoritarian, Katō saw the new critique of the constitutional Japanese state as insufficiently national owing to the multiethnic mix *(sū minzoku kondō)* that colonization had brought to modern Japanese society. Katō maintained that the existence of the majority ethnic Japanese was no obstacle to the integration of other ethnic nations since the transcendental state was not fundamentally a populist or national body. In the end, the people could not be the goal of the state's existence, since "the interests and happiness of the people and the state are contradictory and conflict" (Katō [1913] 1990, 647, 660). In short, Katō tried to deflect the challenge to the state posed from the ethnic national perspective by subordinating ethnic groups to the constitutional state, where they could lend legitimacy to the state without challenging his fundamental concept of the elitist political state as the sole, legitimate representation of Japanese national identity.

Katō's attempt to defend the Japanese multiethnic state was, of course, also a defense of Japanese colonization, specifically the right of a transnational Japanese state to annex the Korean nation, which had just taken place in 1910. Colonization would strongly influence the subsequent direction of debates over national identity, the state, and the meaning of democracy in Japan. Others found it difficult to overlook the attacks on Japanese nationals in China in September of 1913 and found in this incident evidence that seemed to belie Katō's sanguine assessment of the harmonious multiethnic state.

In 1914, Professor Matsumoto Hikojirō of Keiō University suggested that these ethnic attacks on Japanese in China required a consideration of ethnicity as the core of national identity. He noted that many Japanese were increasingly turning to pride in their ethnic identity, and he offered reasons why, suggesting that an interest in the ancient Japanese *Volk (minzoku)* enjoyed a tremendous upsurge in early 1913 by many scholars who were "stimulated by the political crisis of spring 1913, became aware of popular movements, and looked for analogous historical evidence" (Matsumoto 1914, 228). For his part, Matsumoto called for a recognition of the centrality of religion, not as dogma but as an expression of national life. The religion he had in mind was not state Shintoism but a conglomerate religion that included bits and pieces of native Shinto beliefs, indigenized Buddhism, and even Christianity; and he drew on the Ikkō uprisings and the Shimabara rebellion as historical evidence of the populist incorporation of foreign religions. Matsumoto's challenge to Katō rested on a belief that the nation was neither artificial nor rational but rather fundamentally ethnic and emotional. He even criticized his colleague in ethnology, Takagi Toshio, for relying too heavily on natural science instead of idealism, and he invited his colleagues to follow the example of Wilhelm Max Wundt's *Elements of Folk Psychology* as a more appropriate path to understanding the primacy of the *Volk* nation over the modern state (Matsumoto 1914, 234).

However, the Austrian-Hungarian Empire declared war on Serbia, and in the midst of the string of declarations of war that followed, Japan declared war on the German and Austrian-Hungarian empires. Before the year was out, Japan was technically allied with France, the United Kingdom, Belgium, Russia, Italy, Serbia, and Rumania and at war with Germany, Austria-Hungary, Turkey, and Bulgaria. Although Japan played a very minor role in fighting the war, concentrating mainly on acquiring German colonies in East Asia, the symbolic effects of Japan's new alliances were significant in reshaping how ethnic nationality, democracy, and the state were conceived at home. Key among these new alliances was that with Russia against (among others) Turkey. No longer would Turkey seem, as it did to Chogyū, "the Asia of Europe."

WORLD WAR I AND THE GROWTH OF ETHNIC NATIONALISM, 1914–1920

World War I and the events surrounding it had a tremendous, perhaps unparalleled, influence on the evolution of the discourse on state and nationality in early twentieth-century Japan. The most immediate effect was a renewed, positive appraisal of the progressive implications of ethnic nationality. Even Turkey, with its multiethnic empire, no longer seemed a suitable model for democratic aspirations in Asia. Instead, Serbia and its allies represented the progressive hopes of people throughout the world who fought against foreign imperialists. Asano Risaburō made the most extreme case, arguing for nearly a year in the leading historical journal *Shigaku* that the Slavs and Asians had ethnic affinities that stemmed from the thirteenth-century Mongolian invasions of Europe (Asano 1914–1915). In the political climate of the day, Asano's point was as difficult to miss as his serialized article was hard to avoid in the historical profession: the Yugoslavs, an oppressed nationality of the Austrian-Hungarian empire, were Japan's natural allies, as was "Slavic" Russia, now formally aligned with Japan in the European war.

Almost immediately, Katō Hiroyuki sensed the potential for a new challenge to the Japanese state, this time not limited to the radical right but extending as well to those who would use ethnic nationalism to support internationalist and populist causes. He conceded examples of influence across races and nations, specifically noting Asano's argument on the influence of Asian *Volk* in Russian history; but he relegated that kind of cross-fertilization to the ancient past. Such mutual influences were possible only in an age when national identities were less clearly formed and at any rate were "not something one is likely to find in our enlightened age" (Katō [1915] 1990, 3:747). Katō returned to his earlier argument that the Japanese state was well founded on a core ethnic nation, but he now cast the argument with a completely new emphasis:

> The relation between the sovereign and the people [in Japan] is not at all like those in other countries. Ours is that of a natural guardian just like the father of a child, and the way our imperial house looks after its subjects and the way the subjects look up to the imperial house is something other countries cannot even approximate (Katō [1915] 1990, 3:741).

In stressing the uniqueness of the relationship between the sovereign and the people in Japan, Katō had clearly moved back to the right, closer to Hozumi and Uesugi than his earlier stance on universal nature had allowed.

What changes had led Katō to reconsider the uniqueness of the Japanese monarchy? The outbreak of World War I generally had pitted republics and democracies against the empires of Germany and Austria-Hungary, and Japan (eyeing German possessions in China) found itself allied with the nonmonarchies against Katō's favorite, Germany. To differentiate Japan from weak republics like France and China, and from imperial Germany, with whom Japan was now at war, Japan's own monarchy had to be represented as an exception, a unique patriarchy justifiable by its natural claims of ethnicity, while at the same time keeping ethnic nationalism itself at a safe distance from the imperial, multiethnic state. This delicate balancing act required that Katō denounce religion as superstition while attempting to support, in secular terms, a state based on the unique, and supposedly divine, emperor (Katō [1915] 1990, 3:755). Katō's secularism well may have been directed at Matsumoto Hikojirō's call for a return to the religious sentiment of the ethnic nation as the popular foundation for the modern state. Katō still had no illusions about popular democracy: the state would remain in the hands of a rational elite, even if events required more rhetoric about the cultural foundations of the state in the unique traditions of the Japanese ethnic nation.

If Katō's breathtaking redefinition of "natural" from universal law to Japan's specific form of paternalism was meant to neutralize the power of ethnic nationalism's challenge to the Japanese imperial state, it was less than a complete success. Attempts to remove ethnic nationalism from the political realm and relegate it to nature or biology simply yielded more confusion. Professor Yamamoto Miono of Kyoto University also understood ethnicity as a natural product of human instincts, seeing the problem of ethnic nationalism as essentially a racial problem. His confusion of race and ethnicity seemed to him to explain the independence movements in India, Africa, and the Philippines, but it left him baffled by the national liberation movements within Japan's own supposedly monoracial empire. Since independence movements in Taiwan and Korea could not be "racial," they were merely "blind acts by stupid people who are suffering real oppression in their daily lives" (Yamamoto 1916, 59). The solution to relieving this real oppression, Yamamoto suggested, was to be found in Hugh Edward Egerton's proposal that increasing overseas settlements could be used as a means of weakening the independence movements in the colonies. But Yamamoto felt that Japan had to go beyond such a passive role to create a common identity with its colonies on the basis of shared "racial" consciousness. To Yamamoto, this meant that Japan had a great opportunity to educate colonials with a sense of common racial consciousness, a job that would not be too difficult since racial consciousness *(minzoku-teki jikaku)* was, after all, a "natural human instinct" (Yamamoto 1916, 58).

But encouraging *minzoku* consciousness could have vastly different outcomes depending on what precisely *minzoku* was supposed to mean. Most Japanese commentators during the World War I period did not equate *minzoku* with race, as Yamamoto did. Shiozawa Masasada, head of the Department of Political Economy at Waseda University, warned of the perils of a *minzoku tōsō,* by which he meant the increasing nationalist competition (e.g., between England and Germany) that was shaping the global economy (Shiozawa 1916, 28–29). Historian Tanaka Suiichirō, who established the Mita Historiographical Association and would play an increasingly important role in the discourse on the nation, introduced Rudolph Springer's theories on nation *(minzoku)* and state *(kokka)*, in which the two concepts should be kept "as separate as religion and politics" (Tanaka 1916, 21). Perhaps the most widely read attempt to position *minzoku* consciousness in the context of race and nation in Asia during the war was the 1916 volume *The Nations of the Far East,* edited by Tokutomi Sohō. In contrast to the professional historical journals, *The Nations of the Far East* was aimed at a broader audience and was written in clear prose with *furigana* to aid in reading difficult vocabulary.[4]

The author, a certain Nakamura, opened the work by directly addressing the vexing problem of what *minzoku* represents:

> *Minzoku* corresponds to both the English word "nation" and the German word *"Volk."* But these two words in English and German are not precisely defined. *"Volk,"* for example, merely indicates those residents of a certain district or country, but many people use it to mean a composite people [*minshu*] with a single character or a common temperament. More recently, even Germans have been eager to use the word "nation." (Nakamura 1916, 6–7)

As this passage reveals, Nakamura noted that *minzoku,* from its association with the German word *Volk,* carried with it broadly based popular, even democratic *(minshu)* connotations. Moreover, he insisted that *minzoku* is not the same thing as "race" *(jinshu),* as the latter concept is entirely based on physical appearance whereas *minzoku* is a political term. Nakamura's definition of *minzoku* as "nation" and not simply as "race" would prove long lasting, influencing many others in the interwar dialogue on Japanese nationalism, including the liberal Yanaihara Tadao; indeed, his definition remains enshrined today in the authoritative Japanese dictionary, *Kōjien.* But more importantly, his rejection of the racial interpretation of *minzoku* must be seen, first and foremost, as an attempt to refute Yamamoto and (indirectly) Katō, who had tried to equate the nation with the state by relegating the concept of *minzoku* to the natural category of race.

Yet, it is when Nakamura contrasts *minzoku* with *kokumin* (political nation) as variants of the English concept of nation that the complexity of the implications of the debate about nation becomes apparent. First, Nakamura insisted on a distinction between *minzoku* and *kokumin:*

> As I explained above, the two words *minzoku* and *kokumin* are often confused in their usage, but strictly speaking, *kokumin* is a legalistic term. Simply from a common sense, realistic perspective, *kokumin* should be considered an element in the composition of the state, or a unit in the group that is the state. . . . [m]inzoku approaches the problem from a tribal [*shuzoku-teki*] or cultural perspective and *kokumin* approaches the problem from a political or legal perspective. But the two are not the same thing. (Nakamura 1916, 10)

Later Nakamura admitted that the concept of *minzoku* at times includes elements from race and the political nation, but this attempt at a distinction between *minzoku* and *kokumin,* along with his extended analysis of various models of state structures and their ethnic compositions, underscores how well his definition of *minzoku* was influenced by Burgess' notion that the nation refers essentially to an ethnic nation (Nakamura 1916, 11–14).

What this definition of the nation as an ethnic group meant in the context of the changing political world in 1916 is more troubling. Nakamura acknowledged as many as thirteen (including Korean) different ethnic nations in a single Japanese political nation. Yet, the core of his book is a detailed treatment of the various ethnic nations in China, and Nakamura calls the Han ethnic nation an artificial composite of several ethnic groups (Nakamura 1916, 35). To do so, of course, was to undermine the fragile sense of Chinese national identity at a critical moment. A rejection of Chinese Han ethnic national identity might be seen as a defense of other ethnic national minorities in China. Nakamura, however, was more concerned with Japanese national interests. His conclusion that "we must step forth, go to the continent and do our utmost to manage affairs there" (Nakamura 1916, 351) positioned his study on ethnic nations in the Far East alongside such apologists for Japanese colonialism as Uchida Ryōhei, who argued that China, with all its ethnic national tensions, was not yet a state.

Informing much of this subtle shifting of positions on ethnic nationality and the state were changes in the prosecution of the war. From late 1916 to early 1917, it seemed briefly as though the war might end. Germany appealed to the United States to negotiate terms for peace, but Wilson responded instead with his own set of conditions. By January 1917, the Allied Powers made it clear that cessation of hostilities would be predicated on, among other things, political reorganization of Europe on the basis of (ethnic) nationality. This was, of course, unacceptable to imperial Germany, and on April 6 the United States declared war on Germany. The effect of having the United States (represented by the "internationalist" President Wilson) on the side of ethnic nationalism was profound and somewhat confusing. One immediate result was a general reconsideration of the compatibility of ethnic nationalism, liberalism, democracy, and global peace throughout the world.

An early attempt at reviving liberal hopes for ethnic nationalism in Japan was made by Professor Sakaguchi Takakimi of Kyoto Imperial University. Within weeks after the United States entered the war, Sakaguchi wrote that the issue of global racial competition was no longer as compelling as the related problems of the ethnic nation, the political nation, and what he called "world culture" *(sekai bunka)*. Sakaguchi adopted a liberal position on the issue of ethnic identity, rejecting biological determinism and offering instead an argument based on environmental influences and the constant reshaping of cultures. Like Nakamura, Sakaguchi recognized the existence and legitimacy within the Japanese political nation of various other ethnic nations, such as the Ainu, Koreans, and Taiwanese. But more so than Nakamura, Sakaguchi stressed the role of culture as a common national undertaking that elevated citizens beyond the constraints of nature. Thus, he wrote that "historically speaking, the most essential issue when discussing any racial problem, or any racial competition, is what kind of culture accompanies the mixture of blood. . . . And this culture is not determined simply by what kind of blood mixture occurs. It is influenced by all sorts of other factors" (Sakaguchi 1917, 100–101). A people may be a *Kulturnation (bunka kokumin)*, but only when they have formed themselves into a *Staatsnation (kokka kokumin)* have they achieved the final point in national development (Sakaguchi 1917, 103–105; the German terms are Sakaguchi's).

The state was not automatically an inherently unpopular institution, nor was cosmopolitan culture necessarily incompatible with ethnic nationalism. States, Sakaguchi maintained, have historically been based on either the nobility or the people *(minshū)*, but current trends seemed to him to support states based on the people. Given the international trend toward national self-determination as a liberal goal, Sakaguchi rejected a narrow interpretation that posited nationalism as the antithesis of globalism:

> This trend [toward national states] is certainly not a rejection of global culture. It is a trend that, while encouraging the development of ethnic nations *(minzoku kokumin)*, also increasingly requires the propagation and influx of global culture for the sake of the ethnic nation itself. This is because the furthering of global culture refines the national state and its global policies and is absolutely necessary as a means of ensuring the happiness of the people of all states. (Sakaguchi 1917, 114)

In contrast to Sakaguchi's belief that cosmopolitanism and ethnic nationalism were mutually reinforcing, Abe Jirō, writer and editor of the journal *Shichō*, worried about ethnic nationalism being oppressed in the name of universalism and the modern state. "To suppress the special character of an ethnic nation and reduce it to the mean number of a 'humanity,'" Abe insisted, "is just as harmful as to force the particularity of individuals to conform with a concept of ethnic national character" (Abe 1917, 108). In other words, Abe believed that ethnic nationalism was as rife with multiple possibilities as the individual person was. What was important, from his "liberal" ethnic nationalist perspective, was to work toward a more just, ideal world through ethnic nationalism. He rejected Yamamoto Miono's approach for merely confirming a specific ethnic identity that was frozen in the past. Ethnic national consciousness should instead help to "assimilate oneself to the ethnic national spirit that is alive and that connects past, present, and future," and he noted that such a progressive grasp of ethnic nationalism was more compatible with the true meaning of international justice than was "imperialist statism" *(teikokushugi-teki kokkashugi)* (Abe 1917, 116–119).

From late 1917 to early 1918, most serious observers knew the fighting in Europe was all but over, and farsighted minds turned to the question of how the postwar world would be structured. In an address to the Congress on January 8, President Wilson outlined his principle of national self-determination, which was quickly reported all over the world. In Japan, as throughout East Asia, Wilson became known as an advocate of ethnic national self-determination *(minzoku jiketsushugi)*. Professor Tanaka Suiichirō, who a few years earlier had elucidated the difference between "nations" and "states," expressed shock that world reform would be attempted on such contradictory terms as the proposed League of Nations and ethnic nationalism, a principle that, if seriously implemented, ultimately would destroy even the states that formed the League (Tanaka 1918, 23). Tanaka did not favor absolute state supremacy, and he welcomed Wundt's suggestion that the postwar era would be one of humanism instead of the statism of the prewar years. But he was unwilling to believe that humanism and peace were better realized through ethnic nationalism than through the political structure of the state where ethnic identities could, and should, be assimilated.

Tanaka's worries about the League of Nations were dismissed by the legal scholar Matsuda Tomoyuki, who argued that the League was necessary and must support ethnic nationalism even if this meant a further disruption in world peace. Anything less than full support for all ethnic nationalist movements, including Tanaka's professed pacifism, was merely a defense of imperialism (Matsuda 1919, 18). But neither Tanaka nor Matsuda went as far as Yamamoto Miono, who returned to his earlier confusion of ethnicity and race to argue that the League could not really be interested in both ethnic nationalism and global peace if it rejected the Japanese proposal for ending racial discrimination (*jinshu-teki sabetsu*). Yamamoto then presented a spectacular confusion of democracy, ethnic nationalism, and the Monroe Doctrine, concluding that all were equally threats to Japanese national interest (Yamamoto 1919, 52–54).

As the delegates met at Versailles, hopes were raised that ethnic nationalism might hasten the democratic process. Intellectual and social activist Ōyama Ikuo recognized that the principle of ethnic national self-determination was ultimately a form of statism, but he hoped that this new nationalism would not be a "subjugating imperialism" like the old statism but would result in a kind of "international harmonism" (Ōyama 1919, 82–83). Professor Yoshino Sakuzō of Tokyo Imperial University saw the current world reform based on ethnic nationalism as the completion of the democratic movement that began with "nineteenth-century civilization" (Yoshino 1919, 90). Clearly, both men were writing in response to the rise of ethnic nationalism in Korea, where, under the influence of Wilson's principle of ethnic national self-determination, the March First Movement for national independence had just broken out. But as their attention eventually returned to Japanese domestic affairs, their optimism for ethnic nationalism was gradually tempered, for the decade that followed presented an even more complex interweaving of issues related to social democracy, ethnic nationalism, imperialism, and the state.

ETHNIC NATIONALISM AT THE HEIGHT OF TAISHŌ DEMOCRACY, 1920–1930

In the aftermath of World War I, the crumbling of major empires and the growth of nationalist liberation movements that took their place not only ushered in the era of "Taishō democracy" but also prompted various forms of populist movements in Japan, as throughout the world. In evaluating the promise and the shortcomings of "Taishō democracy," it is essential to bear in mind that this broad eclectic challenge to the elitist Meiji state was fundamentally an attempt to reassert the prerogatives of a collectivized view of "the social" against an elite, conceived in various ways. Nor was there agreement on what "the social" was. Some approached the problem of national restructuring from the perspective of ethnicity, others from idealism and "personalism," and others yet held fast to class differences as the key to understanding social oppression. Not surprisingly, given the conceptual and social uncertainty that accompanied the 1920s, some nationalists like Nakano Seigō and some socialists like Sano Manabu could start the decade as liberals and enter the 1930s as "fascists" (on Nakano, see Najita 1971; on Sano, see Hoston 1985). Whether or not the label of fascism best captures their political views, there can no longer be any doubt that nationalism, especially the popular and ethnic version, was a central, perhaps even the defining, ingredient in what has come to be known as "Taishō democracy."

The 1920s opened with the birth of a new world organization and a new world order designed to ensure peace and prosperity in the postwar era. Yet, as I noted above, even before the birth of the League of Nations on January 10, 1920, critics and defenders of the League alike agreed that the League would attempt to restructure the relations between ethnic nations and existing states by redefining state legitimacy on a popular or ethnic basis. In January, the very month that the League was inaugurated, *Chūō kōron* carried a discussion on "a new basis for world reform" that included contributions by such influential legal scholars as Sugimori Kōjirō, Horie Kiichi, and Yoshino Sakuzō. Sugimori called for a new philosophy of the state that would reconcile the claims of the state with those of society, while retaining its foundation in an "individuality" *(kosei)* that would promote humanism. Such a "people's state *(kokumin no kokka)* . . . [would] avoid militarist imperialism abroad and despotism at home" (Sugimori 1920, 164). Yoshino, the "father" of Taishō democracy, argued for a complete overhaul of political science away from the institutionalist assumptions of prewar political science and toward a more cultural approach to understanding the nation:

> In the political science of the prewar era, the state itself, as a compelling institution, was an absolute value. . . . We confuse the state and society in our everyday parlance, so we talk of promoting the culture of the state or boasting of the glories of the Japanese empire. But what we mean by the state in these cases is the social life of the Japanese ethnic nation. When we speak of the state in political science . . . we must not confuse criticism of these kinds of things with criticism of the organized life of the Japanese ethnic nation per se. (Yoshino 1920, 170–171)

Democracy, Yoshino cautioned, cannot be equated with the state since the spirit of democracy ran deeper than such political institutions: it was ultimately a "cultural phenomenon" (Yoshino 1920, 172).

Both Sugimori and Yoshino were attracted to ethnic nationalism as a means of suggesting a popular basis for political culture that would absorb the most appealing aspects of socialism while avoiding the class divisions of socialism itself. In January 1921, only a year after he had proposed a new philosophy for the state, Sugimori noted that the world was experiencing a struggle between socialism and nationalism, and he found nationalism more attractive. Like many socialists, he supported ethnic nationalism when directed toward independence from an imperialist state, but he felt that socialism failed to grasp that life is not reducible to economics and politics. There is also a cultural life, he maintained, and socialists had not paid sufficient attention to it (Sugimori 1921, 45–47). Professor Matsumoto Yoshio of Keio University agreed but took things even farther. He argued that "the Japanese people" referred to those who constituted the core ethnic group in Japan, an identity that had emerged in relation to other ethnic groups. Yet, he rejected the argument that there was interethnic hostility in ancient Japan between the Amaterasu ethnic group and the Izumo ethnic group, emphasizing instead that ethnic national consciousness was only formed with the rise of the Yamato state (Matsumoto 1921, 85–86). That is, Matsumoto rejected those who found social conflict in the earliest incarnations of Japanese culture, and he sought to displace such politicized views with a tight correlation between culture, ethnicity, and the state.

The end of the war and the establishment of the League of Nations required a radical rethinking of the conditions of national identity. As representations of the nation as the political state increasingly intersected with assertions that the nation was a popular, ethnic, or cultural body, the questions of both national identity and the identity of the nation reemerged. The key question was: what standards should govern the evaluation of growing, and sometimes competing, claims by many groups in the world after World War I that they constituted a nation with the right to be represented as a state in the League of Nations? Masaki Masato, a lecturer at Keio University, took up the challenge of defining the nation in his 1921 essay, "What is the ethnic nation?"[5] His essay was an introduction and review of William McDougall's 1920 work, *The Group Mind: A Sketch of the Principles of Collective Psychology with Some Attempt to Apply Them to the Interpretation of National Life and Character*. McDougall had argued that participation in group life was essential to individual happiness and that the highest form of group life was the nation. Masaki's translation of nation in this sense as *minzoku* shares in Abe Jirō's belief that the popular, ethnic nation is consistent with liberal and humanistic goals, even while it contrasts sharply with Katō Hiroyuki and others who had agreed that group life should take precedence over individualism—albeit with the state rather than the nation as the essential group form.

Masaki argued (through McDougall) that not all nations are states nor are all states nation-states, and he cited with approval McDougall's response to Ramsay Muir's answer, "What do we mean by a nation? It is obviously not the same thing as race, and not the same thing as a state" (McDougall 1920, 136–137; cited in Masaki 1921, 151). Muir had argued that the nation was, in the end, simply the sentiment of being a nation, which left him open to ridicule by McDougall. Muir's position, McDougall suggested, was simply to say that "when any population declares itself to be a nation and claims the rights of nationhood, the Statesmen of the Paris Conference are to re-ply—'We do not know whether your claim is well-founded; for the historians and political philosophers cannot tell us the meaning of the word 'nation'. Go to and fight, and, if you survive, we shall recognize the fait accompli and hail you a Nation'" (McDougall 1920, 136–139; cited in Masaki 1921, 151–153). Masaki ended his review with the following lines from McDougall that reinforced the affinities between the nation as *minzoku* and the popu-lism of the Taishō period: "A nation, we must say, is a people or population enjoying some degree of political independence and possessed of a national mind and character, and therefore capable of national deliberation and national volition" (McDougall 1920, 141; cited in Masaki 1921, 154). Masaki's populist intentions were further underscored by his gloss on McDougall's "people or population" in this passage as *jinmin,* an accurate translation but also a term that was close to the heart of many Japanese populists.

Masaki's article accomplished two things: it moved the debate on na-tional identity closer to psychological definitions of the nation, and it forced conservatives to redouble their efforts to support the state just as liberals and socialists were growing more inclined to consider the pragmatic possibilities of ethnic nationalism. Katō Hiroyuki had died in 1916, and his defense of the state was quickly taken up by Professor Uesugi Shinkichi of Tokyo Imperial University. In response to the increasing attention paid to the ethnic nation, Uesugi responded by stressing the synthetic powers of the state. Uesugi knew that statism held little emotional appeal for most Japa-nese, but given the liberal implications that ethnic nationalism had taken on as a challenge to imperialism after World War I, he could hardly join in an unmitigated celebration of ethnicity. Instead Uesugi tried to argue that the state was far more than an artificial institution. He criticized those who would replace the state with some vague concept of a "new society" as anarchists, and he then suggested that society, the ethnic nation, and the state were all one undifferentiated whole that rested fundamentally on what he called the people's "interdependent continuity" (*sōkan renzoku*) (Uesugi 1921, 16–17, 20–22). Utilizing what Irokawa Daikichi has called the politics of "restatement," Uesugi rephrased Masaki's question of "what is the nation?" to "what is the state?":[6]

> A state does not arise merely when a lot of people who have no connection or relationship to each other come together. When they come together with a natural ethnic origin that can give rise to a state, they unite and become one. That is, the state is a nation-state that unites a nation. . . . A nation is not the same as race, nor language, nor religion, although all these are inextricably related to the nation. What makes the nation a nation comes from the existence of national conviction *(minzoku kakushin)* or national sentiment *(minzoku kanjō)*; it is based in a sentiment or belief that each person is part of a mutual solidarity, a same nation. (Uesugi 1921, 24)

As Uesugi's argument for the state as the logical manifestation of the nation revealed, conservatives had little difficulty in adapting the psychological definition of the nation to the modern state. This subordination of the ethnic nation to the state not only could be used to defend the Japanese state from populist attacks, but the Japanese empire overseas could be justified on the grounds of the malleability of such inherently unstable "psychological" national identities (e.g., Korean ethnicity) that allowed for easy assimilation into the Japanese state.[7]

This conservative counterattack on ethnic nationalism, coupled with the outcome of the Washington Conference of November 12, 1921 to February 6, 1922, led liberals and Marxists to a more explicitly political interpretation of ethnic nationalism. Nearly all observers understood that the Washington Conference intended to establish a new order in the Pacific, following the collapse of the old arrangements established by the prewar imperialist treaties. Just before the conference convened, Chen Duxiu, publisher and head of the education department of the Guangdong provincial government in China, effected the image of a united Asian front in the pages of *New Youth* with articles by Japanese leftists Yamakawa Hitoshi and Sakai Toshihiko, as well as his own essay on "The Pacific Conference and the Weak Ethnic Nations of the Pacific." Chen called for Chinese students in the United States to speak out to ensure that the rights of the weak ethnic nations in the Pacific region would not be trampled by the conference of leading capitalist powers in East Asia (i.e., the United States, Great Britain, France, and Japan) (Chen 1921, 1–4).[8] But the signing of the Four-Power Pacific Treaty in Washington on December 13 reaffirmed the signatories' possessions in the Pacific and, to many Chinese and Koreans, seemed to represent Harding's rollback of Wilson and the League of Nations' promise of ethnic national independence. Imperialism had outlived Wilson's presidency and returned to threaten national independence movements in East Asia, just as conservatives were redoubling their efforts to suppress popular nationalism at home.

These concerns were evident early in 1922 when the issue of "the ethnic national struggle and socialist thought" was debated by an eclectic group of political theorists that included Yamakawa and Sakai as well as Takabatake Motoyuki, Mitsukawa Kametarō, and Ayakawa Takeji. Yamakawa and Sakai were highly conscious of their dilemma as socialists committed to ethnic nationalist liberation from capitalist imperialism and as political activists intervening in Japanese politics, where the perils of ethnic nationalism becoming a foundation for the capitalist nation-state were all too evident. Consequently, both men tried to sidestep the question of ethnic nationalism. With the blood spilled between Serbs and Austrians hardly dry, Yamakawa happily announced that ethnic nationalism was rather benign since "wars between ethnic nations, such as were fought in the primitive age, are today no longer fought anywhere." At the same time, he promised that what ethnic hatred still existed at present would soon disappear after the collapse of capitalism. The real evil, as the Washington Conference had demonstrated, remained the capitalist state (Yamakawa 1922, 123–124). Sakai agreed, noting that the issue of ethnic nationalism was "not much to worry about," although he did confess his own preference for socializing with people of a similar racial and cultural background (Sakai 1922, 126–127).

Others were not so ready to dismiss ethnic nationalism. Mitsukawa and Takabatake, like Sakai, were members of the Old and Young Society (Rōsōkai), which Ōkawa Shūmei had founded in 1918, and they had closely followed the rise of populist nationalism at least since World War I. Takabatake argued against what he called "the illusion of ultra-statism," noting that racial sentiment was not economic in nature and therefore was not likely to disappear anytime soon (Takabatake 1922, 146–149). Both Ayakawa and Mitsukawa had an easy time pointing out the contradictions in American democracy as an ostensibly transethnic political philosophy. Ayakawa noted that not only did forcing weaker countries in Asia to submit to the treaties of the Washington Conference violate the democratic principle of popular sovereignty, but that the (white) Americans themselves violated democratic principles in their relations with other ethnic groups all the time. To support this, he pointed to the Haitian occupation, the massacre of native Americans, interventions in Latin America, and violence against blacks in the United States (Ayakawa 1922, 164). Like Ayakawa, Mitsukawa ultimately settled on a view of racial solidarity among the "colored races" as resistance to the white race. Although he praised DeValera's Irish nationalist movement, he suggested that world politics after World War I was best captured in the metaphor of China expanding west against Russian eastern expansion, and he cited approvingly Marcus Garvey's suggestion that "when Europe and Asia clash swords in battle, we blacks should rise up on the side of Asia"

(Mitsukawa 1922, 160). Takayama Chogyū was long dead, but his influence was far from over.

In the midst of this return to Yamamoto Miono's conflation of race and ethnic nationalism, Ōyama Ikuo reopened the question of the ethnic nation both as distinct from the biological concept of race and as a possibility for a more broadly based social foundation for political life. Ōyama believed that the bourgeois, rational approach to social life was no longer possible in the aftermath of the Great War. Consequently, the belief that the political institution of the state was a rational construct had to be reconsidered. Ōyama maintained that the state was not a rational political structure but a product of war and conquest and was fundamentally shaped by the politics of ethnic competition. Teetering dangerously close to Katō and Uesugi's position, he argued that the nation formed the core element in the state, but he insisted that the nation was itself, like the state, a product of war and conquest rather than nature. Ōyama argued that some nineteenth-century political theorists like Walter Bagehot and Gumplowicz had understood the historical nature of the state, but they had confused the concept of the nation with the concept of race. Such nineteenth-century scientific racism would no longer suffice since, as Ōyama argued, "[i]t is no mistake to say that an understanding that the nation and race are not equivalent has become common sense in the field of political science" (Ōyama [1920, 1923] 1947, 4:234–235, 249–250).

Other influential writers agreed that ethnic nationalism could be compatible with liberal political principles. Like Ōyama, the liberal journalist Hasegawa Nyozekan also tried to refashion ethnic nationalism to salvage what he called its "social significance" (Hasegawa 1923, 25–26). For Hasegawa, ethnic nationalism was a product of modernity and therefore essentially progressive, but it had been corrupted by its association with militarism and the state. Yet ethnic national sentiments could be directed in a variety of ways, not all of which were malign. Offering a distinction between environmentally determined ethnic nationalism (good nationalism) and hereditary ethnic nationalism (bad nationalism), Hasegawa called for a "true" ethnic nationalist education that, based on the former, would reflect the interests of the people rather than the dominant class and their institution of the state. No state can trust populism, he noted, and "some day, when this [ethnic national] instinct is manifested permanently in the ethnic national psychology, the state will not be able to preserve its life for even one more day" (Hasegawa 1924, 10–11, 16–19). Tsukamoto Tsuyoshi agreed that ethnic nationalism was ideally a liberal political movement, and he presented a sweeping history of nationalism in the modern world to emphasize the point. "When traced to its essence," he wrote, "ethnic national thought stems from a consciousness of the individual. The roots of class consciousness are the same. . . . To use a very apt description, they are both the embryo of democracy" (Tsukamoto 1925, 17). For Tsukamoto, as well as for Ōyama and Hasegawa, ethnic nationalism could serve the interests of the people, congruent with the aims of social democracy, so long as it was guided in the right direction.

This attempt to assert a democratic ethnic nationalism against the false consciousness of the ethnic nationalism promoted by the capitalist class in their defense of the elitist state came in 1925, just as many right wing organizations, such as Minoda Muneki and Mitsukawa Kametarō's Genri Nihonsha, were forming to espouse national socialism. Also in the same year, Yanagita Kunio and Oka Masao founded a new journal, *Minzoku,* to investigate the ways that "folklore" might retain the populist connotations of ethnic identity outside of the modern national identity offered by the state. When Oka introduced W. H. R. Rivers and the Manchester School's celebration of ethnology as a cultural science that could contest the natural science that supported the state (Rivers 1925, 99, 112), Nishimura Shinji reflected that the Japanese term *minzoku* that Oka and Yanagita had adopted to translate "ethnos" was too easily confused with the "nation," and he urged they at least use different characters to write the word *minzoku.* Nishimura confessed his unease when he saw the journal's first issue since "we always use the word *minzoku* as a synonym for the word nation *(kokumin),* so I felt *minzoku* would be better for a journal with these kinds of [ethnological] concerns" (Nishimura 1926, 121–122).

In spite of the ambiguities of ethnic nationalism as resistance against the state, there was one last attempt to resurrect a liberal version of ethnic nationalism that would remain consistent with the idealism of "Taishō democracy." Former member of the House of Representatives and professor at Tokyo Imperial University Nakatani Takeyo drew from Carlton Hayes, McDougall, Muir, and W. B. Pillsbury to support his view that the nation, along with democracy, was a modern and progressive result of the French Revolution. But he also returned to Abe Jirō's blend of personalism and nationalism as an idealized form of collective political action: "The realization of the national ideal self is, in the sense that it is an ethical effort to establish, develop, and perfect the national personality, none other than national personalism" (Nakatani 1927, 127). Once again, Nakatani emphasized the historical and conceptual difference between the nation and the state, and once again he argued that nationalism was not only compatible with democracy but often the precondition for a democratic and tolerant society.

Nakatani's lengthy study of ethnic nationalism most likely was the inspiration for Hasegawa to reconsider his earlier thoughts on ethnic nationalism as progressive. Although Hasegawa still maintained that ethnic nationality was not reducible to race or the state, he conceded that in light of recent events it could no longer serve as a foundation for effective criticism of the state. Ethnic national consciousness, Hasegawa now concluded, had all the value of an appendix: that is, it was a useless appendage left over from an earlier, by-gone era (Hasegawa 1927, 69, 80, 99).

But not all forms of nationalism were anathema to Hasegawa. One gains a sense of the interconnectedness of domestic and foreign considerations in these critiques of ethnic nationalism when Hasegawa remarks on the attraction of ethnic nationalism for those living under colonialism:

> All peoples in societies such as China and India that suffer from the colonial policies of the white people's states find it impossible to resist a raging ethnic national consciousness, stirred as they are by an instinctual fear of outsider groups that stems from the reality of an invasion which was not only capitalist but backed up by military power. But even in . . . cases like the present where their struggle is more a struggle against capitalism than against military power, once they become snared by an instinctive ethnic national consciousness, there is a real risk that they will fall into the trap of cooperating with the rule of the capitalist social group that dominates their own social group. (Hasegawa 1927, 101)

That is, ethnic nationalism was illegitimate as a form of resistance to (Japanese) imperialism because it simply allowed colonial peoples to imprison themselves at the hands of their own capitalist elites in the name of resistance to foreign oppression. Yet, at the same time that Hasegawa had discounted ethnic nationalism as resistance to the state, in Japan and elsewhere, he retained a sense of nationalist resistance to the state that he called "patriotism" *(aikokushin)*. And while he conceded that patriotism also could be used to support the state, he referred to historical examples in Japan (Saigō Takamori, Sakura Sōgorō, and Kusunoki Masashige) where patriotism had served as the basis of opposition to political authority or the state (Hasegawa 1927, 103). Of course, patriotism had a much weaker historical link to anti-imperialism than ethnic nationalism had.

Tensions over alternatives in national identity were not alleviated with the increasing repression of leftist movements and ideas during the 1930s. Rather, the debate over national identity and the relationship between ethnic nationality and the modern Japanese state continued on during that decade in an equally complicated and fascinating manner (Doak 1994, 1996). But 1930 is an appropriate watershed in nationalist discourse for several reasons. First, it marks the end of a decade of populist attempts to conceive of a collective identity for the Japanese in which nationalism and democracy would be aligned along the same ideological plane. After the Manchurian Incident of 1931, the rise of militarist and national socialist pressures within Japan shaped debates on national identity in profoundly new and disturbing ways. Most notably, the "conversion" *(tenkō)* of many Communists and leftists toward national reconciliation that began around 1930 was often premised on a belief in the oppressed ethnic nation and its defense by the state. As the collapse of Marxist and even liberal political opposition to the elitist state took place under the increasing co-optation of populism by national socialists, the possibility for imagining a liberal, democratic social order based on ethnic nationalist theories also disappeared. But those who had devoted their energies to the possibilities of ethnic nationalism as a foundation for "Taishō democracy" during the 1920s had contributed a great deal, perhaps more than they knew, in preparing the ground for the blood that would flow in the years ahead.

NOTES

Research for this chapter was supported in part by a William and Flora Hewlett Summer International Research Grant for 1995 from the Office for International Programs and Studies of the University of Illinois at Urbana-Champaign. The author also would like to thank Thaddeus Ohta, Luke Roberts, Ronald Toby, and Jinhee Lee for their invaluable research assistance.

1. Sakazaki Sakan (1853–1913), also known as Shiran, was a political activist and writer who had organized the Oriental School of the People's Rights Lecture Group (Tōyō Ippa Minkenkōshaku Hitoza) along with Miyazaki Muryū (1855–1889), whose translation of the French expression "Assemblé Nationale" as *minzoku kaigi* Yasuda Hiroshi identifies as one of the earliest uses of the term *minzoku* (Yasuda 1992, 62).

2. This text sheds further light on Dru Gladney's assertion, based on People's Republic of China texts, that the term *minzu* entered the Chinese vocabulary in 1903 from the "capitalist Swiss-German political theorist and legal scholar Johannes Kaspar Bluntschli" (*Chinese Complete Encyclopedia*, cited in Gladney 1991, 85). Burgess' text draws from Bluntschli, suggesting that Bluntschli's role in the Chinese understanding of the nation may have been indirect and that the concept was familiar to Chinese intellectuals a bit earlier than 1903.

3. Gregory J. Kasza has applied and refined Payne's typology in exploring fascism in Japan with insightful result (Kasza 1984). Still, his conclusion that there were few true fascists in Japan reflects not only his limited time frame but his analytic approach, which did not incorporate the critical question of those who sought to redefine the nation as an ethnic nation.

4. While the author's identity remains uncertain (the text only lists him as a "Nakamura, Bachelor of Arts in Literature") he was in all probability Nakamura Kyūshirō (1874–1961), also known as Nakayama Kyūshirō. The text identifies Nakamura as an instructor of Oriental history at Tokyo Higher Normal School at the same time that Nakamura Kyūshirō was

teaching Oriental history at that school. Yoshinō Sakuzō and Tokutomi both wrote forewords to the book.

5. Note the similarities between the title of Masaki's essay, "Minzoku to wa nani zo," and Ernest Renan's famous 1882 essay, "Qu'est-ce qu'une nation." This question of "what is a nation?"—framed in Masaki's exact syntax—is echoed throughout the 1920s in the vernacular literature on national identity in Japan. Masaki was closely affiliated with Tanaka Suiichirō's Mita Historiographical Association, later serving as the director of the association.

6. Irokawa notes that in the post-Meiji period the logic of political restatement, originally a tool of progressive populists, was used more by rightists and cultural nationalists (Irokawa 1985, 106–107).

7. In 1921, the same year that Uesugi argued for the priority of the state over ethnic identity, the education office of the Korean governor general published the journal *Chōsenjin*, which listed strengths and weaknesses in the Korean ethnic character as part of an overall argument that Korean ethnicity should be assimilated into the Japanese state (Yoon 1993, 25).

8. Compare Chen's term, *ruoxiao minzu* (J: *jakushō minzoku*), which influenced the discussion on ethnic nationalism in Japan in the 1930s, with Stalin's language on "small nations" or "oppressed" nations (sometimes referred to as *narodnosti*, in contrast to the "great power chauvinism" of "oppressor nations") (Cf. Slezkine 1994, 414–452).

REFERENCES

Abe Jirō. 1917. "Shisōjō no minzokushugi." *Shichō* 1:99–120.

Allen, Chizuko T. 1990. "Northeast Asia Centered Around Korea: Ch'oe Namson's View of History." *Journal of Asian Studies* 49:787–806.

Asano Risaburō. 1914–1915. "Ajia minzoku no surabu minzoku ni oyoboseru eikyō o ronzu." *Shigaku* 25 no. 11:35–50, no. 12:37–68, 26 no. 2:201–230, no. 6:18–51, no. 9:48–86.

Ayakawa Takeji. 1922. "Minzoku, minzoku tōsō oyobi sekai kakumei." *Kaihō* (January):162–177.

Burgess, John W. 1893. *Political Science and Comparative Constitutional Law.* Boston: Ginn & Company.

Chen Duxiu. 1921. "Taipingyang huiyi yu taiping ruoxiao minzu." *Xin Qingnian* 9:1–4.

Chow, Kai-Wing. 1994. "Imagining Boundaries of Blood: Zhang Binglin and the Invention of the Chinese Race in Modern China." Manuscript.

Doak, Kevin M. 1994. "Nationalism as Dialectics: Ethnicity, Moralism, and the State in Early Twentieth-Century Japan." In *Rude Awakenings: Zen, the Kyoto School and the Question of Nationalism*, edited by James W. Heisig and John C. Maraldo. Honolulu: University of Hawai'i Press.

———. 1996. "Ethnic Nationalism and Romanticism in Early Twentieth Century Japan." *Journal of Japanese Studies* 22.1:77–103.

Gladney, Dru. 1991. *Muslim Chinese: Ethnic Nationalism in the People's Republic.* Cambridge: Harvard University Press.

Hasegawa Manjirō (Nyozekan). 1923. "Minzoku kanjō no shinri to sono shakaiteki igi." *Warera* 5:9–26.

——. 1924. "Iwayuru minzoku-teki kyōyō no hokai." *Warera* 6:8–24.

——. 1927. "Minzoku ishiki." *Shakai keizai taikei* 13:67–104.

Hoston, Germaine A. 1985. "Emperor, Nation, and the Transformation of Marxism to National Socialism in Prewar Japan: The Case of Sano Manabu." *Studies in Comparative Communism* 18:25–47.

Irokawa Daikichi. 1985. *The Culture of the Meiji Period,* translated by Marius B. Jansen. Princeton: Princeton University Press.

Katō Hiroyuki. [1913] 1990. *Kokka no tōchiken.* Jitsugyō no Nihonsha. Reprinted in *Katō Hiroyuki no bunsho,* 3:629–661. Kyoto: Dōhosha Shuppan.

——. [1915] 1990. *Jinsei no shizen to wagakuni no zento.* Jitsugyō no Nihonsha. Reprinted in *Katō Hiroyuki no bunsho,* 3:701–759. Kyoto: Dōhosha Shuppan.

Kasza, Gregory J. 1984. "Fascism from Below? A Comparative Perspective on the Japanese Right: 1931–1936." *Journal of Contemporary History* 19.4:607–629.

Luo Shishi. 1971. *Minzuzhuyi langchao.* Taipei: Youshi shudian.

Matsuda Tomoyuki. 1919. "Kokusai remmei to minzokushugi no chōwa." *Gaikō jihō* 342:12–23.

Matsumoto Hikojirō. 1914. "Minzoku kenkyū to kojiki." *Shigaku* 25:228–234.

Matsumoto Yoshio. 1921. "Kodai nihonjin no minzoku-teki kannen." *Shigaku* 1:85–100.

Masaki Masato. 1921. "Minzoku to wa nani zo." *Shigaku* 1:148–155.

Mitsukawa Kametarō. 1922. "Sekai kakumei no hanmen o ryōsuru minzoku tōsō." *Kaihō* (January):150–161.

McDougall, William. 1920. *The Group Mind: A Sketch of the Principles of Collective Psychology with Some Attempt to Apply Them to the Interpretation of National Life and Character.* New York: G. P. Putnam's Sons.

Najita, Tetsuo. 1971. "Nakano Seigo and the Spirit of the Meiji Restoration in Twentieth-Century Japan." In *Dilemmas of Growth in Prewar Japan,* edited by James W. Morely. Princeton: Princeton University Press.

Nakamura [Kyūshirō?]. 1916. *Kyokutō no minzoku.* In *Gendai sōsho,* edited by Tokutomi Iichirō. Minyūsha.

Nakatani Takeyo. 1927. "Minzoku ishiki oyobi minzokushugi." *Gaikō jihō* 541:116–128.

Nishimura Shinji. 1926. "Minzoku daiichi-kan dokugo shokan." *Minzoku* 2:121–127.

Ōyama Ikuo. 1919. "Shinkyū nishu no kokkashugi no shōtotsu." *Chūō kōron* 367:74–86.

——. [1920, 1923] 1947. *Minzoku tōsō to kaikyū ishiki.* Reprinted in *Seiji no shakai-teki kiso* and again in *Ōyama Ikuo zenshū* 4:231–286. Chūō Kōron-sha.

Payne, Stanley. 1980. *Fascism: Comparison and Definition*. Madison: University of Wisconsin Press.

Rivers, W. H. R. 1925. "Minzokugaku no mokuteki." Translated by Oka Masao. *Minzoku* 1:99–114.

Sakaguchi Takakimi. 1917. "Minzoku to kokumin to sekai bunka." *Nihon shakai gakuin nempō* 5:97–114.

Sakai Toshihiko. 1922. "Sonna ni shimpai suru koto wa nai." *Kaihō* (January):126–127.

Shiozawa Masasada. 1916. "Kaikei subeki minzoku tōsō." *Tōyō keizai shimpō* 738:28–29.

Slezkine, Yuri. 1994. "The USSR as a Communal Apartment, or How a Socialist State Promoted Ethnic Particularism." *Slavic Review* 53:414–452.

Sugimori Kōjirō. 1920. "Kokka tetsugaku no kōshin." *Chūō kōron* 35:157–164.

———. 1921. "Minzoku-teki danketsu to shisō-teki danketsu." *Chūō kōron* 36:42–47.

Takabatake Motoyuki. 1922. "Chō-kokkashugi no meimō." *Kaihō* (January):146–149.

Takayama Chogyū. [1898, 1900] 1930. *Chogyū zenshū*. Vol. 5. Edited by Anesaki Masaharu and Sasakawa Tanero. Hakubunkan.

Tanaka Suiichirō. 1916. "Minzokushugi no kenkyū." *Mita gakkai zasshi* 10:1–22.

———. 1918. "Kokusai remmei to minzokushugi." *Gaikō jihō* 339:21–39.

Tsukamoto Tsuyoshi. 1925. "Minzoku shisō hassei shi ron." *Gaikō jihō* 491:15–29, 492:63–76.

Uesugi Shinkichi. 1921. "Kokka ketsugō no genryoku." *Chūō kōron* 36:15–37.

Yamakawa Hitoshi. 1922. "Shakaishugi to minzoku tōsō." *Kaihō* (January): 121–125.

Yamamoto Miono. 1916. "Minzoku-teki jikaku to shokuminchi domin no kyōiku." *Keizai ronsō* 2:45–59.

———. 1919. "Minzoku jiketsushugi to shokuminchi mondai." *Gaikō jihō* 343:50–57.

Yasuda Hiroshi. 1992. "Kindai nihon ni okeru 'minzoku' kannen no keisei." *Shisō to gendai* 31:61–72.

Yoon Keun-Cha. 1993. "Minzoku gensō no satetsu." *Shisō* 834:4–37.

Yoshino Sakuzō. 1919. "Sekai kaizō no risō: minzoku-teki jiyū byōdō no risō no jikkō kanō." *Chūō kōron* 367:87–91.

———. 1920. "Seijigaku no kōshin." *Chūō kōron* 35:170–173.

"Zhengzhixue." 1901. *Yi shu hui pien* 8:3–14.

❧ 9 ❦

Writing the National Narrative: Changing Attitudes toward Nation-Building among Japanese Writers, 1900–1930

Roy Starrs

When Japanese writers began to read and translate Western literature in the late nineteenth century, they encountered a very powerful vehicle of national narrative: the Western novel. Just as one of the main features of Western political history over the previous few centuries had been the rise of the modern nation-state, so an equally central feature of Western literary history had been the rise of the novel. These two phenomena were not merely parallel but symbiotic: each had contributed to the other's growth. And this mutually enriching relationship reached its climax and apogee in the nineteenth century—at exactly the historical moment when Japan "re-opened" to the West.

The nineteenth-century novel brought the full scope of national life alive to the imaginations of the newly literate peoples of Europe and America in a way possible to no other artistic form, and perhaps rivaled only by the newly emergent national newspapers—with which, by no coincidence, many novelists were associated and in which they often first published their novels. Nineteenth-century nationalism joined with the nineteenth-century novel to produce some impressive examples of what we might call the "national novel." The paragon of them all was Tolstoy's *War and Peace* (1865–1869), which is undoubtedly the greatest national narrative of the nineteenth century, not only a masterful novel in the usual sense of the term but a grand-scale epic celebrating the Russian people's victory over the invading armies of Napoleon.

Many Meiji Japanese recognized quite early this nation-building function of the Western novel and realized that, like the national flag and the national anthem, the national novel was one of the standard fixtures of the modern nation-state, even though it was a "cultural property" that could not be so easily assimilated. Spurred by the obvious disparity between Western and Japanese images and practices of fiction, the influential Meiji novelist and critic Tsubouchi Shōyō published his stirring call to arms, *Shōsetsu shinzui (The Essence of the Novel)*, in 1885, urging his fellow writers to improve the quality of their fiction so that "we may finally be able to surpass in quality the European novels. . . ." This was obviously an appeal to the nationalism and competitive spirit of Japanese writers, but their response over the following years was not so resoundingly nationalistic as might have been expected. Despite all the pressures on Meiji writers to contribute in their own way to the great nation-building project of the age, no Japanese Tolstoys arose to celebrate their nation's heroic struggle against and ultimate victory over the nineteenth-century imperialist West, which had threatened to reduce the divine land to the status of a colony. Nothing approximating a Tolstoyan, epic treatment of the age appeared until Shimazaki Tōson's *Yoake mae (Before the Dawn)*, which, although written by a writer whose career began in the Meiji period, was written very much in retrospect, several decades after that period had ended. Also, as we shall see, Shimazaki's view of Meiji nation-building as a human experience was more tragic than heroic.

If, then, one were to regard the large-scale nineteenth-century Western novel as the only form of fiction capacious enough to serve as a national narrative, one would have to conclude that Meiji Japan, despite all its frenetic nation-building, produced no national narratives of any significant literary quality. But, of course, developments in the theory and practice of fiction, especially of the short story, since the nineteenth century have taught us the various ways in which fiction may take on metaphorical or symbolic overtones and thus encompass very large areas of meaning within even the smallest areas of text. Using this approach, even a short story can present a meaningful image of an entire nation or period.

The best Meiji fiction writers took easily to the new approaches of symbolic fiction and thus were able to write their own style of what we might describe as national narrative on an intimate scale. Mori Ōgai's short story, "Fushinchū" ("Under Reconstruction," 1910), is an excellent case in point. At first glance, it appears to present a slight if charming vignette from the love life of an upper-class Meiji gentleman, a government official. In a small hotel under reconstruction, he has a brief reencounter with a former lover, a German woman now touring the world as a professional singer. On this immediate level it is a beautifully written, understated story of faded love: the couple find that they cannot rekindle the old flame—sadly, time has taken its toll on their former passion. But the story also works brilliantly on another level—as Ōgai's image of the uneasy mixture of Eastern and Western culture in late Meiji Japan. As the government official himself tells the

German lady, not just the hotel, with its awkward mélange of Western and Japanese decor, but the whole country is "under reconstruction," and the very awkwardness of their meeting, the result not just of lapsed time but of culture clash, echoes the awkwardness of Japan's encounter with the West.

The symbolic approach to fiction, though, was not so much a matter of particular techniques—such as Ōgai's use of synecdoche, a hotel representing the nation as a whole—as it was a whole new attitude toward fiction as symbolic. Any element of the story can function as a symbol—even the characters themselves. Perhaps the first significant example of this kind of symbolic use of character was the "superfluous man" of mid-nineteenth-century Russian literature, an early symbol of the modern social disease of alienation, appearing in writers such as Lermontov, Gogol, Goncharov, and Turgenev. It was precisely from this rather nihilistic tradition of Russian literature, rather than from Tolstoy, that Futabatei Shimei learned what proved to be of most use to him in writing the first significant and successfully modern Meiji novel, *Ukigumo* (*Drifting Cloud*, 1886–1889). As Futabatei himself said, when he began to study Russian literature, he had two motives: a nationalistic one, to know an important potential enemy, and an aesthetic one, to enjoy reading great literature; but soon, he wrote, "my nationalistic fervor was quieted and my passion for literature burned on."

It seems that much the same was true for many Meiji writers. Nevertheless, this did not mean that Futabatei became a pure aesthete without concern for the state of the nation. On the contrary, *Drifting Cloud* may be read as a bitter criticism of the social values encouraged by the Meiji oligarchs. Futabatei's antihero, Bunzō, who loses both his job and his fiancée, is on his way to becoming a superfluous man because he is too honest, in the old samurai way, to prosper or even to survive in the ruthlessly competitive society of early Meiji, a nouveau riche society of self-made men. This theme of the man too sensitive to survive in the brave new world of modern Japan would become a very familiar one, and Futabatei's alienated antihero, his superfluous man, became an archetypal character in modern Japanese literature, reappearing again and again in different forms, often as an obvious alter ego of the author himself, in the work of many of the major writers of twentieth century Japan. Obviously, then, we might say that Futabatei created a powerful national symbol in this character and that his novel, *Drifting Cloud*, came to be accepted, by Japanese intellectuals at least, as a compelling national narrative, albeit of a negative or critical rather than a positive or celebratory kind.

Once we accept this more comprehensive idea of a national narrative—that is, as any work of fiction that attempts to present an image of the nation as a whole, whether literal or symbolic, positive or negative—then it becomes clear that the two major writers who appeared in the late Meiji period, Mori Ōgai and Natsume Sōseki, were national narrators par excellence, and—a point I would particularly like to emphasize—they were national narrators in a way that the writers who came after them were not.

Ōgai, for instance, was so constantly preoccupied with the state of the nation that even in a story that seems entirely personal, "Hannichi" ("Half a Day," 1909), which is about the tensions between his own wife and mother, we still feel larger issues looming in the background. Thus a very perceptive critic, Mishima Yukio, was moved to remark after reading this story: "I believe it is true to say that Ōgai saw in his own household the failure of Japan's modern age" (Keene 1984, 359).

At any rate, to illustrate the way in which both Ōgai and Sōseki were sensitive readers of the pulse of the nation, one could do no better than examine their responses to the disturbing events of late Meiji. The political situation of the late Meiji period was volatile, with a rising tide of liberal democratic and socialist opposition to the status quo and an increasingly authoritarian and oppressive government of elder statesmen. The climax came in 1911 with the execution of the distinguished socialist leader, Kōtoku Shūsui, along with others, because of their supposed plot to assassinate the emperor. Ōgai himself had felt the oppressive weight of intolerant authority just the year before when the censors banned his novel *Vita Sexualis,* a satire on the naturalists' obsession with sex, and the vice-minister of war personally reprimanded Ōgai. As a high official himself in the Imperial Army medical corps, he of course could not afford to criticize openly what he considered to be the irrational behavior of higher officials. But his stories of this period clearly reflect his dissatisfaction—using the symbolic fictional approach he had by now mastered. *Chinmoku no tō (The Tower of Silence,* 1910), for instance, borrows an image from India—the tall towers on Malabar Hill in which the Parsis dispose of their dead—to symbolize the way the Meiji government silences people who read, translate, or write "dangerous books," which are defined as "books about naturalism and socialism." Ōgai ends the story with a bold rhetorical flourish, condemning all forms of censorship:

> Both art and the pursuit of learning must be seen to be dangerous if you look with the conventional eye of the Parsi clan. Why is this? In every country and every age, crowds of reactionaries lurk behind those who walk new paths awaiting an unguarded moment. And when the opportunity arises they inflict persecution. Only the pretext changes, depending upon the country and the times. "Dangerous Western books" is no more than such a pretext. (Mori 1994, 222)

Just two years after this story, Ōgai's work underwent a dramatic transformation, and in an unexpectedly conservative direction—surprisingly for a writer who had seemed so promodern and proreform in his scientific rationalism. The immediate cause was the death of the Meiji emperor and the subsequent *junshi,* or ritual suicide, of his vassal, General Nogi. Like many of his contemporaries, Ōgai was deeply moved by both events: on the one hand, the emperor's death bringing to an end a long and remarkable reign, on the other hand, the general's suicide harking back to the samurai values of an earlier age. These two events naturally produced a mood of nostalgia in many people, but in Ōgai they seem to have produced a lasting change of heart. It was as if they shocked him into realizing what he really valued: now that the world of traditional, heroic values seemed to be passing away, he would devote himself as a writer to preserving its memory. The irony, of course, is that Ōgai himself up to this point, both as a writer and a doctor, had done his best to precipitate the very process of modernization that was destroying the culture he most valued. But he was not alone in his ironic ambivalence; in this too he was emblematic of the whole elite class to which he belonged, the Meiji nation-builders.

Before 1912 there seem to have been two Ōgais: the army officer, a descendant of samurai, and a high-ranking official in the Meiji establishment; and, the writer, a skeptical rationalist and a lover of Western literature and philosophy, somewhat rebellious in spirit and antiestablishment in many of his attitudes. It was as if the army officer used writing as a means of escape from the oppressive confines of his official life. After 1912, however, the two persona seemed to come much closer together: the essential conservatism of the samurai-class army officer found expression in the writing of historical stories and biographies. For many Western readers, the earlier Ōgai may seem a more attractive writer. But Japanese critics generally regard his historical works as his major achievement. One thing brings agreement. In the fiction Ōgai wrote in the last decade of his life, modern Japanese literature finally gained a national narrative of a positive, celebratory kind.

In the four days immediately following General Nogi's *junshi,* Ōgai wrote a story, "Okitsu Yagoemon no isho" ("The Last Testament of Okitsu Yagoemon," 1912), which is a moving tribute to this ultimate act of loyalty. The faithful samurai Yagoemon commits *junshi* to follow his master into death and, like General Nogi, to atone for a mistake he has committed in the distant past—but what is presented as even more admirable is that, like Socrates paying off his debts before his death, Yagoemon allows himself the privilege of committing *junshi* only after he has discharged his various worldly obligations—even leaving behind enough money to pay for his own cremation. In short, he is a paragon of the samurai virtues of loyalty, courage, and dutifulness. Futher, in the second version of the story, published a year after the first, Ōgai makes it clear that he was rewarded with a brilliant posterity, which is described in a genealogical table of almost biblical proportions, down to the eleventh generation!

Since Ōgai's day, of course, samurai stories of this kind have become a standard part of Japan's popular national myth, functioning in much the same way as do Hollywood westerns in the United States. But Ōgai's historical fiction is far above the standard; he performed an important service as a national narrator by bringing the samurai story to a new level of intellectual and literary sophistication.

From our present point of view in the late twentieth century we may judge a story like "Okitsu Yagoemon" to be anachronistic—or worse, potentially to have contributed by its apparent reverence for bushido to the atavistic attitudes and behavior of the ultranationalists and militarists of the early Shōwa period. One could even argue that, by retreating to the past and its traditional values, Ōgai was trying to escape further censure from increasingly intolerant authorities—in effect, caving in to their intimidation and sacrificing his writing for the sake of his career. But even if all this were true or partly true, it would not vitiate the literary quality of Ōgai's historical literature. When reading that literature as a whole, the impression we are given is far from that of a mindless, reactionary traditionalism. He did not abandon his modern education, his scientific rationalism, or his critical intelligence after 1912.

In fact, the very next story he wrote, *Abe ichizoku* (*The Abe Clan,* 1913) is a critical, even satirical treatment of the practice of *junshi.* When a certain daimyo dies, so many men end up killing themselves—even men who hardly knew the daimyo—that we have a farcical as well as tragic *reductio ad absurdum* of the whole custom; on the other hand, choosing not to commit *junshi* in this society could lead to equally tragic consequences, as with Abe Michinobu. Even though he is ordered not to kill himself, a conflict arises between his samurai duty to obey orders and his samurai sense of personal honor; troubled by rumors that he has failed to commit *junshi* because of cowardice, he finally feels obliged to kill himself in front of his five sons. But the matter does not end there. Persecuted by the new daimyo, Abe's whole family is ultimately destroyed, the young and the old, men, women, and children, and the story ends with a bloodbath of more than Shakespearian proportions. But this is with a very modern sense of absurdity rather than with any cathartic sense of tragic greatness; as Ōgai writes of the final fighting in the Abe mansion: "Just as street fighting is far uglier than fighting in the field, the situation here was even more ghastly: a swarm of bugs in a dish devouring one another" (Mori 1977, 66).

Indeed, when one surveys the bulk of Ōgai's historical stories and biographies, one finds that most of them celebrate more quiet virtues than the heroic ones demonstrated in *junshi.* This is especially true of the *shiden,* or historical biographies, and one author of a recent study of them has aptly characterized their subjects as "paragons of the ordinary" (Marcus 1993). Although samurai of the Tokugawa period, they epitomize not so much the martial virtues as the Confucian/samurai virtues of a time of peace, leading quiet lives of moderate, usually scholarly, achievement. These historical biographies are far from being "blood-and-guts" samurai adventure tales; indeed, the problem with them for many readers may be the blandness of their central characters and the uneventfulness of the lives portrayed.

In *Shibue Chūsai*, for instance, Ōgai commemorates the life of a now-forgotten samurai-physician and scholar of that name, whose career, Ōgai felt, "strangely resembled my own." He celebrates Chūsai's devotion to obscure areas of scholarship such as the study of samurai genealogies as well as his more conventional samurai virtues. Chūsai was a man who lived a good life but did not achieve any lasting fame. In rescuing him from obscurity, Ōgai, uniquely among modern writers, created a new order of national narrative, one that celebrates lives of ordinary goodness and achievement. To give further emphasis to this point, he continues the story long past Chūsai's death, to show how he lived on in his descendants and disciples. Thus we are given a powerful sense of the great flow of national life, continuing on from generation to generation, in an undramatic but nonetheless moving way. In this sense it might be said that many of Ōgai's historical works are fundamentally ahistorical rather than anachronistic, in that they aim to present an essentially timeless image of Japanese life as it has existed over many centuries—and still perhaps continues to exist at some subterranean level.

A good expression of this may be found in the story, "Jiisan Baasan" ("Old Man, Old Woman," 1915), a simple but moving account of a woman's loyalty to her husband, a samurai who was sent into exile for a rash act of violence. The faithful wife waits thirty-seven years to be reunited with him, and the couple spend their last few years living together happily and idyllically in a small cottage. Although the story is set in the Tokugawa period, it has the timeless atmosphere and symbolic power of a fairy tale. As Ishikawa Jun once wrote: "The two central characters and their fates stand concretely before us, and the world described in the work seems to be something eternal. It is, so to speak, riding the tide of the lives that Japanese have led without break from ancient times to the present" (Keene 1984, 375). In other words, it is a form of national narrative that attempts to present a timeless, archetypal image of national life—as do fairy tales or folk tales.

It is interesting to compare Ōgai's literary response to the end-of-Meiji events—especially General Nogi's *junshi*—with Natsume Sōseki's: Sōseki's is far more time-bound. That is, in his 1914 novel, *Kokoro*, he emphasizes the anachronistic nature of the general's act. He does so because his purpose in *Kokoro* is not so much to celebrate the Japanese tradition, as Ōgai does in "Okitsu Yagoemon," as to mourn its passing; his mood is elegiac rather than heroic. Thus he emphasizes the fact that the general's act belongs to a now-dead tradition. In the climactic final pages of the novel, when "Sensei" explains his reasons for committing suicide, he explicitly identifies himself with General Nogi as a man of the past and tells the young narrator that he reached this decision just two or three days after hearing of the general's suicide. Then he adds: "Perhaps you will not understand clearly why I am about to die, no more than I can fully understand why General Nogi killed himself. You and I belong to different eras, and so we think differently. There is nothing we can do to bridge the gap between us" (Natsume 1957, 246).

In contrast, then, to Ōgai's apparent belief in certain timeless features of the Japanese national character and mentality, Sōseki's protagonist subscribes to a kind of historical determinism. Especially at a time of rapid modernization, each age has such different values that there is a mutual incomprehension between the different generations. And Sensei identifies himself so closely with the Meiji era that he feels that he cannot survive beyond it. "On the night of the Imperial Funeral," he writes quite majestically, "I sat in my study and listened to the booming of the cannon. To me, it sounded like the last lament for the passing of an age" (Natsume 1957). But, as it turns out, the booming cannon are also his own death knell. As he himself confesses:

> I felt as though the spirit of the Meiji era had begun with the Emperor and had ended with him. I was overcome with the feeling that I and the others, who had been brought up in that era, were now left behind to live as anachronisms. I told my wife so. She laughed and refused to take me seriously. Then she said a curious thing, albeit in jest: "Well then, *junshi* is the solution to your problem." (Natusme 1957, 245)

In this way Sōseki consciously and explicitly creates a correspondence between his characters and crucial events in their lives on the one hand and, on the other, important figures and events in national history. A novel such as *Kokoro* thus becomes a symbolic national narrative—but not of Ōgai's positive, celebratory kind; rather it is a national narrative in an elegiac mode. We may conclude from this as from other of Sōseki's works that he was much more pessimistic than Ōgai about the survival of traditional Japanese values in a rapidly Westernizing and modernizing Japan.

Indeed, Sōseki's pessimism about Japan's future suffuses much of the work he wrote in the latter part of his career, after he abandoned the comic manner of his early novels. In this way the fiction he wrote from about 1908 until his death in 1916, dealing mainly with the historical present, contrasts sharply with Ōgai's Taishō fiction, which is more optimistic, perhaps for the very reason that it deals mainly with the past. A well-known and powerful expression of Sōseki's views is voiced by the central character of *Sore kara* (*And Then*, 1909), Daisuke, a superfluous man like Futabatei's Bunzō but a more intellectually aware one. He wants to believe that modernity does "not necessarily cause anxiety" and that those Japanese writers who deal with "modern anxiety" are merely affecting an imported Western fashion (Natsume 1978, 60–61). But this feigned positivism is contradicted by his own woeful laments on the present state of his nation, especially vis-ǎ-vis the West, which he voices, significantly, as an excuse for his own character as a superfluous man, his idleness and ineffectuality:

> . . . to exaggerate a little, it's because the relationship between Japan and the West is no good that I won't work. . . . The point is, Japan can't get along without borrowing from the West. But it poses as a first-class power. And it's straining to join the ranks of the first-class powers. That's why, in every direction, it puts up the facade of a first-class power and cheats on what's behind. It's like the frog that tried to outdo the cow—look, Japan's belly is bursting. And see, the consequences are reflected in each of us as individuals. A people so oppressed by the West have no mental leisure, they can't do anything worthwhile. They get an education that's stripped to the bare bone, and they're driven with their noses to the grindstone until they're dizzy—that's why they all end up with nervous breakdowns. (Natsume 1978, 72)

This is a far more extreme, and far grimmer, view of Japan's position in the world following the Russo-Japanese War than was presented by Ōgai's "Under Reconstruction," which was written at about the same time. Ōgai's hotel, a rather mild symbol of an incomplete project of modernization and of a half-comic, half-tragic mix of cultures, is now replaced by a sham frontage, not merely unfinished but unfinishable because it is totally false.

Whether in a positive or negative form, however, both Ōgai and Sōseki were exemplary national narrators in their continual engagement with issues of national relevance and in their continual effort to present an image of the nation as they saw it. One of the key questions in the history of modern Japanese literature must be why their immediate successors in the Taishō period were so noticeably deficient in this area, despite the first tentative budding of what is known as Taishō democracy—which one might have expected not only to encourage but to demand the active engagement of writers in a public or civic discourse. Yet Taishō writers such as Shiga Naoya, Akutagawa Ryūnosuke, and Tanizaki Jun'ichirō are remarkably inward-looking, almost exclusively concerned with their own psychological states, seemingly uninterested in the state of the nation as a whole.

Was there something about the spirit of the Meiji period that made writers more public-minded, or was it something in the character of Ōgai and Sōseki themselves? Perhaps this amounts to the same thing, since the two writers were very much products of their age. One could point, for instance, to the fact that, in contrast to the Taishō writers, who were more or less "free agents," both Ōgai and Sōseki were in some sense "government men"—Ōgai more than Sōseki, of course, but even Sōseki taught in government schools for much of his life and was awarded a government grant that enabled him to spend several years studying abroad. One hastens to add that this does not mean that either of them was blindly or uncritically supportive of the government. As we have seen, Ōgai was one of the few writers who dared to challenge the authoritarian intolerance of the Meiji regime, however indirectly; and Sōseki, in the latter part of his career, went out of his way to distance himself from the government—most famously, by resigning his post at a national university and by refusing a doctoral degree offered him by the Ministry of Education. Nevertheless, since both writers benefited, at least in their early careers, from government patronage, they no doubt felt more obliged to contribute to the nation through their writings than did later writers who existed more independently. But this too was very much part of the Meiji reality: as part of its nation-building strategy, the Meiji government sponsored rapid development in all areas of national life, which is why Ōgai was sent to Germany to study army medicine and Sōseki to England to study British literature—in line with the imperial injunction of 1868, which bade citizens to "seek knowledge throughout the world in order to provide for the welfare of the state." Thus in their lives as in their work, Ōgai and Sōseki were typical men of Meiji of the elite class and inevitably felt deeply involved with the nation-building project of that age.

Whether by historical destiny or personal taste, however, the fact remains that these two writers are still unrivaled as the national narrators of modern Japanese literature. No doubt this accounts for the phenomenon of their continuing popularity and prestige—not just with the Japanese establishment, which is happy to use their images on the national currency, but with the Japanese reading public at large.[1] From a strictly literary or aesthetic point of view, there may be modern Japanese writers whose art of fiction is superior to theirs—for instance, Tanizaki or Kawabata. But Ōgai and Sōseki confronted large issues of national identity in such a compelling way and at such a crucial moment in modern Japanese history that they continue to possess a moral authority beyond that of any other Japanese writers of the twentieth century.

All the more striking, then, is the contrasting character of the writers who followed them. The kind of mutual incomprehension caused by a chronic generation gap, described so well by Sōseki's *sensei* in *Kokoro,* an early Taishō novel, became, in fact, a characteristic feature of the Taishō period. In literature as in other realms of national life, Taishō sons seemed intent on liberating themselves in every possible way from the overpowering legacy of their Meiji fathers. Since this legacy included, above all, an intense concern with the state of the nation, the young Taishō writers were almost ostentatious in their rejection of any such concern. Thus it is hardly surprising that intergenerational conflict itself became a major theme of Taishō literature—most famously, in the work of Shiga Naoya, the leading writer of the Shirakaba group, who were in this as in other respects the quintessential Taishō writers. It was the Shirakaba writers, for instance, who most clearly voiced the Taishō generation's negative response to General Nogi's suicide, viewing it, from their Tolstoyan humanist perspective, as an anachronistic and inhumane act.[2]

Of course, the differences and conflicts between the Meiji and Taishō generations were not simply a matter of the commonplace kind of "gap" one finds universally between parents and children, or between the old and the young. A wide range of historical factors widened this gap and exacerbated resultant conflicts. Enormous changes had occurred in Japan in the less than half century that separated the early Meiji from the early Taishō period. By 1912 the Meiji nation-building project had been largely accomplished, and the essential elements of modern Western civilization—even in the literary and artistic realms—had been more or less successfully absorbed. Thus it is hardly surprising that, among the younger, "Taishō generation" of writers, there is a distinctly different attitude toward both the nation and Western or modern culture. Generally speaking, their attitude may be characterized as more "relaxed," or perhaps even as "benignly negligent." It was as if, since both the modern nation-state and the importation of Western civilization were now more or less faits accomplis, the Taishō writers felt that they no longer needed to be much concerned about either one of them as compelling issues about which to write. In the cultural realm this was perhaps all very well: as the first generation of Japanese writers educated more in Western languages and literatures than in the traditional Sino-Japanese canon, they suffered very little of the sense of "cultural conflict" that was quite pronounced in the Meiji writers. The Shirakaba group pronounced themselves to be Tolstoyan humanists, apparently without any sense of incongruity. Akutagawa made such free use of his encyclopedic knowledge of Western literature and philosophy that he seemed to regard it as very much part of his own inheritance. Tanizaki glorified the exotic charms of the *moga* or *modan garu*, the Taishō equivalent of the American flapper. (By the late 1920s, all of these writers would be having second thoughts about these "Western tastes" of their youth, but we are speaking now about the "high Taishō" period when such tastes were still very much in vogue.)

In the social/political realm, however, the Taishō generation's navel-gazing and insouciance toward public issues may seem to have had more dangerous or, at least, less positive consequences. Looking back with the advantage of hindsight, especially with our awareness of the reactionary forces that soon would derail Japan's progress toward modernity and liberal democracy, it may seem to us that they were living in a fool's paradise. Unable to outgrow the shadow of their Meiji fathers, they wrote a kind of *botchan no bungaku*, a literature that took no responsibility for a world created and sustained by the will of their fathers. Thus it was inevitable that, in the aftermath to the Pacific War, the Taishō writers should become the favorite whipping boys of new converts to liberal democracy among Japanese intellectuals who were looking for someone to blame for the failure of "Taishō democracy" (see Arima 1969).

But the issue, of course, is complex and eminently debatable. One may question, for instance, to what extent Taishō writers reasonably could be expected to have had faith in their "democratic rights." I already have mentioned an incident that occurred on the eve of the Taishō period and had a profound impact on the Japanese literary world: the execution of the socialist leader Kōtoku Shūsui and many of his followers. As Nagai Kafū pointed out in his famous essay of 1919, "Hanabi" ("Fireworks"), this incident seemed to have the same meaning for Japanese writers that the Dreyfus affair had for French writers just a few years earlier: a trumped-up charge of treason motivated by the prejudices of the political establishment, although in this case the prejudices were antisocialist rather than anti-Semitic. But, significantly, the response of Japanese writers was quite the opposite of their French counterparts. Even among the Japanese "naturalists," no Zola arose to confront the establishment with a brave and furious "J'accuse." On the contrary, the lesson that most of them seemed to learn from the incident was that they had better not meddle in politics. In "Fireworks," Kafū confesses that, ashamed of his own capitulation to the bullying authorities, he resolved to regard himself thereafter as a writer not worth taking seriously, a mere Edo-style scribbler of light and frivolous fiction:

> Of all the public incidents I had witnessed or heard of, none had filled me with such loathing. I could not, as a man of letters, remain silent in this matter of principle. Had not the novelist Zola, pleading the truth in the Dreyfus Case, had to flee his country? But I, along with the other writers of my land, said nothing. The pangs of conscience that resulted were scarcely endurable. I felt intensely ashamed of myself as a writer. (Quoted in Seidensticker 1968, 46)

In other words, the incident convinced Kafū and many of his colleagues that, despite all the modernization or Westernization since 1868, it was still close enough to a Tokugawa-style "police state" to make the exercise of any antigovernment free speech a very dangerous business. Although what we now refer to as "Taishō democracy" no doubt included such phenomena as a rise in the power of political parties and the extension of male suffrage, it is perhaps understandable that, for many of the writers of the age, it did not seem to include the privilege of speaking out against the government. Indeed, from the writers' perspective, the Taishō period was bracketed by two ominous exercises in government suppression: the Kōtoku incident of

1911 and the Peace Preservation Law of 1925, which initiated a ruthless campaign to extirpate all left-wing opposition to the status quo.

In a well-known study of the intellectuals and writers of the period, Tatsuo Arima claims that their nonengagement with Japan's budding liberal democratic movement resulted ultimately in a "failure of freedom"—that is, in the defeat of "Taishō democracy" by early Shōwa militarism (Arima 1969). But writers who lived through the period might well be puzzled by this claim: after all, how much real "freedom" was theirs to "fail"? There is a definite ex post facto feel about Arima's view: it smacks of the romanticization of the Taishō period that became popular among Japanese intellectuals in the postwar period—perhaps in their overeagerness to prove that Japan had its very own democratic tradition, which had been scuttled by the militarists and their various collaborators. To put it bluntly: Japanese writers did not really begin to feel that it was safe to speak out against the government until the radical restructuring of the political system that occurred after Japan's "second opening" to the West in 1945. If we are to look, then, for historical factors behind the Taishō writers' nonengagement with political issues, the Kōtoku incident of 1911 would be a good place to start.

At any rate, given all the historical forces that were leading Japan, along with Germany and Italy, toward the debacle of the World War II, one may question whether the voices of a few dissenting writers would have made much difference. Germany had quite a few such writers but, unfortunately, they did nothing to slow Hitler's war machine. On the other hand, one could point out that it was precisely such "decadent," "narcissistic" writers as Tanizaki and Nagai Kafū who, later on, were among the most conspicuous non-cooperators with the military, whereas many of the more "committed" Marxist writers were equally conspicuous collaborators.

This is by no means to argue that a writer's social or political views are irrelevant, or that they can have no effect on public life; but it seems that the effectiveness of a writer's views is also contingent upon his or her historical situation. Dickens is often given as the example par excellence of the novelist who shaped public opinion and public policy. But if Dickens had been transplanted from Victorian England to Taishō Japan, and had written novels celebrating democracy and excoriating fascism, one doubts that his views would have had such effectiveness. It is not my intention here, then, to adopt a moralistic or condemnatory tone toward the Taishō writers—like the rest of us, they were simply the products, and perhaps the victims, of their age. I must confess, in fact, that they are among my favorite writers in all of modern Japanese literature. But they are not "national narrators" in the way their Meiji predecessors were, and this fact, it seems to me, is worthy of contemplation for the light it sheds both on them and on their predecessors.

Of the three major writers who emerged in the Taishō period—Tanizaki Jun'ichirō, Shiga Naoya, and Akutagawa Ryūnosuke—Akutagawa seemed most likely, at first, to inherit the mantle of "national narrator" from Ōgai and Sōseki. With his wide knowledge of both East Asian and Western literatures, his interest in writing historical fiction, and his command of a detached, ironic, "intellectual" style, he seemed to promise to succeed Ōgai in particular as historian of the national soul. The fact that he never quite lived up to this promise says something significant not only about Akutagawa himself but about Taishō writers in general.

Like his contemporary Tanizaki, Akutagawa had imbibed the "decadent" aestheticism and world-weary attitudes of fin de siècle Europe, deeply immersing himself in writers such as Baudelaire, Nietzsche, Strindberg, and Wilde. According to the editors of a standard Japanese literary history of the period, it was precisely such aestheticism that was the key new feature of Taishō literature (Kōno et al. 1972). Art took precedence over life, and any concern with political or social issues would be vulgarly unaesthetic. Akutagawa's infatuation with Western culture had a corresponding contempt for a good part of the Japanese cultural tradition—including, especially, those samurai virtues that Ōgai so highly lauded. When Akutagawa did concern himself with the national culture, it was often with a satirical intent. For instance, Ōgai's reverential and Sōseki's elegiac treatments of General Nogi may be compared with Akutagawa's satirical treatment in his story, *Shōgun* (1922). But an even more impressive example of this new "Taishō generation" attitude occurs in his brilliantly effective little story, "Hankechi" (Handkerchief, 1916).

The professorial protagonist of the story, modeled on Nitobe Inazō, author of a famous book on bushido, believes that he has found a splendid example of ancient samurai virtue when he received a visit from the mother of one of his students. She stoically maintains a smile while telling him of the death of her son. But he notices that, at the same time, "probably due to the effort to suppress her emotions, her hands, as they trembled, grasped the handkerchief on her knees so hard that they all but tore it in two" (Akutagawa 1930, 40). The professor's elation at this discovery of living bushido is soon deflated, however, when, by coincidence, he happens to read a passage from Strindberg's book of advice to actors, wherein the great Swedish dramatist mocks the melodramatic mannerism of an actress who tries to convey depth of emotion by smiling and tearing at her handkerchief at the same time. Thus, by an uneasy juxtaposition of traditional Japanese behavior and the cynical thought of a fashionable Western writer, Akutagawa undoubtedly intends to undercut tradition, reducing bushido to the level of a mere mannerism out of an old-fashioned sentimental melodrama.

The few satirical works of this sort that Akutagawa wrote may be regarded as national narratives of a negative kind, or perhaps as antinational narratives. But even *Kappa* (1927), which of all Akutagawa's works comes closest to being a full-scale Swiftian satire of contemporary society and does seem to satirize such things, for instance, as the blind worship of Western culture by Japanese intellectuals (Akutagawa himself not least among them), nonetheless seems driven by a basic satirical thrust that is more general: one might say that it is more an existential satire of the human condition in general than a social satire focusing on any particular nation.

The fact that, as with other Taishō "humanitarians," Akutagawa's real interest lay more in "the state of man" than in "the state of the nation" may be seen even in his "historical" stories. Although, as many Japanese critics and even Akutagawa himself pointed out, he was inspired by Mori Ōgai's historical fiction to try to write his own, there is a very telling difference between Ōgai's historical stories and Akutagawa's. Whereas Ōgai took painstaking efforts to ensure the historical accuracy of his stories in every detail, Akutagawa defended his "artistic license" to distort history in the interest of art. In fact, he confessed that the only reason he set his stories in remote historical periods was to facilitate the reader's suspension of disbelief. He was convinced that, had he given a contemporary setting to his tales of human psychology and behavior in extremis, readers would refuse to believe in them. In a work such as *Jigokuhen* (*Hell Screen*, 1918), perhaps his most powerful historical story, the setting—vaguely Heian—is entirely secondary to Akutagawa's central theme, which is, significantly, that for the artist, art must take precedence over life, even when this necessitates the most extreme sacrifice imaginable. Thus the painter Yoshihide is willing to countenance even the burning of his own beloved daughter so that he might paint a more convincing picture of the agonies of hell. The fact that the story is set in some vague historical past probably does make it more acceptable to our imaginations. Unlike Ōgai, then, Akutagawa's intention was not to present an image of national life in a particular historical period but rather to present a timeless psychological truth in an aesthetically satisfying form. We might even say that in his historical stories, he was a Taishō aesthete disguised as a Meiji national narrator.

Akutagawa's aestheticism certainly was shared by two other writers who began their long careers in the Taishō period and who would go on to become perhaps the two greatest novelists of twentieth-century Japan: Tanizaki Jun'ichirō and Kawabata Yasunari. Both of these writers may also be fairly characterized as "apolitical" in the typical Taishō manner. But the real point of interest, from the perspective of the present essay, is that both must be regarded, nonetheless, as exemplary national narrators, since each developed in his own way a new form of national narrative, one based not on social or political engagement but on a form of cultural nationalism. That this is an obvious fact to the present generation of Japanese writers was made clear to the world in 1994 by Ōe Kenzaburō's Nobel Prize acceptance speech: by titling his speech "Japan the Ambiguous and Myself" (Aimai na Nippon no watashi), Ōe pointedly sought to distance himself from the cultural nationalism of older writers such as Kawabata, a previous winner of the prize, whose own acceptance speech, "Japan, the Beautiful, and Myself" (Utsukushii Nippon no watashi) had been a wholehearted encomium to the Japanese aesthetic and spiritual tradition (Ōe 1995; see also Kawabata 1969). As someone who had grown up in wartime and postwar Japan, Ōe felt that he could not share Kawabata's unambivalent enthusiasm for the glories of Japanese culture.

Nevertheless, the gentle cultural nationalism of Kawabata and Tanizaki should in no way be equated with the fanatic ultranationalism of their contemporaries, the early Shōwa militarists. Although, from a historical point of view, both phenomena may be seen as manifestations of the conservative "back to Japan" movement of the period, the resultant world views were quite literally "worlds apart." Both Kawabata and Tanizaki may be said to have created an "alternate Japan," very different from the pseudosamurai Japan of the militarists—equally idealized perhaps, but following a very different ideal, closer to the "feminine" tradition of the Heian courtiers than to the "masculine" tradition of the more violent middle ages so often evoked by the militarists. It also is important to note that neither Kawabata nor Tanizaki sought chauvinistically to exclude the West from his vision of a Japanese cultural renaissance. On the contrary, both profited enormously as artists from the dialectical interplay between Western culture and their own tradition. Indeed, much of the dynamism and originality of their work derives precisely from this cultural interplay.

As long as Tanizaki, for instance, confined himself to an ardent devotion to all things Western, from the *esthétique du mal* of Baudelaire and Poe to the more vulgar pleasures of such new Taishō fads as Hollywood movies and ballroom dancing, his fiction rarely rose above the level of a rather superficial sensationalism. It was only after the Great Kantō Earthquake of 1923 forced him to move to the Kansai area and to rediscover the pleasures of Japanese tradition that his work may be said to have acquired the depth of serious literature. It seems that he needed the inspiration of the theme of East-West cultural conflict to give his work this necessary depth. Thus his first major novel, *A Fool's Love* (*Chijin no ai,* 1924),[3] brilliantly satirizes his own earlier infatuation with Western culture, borrowing the basic plotline of Somerset Maugham's *Of Human Bondage* but giving it a new cross-cultural twist: the femme fatale with whom the male protagonist is foolishly infatuated is a monster created by his own desire for a self-assertive, exotically "Western" woman. *Some Prefer Nettles* (*Tade kuu mushi,* 1929), written five years later, is a more elegant and mature expression of Tanizaki's "rediscovery" of traditional pleasures. Here the male hero, unlike the "fool" of the earlier novel, consciously chooses to "revert" to native tastes in art, women, and even domestic architecture—and ends up a happier and a wiser man.

Judging, then, by the vastly improved quality of Tanizaki's fiction at this time, which occurred with a startling suddenness and permanency, the move to Kansai seems to have precipitated the major creative breakthrough of his life. The erstwhile connoisseur of all things Western and modern now felt the pull of a counterattraction: the great charm and value of the old native traditions of the Kansai area. What occurred for him was not simply an "exchange" of Japan for the West, or of tradition for modernity—this would hardly have served as such a powerful creative stimulus. Rather a new dialectical tension was introduced into his thinking and his work. Unlike the ultranationalists of the day, he never adopted a xenophobic tone or favored a one-way pendulum swing away from the West or modernity and toward Japan or tradition. He preferred to keep the pendulum swinging both ways. Even in *A Fool's Love* he obviously relishes the male hero's "Occidentalism"—to the extent of taking some pleasure in his masochistic submission to the "Westernized" female's arbitrary and dictatorial treatment of her male lover—at the same time that he satirizes this example of male "folly."

One of the outstanding features of works of Tanizaki's later career such as *The Key* (*Kagi*, 1956) and *Diary of a Mad Old Man* (*Fūten rōjin nikki*, 1962) is the charming and effortless way in which his "mad old men" take as much pleasure in, say, a gleaming new swimming pool as in a statue of the boddhisattva Kannon. Always more the tolerant hedonist than the closed-minded ideologue, Tanizaki was happy to take his pleasures wherever he could find them and thus was often pulled in two directions at once. But, like other Taishō writers and unlike the older, more politically or ideologically inclined Meiji writers, he never seemed to suffer any great psychological pain on account of the resultant "culture clash." Tanizaki's down-to-earth, laissez-faire attitude is nicely epitomized by a story his wife once told. An architect whom he had hired to build a new house had dutifully read his essay, *In Praise of Shadows* (*In'ei raisan*, 1933–1934), which waxes lyrical about traditional domestic architecture, and thus confidently assured the writer that he knew exactly what he wanted. But Tanizaki promptly responded that he could never actually *live* in such a house—when aesthetics clashed with comfort, there was no doubt as to which took precedence with Tanizaki![4]

In contrast to that of Tanizaki, Kawabata's intercultural or East-West drama was played out in more purely formal literary terms. When he first appeared on the literary scene in the late Taishō period, it was as a leading spokesman of the *shinkankaku-ha*, the so-called neosensory school of young writers who, inspired by the European modernism of the 1920s, were eager to develop radical new techniques of literary expression. In conscious opposition to the Marxist "proletarian literature" school that also appeared at this time, these writers insisted on the primacy of aesthetics over politics or any other "extraliterary" considerations.[5] The young Kawabata tried his hand at a variety of the latest modernist experimental techniques—most notably, a remarkably successful exercise in Joycean stream-of-consciousness narrative, *Crystal Fantasies* (*Suishō gensō,* 1931), which also made good use of the recently fashionable Freudian concept of the unconscious for an in-depth analysis of the psychology of an infertile woman. This early "flirtation" with Western ideas and styles was, sure enough, followed by a "return" to a more traditionally Japanese style of writing in the mid 1930s. Still, looking more closely, we find that, as with Tanizaki, what this "conservative reaction" involved was less a divorce from the foreign culture than a marriage between that and Japanese culture. Certainly, the great "haiku novels" that Kawabata wrote over the next twenty years—masterpieces such as *Snow Country* (*Yukiguni,* 1935–1947), *Thousand Cranes* (*Sembazuru,* 1952), and *The Sound of the Mountain* (*Yama no oto,* 1954)—may be properly regarded as celebrations of Japanese tradition; at the same time, they successfully revitalize that tradition precisely by a subtle incorporation of much that Kawabata had learned from Western modernism. In particular, a close analysis of these texts reveals that he never lost his taste for surrealistic imagery and stream-of-consciousness narrative.[6] And the fact that he never really abandoned modernism was made even clearer by the powerful surrealist stories he wrote in the last decade of his career: *Sleeping Beauties* (*Nemureru bijo,* 1961), "One Arm" (Kata ude, 1965), and *Dandelions* (*Tanpopo,* 1972).

One may question whether Tanizaki's and Kawabata's highly aesthetic form of cultural nationalism contributed as concretely to the nation-building enterprise as Ōgai's and Sōseki's more direct concern with the health of the body politic. Of course, it is to the more insubstantial but nonetheless indispensable ingredients of nationhood that such "aesthetic" literature contributes, those ingredients that Ernest Renan judged to be of paramount importance in his celebrated talk of 1882, "What is a nation?":

> A nation is a soul, a spiritual principle. . . . More valuable by far than common custom posts and frontiers conforming to strategic ideas is the fact of sharing, in the past, a glorious heritage and regrets . . . or the fact of having suffered, enjoyed, and hoped together. (Renan 1990, 19)

In the Japanese context in particular, purely "aesthetic" literature had long been assigned a central place in definitions of national identity. Since so much of the nation's religious and philosophical culture was imported from continental Asia, it was to the native language and literature that nationalists often turned in their search for the defining characteristics of "Japaneseness." We may see this brand of cultural nationalism at work especially in such Tokugawa nativist scholars and revivalists of Shinto as Kamo Mabuchi (1697–1769) and Motoori Norinaga (1730–1817), who held up literary classics such as the *Manyōshū,* the *Tale of Genji,* and the *Shinkokinshū* as pure expressions of Japanese sentiment—or, in Mabuchi's words, as the "voice of our divine land."

But the importance to the nation of Tanizaki's and Kawabata's form of cultural nationalism did not become fully apparent until after 1945. By providing a positive model of an "alternate Japan" that was uncontaminated by the militarist ethos, they played a key role in the difficult task of nation-rebuilding that Japan had to undertake in the dark days following its defeat in the Pacific War. By showing that there remained much of value in the native tradition, and much that could still be successfully integrated into modern culture, they provided a salutary alternative to those intellectuals who, in their eagerness to distance themselves from the evils of the immediate past, were prepared to scuttle the whole of Japanese tradition—Bashō's haiku along with Tōjō's bushido. And when Kawabata was awarded the Nobel Prize for literature in 1968, to many Japanese this seemed an important milestone in their postwar history, one marking Japan's acceptance back into the community of civilized nations. It was made all the sweeter by the fact that, as the Nobel committee acknowledged, the prize was awarded to recognize Kawabata's achievement in revitalizing a distinctly Japanese tradition.

To return now, though, to the period more particularly under consideration here: toward the very end of that period, in April 1929, there finally began to appear, serialized in the journal *Chūō kōron*, a large-scale novel that in many respects may be regarded as the culminating achievement of Japanese writers' long struggle, after 1868, to create a satisfying national narrative. This, of course, was the work of Shimazaki Tōson I have already mentioned, *Before the Dawn* (1929–1935). What is particularly interesting about Shimazaki's work, in light of the other works discussed here, is that it achieves this culminating status by conflating the public dimension of Meiji fiction with the private dimension of Taishō fiction, the concern with history with the concern with family relations—and, in particular, with the relation between father and son. In other words, it combines elements of Meiji historical fiction ň la Mori Ōgai with elements of the Taishō *shishōsetsu* ň la Shiga Naoya—and so it may legitimately be regarded as the culmination of the two major, although apparently antithetical, tendencies in the Japanese fiction of the first three decades of this century.

Shimazaki's father, who had been a village headman under the Tokugawa feudal system, found himself suddenly dispossessed of his power and even of his social usefulness by the new Meiji order, and this led to his steady moral decline and ultimate descent into madness. This tragic father figure had haunted and also embarrassed Tōson since his youth. Thus when, in his late fifties, he resolved to write his first historical novel and confront the complex reality of the transformation Japan had undergone in the late Tokugawa and early Meiji period, this also became, inevitably, a resolve to confront his own troubled family history. On a personal level, the novel is both an elegy and an exorcism. But, unlike a *shishōsetsu*, Shimazaki's novel also attains to a much wider dimension: by using his own father's tragic story in a symbolic way, to represent the human costs of nineteenth-century Japan's nation-building and modernization, Shimazaki both achieves a Shiga-style "reconciliation" with his traditionalist father and creates an exemplary national narrative in the tradition—if not quite in the style—of Ōgai. As the translator who accomplished the herculean labor of rendering the novel into English, William E. Naff, has written: ". . . Tōson's version of the story of the Meiji restoration has played a major role in defining the form in which those great events of the middle third of the nineteenth century have entered the Japanese national consciousness" (Shimazaki 1987, XI).

From a historical point of view, of course, this may not have been an entirely good thing: it may have been preferable if the "Japanese national consciousness" had taken its view of late Tokugawa and early Meiji history from a less passionate, more disinterested source than Shimazaki's novel. *Before the Dawn*'s conflation of family history with national history is its weakness as well as its strength. The novel's tragic father figure, Aoyama Hanzō, is a passionate devotee of the Hirata school of nationalist ideology, and thus, for him, the only legitimate response to the challenge of the West is a revitalization of Japanese tradition: "'The more the foreign countries provoke us, the more we'll look back to our own past'" (Shimazaki 1987, 84). Unfortunately for him, however, this "we" did not include the early Meiji leadership; instead of the restoration of "pure" Japanese and imperial tradition that had been promised, they engineered a renewed opening to the West on an unprecedented scale. Even the sacred imperial court itself was not untouched. Even there European fashions and manners became ň la mode. For a simple country traditionalist and nationalist like Hanzō, it seemed that the new Meiji regime was intent on destroying millennia of Japanese tradition and turning Japan into a foreign country, a country in which there would be no room for men like himself. Of course, he was not alone in his disaffection, and people who called for a return to tradition and a new imperial restoration by no means died out with his generation. Indeed, at the very time Shimazaki was publishing this novel they were in the process of taking over the national government.

Looking back on *Before the Dawn* from our present historical perspective, then, we may feel uncomfortable about its tendency to idealize and romanticize the Japanese past, its presenting of Tokugawa village life as a model of law and order and as a kind of sweet pastoral idyll, its championing of the more noble qualities of *kokugaku* nationalism and agrarianism, and, on the other hand, its demonization of the Meiji government and of the Western powers, who are seen standing threateningly behind it. Whether or not such was Shimazaki's intention, this unbalanced and rather simplistic view of history obviously fed very nicely into the simple pieties of the nationalist ideology that was very much on the rise in the early 1930s.

Of course, any historical novel runs the risk of being judged as history rather than as fiction—a price to be paid for the ambiguous status of the genre. Although *Before the Dawn,* given the time at which it was written, may be a particularly sensitive case in point, even the most innocuous historical romance may be condemned for misleading its readers with its historical distortions. But a historical novel is first and foremost a novel and must be judged as such; questions of its historical accuracy are secondary. As fiction, Shimazaki's presentation of late Tokugawa and early Meiji history is eminently successful, because it represents so well the world view of its central protagonist, Aoyama Hanzō, and provides a more than sufficient "objective correlative" for his descent into madness. As for the novel's wider historical meaning, although one would not want it taken as the last word on mid-nineteenth-century Japanese history, the fact that there were many others like Hanzō, and that their disaffection and rage ultimately would erupt onto the world stage with such disastrous consequences, surely gives the novel profound significance as an historical document as well.

NOTES

1. Although it is Sōseki's image that now graces the thousand-yen bill, apparently the Finance Ministry's first choice had been Ōgai—a choice that seems somehow more appropriate—but a suitable portrait or photograph of him could not be found (according to a Finance Ministry official who spoke at the Nichibunken Conference, Kyoto, October 1994).
2. For a thorough account of the Taishō generation's response to General Nogi's suicide as one of the defining events of their youth, see Yanagida, Katsumoto, and Ino 1965, 4–7.
3. Translated into English as *Naomi* by Anthony H. Chambers (1990).
4. The story is recounted by Tanizaki 1977, 48.
5. For reasons of space, I confine myself to dealing with major writers here and do not deal with the Marxist writers, despite their undoubted historical importance: the movement produced no major creative writers, although it did make a significant contribution to the development of literary theory in Japan.
6. For a fuller account, see my forthcoming *Soundings in Time: The Fictive Art of Kawabata Yasunari.*

REFERENCES

Akutagawa Ryūnosuke. 1930. *Tales Grotesque and Curious,* translated by Glenn Shaw. Hokuseido.
Arima, Tatsuo. 1969. *The Failure of Freedom: A Portrait of Modern Japanese Intellectuals.* Cambridge: Harvard University Press.
Kawabata Yasunari. 1969. *Japan, the Beautiful, and Myself.* Kodansha.

Keene, Donald. 1984. *Dawn to the West: Japanese Literature in the Modern Era* (Fiction). New York: Holt, Rinehart & Winston.

Kōno Toshirō, Miyoshi Yukio, Takemori Tenyū, and Hiraoka Toshino, eds. 1972. *Taishō no bungaku.* Yūhikaku.

Marcus, Marvin. 1993. *Paragons of the Ordinary: The Biographical Literature of Mori Ōgai.* Honolulu: University of Hawai'i Press.

Mori Ōgai. 1977. *The Incident at Sakai and Other Stories,* edited by David Dilworth and J. Thomas Rimer. Honolulu: University of Hawai'i Press.

———. 1994. *Youth and Other Stories,* edited by J. Thomas Rimer. Honolulu: University of Hawai'i Press.

Natsume Sōseki. 1978. *And Then,* translated by Norma Moore Field. Baton Rouge: Louisiana State University Press.

———. 1957. *Kokoro,* translated by Edwin McClellan. Chicago: Henry Regnery.

Ōe Kenzaburō. 1995. *Japan, the Ambigious, and Myself.* Kodansha.

Renan, Ernest. 1990. "What is a Nation?" In *Nation and Narration,* edited by Homi K. Bhabha. London: Routledge.

Seidensticker, Edward. 1968. *Kafū the Scribbler: The Life and Writings of Nagai Kafū, 1879–1959.* Stanford: Stanford University Press.

Shimazaki Tōson. 1987. *Before the Dawn,* translated by William E. Naff. Honolulu: University of Hawai'i Press.

Tanizaki Jun'ichirō. 1977. *In Praise of Shadows,* translated by Thomas J. Harper. New Haven: Leete's Island Books.

———. 1990. *Naomi,* translated by Anthony Chambers. New York: North Point Press.

Yanagida Izumi, Katsumoto Seiichirō, and Ino Kenji, eds. 1965. *Zadankai: Taishō bungaku shi.* Iwanami Shoten.

The Bunriha and the Problem of "Tradition" for Modernist Architecture in Japan, 1920–1928

JONATHAN M. REYNOLDS

In 1920, a group of young architects launched Japan's first modernist architectural movement. They called themselves the Bunriha Kenchikukai, or Secessionist Architectural Group, a name that at once linked them with contemporary movements in Europe and distanced them from the professional establishment both in the West and in Japan. At the heart of the Bunriha project was a particular vision of history. These architects sought to break with the past as it had been constructed in recent architectural practice. At the same time, they proposed to replace this problematic "past" with an architecture firmly situated in the present yet resonant with their own conception of a more vital and authentic "tradition." The Bunriha's effort to grapple with the burden of the "past" is representative of the complex process through which Japanese society was attempting to come to terms with its ambivalence toward modernization and the crisis of identity that it produced. This essay will first examine the Bunriha architects' treatment of history in their writings and will then discuss their efforts to synthesize a new historically situated identity through architectural design.

THE BUNRIHA KENCHIKUKAI

The Bunriha Kenchikukai was formed by six graduating students from the architecture department at Tokyo Imperial University.[1] The group first displayed its designs in a waiting room at the university in February of 1920. That summer the Bunriha held an exhibition at the Shirokiya department store at Nihonbashi in Tokyo and produced a catalogue containing designs and essays by its members.[2]

The Vienna Secession undoubtedly inspired the choice of the name Bunriha (Secessionist group). The group did not, however, perceive itself merely as an offshoot of the dynamic Viennese movement of artists and architects active at the turn of the century.[3] One of the Bunriha members, Yamada Mamoru (1894–1966), emphatically asserted that the word *secessionist* should not be interpreted narrowly as a reference to the Vienna Secession. Rather, Yamada insisted that the name should be understood more generally as an expression of the group's intention to secede from certain practices current in the architectural profession at that time. Yamada even stated that when the group's name was rendered in Roman letters it should be written as "Bunriha" and not translated as "Secessionist Group" in order to avoid any confusion (Yamada 1921, 25–26). The group's members were careful to affirm their independence and not to substitute the encumbrances of one affiliation for another.

The Bunriha issued a dramatic manifesto that featured prominently in its exhibition catalogues. The architects declared:

> We arise!
> We break away *(bunri shite)* from the realm of past architecture so that we might create a new architectural realm where all of the architecture that we produce is given genuine significance
> We arise!
> In order to awaken all that is sleeping in the realm of past architecture
> In order to rescue all that is in the process of drowning
> In a state of joy, we dedicate everything that we have to the attainment of this ideal and we will wait expectantly for it until we collapse and die
> In unison, we declare this to the world!
> (Bunriha Kenchikukai 1920, n.p.)[4]

This emotionally charged declaration is a call to action—a commitment to free the profession from the fetters of a complacent architectural establishment. The message is driven by a sincere and idealistic spirit and is expressed in intense—even ecstatic—language. These architects pledged to achieve their goals or die making the attempt.

The Bunriha's manifesto has many points in common with the pronouncements of other Japanese student groups during this period. The initial statement of purpose of the Shinjinkai, a leftist student group at Tokyo Imperial University formed in December of 1918, stated:

> I. We will work for and seek to advance the new trends towards the liberation of mankind which is a universal cultural force.

II. We will engage ourselves in the movement for the rational
reform of contemporary Japan. (Smith 1972, 52)

Both the Bunriha and the Shinjinkai grounded their idealistic endeavors in
the particular conditions that they found in Japan and yet called for a total
transformation of these conditions and claimed that their project held universal significance.[5] They were in search of a new order. What distinguished
the Bunriha from their Shinjinkai classmates was the degree to which a lost
past would play a role in their vision of the future.

The authors of the manifesto were participating in a modernist discourse that links them directly with colleagues in Europe. One might, for
example, compare it with Bruno Taut's essay of 1919:

> Art seeks to be an image of death. . . . to furnish the threshold at which
> mean preoccupation with earthly things dissolves in contemplation of
> that which opens up beyond death . . . . [the artist] assigns everything
> to its place. . . . Light casts its radiance over all. . . . The earth itself
> sparkles with the New; as the impossible becomes possible, "hard"
> reality yields up miracles. (Pehnt 1973, 55)

In both cases the authors wield a vivid, proselytizing rhetoric. Each passage
raises the specter of death, a move that acknowledges the only meaningful
limits to human endeavor and highlights what is at stake in the artistic
process. Most importantly, these modernists share a fascination with the
"New." The Bunriha architects, like Taut, express faith in the possibility of
transformation and renewal through art.

THE PROBLEM OF "TRADITION"

The Bunriha members were exceptionally self-conscious about the historical
process. The rejection of some uses of the past was not a denial of history
itself. In fact, Horiguchi Sutemi (1895–1984), one of the leaders, argued that
any effort to attempt to place oneself outside of history was itself a historically constituted act (Horiguchi 1921, 7; also Fujii and Yamaguchi 1973,
153). The Bunriha's historical perspective was emphatically international in
its scope. Many of the group's published essays placed their works in a broad
context by citing the architecture of ancient Greece and of medieval Europe
as well as Buddhist temples and Shinto shrines (for example, Ishimoto 1920,
1). These writings emphasized the development of architecture resulting
from social transformation or technological development. History was being
represented not as millstone fixing architectural practice in place but as
proof for the inevitability of change. The Bunriha architects, of course, saw
themselves as leaders at the vanguard of this ongoing process.

When the Bunriha members declared their break with the past, what they were objecting to was the academic historicism that dominated their profession. These architects studied in the oldest architecture program in the country, at Tokyo Imperial University. This program, originally established at the Imperial Engineering College, had been organized by the Japanese government in the 1870s as one facet of its sweeping modernization effort. The purpose had been to facilitate the adaptation of Western building technology and Western architectural styles in Japan. The government itself was a generous patron of Western building and was the primary employer of the early graduates of the architecture program. In fact, the early graduates were obligated to work for the government for seven years after graduation in exchange for their training. Masonry structures with pedimented porticos and neo-Baroque domes came to characterize the public space of the Meiji era. The Bunriha architects, like two generations of academically trained architects before them, were still expected to design with a palette of styles such as Romanesque, Gothic, and Italian Renaissance, all derived from European architectural practice. In the 1870s, the systematic use of historically based styles—historicism—was still seen as "progressive," but in the eyes of these newly minted architects of the 1920s, the historicizing styles had become the stale conventions of an architectural establishment divorced from modern life.

Modernists questioned not only the predominance of historicism but the process through which the styles were selected and applied in any given design. In the profession as it was being practiced in Europe and Japan, each historical style had meaning, and certain styles were thought to be more appropriate for a given project than others. Nonetheless, architects would readily substitute one style for another in accordance with the whims of a patron.[6] As a result, for a growing number of architects, the choice of styles seemed arbitrary.[7] Furthermore, these styles were developed originally in conjunction with earlier building methods. Yet architects continued to incorporate them into buildings even when those structures were constructed with modern materials. In Europe, from the late nineteenth century onward, a growing number of architects began to reject this approach, believing that it resulted in work that lacked integrity and coherence.[8] The Bunriha agreed with the European critics that architectural design had been reduced to a process of choosing from a wardrobe of styles and to the superficial manipulation of ornament. Horiguchi likened traditional forms pasted onto contemporary architecture to moss and duckweed floating on stagnant water (Horiguchi 1921, 8; also Fujii and Yamaguchi 1973, 154). If an architect was to employ ornament, it was crucial that the ornament be appropriate to and properly integrated with the project at hand.

Although the Bunriha as a group condemned the misuse of past architectural forms, its members did not all turn their backs on the various architectural practices that they had inherited. Horiguchi was concerned that critics had misunderstood the Bunriha's call to "secede from the realm of past architecture" as a total rejection of "tradition." He offered a nuanced interpretation of this pronouncement in an essay titled "Thoughts on Art and Architecture" from the Bunriha's second catalogue in 1921. Horiguchi wrote:

> There is no doubt that modern architecture could not have come into being detached from architecture of the past. In this sense, we have absorbed tradition deeply into our blood and muscle and it has matured in every cell in our bodies—we could never just decide to separate ourselves from it. (Horiguchi 1921, 8; also Fujii and Yamaguchi 1973, 154)

Here as elsewhere in his writings, Horiguchi appears to be making a subtle distinction between an undifferentiated "architecture of the past" and a more selective, coherent, and meaningful "tradition." It would have been both impossible and undesirable to abandon "tradition." As Horiguchi indicates with his corporeal metaphor, he viewed "tradition" as an integral part of who the Bunriha architects were. This level of intimacy with the past would inevitably manifest itself in practice as more than a mere collection of "molds and forms that restrict expression" (Horiguchi 1921, 8; also Fujii and Yamaguchi 1973, 153).

Some Bunriha architects were more impatient with the burdens of history than others. Okamura Bunzō (1902–1978) wanted to wipe the slate clean. In the catalogue of 1924, he wrote:

> Smash the conventions and rigid customs that have piled up over
>   the past several thousand years,
> The acanthus motif, the Roman orders (of column ornamentation)
> The Gothic, the Renaissance
> Throw away all "tradition" *(arayuru dentō)* without regret
> Become naked and wash away the impure grime that has been such
>   a curse up to now
> And just like that pure poem, let us restore the world to its original
>   state of long ago
> Reform from that point forward and dance out into the heaven of
>   creation.
>
> (Okamura 1924, 27)

Okamura, who was a late arrival to the Bunriha, was one of the most uncompromising affiliates of the group. His vision of his architectural mission was as romantic as that of his colleagues, but there was a sharper edge to his attack on the past. Significantly, Okamura's writings became increasingly political later in the 1920s, and his vigorous rejection of "tradition" became transformed into a Marxist critique of society.

The question of the role of "tradition" in architectural practice is further complicated by a long-standing, fractious debate over national identity within the Japanese architectural community. As mentioned above, the modern architectural profession in Japan was established in order to produce Western-style buildings using modern—in this context, Western—construction methods. In the first decade of its existence, the architecture program virtually ignored Japan's own architectural legacy. This began to change in a limited way in the late 1880s. By the 1890s academically trained architects such as Itō Chūta (1867–1954) championed Japanese architectural history and even advocated the formation of a new architectural style that would reflect Japan's unique architectural position by combining Western and Japanese elements.

Itō participated in several projects to restore or replicate premodern Japanese buildings (for example, the construction in 1895 of Heian Shrine modeled on the Administrative Court, the *Chōdōin* of the ninth-century Imperial Palace). In these instances, he relied primarily on materials appropriate to the historic structures. In most cases, however, he relied on contemporary methods and materials. Throughout his career, Itō designed

Itō Chūta, Great Kantō Earthquake Memorial Hall, Tokyo, 1927. (Photo by Jonathan M. Reynolds.)

buildings in unambiguously Western styles, such as his Romanesque Kane-matsu Lecture Hall at Hitotsubashi University, completed in 1927. He also produced works that appropriated Japanese architectural elements. The Great Kantō Earthquake Memorial Hall (also 1927) was constructed with the most earthquake- and fire-resistant methods available to Itō, including steel and steel reinforced concrete. Yet the main entrance is covered by a roof in the form of a *karahafu* (Chinese-style gable), in a manner similar to the formal entrances of Edo-period estates. The main hall has a tiled hipped-and-gabled roof characteristic of premodern public structures in Japan, including many Buddhist halls. At the rear of the building is an ossuary in the form of a three-story pagoda. Itō extended his new vocabulary of decorative ornament to smaller architectural details, as well. The electric light fixtures in the main sanctuary, for example, are in the form of the Buddhist lotus. Itō applied this ornament to the hall's modern structure in the same way that other programs of ornament in the Western academic mode might have been applied, but instead of looking to ancient Greece or Renaissance Italy, he turned to premodern Japanese sources.

Itō was in effect constructing a new "tradition" for contemporary practice. As Raymond Williams has observed:

> It [tradition] is always more than an inert historicized segment; indeed it is the most powerful practical means of incorporation. What we have to see is not just "a tradition" but a *selective tradition:* an intentionally selective version of a shaping past and a preshaped present, which is then powerfully operative in the process of social and cultural definition and identification. (Williams 1977, 115; emphasis in original)

Itō's Earthquake Memorial is a particularly graphic example of the process that Williams is describing. Itō and others of his generation were concerned that Japan might lose its cultural identity as a consequence of the modernization that had been promoted to preserve the nation's political autonomy. It is unlikely that anyone would mistake Itō's Earthquake Memorial for an "authentically traditional" building. Its hybrid quality is readily apparent. And yet, the inclusion of selective citations from Japan's architectural past creates tangible connections with an imagined pre-Westernized and hence more "authentically Japanese" Japan.

Within the architectural profession the Bunriha architects were entering, there were diverse opinions on the relationship between style and cultural identity. Itō's approach was only one among many. Professionals debated this issue for years in articles and panel discussions. A panel discussion sponsored by the Architectural Association (Kenchiku Gakkai) in May of 1910 titled "What should our country's future architectural style be?" provides a cross section of opinion within the profession's leadership. Some participants were not troubled by the Western origins of the architectural styles that they employed. Nagano Uheiji (1867–1837) argued that it had been necessary to adopt Western dress and weaponry after the Meiji Restoration but that this did not mean that Japan had lost its national essence (here Nagano uses both the term *kokusui* and the loanword *nashonaritei*). Nagano also pointed out that in the distant past Japan had incorporated architecture from China without losing its identity. With all of this in mind, he advocated the European architectural styles for Japan (Nagano 1910, 260–264). Itō argued for "the creation of a new Japanese style based on a careful study of architecture of the past and present in the East and the West" (Itō 1910, 266). Others were even more traditionalist than Itō.[9] Architects never really formed a consensus on the matter.

The concern over whether cultural practices closely linked to practices in the West were still "Japanese" was not limited to the field of architecture. In 1910, the same year the Kenchiku Gakkai sponsored its panel on Japan's architectural future, the artist Takamura Kōtarō published a celebrated essay titled "The Green Sun" ("Midori iro no taiyō"). He wrote:

> I hope Japanese artists will try to use all *möglich* techniques without being put out by interpretation. I pray that when they do so, consequent on their interior psychological demands, they are not afraid of what is un-Japanese. However, un-Japanese this might be, if a Japanese person creates it, it must be Japanese. (Clark 1994, 41–42)

For Takamura, a work need not have any formal characteristics that would distinguish it as "Japanese." The work would be "Japanese" simply by benefit of having been produced by a Japanese. It is testimony to the pervasiveness of the anxiety over cultural identity at this time that this avant-garde artist felt compelled to affirm the "Japaneseness" of Japanese artistic production.

Some Bunriha members also felt compelled to address this issue. There was an interest in affirming the "Japaneseness" of the group's work, perhaps because it was so closely identified with European movements. Yada Shigeru (1896–1958) touched on the issue obliquely in an article that criticized the Meiji generation for adopting Western methods wholesale without regard to prevailing conditions in Japan. The essay does not, however, press the "Japaneseness" of the more modern work that he and his colleagues advocated (Yada 1920, 15–28). Horiguchi seemed especially concerned with the problem. He observed that there should be a close connection between a place and the architecture produced there. He wrote: "Because of its intimate relationship to real life, [architecture] cannot be separated from the locality and country [in which it is produced]. Greek architecture is Greek, Indian architecture is Indian, and in Japan architecture is Japanese" (Horiguchi 1920, 10). Horiguchi stressed that architecture needed to be adapted to the unique climate of a given location. In turn, architectural styles would necessarily vary in accord with differences in physical conditions and local history. In this essay, Horiguchi did not elaborate in detail how the Japaneseness of Japanese architecture might manifest itself, but some of his designs of the 1920s explore this question in an illuminating fashion.

ARTISTIC EXPRESSION

The Bunriha architects asserted that artistic expression was essential to architectural practice. Ishimoto Kikuji (1894–1963) declared in the first line of his essay in the group's first catalogue "Architecture is one of the arts. Please recognize this fact!" (Ishimoto 1920, 1). The Bunriha's concern with affirming architecture as an art is a response to the work of one of the most influential architectural critics at the time, Noda Toshihiko (1891–1921). Noda published an essay in 1915 in which he challenged the broadly accepted belief that architecture should be considered one of the fine arts. He wrote: "Architecture is not art *(geijutsu)*" (Noda 1915, 28).[10] Noda's argument is sympathetic with the functionalist approach of Sano Riki (1880–1956), an architect, engineer, and Noda's professor at Tokyo Imperial University. He also may have been indebted to the Viennese architect and theorist Adolf Loos (1870–1933) and his controversial polemic "Ornament and Crime" and other writings (Loos 1964, 19–24).[11] Noda distinguished the arts that were intended to express feelings to others from practices that were primarily functional. Noda viewed architecture as a practical object to serve specific functions. It can be argued that this Loosian distinction was more radically modernist than the Bunriha's position; but despite this, it was well received in certain segments of the architectural profession that had always been heavily oriented toward engineering.

Horiguchi discussed this issue at some length in "Thoughts on Art and Architecture." Horiguchi agreed with Noda and Sano that structural and economic factors had to be taken into account in any architectural project. Still, he was wary of placing too much emphasis on structural considerations. He stated:

> The art of expression in architecture is structural in nature. Therefore, the study of structures is necessary [to the practice of architecture]. I believe that the problem of structures is the first subject that architects must study. However, the study of structures is meant to aid in construction; it should not be an end in itself. (Horiguchi 1921, 3; also Fujii and Yamaguchi 1973, 150–151)

According to Horiguchi, the architect must base his designs on utilitarian needs *(kōriteki hitsuyō)*, but the engineering-oriented architects had far too narrow a definition of what these basic needs were. He wrote: "naturally utilitarian needs don't consist solely of material needs—one must include spiritual aspiration *(seishinteki yokkyū)* as well" (Horiguchi 1921, 4; also in Fujii and Yamaguchi 1973, 152).

Horiguchi's argument was, to some extent, reminiscent of the position Itō Chūta articulated in an essay of 1894. In his piece, Itō was challenging the engineering bias of his profession in the 1890s, just as Horiguchi was resisting Noda's "anti-aestheticism" of the 1910s (Itō 1894; also in Fujii and Yamaguchi 1973, 4–9). Both architects insisted that artistic expression was at least as important as structure to architecture. Yet, these architects conceived of artistic expression and the purposes of art in different ways. When Itō began his career, there was still a sense of national crisis, and "national spirit" affected people's outlook on a surprisingly wide range of activities.[12] Itō's efforts to convince his colleagues of the importance of aesthetics in architecture and his related campaign to reestablish links with Japan's architectural heritage were intended at least at one level as contributions to the strengthening of the nation.

The sense of national crisis that was still so acute in the 1890s seemed to be less pressing in the early 1920s. Japan's economy was stronger and its position in the world seemed somewhat more secure. In this context, Horiguchi and his fellow Bunriha members did not feel compelled to relate their work as directly to the cause of national development. They directed their attention inward.[13] The Bunriha placed a strong emphasis on the individual, seeking in the personal, inner world a new source for artistic inspiration. According to Horiguchi,

> The freedom of our inner lives can be obtained only when we stand independent of others and form a style that is most appropriate to ourselves; only then will there emerge a world of individuality *(kosei no sekai)*, and the style of this world will come to be expressed through our creations. (Horiguchi 1921, 7)

In order for the architect's art to remain vital, he must strive for personal expression.

BUNRIHA DESIGNS

The Bunriha was not defined by any particular style or method of design. The group's designs reflected a wide variety of stylistic sources, including that of the Vienna Secession, Expressionism, the Amsterdam School, and the Bauhaus. There was, however, little mention of American architecture in this circle.[14] When the Bunriha was established in 1920, members relied primarily on architectural magazines for information about European modernism.

Within a few years, several members traveled to Europe to meet leading modernist architects and see their work. Horiguchi Sutemi visited Vienna, Paris, Brussels, Amsterdam, and the Bauhaus in Weimar from 1923 to 1924. Ishimoto Kikuji traveled to Germany to work with Gropius in 1922. Yamada Mamoru also made a pilgrimage to Europe, but not until 1929, after the group had disbanded.

The impact of Expressionism was particularly strong among the Bunriha architects. Yamada Mamoru, a founding member of the group and an architect in the Communications Ministry, produced several expressionist designs. A design that he included in the Bunriha exhibition of 1921 as "An Office Building" eventually developed into the Tokyo Central Telephone Office, which was completed under the auspices of the Communications Ministry in 1925. Across one facade of the Central Telegraph Office, Yamada placed a row of thin vertical windows running the entire height of the building. These narrow bays were capped with slightly rounded Gothic arched gables reminiscent of French Gothic lancet windows. Hans Poelzig's Grosse Schauspielhaus in Berlin of 1918–1919 and Peder Vilhelm Jensen-Klint's St. Hans Tveje at Odense of 1919 are possible sources for this treatment of the facade.

Expressionism is also evident in Takizawa Mayumi's (1896–?) dramatic model of "A Mountain House," which was included in the second Bunriha exhibition in 1921. Like so much of Expressionist work, there is a strong suggestion of a highly romanticized vision of medieval Europe in the design, both in terms of the Gothic windows and irregularity of the form. With an entry court like the entrance to a cave, and with sloping and concave walls, the house looks like it was carved out of a mountainside. Takizawa's design is strongly suggestive of European works, such as Hermann Orbrist's Monumental Building on a Rock of 1908.

Yada Shigeru's classical design for a Community Hall for an Artists' Colony of 1920 is a startling contrast with the previous works. The entry portico is marked with a monumental colonnade. Enclosed gardens flank the entrance on both sides. The historicizing detail, however, has been suppressed. The columns do not have clearly articulated capitals. There is not a pronounced cornice but only a thin, elegant molding outlining the cornice and the side corners of the exterior walls. Josef Hoffmann was frequently cited in Bunriha writings, and his Stoclet House (begun in 1905) could have provided a model for Yada.

All three of the preceding designs included allusions to contemporary European architects, and like those colleagues, Yamada, Takizawa, and Yada also included allusions to European historical styles, such as the classical and the Gothic. Although they drew from historical sources, these modernist appropriations were a far cry from the systematic application of historical styles that was common in the profession as a whole. The historicizing

Takizawa Mayumi, A Mountain House, project, 1921. (Bunriha kenchikukai sakuhinshū, vol. 2. Iwanami, 1921.)

elements are subdued and radically simplified—these citations establish an atmosphere but do not dominate the overall form of the design. There are no tangible signs of Japanese architectural "tradition" in any of these works.

Horiguchi's early designs were closely related to the designs of architects associated with the Vienna Succession such as Joseph Maria Olbrich (1867–1908). This is evident in Horiguchi's tower for the Peace Memorial Exposition in Ueno Park of 1922, which is based on Olbrich's Wedding Tower at Darmstadt from 1908. When Horiguchi returned from his trip to Europe in January of 1924, he brought many new ideas back with him. He was so impressed with the Amsterdam School that, on his return to Japan, he published a study of contemporary Dutch architecture (Horiguchi 1924; also reprinted in Horiguchi 1978). Horiguchi combined Dutch elements with premodern Japanese features in his Shiensō, a private residence he completed in Warabi, Saitama prefecture, in 1926.

One remarkable feature of the Shiensō was a steeply pitched, thatched, pyramidal roof. Horiguchi juxtaposed this thick roof thatching with comparatively thin horizontal roof slabs placed over one corner of the first floor, over the entry way, and over a second-floor gable. A number of Amsterdam architects who Horiguchi presented in his publication on Dutch architecture employed thickly thatched roofs. Horiguchi characterized works such

Yada Shigeru, Community Hall for an Artists' Colony, 1920. (Bunriha kenchi-kukai sakuhinshū, *vol. 1. Iwanami, 1920.*)

as Margaret Kropholler's thatch-roofed Huize de Beukenhoek at Park Meerwijk as examples of "the bravest and freest expression . . . " (Horiguchi 1978, 141). The Shiensō's patron had read Horiguchi's book and requested a Western-style house with a similar thatched roof for his house (Fujioka 1996, 38).

One also can view the Shiensō's thatch roof as an allusion to Japan's own rustic teahouse *(sōan)* tradition. Although the designers of the early *sōan* teahouses and the Dutch architects were widely separated by time and geography, they followed the same strategy of borrowing from modest local vernacular structures, and in the process arrived at some remarkably similar roof shapes. Horiguchi commented on this use of humble materials such as thatch in elite architecture in his study of the Amsterdam School. He cited other precedents ranging from Hoffmann's Primavesi Country House (Winkelsdorf, Czechoslovakia, 1913–1914) to Marie Antoinette's elaborate cottage at the Petit Trianon at Versailles (1783). Horiguchi was struck by the dramatic contrast between the luxury of Versailles grand palaces and the rusticity of the cottage retreat. Here, he suggested a parallel between Versailles and Japanese Muromachi era estates that ran the gamut from glittering formal audience halls to refined, restrained tea houses (Horiguchi 1978, 145–146). The Shiensō was certainly not intended to duplicate any of these earlier works, but Horiguchi must have seen the design as part of this dual European and Japanese legacy.

Horiguchi Sutemi, Shiensō, exterior, Warabi-shi, Saitama, 1926. (Horiguchi Sutemi, Shiensō zushū. Kōyōsha, 1927.)

The first-floor interior is in Western style with hardwood floors (rather than *tatami* mats) and with Western-style furniture. The second-floor room has *tatami* in Japanese style. The living room has five round windows with thin mullions set in various rectilinear patterns. This motif is undoubtedly based on Japanese prototypes. Large round windows with irregular mullions were frequently used in teahouses and in larger residential complexes of the related *sukiya* style. Although the arrangement of suites of these types of windows is less common, there are some examples, such as the six round windows placed across a transom at the Shoi-ken teahouse on the grounds of the Katsura Villa.[15] Horiguchi did not blindly reproduced this motif. He brought the windows up to date, by covering them with marbled or rippled translucent glass, rather than with translucent paper. He placed round windows near the front entrance and on the pump house at the edge of the enclosed garden making them an important unifying theme for the design as whole.

The combination of Western and premodern Japanese sources in the Shiensō might, at first, appear to be inconsistent with Horiguchi's own criticism of historicism. I would argue, however, that the sources in the Shiensō are both more thoroughly integrated and ambiguous (is the roof

*Horiguchi Sutemi, Shiensō, living room, Warabi-shi, Saitama,
1926. (Horiguchi Sutemi, Shiensō zushū. Kōyōsha, 1927.)*

Dutch or Japanese? are the windows "traditional" or modern?) than in the
designs of academic eclectics such as Itō. The complex layering of Japanese
and European modernist sources suggests the complex and layered nature
of the historical situation in which Horiguchi and his Bunriha colleagues
found themselves. Modern materials and technology were as much a part of
their experience as they were for European contemporaries. If we accept
Horiguchi at his word that he had "absorbed tradition deeply into their blood
and muscles," that "tradition" included the architectural legacy of both Japan
and Europe. In Horiguchi's Shiensō those sources were brought together in
a fundamentally new way.

The Bunriha remained active for eight years. By the time it disbanded,
its catalogues had already begun to look old-fashioned in comparison with
the more starkly modern designs presented by new modernist organizations
such as the Sōūsha (founded by a Bunriha member, Okamura Bunzō, and

others in 1923). Even the Bunriha's defense of architecture as a mode of personal expression seemed out of date in the face of a growing call from Okamura and others to exploit architecture as a vehicle for social change. Members got involved in other organizations and other projects, and the architects went their own ways after their seventh exhibition in 1928.[16]

Nonetheless, the establishment of the Bunriha had tremendous significance for the development of modernism in Japan. The Bunriha's exhibitions provided these architects with a forum in which to present their ideas to the public. The group explored new developments in European architecture and played an important role in promoting these ideas within Japan's architectural community. When these young architects, who were trained within the architectural establishment, declared forcefully that they were breaking away from that establishment and were embarking on the pursuit of a new architecture, they were acting as a catalyst in the crystallization of a modernist identity. The group's visionary rhetoric helped to shape Japanese modernist discourse for years to come (Reynolds 1991, 107–122, 135–140). The act of forming an association to exhibit modernist designs and to advocate modernist ideas was equally important, because it provided a model for the kind of social institution that was essential for the emergence of a viable modernist architectural movement.

The tensions over cultural identity as expressed through architecture continued to increase in the years after the Bunriha broke up. In the late 1920s and early 1930s a number of high-profile public competitions required that buildings reflect "Japanese taste" by including unambiguous citations of premodern Japanese architectural forms, and a number of Bunriha members opposed this development. At the same time, some of these architects continued to explore Japan's architectural "traditions" in their own ways. In fact, Horiguchi became deeply involved in research on Japanese architectural history and produced a number of substantial studies on various topics including tea architecture. He also completed several important commissions in a modified *sukiya* style (such as the Hasshokan of 1967). Even Okamura Bunzō's own residence of 1940 contained many "traditional" features. Architects in Japan are as absorbed by the politics of cultural identity now as they were in the 1920s. The flexibility and imagination with which the Bunriha architects integrated the disparate sources of their works may in the end be one of the group's most important contributions to the modernist movement in Japan.

NOTES

1. The six founding members of the Bunriha were Horiguchi Sutemi, Yamada Mamoru, Ishimoto Kikuji, Takizawa Mayumi, Morita Keiichi, and Yada Shigeru. Okamura Bunzō (later known as Yamaguchi Bunzō), Hamaoka

Chikatada (later known as Kurata Chikatada), and eight others joined the Bunriha several years later.

2. By the 1910s, department stores, such as the Shirokiya, were popular venues for art exhibitions.

3. Two architects closely associated with the Vienna Secession were Otto Wagner and Joseph Maria Olbrich. Their work often included elaborate surface decoration that linked them with the Art Nouveau. At the same time, Wagner, in particular, moved away from historicizing ornament in some designs and incorporated industrial building materials in an innovative fashion that presaged later modernist developments.

4. The manifesto was included in the group's later catalogues as well (reprinted in Fujii and Yamaguchi 1973, 126).

5. Henry Smith has identified the emphasis on the new, the total, and the universal as some of the salient tropes in the Shinjinkai's rhetoric (see Smith 1972, 52–58). I would like to thank the anonymous reader who suggested this comparison.

6. One famous example of this kind of switch occurred with the design for Great Britain's War Office and Foreign Office. The commission was awarded for a Gothic design by George Gilbert Scott through a competition in 1856, but when Lord Palmerston came to power in 1859, he insisted that Scott redesign the buildings in Italian neoclassical style. See Summerson 1970, 79–90.

7. Summerson characterizes George Gilbert Scott's approach to style this way:

This is a remarkable confession of what "style" meant to Scott and, indeed, many of his contemporaries—it meant, in effect, a sum of details. The plan was something else. It needed, of course, to be practical and a practical plan often turned out not wholly unlike a traditional Neoclassical plan. And why not? The "art" was in the ornaments. (Summerson 1970, 86)

8. Past academic formulas for the use of ornament were being widely challenged in Europe at this time. As Reyner Banham points out, however, while architects such as Muthesius, Behrens, Gropius, and even Loos attacked "superfluous ornament," they did not advocate eliminating ornament altogether. See Banham 1960, 90–97.

9. See Yamaguchi's characterization of this panel discussion in Suzuki and Yamaguchi 1993, 311–312.

10. This essay was one portion of Noda's graduation thesis from Tokyo Imperial University from 1915.

11. See also the discussion of Loos in Janik and Toulmin 1973, 98–100.

12. Carol Gluck writes of this period:

National spirit, national thought, national doctrine, national essence, nationality—this outburst of nation-mindedness included explorations of national character, reassertions of indigenous ways, and projections of Japan into the world order as the nineteenth-century West defined it. Indeed the word "empire" (*teikoku*) became so fashionable in the names of schools, magazines, and insurance companies that one caricature condescendingly warned that "imperial rickshaw pullers" and "imperial nightsoilmen" would be next. This was precisely the point, as the invocations of nation included, more and more pressingly, the effort to draw all the people into the state, to have them thinking national thoughts, to make *kokumin* of them, new Japanese for what was called "the new Japan." (Gluck 1985, 23)

13. See also Mariko Tamanoi's discussion of the concept of *bunka seikatsu* in the Taishō period in her essay in this volume.

14. This is striking in that Frank Lloyd Wright's early "prairie" designs had had an impact on some of the European architects to whom the Bunriha architects were drawn and that Wright produced several designs for Japan during the Bunriha's early years. This may, in part, be a reflection of the long-standing European focus of the architectural program at Tokyo Imperial University. In addition, the unusually heavy and decorative quality of Wright's work in Japan, such as the Imperial Hotel, may not have appealed to the Bunriha architects as much as European alternatives.

15. At present, I do not have firm evidence that Horiguchi was aware of this particular structure in 1926, but within a few years of the construction of the Shiensō, Katsura would gain widespread recognition in modernist circles in Japan and abroad. Horiguchi himself published a study of Katsura in 1952. Furthermore, similar features can be found in other Edo-period structures.

16. Two of the founding members of the group, Ishimoto Kikuji and Yamada Mamoru, were not included in the final exhibition in 1928. Apparently, Ishimoto was expelled because of his involvement in the International Architecture Association of Japan (Nihon Intaanashonaru Kenchikukai), and his associate, Yamaguchi, left the Bunriha at the same time (RIA Sōgō Kenkyūjo 1982, 213).

REFERENCES

Banham, Reyner. 1960. *Theory and Design in the First Machine Age.* Cambridge: MIT Press.

Bunriha Kenchikukai. 1920 "Bunriha kenchikukai sengen." *Bunriha kenchikukai sakuhinshū.* Iwanami Shoten 1, n. p.

Clark, John. 1994. "Artistic Subjectivity in the Taishō and Early Showa Avant-Garde." In *Japanese Art After 1945: Scream Against the Sky,* edited by Alexandra Munroe. New York: Harry N. Abrams.

Fujii Shōichirō and Yamaguchi Hiroshi, ed. 1973. *Nihon kenchiku sengen bunshū.* Shōkokusha.

Fujioka Hiroyasu, et al. 1996. *Horiguchi Sutemi no "Nihon": Kūkan kōsei ni yoru bi no sekai.* Kenchikubunka.

Horiguchi Sutemi. 1920. "Kenchiku ni tai suru watashi no kansō to taidō." *Bunriha kenchikukai sakuhinshū*, 1:4–12. Iwanami Shoten.

———. 1921. "Geijutsu to kenchiku to no kansō." In *Bunriha kenchikukai sakuhinshū*, 2:1–9. Iwanami Shoten.

———. 1924. *Gendai Oranda kenchiku*. Iwanami Shoten.

———. 1978. *Kenchiku ronsō*. Kajima Shuppankai.

Gluck, Carol. 1985. *Japan's Modern Myths: Ideology in the Late Meiji Period*. Princeton: Princeton University Press.

Ishimoto Kikuji. 1920. "Kenchiku kangenron." *Bunriha kenchikukai sakuhinshū*, 1:1–3. Iwanami Shoten.

Itō Chūta. 1894. "Aakitekuchūru no hongi." *Kenchiku zasshi* 90:595–597.

———. 1910. "Wagakuni shōrai no kenchiku yōshiki o ika ni subeki ka?" *Kenchiku zasshi* 24.282 (June):16–19.

Janik, Allan, and Stephen Toulmin. 1973. *Wittgenstein's Vienna*. New York: Touchstone.

Loos, Adolf. 1964. "Ornament and Crime." In *Programs and Manifestos on 20th Century Architecture*, edited by Ulrich Conrads, 19–24. Cambridge: MIT Press.

Nagano Uheiji. 1910. "Wagakuni shōrai no kenchiku yōshiki o ika ni subeki ka?" *Kenchiku zasshi* 24.282 (June):12–16.

Noda Toshihiko. 1915. "Kenchiku higeitsu ron." *Kenchiku zasshi* 29.346 (October):28.

Okamura Bunzō. 1924. "Seisaku suru kokoro." *Bunriha kenchikukai sakuhinshū*, 3:27–28. Iwanami Shoten.

Pehnt, Wolfgang. 1973. *Expressionist Architecture*. New York: Praeger.

Reynolds, Jonathan. 1991. "Maekawa Kunio and the Emergence of Modernism in Japanese Architecture." Ph.D. diss., Stanford University.

RIA Sōgō Kenkyūjo, ed. 1982. *Kenchikuka Yamaguchi Bunzō*. Sagami Shobō.

Smith, Henry Dewitt, II. 1972. *Japan's First Student Radicals*. Cambridge: Harvard University Press.

Summerson, John. 1970. *Victorian Architecture in England: Four Studies in Evaluation*. New York: W. W. Norton.

Suzuki Hiroyuki and Yamaguchi Hiroshi, eds. 1993. *Kindai Gendai kenchikushi*.

Uchida Yoshichika, et al., eds. *Shin kenchikugaku taikei*. Vol. 5. Shōkokusha.

Williams, Raymond. 1977. *Marxism and Literature*. Oxford: Oxford University Press.

Yada Shigeru. 1920. "Kaigi yori jikaku e." *Bunriha kenchikukai sakuhinshū*, 1:15–28. Iwanami Shoten.

Yamada Mamoru. 1921. "Dai ni kai Bunriha tenrankai ni okeru watakushi no kenchikukan." *Bunriha kenchikukai sakuhinshū*, 2:25–26. Iwanami Shoten.

⇒ 11 ⇐

Defining the Modern Nation in
Japanese Popular Song, 1914–1932

CHRISTINE R. YANO

One of the most significant social aspects of the Taishō period (1912–1926) was the mass migration from rural to urban areas. Modern Taishō life was characterized by a reformulation of the existing urban culture, based in part upon a keen sense of displacement of these new urbanites. This new urbanism became the nexus of the nation and the modern in Japan. This essay examines representations of the modern Japanese nation found in popular songs from 1914 to 1932. These songs document an unofficial but no less important history of urban life filled with heady intoxication, as well as poignant loneliness (cf. Hane 1982).

The main question I address is, in what ways did themes in popular songs forge a sense of the modern and the nation in Taishō Japan? My assumptions concerning these songs are: (1) their production was not the spontaneous outpouring of people's sentiments but the calculated outcome of market strategies based upon economic gain (cf. Ivy 1993, 240), and (2) their consumption was varied but included active choices to sing or listen for individual purposes (cf. Hanes, this volume). Moreover, the familiarity with which a large segment of the adult population in Japan in the 1990s is able to recognize many of the songs, in particular as foundations of popular music today, suggests a continuing interaction with the texts and music. Although the readings I give the songs are my own, I acknowledge the multiple readings that may have been given them during the period in question, including those of consensus, defiance, nostalgia, and irony.

I base my findings primarily on song-text analysis and background readings. The song texts come from two sources: *Ryūkō kayō hyakkyoku-shū*

(Collection of One Hundred Popular Songs), compiled by Nagata Gyōji, 1967, and *Nihon ryūkōka-shi (Sengo-hen)* *(A History of Japanese Popular Songs—Prewar)*, by Komota Nobuo, Shimada Yoshifumi, Yazawa Tamotsu, and Yokozawa Chiaki, 1981, a history and anthology of songs from 1868 to 1945. For the period that I examined, 1914–1932, the sources provided more than two hundred songs.

The period that I selected spans the formative years of what is considered modern popular music in Japan. I define modern popular music in Japan as primarily vocal music written by a known composer, disseminated through mass media, sold in the form of recordings or printed sheets, and having a broad base of popularity (cf. Fujie 1989, 197–199). My study begins in 1914, when the song "Kachusha no uta" (Kachusha's Song) became a national hit, and ends in 1932, with songs composed by Koga Masao (1904–1978) setting the standard formula by which much popular music continues to be composed even today.[1] These songs, I feel, provide a unique lens illuminating some of the complexities of modern life in Taishō Japan.

My discussion of nationhood borrows from Anderson's conceptualization of the nation as built around a sense of belonging to an "imagined community" (Anderson 1983). I take these songs and their reception to be part of the process of imagining peoplehood/nationhood, differentiating between the nation *(minzoku)* and the state *(kokka)*.[2] In preserving this distinction, I place these as songs sung in service to the nation, building affective linkages among members.

JAPANESE POPULAR MUSIC, 1914–1932

Many consider the Taishō and early Shōwa eras to be the founding period of what is generically known as *ryūkōka* (popular song) in Japan. Western elements such as diatonic scales, strophic forms, harmonization, and instrumentation had been introduced through songs taught in the public school system and military bands during the Meiji era.[3] By the middle of the Taishō period, these elements had become part of the musical vocabulary of the general public and incorporated in popular songs. Nakayama Shimpei (1887–1952), composer of many hit songs of this period, was among the first generation to be educated in the Meiji-established school system with its Western-derived music education program (Mita 1992, 55). Nakayama deliberately created the Japanese *yonanuki* minor pentatonic scale (literally, without four and seven; five-note scale differing from a Western diatonic scale by deletion of the fourth and seventh degrees—solfege fa and ti) as a synthesis of Western diatonicism with the melodic structure of nineteenth-century Japanese songs.[4] One of his most influential compositions, "Sendō kouta" (Boatman's Song, 1923) was the first popular hit to use this scale.

In many instances, Western elements combined with more indigenous elements: method of vocal production and ornamentation; emphasis upon narrative genres; rhythmic structures; importance of timbre and texture over melody; heterophony (voice and accompaniment performing the same basic melody, but with slight variations); melisma (text setting of several melodic notes to one syllable of text); poetic structures; and a preponderance of melancholy rather than cheerful themes. Japanese popular songs of the period relied upon the above elements, but with a veneer of modernity achieved through Western instrumentation, harmonization, and strophic forms.

One may also see the Taishō and early Shōwa era as the founding period of modern popular song in its introduction and growth of mass media by which songs were increasingly popularized. Mass media worked toward creating a nation of listeners, connected and defined through song. The same media, which during the 1930s and 1940s effectively became a basis for military control, found its fledgling start in the 1920s. During this period, the transition from human to electronic transmission of songs helped draw the nation into an affective body.

Earlier, songs were popularized primarily by street singers known as *enkashi* (balladeers), who sold printed lyric sheets and sang songs as a way of promoting sales. The word *enka* (literally, performed speech-song) originated in the 1880s to describe antigovernment protest song sung in the streets as an expression of the *jiyū minken undō* (freedom and people's rights movement) of 1874–1890. At the time, intellectual leaders of the movement sought the support of the general public through song. Song was important to the movement because it communicated to a public with relatively low level of literacy, averted governmental restrictions on speeches and large gatherings, and appealed to the public as entertainment (Nakamura 1991, 270).[5] When the movement died out, *enkashi* sang other, less political songs dealing with everyday life. As with other street entertainers in premodern and early modern Japan, *enkashi* held very low social status.[6]

In 1993 I interviewed eighty-three-year-old Sakurai Toshio, the last performing *enkashi*, whose life experiences document some of the changes of the period. Tokyo-born Sakurai began performing as an *enkashi* at the age of thirteen, following the Great Kantō Earthquake of 1923. The earthquake destroyed much of his family home and surroundings. Sakurai shunned the white-collar profession of his family in favor of the unorthodox trade of singing on the streets. He worked as an *enkashi* from 1923 to 1929 and then from 1948 on in a rapidly shrinking market overtaken by electronic media. His main job at the beginning was to sell sheet music. As bookstores and music stores proliferated, however, he became more of a balladeer. With a "menu" of songs, he traveled from bar to bar, singing and getting paid per song. He worked hard and was able to provide for his family; however because of the low status of the profession, he never wanted his children to tell their friends his occupation. He proudly told me that he was the first in his neighborhood with a radio, first with a television. He bought high-status, "modern" accoutrements with earnings from his low-status job. By 1993, Sakurai was considered a relic of the past, dubbed "the last *enkashi*," performing at limited venues such as museums and special events. His performance at these events serves as a poignant reminder of the immediacy of live, unamplified music, circumscribing the audience within its limited range. This stands in stark contrast to the seemingly limitless transmission afforded by mass media, with its distance-spanning audiences.

This distance-spanning, however, is the very point. Electronic transmission of popular songs (and other broadcast messages), begun in the 1920s, became part of the construction of the modern nation. Electronic media not only created mass audiences and the potential for mass nationhood but also developed a qualitatively different kind of relationship between performer, performance, and audience.[7] Whereas previously audiences typically had to go to the place of performance to listen to the performer, now the performance could be brought into the home—or at least into those homes with radios or phonographs. In 1932, just over 25 percent of urban households owned radios, while less than 5 percent of rural households did (Kasza 1988, 88). This urban-rural divide became part of the divide of the nation, centering on control of and access to electronic media. For radio owners, what was public became private. At the same time, the extension of nationhood into the home through mass media suggested a potential encroachment on the private by the public. The music of the streets could be heard in the home through radio broadcasts and recordings. What was private (the home) became subject to public messages and music. Those with access to the media thus became crucial in molding a populist sense of the nation borne through the new mass culture.[8] Electronic media also helped legitimize the work of entertainers. Far from beggars, they were situated on at least one cutting edge of modernity—that of technology and the new mass media industries.

The first radio stations began broadcasting in 1925 in Tokyo, Nagoya, and Osaka, the first in all of Asia. From the beginning, the Japanese government recognized the ideological power of electronic media such as radio and placed it under tight controls (Kasza 1988, 72). In 1926 the government established the Nihon Hōsō Kyōkai (NHK; Japan Broadcasting Corporation), which controlled all radio broadcasting until the 1950s through the Communications Ministry. The creation of an electronically united country was pivotal to Japan's militaristic buildup of the 1930s and 1940s. The government therefore made a concerted effort during the 1930s to extend radio access to its citizens. By 1941, Japan had the fourth highest number of radio receivers in the world, with more than 45 percent of all households owning a radio (Kasza 1988, 253). Although the electronic mass media society had not yet been firmly established in the 1920s and 1930s, this period marks its beginning, as well as the subsequent demise of street arts.

Recording technology also improved and phonographs became more affordable to a wider segment of the population during this period.[9] The year 1927 may be considered the birth of a technologically advanced recording industry in Japan. In that one year, three major recording companies were established: American Columbia and British Columbia invested heavily in an existing Japanese company (which started in 1907) to create Nippon Columbia; American Victor supplied all the capital to establish Nippon Victor; and Deutsche Polydor established Nippon Polydor. To Japan's benefit, this occurred at a pivotal time when technology in America and elsewhere was switching over from acoustic to electric recording, so these new companies set up recording facilities with the latest equipment.

The interrelationship between song and media shifted during the period. At the beginning, songs were popularized by street singers in the cities, then picked up by record companies, who capitalized upon the song's popularity to sell records. For example, "Kachusha no uta," with words by Shimamura Hōgetsu (1871–1918) and Sōma Gyofū (1883–1950) and music by Nakayama Shimpei, was first sung during Shimamura's popular 1914 *shingeki* (new theater) dramatization of Tolstoy's novel *Resurrection.* After gaining tremendous popularity, Orient Records recorded and sold the song with great success. According to Nakamura, "Kachusha's Song" may be considered "firmly in the spirit of the modern popular song production" in its "conscious attention to audience susceptibilities by both composer and lyricist, and in their estimate of audience impact" (Nakamura 1991, 264–265). Another song, "Sendō kouta" (Boatman's Song), became the basis for a 1923 film released to take advantage of the song's popularity. A third song, "Habu no minato" (Harbor of Habu), written by the same combination of Noguchi Ujō and Nakayama Shimpei and recorded by Victor Records in 1928, originated as a thematic suggestion by a women's magazine editor. In these three typical examples, songs originated outside record companies, became popular, and then were recorded and sold by record companies, which profited from the songs' pre-existing popularity.

Soon thereafter, the process reversed. Record companies increasingly became hit-makers, hiring composers, lyricists, arrangers, and singers to generate new songs, which then became popular in the streets. The first such hit was "Kimi koishi" (I Long for You), written and recorded in 1928 by Nippon Victor with words by Shigure Otowa (1899–1980) and music by Sasa Kōka (1886–1961). Moreover, record companies worked together with film companies and radio broadcasters to saturate the public with their songs. In this way, popular music was integrated with other media-driven cultural products in an upward spiral of mass consumption and mass sentiment from which could be derived an imagining of mass nationhood.

DEFINING MODERNITY IN SONG

Popular songs define the modern as much by concrete elements such as place and things as by intangible elements such as thoughts and sentiments. Through song, modernity becomes spatialized, temporalized, emotionalized, compartmentalized, commodified. One of the most dominant constructions is the locus of the modern in cities. According to these songs, to be modern is to live in a city.[10] Although urbanism has a long history in Japanese society, it is the particular nature of cities in this era that became a focus of notions of modernity.[11] Taishō songs lauded cities for their material goods and pleasures. Various songs sing of cities as a parade of modernity. In these, modernity suggests a conflation of political power, material wealth, and technological progress.

> At the center of Tokyo is Marunouchi,
> Hibiya Park, both Houses of Representatives and Peers,
> Along with the fashionable Imperial Theater.
> On the other side are the imposing buildings of the Metropolitan
>   Police Department.
> The various government offices stand in array in the Babasakimon
>   district.
> And there is Tokyo station in the Kaijo Building.[12]
>   "Tokyo bushi" (Tokyo Song, 1919)

Modernity also suggests an increased quantity and variety of goods, sensations, choices. These choices pile atop each other in a consumer's dream.[13]

> Tokyo is a great place,[14] full of interesting things.
> Tōfu, soybeans, *nattō* [fermented soybeans], coopers,
> Bamboo pipestem stores, candy stores, and stores selling sweet *sake*,
> Chili pepper seasonings and salted fish.
> "Kuzuui, kuzuui!" Hear the sound of the wooden clogs being made!
> Here you can get a massage! There you can eat stew! And there
>   they are selling Chinese dumplings!
> There is a song peddler! How about all this! . . .
> Bustling Asakusa in Tokyo
> Has in it the Kaminari Gate, Nakamise shopping street, and
>   Asakusa temple. . . .
> Movies! Twelve-story buildings! Flower gardens!
> Sushi, candy, beef, tempura!
>   "Tokyo bushi"

The feast of consumption includes a cosmopolitan mix of both the indigenous and nonindigenous.

Coupled with this positive, exhilarating, and seductive view of modern urban life is its opposite. One sometimes finds both sides of modernity within various verses of the same song. In contrast to the verses of "Tokyo bushi" quoted above, for example, other verses characterize modernity as overcrowded cities suffering from depleted resources, corrupt politicians, and worse yet, a public that meekly accepts all of the above.

> Upon what do you suppose Tokyo rests her pride?
> Crawling with 3,000,000 people
> Who live without manufacturing their own rice,
> Looking up to the mayor.
> Admirably, everybody conscientiously
> Listens closely to what the mayor says.
> Eating the scraps from the soybeans, growing thinner and thinner.
> "Tokyo bushi"

Amidst a panoply of goods, at least some urban dwellers go hungry. The song—itself an urban product—criticizes Tokyoites as leeches of the countryside, incapable of adequately sustaining either their bodies or spirits.

Oftentimes the complaints of these songs are those common to urban dwellers. Modernity means putting up with modern irritations, urban frustrations—the suffering of individuals from whom control over their surroundings has been wrested. The Taishō urban dweller sometimes seethes.

> Tokyo is famous for its packed trains.
> No matter how long you wait, you cannot get on.
> When you try to get on, there's a life-or-death struggle awaiting you.
> Even when an empty train finally approaches, the car passes
>   without stopping.
> No, no, waves a hand to those of us who wait.
> Again and again, without stopping, the trains pass.
> What! Is this a broken-down car? What a jalopy of a train!
> "Tokyo bushi"

At other times, the critique is more sharply directed at its target. Tokyo, the pinnacle of modern urban life, lifts its glittery facade to show itself as little more than a sewer.

> In Tokyo, even the underside has an underside.
> It is an island where birds do not fly,

And even the sun does not appear.
Dark and smelly, like a hole,
One might wonder if it is a dog house.
Why, on the contrary, human beings
Are alive and well in this hovel!

"Tokyo bushi"

Tokyo, the heart of modernity, here becomes the center of discontent, its inhabitants reduced to sub-humans. The city both rises and falls as a peak of civilization and a pit of degradation. The resultant multilayered view of modernity shows the complexity of the phenomenon.

Songs of the period express this discontent in several ways. The most obvious expressions are those that directly criticize urban life and the experiences of modernity that it encompasses, as in "Tokyo bushi" above. Other songs express discontent by describing the empty escapism of urban life. Here life rushes by in a flurry of activity, masking the loneliness that lies at its root.

Dancing to jazz, staying up until all hours, drinking liqueur.
At daybreak, the dancers shed their tears. . . .
During rush hour I picked up a rose,
And in that rose I found memories of my sweetheart.

"Tokyo kōshinkyoku" (Tokyo March, 1929)

The juxtaposition of urban phenomena such as all-night entertainment and rush hours with heart-felt memories deliberately points up the incompatibility of the two. Public modernity rushes ahead, leaving private emotions behind.

A more light-hearted approach to discontent can be found in songs that mock urban life and its influx of Western (i.e., "modern") trappings.

I had a wife and was so happy,
But all she ever cooks is
Croquettes, croquettes!
Today it's croquettes, tomorrow it will be croquettes!
That's the way it is, every year, all year long.
Whee! Croquettes!
Ah-ha-ha-ha! Ah-ha-ha-ha!
This is so funny!

"Korokke no uta" (The Song of Croquettes, 1921)

The song criticizes not only Western food (croquettes), but more importantly, Westernized wives who think to cook nothing but Western food. In the third verse, the song takes a further turn, lamenting the urbanite's economic dreams, which are easily shattered with so little as a sneeze.

> I found a purse and was so happy!
> And when I opened it and looked inside,
> The coins went jingle-jingle, jingle-jingle!
> Shall I buy some stocks? Shall I buy some land?
> In the midst of my reveries—
> Ah-a-ah-a-choo!
> I suddenly awoke!
> Ah-ha-ha-ha! Ah-ha-ha-ha!
> This is so funny!
>
> "Korokke no uta"

The disillusionment of economic hopes remains a prominent feature of the popular imagination. The song's laughter becomes a mockery of the urban dweller's own economic plight and helplessness.

> Songs also mock those in power, in particular intellectuals and
>   their ideas.
> Democracy is so popular these days!
> Leaning back arrogantly, sitting on a high platform,
> They argue heatedly, foaming at the mouth.
> This is the source of fodder for intellectuals,
> Yes, the source of fodder.
>
> "Demokurashii bushi" (Democracy Song, 1919)

> This [stinking hole of Tokyo exists], amidst their [intellectuals']
>   uppity theories of hygiene, their theories of dignity.
>
> "Tokyo bushi"

The mockery runs from high to low, targeting not only intellectuals, but also destitute urban dwellers.

Mockery also makes fun of those in between, such as some of the most famous urban dwellers—the *mobo* ("modern boy").[15]

> The guys who strut around Ginza are stupid. . . .
> With sailor pants and painted eyebrows,
> Their Eton-cropped hair—they're so happy, aren't they?
>
> "Tōsei Ginza bushi" (Song of Fashionable Ginza)

The song's critique of the *mobo* asserts the superficiality of his Westernisms, the laughability of his "modernisms." I quote the following song at length to detail various aspects of the *mobo*. For one, his dandyism is mockingly complete, and he is able to describe the style of the times (i.e., his own) down to the last detail. More important, he is from the country, not the city, making his strutting that of a country boy in the big city. By his own definition, he is "vain, conceited, smug"; however, all of his conceit in the end vanishes along with his wallet and girlfriend.

> In the village I am the one they call
> The number one *mobo*.
> Vain, conceited, smug,
> I came to Ginza in Tokyo.
> To begin with, my style consists of
> A blue shirt with crimson necktie,
> A derby hat and horn-rimmed glasses,
> And baggy sailor pants.
> The woman that I have fallen in love with
> Has jet black eyes and bobbed hair.
> She's short and curvaceous,
> And she is brazen down to her toes.
> I first got to know her at the cafe,
> Where I work. . . .
> Do you know? My Father is the landlord, the head of the village.
> The village head is a rich man and I, his son,
> Am single even now, a bachelor! . . .
> If you've got the prestige and the money,
> Even if you have no looks— . . .
> [Women are still attracted to you.]
> Is it a dream or is it a figment of my imagination?
> Just then, the woman's husband comes rushing at me.
> Without saying a word, I am engulfed by a flurry of fists.
> Beaten to a pulp, I faint.
> My wallet, my watch have been taken!
> My precious woman is gone!
> What a fearsome place Tokyo's Ginza is!
> I am a *mobo* who cannot cry, even if I feel like it.
>
> "Share otoko" (The Dandy, 1924)

In the end, the *mobo*'s would-be tears are those of a would-be sophisticate, in reality a bumpkin trying to act beyond his scope. Those laughing at him are other urban dwellers, many of whom are from the countryside. In laughing at him, they laugh at themselves. The *mobo* here becomes an example of modernity as effete superficiality. One may purchase modernity's accoutrements, don its vestments, tout one's place in the modern world, and lose it all in an instant.

Part of that superficiality lies in the uncritical embracing of things Western. As in "Korokke no uta," the *mobo* songs express ambivalence toward Westernisms as modernisms. For example, one song, "Zattsu okei" (That's Okay!, 1930) adopts the popular American expression as a refrain. Although the rest of the song includes serious discussion of lovers parting and vows of love, each verse ends with the trivializing, *Okei, okei, zattsu okei* (Okay, okay, that's okay!).

Other foreign borrowings in song include constructions of the exotic. Among the songs in the collections I examined were two translated lyrics, "Arabiya" (Arabia, 1928) and "Barenshia" (Valencia, 1929). These both—taken from the Western originals—genderize distant lands as exotic female lovers.

> Valencia! Faintly, the sound of your voice calling to me
> Comes to my ears.
> Valencia! You are a tender lover in the country of my dreams.
> Valencia! The orange
> Blossoms' fragrance
> Drifts to me from your distant shores,
> Borne by the winds.
>
> "Barenshia"

To be modern here is to desire exotic Others, as those in the West do.

One way to approach modernity in twentieth-century Japan is to examine what it is not. Being unmodern means living away from the cities, in rural areas, in one's *furusato* (hometown). Several songs use the concept of *furusato* to create a generalized nostalgia.[16] One's hometown becomes everyone's hometown, linked by a pervading sense of nostalgia and longing, as in the following example.

> The mountains are full of rabbits,
> The rivers are full of carp.
> Even now, my dream comes back to me
> Of *furusato*, which I will never forget.
> How are my mother and father?
> Are my friends all right?
> Regardless of the rain or wind,
> My thoughts are always upon *furusato*. . . .
> *Furusato,* where mountains are covered with green.
> *Furusato,* where water runs clear.
>
> "Furusato" (1914)

This is *furusato* not as lived but as remembered, as dreamed. What is remembered is everything linked or constructed as Japan's past—nature, abundance, beauty, purity, family, emotions of warmth and sense of belonging.[17] What is shaped by negation, then, is the modern—the unnatural, impoverished, ugly, impure, lonesome, cold.

The irony lies in the contradictory shapings of nationhood vis-ň-vis modernity. On the one hand, nationhood may be considered a modern project, conceived in the late nineteenth century, gaining force in the early twentieth century. On the other hand, nationhood is linked in song with premodern *furusato*, family, and nature. The discrepancy lies in the different definitions of nationhood. The first rests upon the conceptualization of *kokka*, whose nationalism was statist and political. The second embraces *minzoku*, whose nationalism was populist and cultural. Although *kokka* eventually absorbed *minzoku* during the 1930s and 1940s, in the 1920s the two retained their distinctiveness. Moreover, part of that absorption was the process of placing modernity in service to political nationhood, to *kokka*.

To be modern is to live in the city, but, as constructed in several songs, to remain not entirely of it, to be rootless.[18] The 1917 song "Sasurai no uta" (Song of Wandering) is considered the first modern popular song dealing with the loneliness of rootlessness (Mita 1992, 96).

> I am just like a water grass,
> Blowing in the wind,
> Flowing and flowing, without end.
> I travel by day and dance by night.
> I wonder where I shall meet my end?
> "Sasurai no uta" (1917)

By definition, a wanderer is one who lives without roots, a water grass. The sense of transience gives rise not only to loneliness but also loss. The wanderer is one who has been set adrift from his or her homeland, whose roots have been lost in the urban shuffle. This construction of modernity, then, lies in the anomie of the urban wanderer.

Within representations of romance, a notable shift occurs between 1914 and the 1930s. Most popular love songs sing of failed love. However, earlier songs depict love's sadness in an earnest, but benign manner.

> My dear Kachusha,
> The pain of parting!
> The snow which falls tonight
> Will hide the path through hills and fields in the morning.
> My dear Kachusha,

The pain of parting!
At least until we meet again,
Stay the same as you are.

"Kachusha no uta"

I am a withered eulalia tree on a dry riverbed.
You, too, are a withered eulalia tree.
After all, the two of us in this world
Are like withered eulalia trees which do not bloom.
My dear, even in death, even in life,
The water's flow never changes.

"Sendō kouta"

These songs express the pain of love, but not with the kind of darkness characterized by later songs.

When the moonless night draws near, my anguish knows no end.
In my tumultuous heart, whose image appears?
I long for you, and though the color of my lips refuses to fade,
My eyes fill with tears, and the night grows late.
Although my voice sings and my footsteps resound,
Where shall I go to look for your visage in my heart?
I long for you, and my thoughts are a-jumble.
For whom am I going to bear so many painful nights like this?

"Kimi koishi"

Is *sake* a tear or a sigh?
It is something to make one forget one's woes.
That person whom I loved long ago
Moves me to sorrow in my dreams every night.
Is *sake* a tear or a sigh?
It is something to make one forget love's sorrows.
That person whom I managed to forget at one time—
What shall I do with my lingering heart?

"Sake wa namida ka tameiki ka"
(Is *Sake* a Tear or a Sigh? 1931)

The motifs established by these later songs—broken hearts, tears, and drink—soon became the standard of many popular songs, including those written today. Within the span of approximately fifteen years, during which people's attempts at financial and political gain were increasingly thwarted by economic depression, governmental suppression, and natural disaster, what became patterned, and even mannered, was the expression of modernity as despair.[19]

CONCLUSION: DEFINING THE NATION IN SONG

During this period, a sense of the nation, of *minzoku,* began to emerge electronically. What the Meiji leaders had tried so diligently to impose fifty years earlier arose through the seductiveness of mass media. Limited audiences became seemingly limitless ones, as wave after wave of fad, information, and consumption connected households. At the same time, the interweaving of public and private through the media and its music increasingly blurred the distinction between the two, making of the home a platform for the nation writ small.

There was also an affective sense by which the modern nation began its construction during this period. Listeners in rural Niigata—gradually increasing in numbers—could imagine greater kinship to fellow listeners in urban Tokyo. Although we cannot assume uniform reception of these songs or interpretation of their meanings, we can address their widespread popularity to suggest the beginnings of an emergent electronic community of listeners. These listeners were captivated not only by the emotions of the songs but also by the miracle of their transmission. Theirs was nationhood built upon the intimacy of simultaneity. The titillation lay in listening, breathing, and potentially crying together. The gap between the far reaches of the country, especially between urban and rural parts, were not erased immediately. Innovations and technological changes came far later to rural areas. Moreover, certain gaps between the reception of the music in urban and rural areas, or even within the same urban area, were not erased either. Urban cultures continued to be highly segmented and contested. Yet, the foundation for the emergent nation was laid during this period, electronically mobilized, affectively deployed.

What helped give a sense of nationhood to the urban populace was its negotiation with aspects of modernity—technology, consumership, expression of the individual—all of which came together in popular music. In these popular songs, modernity was not only temporalized but also spatialized to suggest domestic urban scapes, distant Western countries, and yearning toward even more distant "exotic" lands. Modernity was also moralized, these songs expressing a pervasive denigration of superficial Westernisms. Moreover, modernity was emotionalized in the exhilaration and frustration of urban life, glee in escapist activities, wrenching loneliness, and dark despair.

In the texts as well as songs themselves, modernity became a concept whose boundaries were both elusive and permeable. Modernity possessed an amnesiac quality whose self-definition changed by the vagaries of who got to decide what constituted it. Although the goals differed, various actors pursued the project of modernity in Japan, from "middle-class professions and village elites to higher civil servants," creating unexpected alignments (Garon 1994, 347). As actors changed and needs shifted, so, too, did definitions of modernity.

Popular songs of this formative period constructed modernity in terms of desire. The desires were those of the consumer—buying, imbibing, displaying. The desires were also those of the displaced urban dweller. One's *furusato* became the nation's *furusato*—an object of yearning and metaphor for the past and nearly distant, reconstructed to emphasize "traditional" values, human relationships, and close contact with nature. Romance became the basis for a different kind of desire, more sensually derived and individualistic. Romance also became a metaphor for frustrated dreams, the obstacle of which was often civil society. Through both seemingly apolitical topics of nostalgia and romance, what might be interpreted as a highly political message could be wrought, critical of the emergent state. If Taishō *demokurashii* may be thought of as a reformulation of Western democratic ideals to suit the needs the Japanese state, then popular song provided some of the emotional grist and resistance by which those needs were mediated.

APPENDIX: SONGS ANALYZED

Arabiya (Arabia)	1928
Barenshia (Valencia)	1929
Bazoku no uta (Song of the Horseman)	1922
Demokurashii bushi (Democracy Song)	1919
Defune (Departing Ship)	1928
Dōtonbori Kōshinkyoku (Dōtonbori March)	1929
Fukō bushi (Reconstruction Song)	1924
Hanazono no koi (Love in the Flower Garden)	1919
Jokyū no uta (Barmaid's Song)	1930
Kachusha no uta (Kachusha's Song)	1914
Kage o shitaite (Yearning for Shadows)	1932
Kago no tori (The Caged Bird)	1925
Kimi koishi (I Long for You)	1928
Koi no tori (Bird of Love)	1919
Konjiki no yasha no uta (Song of the Golden Female Dragon)	1917

Kono taiyō (This Sun)	1930
Korokke no uta (The Song of Croquettes)	1921
Nihonbashi kara (From Nihonbashi)	1931
Sakaba no uta (Song of the Bar)	1919
Sake wa namida ka tameiki ka (Is *Sake* a Tear or a Sigh?)	1931
Sasurai no uta (Song of Wandering)	1917
Sendō kouta (The Boatman's Song)	1923
Share otoko (The Dandy)	1924
Shichirigahama no aika (Elegy of Shichirigahama)	1916
Sutare-mono (The Useless One)	1924
Tokyo bushi (Tokyo Song) (two versions)	1919
Tokyo kōshinkyoku (Tokyo March)	1929
Wakare no uta (Song of Parting)	1919
Zattsu okei (That's Okay!)	1930

NOTES

Research for this paper was conducted in part under a Japan Foundation Dissertation Fellowship, 1992–1993, which I gratefully acknowledge. I would like to thank Dr. Sharon A. Minichiello and other members of the conference for their comments on this paper. I also would like to thank Mr. Harry Urata and Mrs. Takako Ishida for their help with song text translations and interpretations.

1. The songs I examined were by no means the only kinds of music of the period. Other genres popularly recorded and broadcast include *naniwabushi* (narrative ballad with lute accompaniment), which focused on historical events or well-known stories, often with an emphasis upon such moral dilemmas as *giri-ninjō* (duty vs. human feelings).
2. I gratefully acknowledge the help of Kevin Doak for pointing out this distinction.
3. For more on Western music during the Meiji era, see Malm 1971.
4. See Kitahara 1966 for further discussion of these scales as an example of syncretism in the composition of modern Japanese popular song.
5. For more on *enka* of this period, see Soeda 1963.
6. Entertainers, especially wandering ones, were considered among the outcasts of premodern Japan. For more on one kind of outcast entertainer, see Ohnuki-Tierney 1987.
7. My emphasis here is on potential nationhood, well recognized by the government as evidenced by their state monopoly of airwaves, as well as censorship controls. In contrast, see papers in this volume by Robinson and Hanes, which highlight the divisive potential of mass media.
8. For further discussion on the creation of mass culture during the 1920s, see Ivy 1993, Kato 1974, Seidensticker 1985, Maruyama 1982.
9. Although phonographs were not so widespread as radios, I include a dis-

cussion of recordings here because their sales and promotion so critically shaped the music industry as a field of cultural production.

10. Here I focus on the representation of modernity in popular songs, regardless of the potential "metonymic misrepresentation" (cf. Tamanoi, this volume). Although the potential of misrepresentation that Tamanoi points out—the conflation of modern with Western and modern with urban—is real, my focus is on the representations themselves.

11. See Yazaki 1968 for a historical overview of urbanism in Japan from antiquity to the 1920s.

12. This and all other song translations are my own.

13. Garon characterizes the 1920s in Japan as a period during which both consumption and frugality increased in separate campaigns whose bridge may be found in modernity/rationality (this volume). See Silverberg 1992 for further discussion of consumption and its relation to the state.

14. This kind of paean to a particular place follows a common form of various folk songs that begin, "X *wa yoi toko*" ("X is a fine place").

15. I have not come across songs critical of the *moga* (modern girl), the female companion to the *mobo*. I view the difference in public reaction as resulting from a cultural critique of the *mobo* as an unproductive male member of society, a feminized dandy. This kind of creature calls for greater social scorn than the *moga*. Although she was a multivalent figure, as analyzed by Silverberg (1991), in general she represented tantalizing Westernization/modernization; he, on the other hand, represented effete decadence.

16. One genre that focused on *furusato* was *shin min'yō* (new folk song), newly composed songs deliberately created to evoke rural associations of folk song. For more on *shin min'yō*, see Hughes 1985.

17. See Thomas (this volume) for discussion of the nationalizing of nature (and the concomitant "naturalization" of nationhood) during this period.

18. Ethnographic evidence to the contrary suggests certain urban social and cultural institutions mitigate against anomie (e.g., Bestor 1989). However, here as elsewhere, my focus is on representations of modernity.

19. This is not to say that themes of despair, loneliness, and sadness did not pervade Japanese songs and poetry before this time. They did. Yet there is a sense in the love songs from the 1930s on of dark melodrama, of individual anguish, whose formulaic patterning is striking—and which signals a shift in the commodification of emotion.

REFERENCES

Anderson, Benedict. 1983. *Imagined Communities; Reflections on the Origin and Spread of Nationalism.* London: Verso.

Bestor, Theodore C. 1989. *Neighborhood Tokyo.* Stanford: Stanford University Press.

Fujie, Linda. 1989. "Popular Music." In *Handbook of Japanese Popular Culture,* edited by Richard G. Powers and Hidetoshi Kato, 197–220. New York: Greenwood Press.

Garon, Sheldon. 1994. "Rethinking Modernization and Modernity in Japanese History." *Journal of Asian Studies* 53.2:346–366.

Hane Mikiso. 1982. *Peasants, Rebels and Outcastes: The Underside of Modern Japan.* New York: Pantheon Books.

Hughes, David. 1985. "The Heart's Home Town: Traditional Folk Song in Modern Japan." Ph.D. diss., University of Michigan.

Ivy, Marilyn. 1993. "Formations of Mass Culture." In *Postwar Japan as History,* edited by Andrew Gordon, 239–258. Berkeley: University of California Press.

Kasza, Gregory. 1988. *The State and the Mass Media in Japan, 1918–1945.* Berkeley: University of California Press.

Kato Shūichi. 1974. "Taishō Democracy as the Pre-stage for Japanese Militarism." In *Japan in Crisis: Essays on Taishō Democracy,* edited by Bernard S. Silberman and Harry D. Harootunian, 217–236. Princeton: Princeton University Press.

Kitahara Michio. 1966. "*Kayokyoku*: An Example of Syncretism Involving Scale and Mode." *Ethnomusicology* 10.3:271–284.

Komota Nobuo, Shimada Yoshifumi, Yazawa Tamotsu, and Yokozawa Chiaki. 1981. *Nihon ryūkōka-shi (Senzen-hen).* Shakai Shisō-sha.

Malm, William P. 1971. "The Modern Music of Meiji Japan." In *Tradition and Modernization in Japanese Culture,* edited by Donald H. Shively, 257–300. Princeton: Princeton University Press.

Maruyama Masao. 1982. "Patterns of Individuation and the Case of Japan." In *Changing Japanese Attitudes toward Modernization,* edited by Marius B. Jansen, 489–531. Rutland, Vermont: Charles E. Tuttle.

Mita Munesuke. 1992. *Social Psychology of Modern Japan,* translated by Stephen Suloway. London: Kegan Paul International.

Nagata Gyōji, comp. 1967. *Ryūkō kayō hyakkyoku-shū.* Zen-on Music Publishers.

Nakamura Toyo. 1991. "Early Pop Song Writers and Their Backgrounds." *Popular Music* 10.3:263–282.

Ohnuki-Tierney, Emiko. 1987. *The Monkey as Mirror: Symbolic Transformations in Japanese History and Ritual.* Princeton: Princeton University Press.

Seidensticker, Edward. 1985. *Low City, High City: Tokyo from Edo to the Earthquake.* San Francisco: Donald S. Ellis.

Silverberg, Miriam. 1991. "The Modern Girl as Militant." In *Recreating Japanese Women, 1600–1945,* edited by Gail L. Bernstein, 239–266. Berkeley: University of California Press.

———. 1992. "Constructing the Japanese Ethnography of Modernity." *Journal of Asian Studies* 51.1:30–54.

Soeda Tomomichi. 1963. *Enka no Meiji Taishō-shi.* Iwanami Shinsho.

Yazaki Takeo. 1968. *Social Change and the City in Japan.* Japan Publications.

⇒ III ⇐

Diversity, Autonomy, and Integration

≫ 12 ≪

Media Culture in Taishō Osaka

JEFFREY E. HANES

In 1920, Ōbayashi Sōshi set out to conduct a comprehensive survey of "popular recreation" *(minshū goraku)* in the city of Osaka. By the time he released his hefty 380-page study in 1922, however, he had restricted his purview to the "for-profit entertainment industry" *(eiriteki kōgyō goraku)* in four discrete amusement quarters—Dōtonbori-Sennichimae, Shin Sekai, Tamatsukuri, and Kujō (Ōbayashi 1922). This essay retraces the topical and spatial boundaries of Ōbayashi's pioneering survey, revisiting the alluring amusement quarters of Taishō Osaka, but it also asks why Ōbayashi put this particular form of popular recreation at center stage. I will suggest that this social scientist, trained to look for signs of social and cultural change, was ultimately mesmerized by the same staged spectacle of mass media entertainments that drew "the people" *(minshū)* of his study into its net. The unprecedented sight of Osakans by the thousands descending on the city's electric-lit amusement quarters, week in and week out, was merely the lure. The entertainment industry itself reeled Ōbayashi in, making a believer out of the skeptic.

Inclined by his popular sympathies to unmask the hucksterism of Osaka's "for-profit entertainment industry"—but enjoined by the objectivist spirit of modern social science to suspend disbelief—Ōbayashi left himself open to the power of suggestion. That the entertainment industry wielded this power, in the amusements it staged and the marketing and advertising schemes it launched, placed the interrogator in a deliciously compromising position. And, to judge from the trajectory of Ōbayashi's analysis, the industry ate him up. While Ōbayashi took to the streets as a professionally trained social scientist of the people, he went to press as a self-styled media maven of the masses. That he was gradually implicated in the object of his own inquiry raises important questions about the persuasive power of the entertainment industry—questions that require us to take a closer look at the processes of cultural production and cultural consumption.

The moneymaking entertainments that Ōbayashi dispassionately identified as popular venues of the "for-profit entertainment industry" in the amusement quarters of Taishō Osaka were part of a larger cultural phenomenon triggered by technological change. While Osaka had long been a lively locus of popular entertainment (so lively that Englebert Kaempfer fancied it a "universal theater of pleasures and diversions" in the 1690s), it spawned an entirely new entertainment culture under the influence of the mass media. The revolutionary technologies that made newspapers, magazines, and movies accessible to a "mass" audience, combined with the marketing and advertising schemes that drew them into the nexus of urban consumption, changed the face of Osaka. Once marshaled by the entertainment industry, the power of the mass media to attract a "mass" audience seemed infinite. It is not surprising, therefore, that historians of the era have identified a "mass culture" in the making. As a theoretical formulation, however, this term has limited reach. Lifted wholesale from the European and American literatures on cultural modernity, it never fully grasped the Japanese case. Now that cultural historians across the world have begun to question its utility, the writing would seem to be on the wall. It has come time to introduce new formulations that resonate with the realities of cultural change in modern Japan. I hope to do so here.

As Ōbayashi amply illustrates in his survey of Taishō Osaka's amusement quarters, the entertainment industry did not even attempt to ensnare "the masses." And for good reason—it could not identify any such classless, androgynous, ageless social animal. The audiences it did identify were nothing if not diverse, and they also were discriminating. Hence, far from trying to homogenize popular tastes, the entertainment industry strove to diversify its offerings. It did so by wedding mass cultural forms (mass media) to subcultural norms (the tastes and values of identifiable urban interest groups). Douglas Kellner identifies this dynamic cultural configuration with what he calls "media cultures." As he summarizes their common credo, "Difference sells. Capitalism must constantly multiply markets, styles, fads, and artifacts to keep absorbing consumers into its practices and lifestyles" (Kellner 1995, 40). The "media culture" of Ōbayashi's Osaka in the 1920s followed much the same capitalist logic of cultural reproduction as the "media culture" of Kellner's America in the 1990s. In these settings, as elsewhere in the modern capitalist world, the culture industry in general and the entertainment industry in particular have marshaled the mass media in the endless quest for consumers.

It is one thing to acknowledge that consumer marketing matters, however, and yet another to make it work. The medium might well carry the message, but that is not to say it will be received as its sender intends. While cultural producers in Taishō Osaka clearly used the media to promote what Kellner terms "structures of [cultural] domination" (Kellner 1995, 32), they understood full well that these could not be erected without the complicity of cultural consumers. So it went, and so it goes, under capitalism: producers and consumers shaping popular culture through a multifaceted process of negotiation. While cultural producers have always brought their bag of tricks to this capitalist dance—whether it be marketing surveys, advertising, or free samples—cultural consumers likewise have proven themselves to be anything but passive partners. Their capacity for resistance and reinvention is legendary, as many an advertising executive would grudgingly concede, and few are those cultural producers who have managed to channel consumption into the patterns they anticipate.[1] Thus, cultural producers have learned to woo, cultural consumers to be coy, and both to wheel and deal.

With just such a characterization of cultural production and consumption in mind, Kellner has endeavored to propel cultural studies in a new direction. In an effort to reconcile the radically different perspectives of modern culture offered by the Frankfurt School ("sovereign producers" creating a mass culture) and the Birmingham School ("sovereign consumers" creating a popular culture),[2] he has adopted the term "media culture." This new formulation, he insists, "avoids ideological terms like 'mass culture' and 'popular culture' and calls attention to the circuit of production, distribution, and reception through which media culture is produced, distributed, and consumed" (Kellner 1995, 34). If there seems a certain circular logic to Kellner's explanation, it is because the term he has selected oscillates between two contingent associations: "Media culture" signifies "both the nature and form of the artifacts of the culture industries (i.e. culture) and their mode of production and distribution (i.e. media technologies and industries)" (Kellner 1995, 34). We might add that by definition media mediate: Cultural producers and consumers could not reach one another without the "mediation" they provide.[3] The mass media, for their part, have progressively intensified the relationship.

Kellner's formulation aptly describes the urban culture that Ōbayashi surveyed in Osaka in 1920. Not only was the city awash with signboard advertisements for everything from soap to garden suburbs, its supercharged *sakariba* (amusement quarters) were bathed in electric light and inundated with amplified sound. In the cafés, movie theaters, and amusement parks that transmogrified Osaka's culture industry, stimulation was the name of the game: Jazz music wailed as patrons tippled alcohol and tickled waitresses in the Union Cafe; *benshi* (narrators for silent picture shows) intoned their lines over the whir of the movie projector and against the mesmerizing images it cast on the big screen in the multiplex performance center of Entertainment Heaven (Rakutenchi); and carnies lightheartedly cajoled thrill-seekers into elevator rides up Tsūtenkaku Tower at the entrance to Luna Park in The New World (Shin Sekai) amusement park. The epoch-making technologies that embodied this new "media culture" defined the spectacle of urban life; and the cultural processes of importation, adaptation, amplification, production, distribution, reproduction, and reinvention that helped assimilate these technologies into the everyday world had begun to work a powerful influence on the urban identity.

To explain at the outset how and why this culture appeared when it did, we need to turn back the clock to the mid-1910s—to the Great War that sent Europe to its knees and brought Japan to its feet. World War I was as much a watershed event for Japan as it was for Europe. Deprived from the war's outbreak of further access to the modern technologies that Europe had provided since the Meiji Restoration (1868)—and disabused by the war's utter barbarism of the romantic notion that technology and civilization went hand-in-hand—Japan found itself dazed and confused in 1914. But not for long. Poignantly confronting its own technological dependency, Japan was swept (and swept itself) into the world of mass production perfected by the United States. It enjoined American expertise, entering into business partnerships and forging a new trail of technological and organizational innovation. In the process, Japan grew into an industrial dynamo (Yamamura 1986, 65–94; Morris-Suzuki 1994, 107–108).

Social and cultural historians have long since observed that the character and the scale of Japan's economic success brought fundamental changes in daily life, especially in the big cities where industrialization was centered (Takemura 1980; Minami 1965; Silverberg 1993). Not only did the famed *narikin* (nouveaux riches) work and spend on an epic scale, they carried the rest of the urban populace along in their wake. Rising employment and wages instigated a rise in the worker's standard of living that did not peak until 1922 (Ishikawa 1981, 99). While *narikin* extravagance jump-started the culture of mass consumption, white-collar and blue-collar spending kept its engine running. Inexplicably, given the recent proliferation of reprinted primary sources and popular cultural histories that tell this story in all its complexity, illustrating the *diversity* of urban life,[4] many historians persist in characterizing modish elites as the pioneers and role models of a *homogeneous* mass culture in the making. It is time to put this urban myth to rest.

As anyone familiar with the history of interwar Japan knows, its cities were a mosaic of segmented subcultures—*narikin, mobo* and *moga* (modern boys and modern girls), housewives, *sarariiman* (salarymen), *yōfuku saimin* (the so-called Western-dressed poor: low-level salaried employees), the petit bourgeoisie, working-class families, *shinheimin* (a euphemism for hereditary outcastes), newspaper boys, café waitresses, Korean immigrants, and students—to name just a few. What seems less well known is that many of these subcultures were identified by, and identified themselves to, a consumer industry that recognized market segmentation when it saw it. As a case in point, let us look briefly at a subculture that drew considerable attention throughout the Taishō era: urban working-class consumers.

In his pathbreaking study of prewar recreation, Ishikawa Hiroyoshi punctuates his account of working-class entertainments by tracing a chronological trajectory of popular consumerism that confounds the conventional wisdom that interwar Japan witnessed a mass mania for conspicuous consumption fueled by status envy. His account of the "formation of a lifestyle framework" by interwar industrial laborers illustrates that their expectations rose progressively from food and drink (1916–1919), to housing and clothing (1919–1922), and finally to society and culture (1922–1927) (Ishikawa 1981, 100–102). While he is right on target when he observes that urban workers gradually internalized the consumerist ethos of interwar Japan, he misses the mark altogether when he infers that they were also progressively assimilating to the mass consumer market of a nascent mass culture (Ishikawa 1981, 109). Workers and their families were not absorbed into the mass consumer market. With the help of able and willing (even enthusiastic) cultural producers, they carved out a distinct niche within it.

A cursory examination of Taishō cost-of-living surveys illustrates that working-class families had to make a practical distinction between necessities and luxuries (Hazama 1976, 39–43). While their standard of living rose significantly in the late 1910s, it hardly rose so dramatically as to provide them with disposable income or to wean them from budgetary conservatism. This is not to say, on the other hand, that workers were either estranged from or oblivious to the consumer society that had been sprouting around them. Their replies to questions about popular recreation—already a major bone of contention by the 1920s—were frequently laced with cynicism. Behind their common refrain—"no time, no money, no fun"—lay the suggestion that workers knew exactly what they were missing (Ishikawa 1981, 106).

As it happens, the City of Osaka published a survey of the cost of living among its laborers at the same moment Ōbayashi released his survey of their popular recreational habits. While the city's survey recorded low levels of spending for "pleasure" by most working-class families—between 0.12 and 11.34 yen per family, or 1 to 5 percent of a family's total yearly income—it also observed that such spending was going up, and tended to rise with increasing income (Municipal Bureau of Labor Research of Osaka 1976, 73). I might add, as an amusing aside, that on each of the three occasions city officials asked families to complete survey questionnaires, they brought a gift valued at one yen: tickets to a variety show or a moving picture, whichever the family preferred.

If these city officials meant to put their finger on the pulse of the Taishō consumer economy, the entertainment industry for one aimed to place it under its thumb. Put in terms only slightly more fanciful and obsequious than the industry itself employed, media marketers offered to salve the workers' wounded spirits, interpret their unspoken dreams, and sell them an afternoon's excursion into a liminal world of sensory pleasure. As the industry appealed to new notions and rhythms of work and leisure, it also contrived to create more alluring, accessible, and affordable forms of popular entertainment. By the 1920s, most especially in its promotion of motion pictures as a "mass" entertainment, the entertainment industry had secured the massive audiences that spelled success.

Within the city limits of Osaka alone in 1920, the motion picture audience totaled 740,498: roughly one-half of the recorded total for all moneymaking entertainments (Ōbayashi 1922, 57–58). These aggregate figures do not reveal what percentage of moviegoers came from the working class. But if we can extrapolate from the recreational preferences indicated by factory workers in a 1924 Ministry of Education survey—where motion pictures (katsudō shashin) ranked second only to minstrel shows (naniwabushi) in popularity—the working class was certainly lining up at the box office (Nakata 1924, 53–58). As I shall soon suggest, they lined up at least in part because Japanese movie producers and theater managers (often one and the same under Japan's "rationalized" studio system), catered to working-class tastes, work schedules, and pocketbooks.

The cultural shift I have sketched in outline here was not limited to cities, but it certainly was centered there. Two cities in particular came to epitomize it—Tokyo and Osaka. In both, cultural critics, ethnographers, surveyists, and government officials brought attention to the changes sweeping city life. At that point in the early 1920s when public interest in popular recreation became a public concern and the term "recreational question" (goraku mondai) crept into the Japanese vocabulary, the ideological lines that later separated these social commentators had yet to be drawn. Thus, the cultural critic–social surveyist Gonda Yasunosuke could work concurrently for the progressive Ōhara Institute for the Study of Social Problems (Ōhara Shakai Mondai Kenkyūjo) and the conservative Education and Home ministries (Silverberg 1992, 46).

From Tokyo, the redoubtable Gonda measured the cultural fallout from consumerism. His earliest collection of essays on popular pastimes, published as The Keynote of Popular Recreation (Minshū goraku no kichō) in 1922, identified what he took to be an epoch-making cultural trend. While many in Japan hailed the advent of leisure time as a well-earned reward for the hardworking laborers of industrial society, just as many recoiled at the thought of setting them free from labor to squander their time and money on the fleeting pleasures provided by the culture industry.[5] Gonda stood squarely with the former, and his work would soon set the critical standard for studies of popular recreation. Miriam Silverberg has introduced Gonda to Western readers, showing us just how sharp an eye he had in the 1920s for the pivotal importance of "new popular play" (Silverberg 1992, 46). Here, I would like to push the theoretical/interpretive envelope she has opened.

In a manner that anticipated the cultural populism of Raymond Williams and the Birmingham School, Gonda observed that "Popular recreation does not create the popular way of life; the popular way of life creates popular recreation." His advice to aspiring students of the subject was to get their noses out of Western books and to open their eyes to Japanese experience. Steering them away from the Western theoretical texts stocked by the Maruzen bookstore, he urged them to seek out the Japanese primary texts proffered by experience (Gonda 1922, 22). Silverberg's translation captures the spirit of his advice: "Go to Asakusa—Asakusa's your text." Gonda's clever juxtaposition of Tokyo's famous emporium of Western books to its (in)famous center of mass amusements alerts us to a critical ideological turn in Japanese culture and cultural studies alike (Silverberg 1992, 30–31).

Gonda Yasunosuke was every bit the discriminating Taishō intellectual, most especially in his refusal to view Japanese cultural change through a Western theoretical lens. If Japan had learned anything from World War I, he suggested, it was that the mistaken Meiji faith in the universalism of advanced civilization *(bunmei)* had prevented Japan from exploiting the particularities of its own dynamic culture *(bunka)*. As I argue elsewhere, the displacement of *bunmei* by *bunka* at this historical juncture signaled a revolutionary epistemological shift: the recognition that "modernity was not *inherited* by the many, but *invented* by the few" (Hanes 1996). Gonda took his own inspiration on this point from the "inventive" popular energy he witnessed on the streets of Tokyo: The kaleidoscopic variety of entertainments in Asakusa affirmed to him the liberation of "the people" from the "vacuous dilettantism" of (Western-inspired) high culture (Gonda 1922, 6). That Gonda wore his popular sympathies on his sleeve does not diminish the significance of his central insight: that "the people," broadly conceived, had neither been duped by the culture industry nor mesmerized by their supposed betters, but had created a subculture of their own from the possibilities held out by the new media culture.

From Osaka, Ōbayashi Sōshi put a rather different spin on urban cultural change in Taishō Japan. While instinctively sympathetic to Gonda's populism (both men, after all, were employed by the Ōhara Institute), he came at the issue of popular recreation from a much more orthodox social scientific perspective. Ōbayashi's survey of Osakan amusement was a paean to social scientific objectivity. He flatly denied any impulse to extrapolate from the data he had obtained so scrupulously and accordingly prefaced his study with the following disclaimer: "I will not attempt to draw any conclusions about popular recreation in Japan as a whole from this narrowly defined study. I will be gratified if this research serves to document the trends in popular recreation of one small part of the Kansai region" (Ōbayashi 1922, preface). In a lengthy theoretical preamble that drew heavily on the Western literature Gonda disdained, Ōbayashi provided an elaborate justification for his survey's narrow focus. While the Western sources he consulted certainly planted preconceptions—as he worked backward covertly, like Western social science itself, from Euro-American experience to universal law—it also gave form to his interpretation. It is not surprising, in this sense, that the almost obsessively theoretical Ōbayashi inflated all "popular recreation" (minshū goraku) to system while the antitheoretical Gonda reduced it to play (Silverberg 1992, 44–45).

Ōbayashi's interest in popular recreation placed him among a growing cohort of Japanese intellectuals and officials who had begun to project a new cultural trajectory for modern Japan. They were stimulated at once by both experience and example. Emboldened by the wartime boom years in Japan to extrapolate an ever-rising standard of living—and awed by the dramatic image of post–World War I America as a nation that promised the universal fulfillment of physical needs—Ōbayashi and many others anticipated a sea change in advanced industrial society. Yet, as the historian Gary Cross so astutely observed of the interwar ideological turn in Western cultural thought that both anticipated and reinforced Japan's, the American example of economic growth based on mass production and mass distribution did not initially conjure up dreams of mass consumerism, but of a mass leisure society: "the common assumption in 1920 [was] that free time, not the endless increase of consumption, was the inevitable consequence of growth" (Cross 1993, 7).

Ōbayashi did not simply echo this assumption; he parroted the social scientific paradigms produced to promote it. Prefacing his survey with a grandiloquent pronouncement about "the complete way of life," he reversed the conventional wisdom about human priorities. Ōbayashi noted that, while it was commonplace to assume that people worked, slept, and recreated in the interest of securing food, clothing, and shelter, the inverse was true. In short, he reversed means and ends, essentializing work, sleep, and recreation as the be-all and end-all of modern life (Ōbayashi 1922, 1). He then recited the theoretical wisdom of Western social scientists—to wit, that modern life should *naturally* be divided into three equal, eight-hour segments of work, sleep, and play (Ōbayashi 1922, 1–3, 26–27). This social reformist model, offered as a challenge to the prevailing industrial productionist model of lives divided equally between work and rest, dovetailed neatly with the international labor standard adopted by many Taishō reformers (Ujihara 1970, 65–68). Making the obligatory progressive reference to overwork as a pressing social problem, a perspective unequivocally endorsed by his institutional employer, Ōbayashi then pressed his social reformist agenda by drawing out the connection between reduced working hours and social psychological well-being. Recreation, he insisted, was the missing element in this human equation. Quite simply, it represented the key to "preserv[ing] equilibrium of mind and body" (Ōbayashi 1922, 5).

Ōbayashi considered recreation essential to the maintenance of "civilization." And civilization, broadly conceived as the setting of modern human experience, could be characterized most meaningfully as the social psychological state of "ever-increasing stimuli." Drawing on Western psychology, Ōbayashi noted that these stimuli produced such static in contemporary life that people naturally fell ill with various physical and spiritual ailments—most ominously, exhaustion and hysteria. Then he threw in the clincher. Given that it was instinctual for human beings to pursue recreation, and that the people of Japan were deprived of it, the inevitable result was sick individuals in an unhealthy society (Ōbayashi 1922, 9–11). With this in mind, Ōbayashi recalled the root meaning of *goraku* in English: "re-creation" or "to create anew." Associating this impulse with "higher animals," he touted it at once as the essential means for individuals to renew body and spirit and for society to realize progress (Ōbayashi 1922, 25). Nowhere, in his view, was "re-creation" more important than in industrial societies, where the rigid division of labor had rendered factory work "bland and monotonous" (Ōbayashi 1922, 27).

Ōbayashi set out next to examine and dissect the modern incarnation of popular recreation. He began by cataloguing and categorizing the bewildering variety of leisure activities in which Japanese indulged. His intricate classification system was a model of social scientific sophistication. After establishing recreation as an essential element of life, and asserting its autonomy from other forms of human activity, he laid out the recreational grid of modern life. Then he got down to brass tacks, producing an extraordinary series of sensorially ordered lists meant to run the gamut of recreational activities. There was "mental recreation" (*chiteki goraku*: trumps, chess, riddles, linked verse), "observational recreation" (*kansatsuteki goraku*: sightseeing, museum-going, aquarium viewing), "inclinational recreation" (*iteki goraku*: archery, judo, sumo), "instinctual recreation" (*honnōteki goraku*: summering, traveling, competitive sports, stamp, coin, and rare-book collecting), "emotional recreation" (*jōkanteki goraku*: playing musical instruments), "literary recreation" (*bungakuteki goraku*: reading and reciting), "constructive recreation" (*zōgeiteki goraku*: model building), "performance recreation" (*geijutsuteki goraku*: dance, theater, opera, motion pictures), and "spiritual recreation" (*seishinteki goraku*: pilgrimages) (Ōbayashi 1922, 35–38).

After chaining these types of recreation to four criteria of classification (psychological, practical, social, and economic) and linking them in turn to one or more of four further categories within them (moneymaking, public, sociable, and individual), Ōbayashi mercifully abandoned theory for reality. But this was not before he informed readers that he would be limiting his purview to only one type of recreation from the multitudes with which he had just regaled them: "moneymaking entertainment" *(eiriteki kōgyō)*. In observing bluntly that it was "the most ubiquitous and powerful [form of] popular recreation in the city of Osaka," Ōbayashi clearly meant to justify the survey's seemingly narrow focus (Ōbayashi 1922, 49). Still, he was being slightly disingenuous. A close rereading of the first chapter reveals something more than the mind of a dispassionate social scientist at work. One can sense the alarms going off in Ōbayashi's mind as he considered the implications of unregulated, popular, moneymaking entertainment on a metropolitan scale. Distinct from work and home life alike, and inextricably intertwined with money and the profit motive, this sort of entertainment was also saturated with the static of civilization—precisely the sort of sensory stimuli Ōbayashi condemned as a threat to the health of society. Throughout, Ōbayashi's "objective" survey of "the ubiquity and power" of the culture industry reverberates between two judgmental poles: ill-concealed respect for the cultural producers who knew how to capture audiences and ill-disguised suspicion of the media culture into which those audiences were immersed.

I have already suggested why Ōbayashi narrowed his *thematic* scope to moneymaking entertainment; allow me now to suggest why he narrowed his *spatial* scope to its activities in four discrete amusement quarters of Osaka. In one very real sense, his decision had to have been pragmatic. Osaka, after all, was then a city of one-and-a-half-million people who had found a million things to do in their spare time. Not only did these people live in a sprawling city whose area and population would soon exceed Tokyo's, they lived in one whose historical and contemporary identity were inextricably intertwined with commerce and industry. More properly characterized as a metropolis, in deference at once to its size and situation, Osaka was the urban magnet of the Kansai region. Fifty years earlier, following two centuries as the nation's commercial entrepôt, Osaka's economy nearly collapsed. Only when the business community rallied to its own defense, by dredging the city's outdated harbor and outfitting its port for oceangoing ships, did Osaka begin to relive its glory days as the Capital of Water *(Mizu no Miyako)*.

The industrial revolution that followed closely upon Osaka's commercial revival prompted the coinage of a new sobriquet: the Capital of Smoke *(Kemuri no Miyako)*. Osaka's unmatched industrial growth from mid-Meiji had transformed it into a sprawling metropolis whose skyline bristled forestlike with smokestacks. For those who clung proudly to the late Meiji ideology of "developing industry and promoting enterprise" *(shokusan kōgyō)*, the haze of smoke and smog that hung in its sky evoked a positively grimy comparison with the quintessential European industrial city. They called Osaka "the Manchester of the Orient."

Such capitalist hubris aside, the Osaka that Osakans called home was a social disaster in the making. Unplanned, overcrowded, and polluted, it inspired the muckraking urban reformer, Kagawa Toyohiko, to write a science fiction send-up set in the twenty-first century. *Mastery of the Air (Kūchū seifuku)*, published in 1922, envisioned the residents of Osaka suspended above its smog-laden sky in an aerial city of hot-air balloons. Plodding the streets below with oxygen tanks on their backs and hermetically sealed helmets on their heads—sporting metallic masks that gave credence to the names inscribed in roman letters on their carpetbags, A. Tengu (Mr. Hawk-nosed Demon) and Y. Hanatare (Mr. Runny-nose)—were the Tokyo-based inventors of said technology. That these interlopers amused themselves by contrasting the fresh air of Tokyo to Osaka's "putrid" atmosphere was bad enough. By moving about under a cinder-repellent umbrella, of all things, they added insult to injury (Kagawa 1974).

Yet, if Osaka as an industrialized place inspired awe of different sorts in its entrepreneurs and its residents, Osaka as a metropolitan space spurred the imagination of virtually everyone. As a magnet for the magnates who epitomized nouveaux riches-dom, it quickly spawned a flashy consumer culture of cafés, dance halls, and department stores rivaling Tokyo's. And contemporary commentators, concerned less with currency per se than with the culture it capitalized and patronized, paid increasing attention to Osaka in its Taishō incarnation.

In a fanciful essay contrasting the famed flâneurs of the Ginza in Tokyo to the grand gourmands of (the) Dōtonbori in Osaka, Gonda Yasunosuke took both a closer look at Japanese urban culture and a casual swipe at its Osakan manifestation. While the term "Ginza cruising"[6] *(Ginbura)* aptly expressed the all-consuming passion of Tokyo's legendary loungers, in Gonda's view, the term "Dōtonbori cruising" *(Dōbura)* was an infelicitous malapropism that elided the critical distinction between the flâneur and the gourmand. After all, cruisers cruised the Ginza for the sake of cruising, while strollers strolled Dōtonbori in search of seats and eats (Gonda 1975, 68–71). Gonda was right as rain on this point, but he arguably made it in the first place to put another, larger issue in high relief: By juxtaposing the trademark activities of these emblematic entertainment districts in distant Osaka and Tokyo, he meant to draw out the difference in ethos between the two cities. Gonda's portrayal of Dōtonbori played on Osaka's legendary reputation as a place where victuals were so plentiful and irresistible as to compel people to "eat 'til they dropped" *(kuidaore)*.

Gonda's ethnographic commentary doubtless set some Osakan ears ringing—dissonantly. For despite his "constructivist fondness for street life" (Silverberg 1992, 48), he apparently strolled a narrow urban circuit himself.

Even with his eyes open, Gonda pinned the tail on the wrong Osakan donkey. Had he followed his own advice and "read" the urban "text" of downtown Osaka, he might have discovered the equivalent of *Ginbura* in *Shinbura*. The latter term, which came into currency in the 1920s, described the window shopping and stroll-to-be-seen cruises of modish young Osakans along Shinsaibashi—the fashionable shopping street that would soon become Japan's first covered arcade.[7] That Shinsaibashi adjoined Dōtonbori, and Dōtonbori lay adjacent to the amusement quarter of Sennichimae, was something Gonda himself observed. But while he looked, apparently, he did not see. For his essay trailed off into an impressionistic effort at evoking the different "moods" of Tokyo, Osaka, and Kyoto (Gonda 1975, 70–71).

What escaped the eyes of Gonda Yasunosuke opened those of Ōbayashi Sōshi. As Ōbayashi discovered when he consulted Osaka's urban "text," it was immensely difficult and, in some respects, quite painful to read. No sooner did he take to the streets of Osaka than he encountered streetwalkers, in a way of speaking. Based on his observations of city life, Ōbayashi was forced to concede that prostitution fit his own definition of moneymaking entertainment. Noting that all four of Osaka's liveliest amusement quarters were within hailing distance of one or another of its pleasure quarters, the social scientist asked "Why?" as his alter ego whispered "Why ask?" The answer "they" came up with, which ultimately begged the question, was that there "appeared to be" an intimate connection between the "carnal" *(kannōteki)* and "performative" *(kōgyōteki)* forms of recreation (Ōbayashi 1922, 52). While Ōbayashi did not pursue this insight further, it clearly shocked him out of the dispassionate complacency of his social scientific persona. His subsequent survey of other, less intimate, moneymaking entertainments was charged with misgivings about the extent to which cultural producers and cultural consumers seemed anxious to enjoin and enjoy the cash nexus of Osaka's media culture.

Turning his attention first to the Dōtonbori and Sennichimae amusement quarters, whose proximity had initially prompted him to treat them as one, Ōbayashi found himself telling a tale of two cities. These two meccas of popular entertainment, separated by barely two blocks, were as different as night and day. While Dōtonbori was an orderly complex of theaters, movie houses, restaurants, and cafés whose settled quality emanated from long-established customs of entertainment, Sennichimae was a "higgledy-piggledy" collection of fly-by-night variety halls and movie houses anchored by a multiplex media center that pandered shamelessly to faddism (Ōbayashi 1922, 92). Before we take a look around the place that pulled Ōbayashi in, however, perhaps we should visit the one he fled.

Given Sennichimae's sordid history, it is hardly surprising that the district was virtually devoid of an entertainment tradition: An execution ground, a crematorium, and graveyards occupied the site through the Edo era.

Sennichimae's subsequent transformation into an amusement quarter reputedly was due to the entrepreneurship of a creative Meiji developer who, after purchasing the land for a song, first gave it over to a monkey show and dog act, then to a night fair and bar, and finally to a small amusement park. When Ōbayashi made his way to Sennichimae in 1920, the entire amusement quarter seemed suspended in an unremitting state of self-reinvention. The history of the Minami-za theater tells it all: A Nikkatsu Cinema movie house in 1913, it was redesigned for minstrel shows in 1914, was made back into a movie house in 1919, then was renovated and renamed The Cinema Club in 1920 (Shibata 1975, 5, 9). Ōbayashi counted twelve such small theaters in Sennichimae; and in each, as the saying goes, it was deja vu all over again. They supported every entertainment imaginable—from variety shows and stand-up comedy teams to minstrel shows and motion pictures (Ōbayashi 1922, 91–97). Sennichimae's movie houses, such as they were, screened so many different genres of film that their bill of fare went by the euphemism "a hefty serving" *(mori takusan)*. Three of its other theaters mixed and matched such a variety of entertainments that Ōbayashi was compelled to list their bill of fare as "miscellaneous" (Ōbayashi 1922, 99–101).

So, what made the owners do it? According to Ōbayashi, they were just trying to keep up with the Rakutenchi's. This place known as Entertainment Heaven, erected expressly to act as what Ōbayashi called a "crowd-pulling recreational magnet," was the jewel in Sennichimae's tinsel crown (Ōbayashi 1922, 92). It was a garishly illuminated venue where motion pictures danced across the screen on one stage as a dance troupe tripped the light fantastic next door. And that was not all: There were two more stages for "adaptations of Western drama" *(honyakugeki)* and comedies, a merry-go-round, a Western restaurant, souvenir booths, and a photo portrait studio strewn about the sprawling 4,300-square-meter complex. Best of all, however, one entered this entertainment paradise through the gate of heaven, an archway reputedly worthy of Tokyo Station, for the cost of a single, moderately priced (1 yen 50 sen) ticket (Ōbayashi 1922, 91–93).

It is little wonder that Ōbayashi was amazed by the spectacle of Sennichimae, and it is equally unsurprising that he reacted with profound ambivalence to what he saw. Bound as he was by the social scientific credo of objectivity, he was compelled to report that Sennichimae was less expensive (on average, by a full yen) and more diverse than neighboring Dōtonbori. And he had to admit that it was more "popular" as well, in both senses we use that term today. But the motley mixture of workers, salarymen, and students he spotted, combined with the "unsettled ambience" and "crowd-pulling promiscuity" of Sennichimae's media culture, both unsettled the social scientist and aroused the cultural ideologue within him. So seriously conflicted was Ōbayashi that he finally conveyed what I take to be a pensive projection of his fears for the future. "As a place of popular recreation gotten up in contemporary garb," he solemnly concluded, "Sennichimae may well be closer to the cutting edge [of popular entertainment] than Dōtonbori" (Ōbayashi 1922, 101). Nearer the recreational ideal of this erstwhile social progressive—but damned by the contrast to "wannabe" status—was that Osakan mecca of popular entertainment called The New World. Here, Ōbayashi observed, workers, shop clerks, and their families could and did enjoy "an inexpensive day of amusement" amidst movie theaters, variety shows, exhibit halls, carnival booths, and a merry-go-round (Ōbayashi 1922, 114–116). That The New World attracted an overwhelmingly lower-class clientele raised certain moral issues in Ōbayashi's mind, specifically about the wholesomeness of its amusements and the wisdom in allowing youthful consumers to indulge in them freely, but he was mollified by the fact that it *looked* every bit like a "civilized" amusement quarter (Ōbayashi 1922, 115–116).

Laid out in the fashion of a futuristic urban utopia, The New World was anchored at one end by an Eiffel tower look-alike, Tsūtenkaku, and at the other by an orderly amusement park that bore the name of its Coney Island inspiration, Luna Park. What spared the amusement park Ōbayashi's scorn, aside from its "civilized" orderliness, were its unique "radium baths" and "national sports hall." In this judgment, he gave his values away. Here, after all, were tangible symbols of good, clean, family fun (Ōbayashi 1922, 113).

For all its appeal as a decent and affordable amusement quarter, however, The New World was devoid of one crucial quality: cultural elevation. And while Ōbayashi searched for it in three more of Osaka's amusement quarters, he found it in one alone: Dōtonbori. Everyplace else in the end, including The New World, paled by comparison.[8] Long the darling of metropolitan night life in Osaka, to hear its aficionados tell it, Dōtonbori had veritably seethed with sensual energy since the Edo era. In its modern incarnation, it was a feast for the eyes, the ears, and the stomach. That its media culture preserved the patina of Dōtonbori's illustrious past, while pointing toward the future with its masterfully marketed entertainments, made the place positively alluring to Ōbayashi: Here was a time-honored amusement quarter that had kept pace with the times.

Anchored by the so-called Five Theaters, which were ranged along and just off its main thoroughfare, Dōtonbori supported an exotic menagerie of popular entertainments. And, like the attractions it showcased, Dōtonbori's entertainment industry arranged its human clientele with an ethnologist's eye for social difference. Ōbayashi's impressionistic "customer profile" (*kyakusuji*) revealed that each of its theaters had a unique box-office draw geared toward specific audiences. Naka-za, a theater that produced traditional drama, catered to an "upper-class audience" (*jōryū kankyaku*); Naniwa-za, a playhouse that presented avant-garde theater, pulled in "the middle class and above" (*chūryū ijō no kaikyū*); Kado-za, which specialized in new contemporary drama, brought in the "middle stratum" (*chūryū no*

場樂娛前日千堀頓道

A tale of two cities: The Dōtonbori and Sennichimae amusement quarters. (Ōbayashi Sōshi, Minshū goraku no jissai kenkyū: Osaka-shi minshū goraku chōsa. *Ōhara Shakai Mondai Kenkyūjo, 75.*)

hitobito); Benten-za, which showed motion pictures, priced tickets low enough for the "working classes" *(rōdōsha kaikyū)*; and Asahi-za, a true movie theater, reputedly accommodated the entire social spectrum (Ōbayashi 1922, 75–76).

If this consumer profile is intrinsically interesting for what it says about the diversity of Dōtonbori's paying public, it becomes more fascinating when one considers its source. For this profile, Ōbayashi drew unabashedly on the information offered him in an interview with one Oka Seizaburō, who was

The New World, day and night. (Utsusareta Osaka: Kindai hyaku-nen
no ayumi. *Osaka Shiritsu Hakubutsukan*, 114th printing, 1989, 42.)

none other than the manager of the Naniwa-za theater. This theater was
owned by one of Japan's most successful culture industries, the Shōchiku
Corporation; and speaking for the ownership, Oka offered Ōbayashi an
insider's view of the entertainment business. Shōchiku, which had recently
set the basis for what would become one of Japan's two film production
empires (along with Nikkatsu), had long been in the theater business. But
by 1920, as Ōbayashi learned, it had assumed control of all of the Five
Theaters in Dōtonbori.[9] One might imagine Ōbayashi, as a friend of "the
people," seeing this enterprise for what it was: a monument to the success

Dōtonbori. (Utsusareta Osaka: Kindai hyaku-nen no ayumi. *Osaka Shiritsu Hakubutsukan*, 114th printing, 1989, 43.)

of monopoly capitalism. But his instincts were not nearly so unambiguous. Ōbayashi was sufficiently impressed, in fact, with what his industry inform-ant told him next that he quoted him at length:

> Shōchiku policy with respect to the various entertainments in the Five Theaters is to run them in a way that reflects the diverse tastes and meets the diverse demands of a wide variety of people. For example, Naka-za takes account of the tastes and demands of a wealthy, upper middle-class clientele and selects performances and dramatic themes that will draw them in, while Naniwa-za aims to pull in middle-class people by offering performances of the newest contemporary drama. Kado-za and Benten-za, on the other hand, are run largely to meet the tastes and demands of the working class. And Asahi-za, as a movie palace screening motion pictures almost exclusively, aims to meet the tastes and needs of all audiences. Accordingly, there is little attempt to allow audiences—especially the tastes of low-class audiences—to de-termine theater programs. It is absolutely not company policy to pander to the public; we are able to offer programs that address [the tastes and demands of] people from various walks of life. (Ōbayashi 1922, 76)

What this media marketing spiel illustrates is that Osaka's entertain-ment industry openly acknowledged the diversity of its consumers. Neither pandering to popular tastes nor seeking to manipulate them, the Shōchiku Corporation *actively catered to* the different audiences it hoped to capture. That Ōbayashi gleefully acknowledged the agency of Osaka's consumers is hardly surpising, but he did not stop there. With tragic irony, he also celebrated what can be described only as a shameless Shōchiku marketing ploy: the "Glory Day" specials, run regularly in the company's movie theaters, offering workers free admission. As reported by Ōbayashi, this enlightened company policy anticipated "the deliverance" of workers from the "labor problem" (Ōbayashi 1922, 82).

Shōchiku was hardly alone, of course, in wooing working-class audiences. In Osaka, Kobayashi Ichizō, the Hankyū railway magnate and entertainment industry mogul, strove to meet working class demand in his Kansai movie houses by scheduling show times and setting ticket prices to meet workers' needs and desires (Tanaka 1976, 242–243). Indeed, it was the competition with Kobayashi for Kansai audiences that prompted Shōchiku to market its theaters so aggressively. Their subsequent decision in 1923 to construct the Shōchiku-za movie palace in Dōtonbori, featuring twin bills that included both movies and stage reviews, was an explicit challenge to Kobayashi's success at Takarazuka.

By Ōbayashi's account, Shōchiku's success in Dōtonbori owed to the creation of an urban "recreational system" (*goraku shisetsu:* Ōbayashi's own translation). Throwing his popular sympathies to the wind at last, Ōbayashi expressed unreserved admiration for the enterprising industry executives who had rationalized the movie theater market. By buying up theaters across Japan and creating theater chains, argued Ōbayashi, the industry had not only reduced costs but passed these savings on to the public (Ōbayashi 1922, 56–57). What he could not have known (but might have suspected had he not been taken in himself by Shōchiku's marketing strategy) was that the industry powers would soon transform their emergent production/theater empires into a studio system not unlike the one created by Hollywood. Already by 1920, as confirmed by Ōbayashi, they had made significant progress toward that end.

The very same company that reached out so obsequiously to working-class audiences in Dōtonbori would soon hire the indomitable Henry Kotani away from Hollywood to see that the films it produced held the necessary allure to bring them in, then keep them coming (Bordwell 1988, 18). Hardly oblivious to this aspect of the culture industry—indeed, sufficiently fascinated by it to devote fifty pages to a discussion of the motion picture medium and its mavens—Ōbayashi arguably had been sold on the new media culture by the culture industry's best salesmen. In the end, I would argue, he became a media maven himself. Concluding his survey of popular recreation quite differently than he began it, Ōbayashi celebrated the media culture of Taishō Japan as if its exponents were guileless innovators rather than greedy capitalists: "When the people are no longer satisfied with what's come before in the way of popular recreation, they must create something new appropriate to the new age." Shōchiku's "people," by his lights, had accomplished just that with their films and theaters. But even Ōbayashi recognized that this revelation put an ironic twist on his message. So, he took a page out of Oka's marketing manual. Acknowledging that only "the intellectual public" *(chishikiteki minshū)* had thus far embraced the new media culture, producing a cinematic simulacrum of their own lifestyle, he exhorted "the masses" *(ippan minshū)* to seize their turn. Then, in a parting ideological salvo that recalls nothing so much as America's media debate today, Ōbayashi cast the issue as one of "equal opportunity" *(kikai kintōshugi)* (Ōbayashi 1922, 378–380).

Ōbayashi was right. Then as now, intellectual elites exerted inordinate control over the media. But he failed to grasp the obvious: that he himself was captivated by the power they seemed to possess. Seduced by the media culture of which he was once so suspicious, Ōbayashi now spoke of empowering "the masses" as media mavens in their own right. Had he returned to Dōtonbori and conveyed this news to his industry informant, Oka Seizaburō, he would have been set straight on at least one account: that the "masses" he championed were a figment of his imagination. Oka might even have toyed with the idea of lecturing his idealistic friend on the realities of urban life, reminding him of the mosaic of segmented subcultures that composed his company's consumer market. Whether Oka would have gone on to speak of the power these people already possessed as consumers is doubtful, however. He was, after all, speaking to a neophyte. Sitting before him was an intellectual enchanted by the power of the media, but oblivious to the social and cultural realities it engaged. Can you hear Oka laughing?[10]

NOTES

1. See especially Schudson 1993 for a gainsayer's view on the power of advertising enterprise.
2. I borrow the language of T. J. Jackson Lears (1992) here.
3. I am indebted to Ron Toby for this and other insights. In addition, I would like to thank the Social Science Research Council, the Japan Foundation, and the University of Oregon for research funding; the School of Policy Studies at Ritsumeikan University in Kyoto for a luxurious office; the Fox-Murotanis for welcoming me into their home; and Gary Allinson, Charlie Fox, Bill Hauser, and Jennifer Rondeau for helpful comments on this essay.
4. Two outstanding, multivolume collections of primary sources are Minami 1984–1995 and Ishikawa 1989.
5. Fueled by fears of creeping moral decay, city and central government agencies alike began to season their surveys of popular recreation with

sizable doses of moralistic rhetoric slamming commercialized entertainment as a corrupting influence. See, for example, Osaka-shi Shakai-bu Chōsa-ka 1923 and Nakata 1924.

6. I am using Miriam Silverberg's vivid translation of the term.

7. It is not clear when the terms *Dōbura* and *Shinbura* entered the Osakan vocabulary, but both were reputedly in use by 1930 (see Hibi 1984, 187).

8. The Kujō district, which was literally an island, became one figuratively as well in Ōbayashi's account: It was little more than a garish collection of honky-tonks whose fate was tied to the Matsushima gay quarter. Tamatsukuri, on the other hand, had none of the "glitter" of The New World and Dōtonbori/Sennichimae: It was a lackluster throwback to an earlier age of urban entertainments (see Ōbayashi 1922, 123–131).

9. See Shibata 1975 for a historical survey of Shōchiku's theater interests in the Hanshin area.

10. After the closing line of Asada 1989.

REFERENCES

Asada Akira. 1989. "Infantile Capitalism and Japan's Postmodernism: A Fairy Tale." In *Postmodernism and Japan,* edited by Masao Miyoshi and H. D. Harootunian. Durham: Duke University Press.

Bordwell, David. 1988. *Ozu and the Poetics of Cinema.* Princeton: Princeton University Press.

Cross, Gary. 1993. *Time and Money: The Making of Consumer Culture.* London: Routledge.

Gonda Yasunosuke. [1922] 1975. "Ginbura to Dōbura: santo jōshu." In *Gonda Yasunosuke chōsakushū.* Vol. 4. Bunwa Shobō.

———. 1922. *Minshū goraku no kichō.* Dōjinsha.

Hanes, Jeffrey. 1996. "Taishū bunka/ka'i bunka/minshū bunka: senkan-ki no Nihon no toshi ni okeru kindai seikatsu." In *Toshi no kūkan/toshi no shintai,* edited by Yoshimi Shunya. Keisō Shobō.

Hazama, Hiroshi. 1976. "Historical Changes in the Life Style of Industrial Workers." In *Japanese Industrialization and Its Social Consequences,* edited by Hugh Patrick. Berkeley: University of California Press.

Hibi Hanjirō. [1930] 1984. "Dōtonbori tsū." In *Kindai shomin seikatsu shi.* Vol. 2. Edited by Minami Hiroshi. San'ichi Shobō.

Ishikawa Hiroyoshi. 1981. *Goraku no senzen shi.* Tōsho Sensho.

———. 1989. *Yoka/goraku kenkyū kisō bunken shū: dai ikki.* 12 vols. Ōzorasha.

Kagawa Toyohiko. [1922] 1974. *Kūchū seifuku.* In *Kagawa Toyohiko zenshū.* Vol. 15. Kirisuto Shinbunsha.

Kellner, Douglas. 1995. *Media Culture: Cultural studies, identity and politics between the modern and the postmodern.* London: Routledge.

Lears, T. J. Jackson. 1992. "Making Fun of Popular Culture." *American Historical Review* 97.5:1417–1426.

Minami Hiroshi, ed. 1965. *Taishō bunka*. Keisō Shobō.

———, ed. 1984–1995. *Kindai shomin seikatsu shi*. 20 vols. San'ichi Shobō.

Morris-Suzuki, Tessa. 1994. *The Technological Transformation of Japan; from the Seventeenth to the Twenty-First Century*. Cambridge: Cambridge University Press.

Municipal Bureau of Labor Research of Osaka. [1921] 1976. "Cost of Living Among Laborers in Osaka, Japan." In *Rōdō chōsa hōkoku*, edited by Osaka Shiyakusho. Osaka: Osaka Shiritsu Chūō Toshokan.

Nakata Shunzō. 1924. *Goraku no kenkyū*. Shakai Kyōiku Kyōkai.

Ōbayashi Sōshi. 1922. *Minshū goraku no jissai kenkyū: Osaka-shi no minshū goraku chōsa*. Osaka: Ōhara Shakai Mondai Kenkyūjo.

Osaka-shi Shakai-bu Chōsa-ka, ed. 1923. *Yoka seikatsu no kenkyū*. Kyoto: Kōbundō.

Schudson, Michael. 1993. *Advertising, the Uneasy Persuasion: Its Dubious Impact on American Society*. London: Routledge.

Shibata Masaru. 1975. Osaka, Dōtonbori, Sennichimae, Kobe, Shinkaichi, Sannomiya shūhen eiga jōsetsukan no kiroku. Typescript. Shōchiku.

Silverberg, Miriam. 1992. "Constructing the Japanese Ethnography of Modernity." *Journal of Asian Studies* 51.1:30–54.

———. 1993. "Constructing a New Cultural History of Prewar Japan." In *Japan in the World*, edited by Masao Miyoshi and Harry Harootunian. Durham: Duke University Press.

Takemura Tamio. 1980. *Taishō bunka*. Kodansha.

Tanaka Jun'ichirō. 1976. *Nihon eiga hattatsu shi*. Vol. 2. Chūō Kōronsha.

Ujihara Shōjirō. 1970. "Daiichiji taisen-go no rōdō chōsa to yoka seikatsu no kenkyū." In *Yoka seikatsu no kenkyū*. Kōseikan.

Yamamura, Kozo. 1986. "Japan's Deus ex Machina: Western Technology in the 1920s." *Journal of Japanese Studies* 12.1:65–94.

❧ 13 ❧

Zaikai *and Taishō* Demokurashii, 1900–1930

LONNY E. CARLILE

Various chapters in this volume demonstrate that during the Taishō years "modernity" permeated all classes of Japanese society in a variety of economic and political guises. Indeed, one of the themes to emerge strongly from many of the contributions to this volume is the stunningly populist quality of much of Taishō modernity. Clearly, modernity in Taishō had a mass dimension of a greater magnitude than had been realized in past scholarship. Despite this, it remains the case that there were clear and profound limits on the degree to which the "massification" of Taishō *demokurashii* could unfold. Nowhere were these limits more conspicuous and significant than at the "commanding heights" of the Japanese political economy. There, despite concessions to populist pressures, a small nexus of elites, whose roots were traceable to the immediate post-Restoration period, maintained a firm grip on key levers of political economic power.

This essay deals with the arrival of modernity in the arena of elite-level business-state relations. It focuses on the evolution of *zaikai* during the Greater Taishō period of 1900–1930.[1] *Zaikai* refers to that small group of individuals who as a rule served in executive positions in Japan's leading business associations and who, collectively, were recognized to be the representative spokespersons for the big business community. This definition corresponds to current usage more than to the usage of the term at the time. It is a somewhat "fuzzy" term in that who qualifies as a member of *zaikai* is a matter of subjective attribution and therefore prone to varying interpretations. In practice, however, the term generates a surprisingly solid consensus about who the core members of *zaikai* are at any given time. By focusing on the 1900–1930 period, we are observing *zaikai* as it evolved from a loose, informally organized set of individuals with personal connections to individual Meiji government officials (traditionally referred to as *seishō*, or political merchant) into a formalized structure of interest representation built around national business associations that were the forerunners of the *zaikai* associations that speak for Japanese business today.

Using one or more formally organized *zaikai* associations to anchor the discussion, the sections that follow relate *zaikai*'s evolving structural features to the changing social, political, and economic contexts of Taishō *demokurashii* and through these attempt to assess the character and impact of *zaikai* on the evolution of the prewar Japanese polity. The picture that unfolds is one of increasing *zaikai* autonomy and policymaking influence and growing formalization and "rationalization" of the institutional mechanisms for exercising that influence. The essential argument that emerges is that, despite being fraught with contradictions and far from perfect from *zaikai*'s standpoint, the authoritarian Meiji constitutional order simply provided too many opportunities for organized business to advance its interests through direct interaction with the state bureaucracy and too few incentives for it to act as a liberal, proparliamentary force in the evolving political economic order. These circumstances, in turn, suggest at least a partial explanation of why the populism of Taishō *demokurashii* could progress only so far and why the period would eventually set the stage for the explosion of social, political, and economic tensions of the 1930s.

FINANCE AND MEIJI PARTY POLITICS

In setting the stage for the discussion of Taishō *zaikai*, it is useful to point out that in the classic formulation, industrialization and the emergence of modern capitalism give rise in the sociopolitical arena to an era of political and economic liberalism. Whether and to what extent this formulation constitutes a valid universal principle applicable beyond the early industrialization of England remains an open question and is not an issue that will be dealt with here (see, among others, Bendix 1974). It is noteworthy, nonetheless, that early industrialization in Japan in fact produced political forces and tendencies of the sort described by the classic formulation. The "popular" parties in the years immediately following the opening of the Diet in 1890 battled the entrenched *hanbatsu* oligarchs over "freedom and popular rights" in the political arena and lower taxes and greater scope for private activities in the economic arena. Backing them, as is consistent with the classic formula, was a movement of merchants and industrialists aligned, in the Japanese case, with a nonaristocratic landlord elite (Najita 1967; Mitani 1988; Masumi 1988, 4–5). The nonelected *hanbatsu* governments contributed significantly albeit unintentionally to the mobilizational capacity of the commercial and landlord classes by organizing a nationwide, compulsory-membership network of chambers of commerce *(shōhō kaigisho)* and agri-cultural associations *(nōkai)* that served as the backbone of the movement. These governments also granted the right to vote to the moneyed classes. Mass agitation and protest by the commercial and industrial classes against increased taxes, led by the chambers of commerce, were particularly con-spicuous between 1890 and 1910, the time span that is widely viewed as constituting Japan's industrial revolution (Eguchi 1971).

Despite the existence of a mass base for political and economic liberal-ism as well as, initially, a majoritarian parliamentary movement willing to champion its cause, the Meiji constitutional order was profoundly biased against the playing out of the classic scenario. It was in fact a system deliberately designed to limit the influence of the Diet-based popular par-ties (Mitani 1988; Akita 1967). Eventually, the parties were able to expand their power and influence to the point that party governments could be established; but as Tetsuo Najita and others have demonstrated, this was the result of a series of strategic and tactical compromises with the entrenched extraparliamentary elites (Najita 1967; Mitani 1988). Fiscal and economic policy was at the heart of these compromises.

The primary axis of conflict over policy during the initial years of the Meiji constitutional order was that which pitted the low tax/small govern-ment *minryoku kyūyō* (relief for the people) agenda of the popular parties against the high tax/big government *fukoku kyōhei* (rich country strong military) program of the *hanbatsu* cabinets. The centrality of fiscally based confrontation was not coincidental. The lower house's power to block in-creases in the annual government budget was one of the few meaningful levers that the popular parties had available to use against the Meiji oli-garchs, while the attainment of an international status for Japan equal to that of the great powers via the fiscally burdensome construction of a modern military force and associated infrastructure remained the foremost goal of all of the *genrō*. Enhancing the political significance of the demands of the military was the special status of the armed services in the Meiji Constitu-tion. It was hardly coincidental, therefore, that the securing of Seiyūkai parliamentary dominance and cabinet participation during the first decade of this century was premised on the party's decision to go along with the military build-up and modernization that was so dear to the hearts of Yama-gata Aritomo and other hard-line *hanbatsu* figures. The Seiyūkai's "fiscal positivism"—increased military spending *and* pork-barrel-producing do-mestic infrastructural development—was an attractive option to pursue un-der the circumstances and perhaps even the only viable long-term route to power under the Meiji constitutional system (Banno 1975). But it also set an important precedent. Although the parties were granted some say in how government spending was to be distributed, the determination of the goals and the general framework of economic policy were left in the hands of nonelected extraparliamentary elites. It is in this historical context that the emergence of *zaikai* must be understood.

THE YŪRAKUKAI

The Yūrakukai was established on January 29, 1900, in the Mitsui Building in the Yūrakuchō district of Tokyo (Yamashita 1978; Takahashi 1973, 5). It continued to hold meetings until 1905. The bulk of its initial membership of sixty-four consisted of individuals of three types: prominent *seishō* like Masuda Takashi of Mitsui, Iwasaki Hisaya of Mitsubishi, Yasuda Zenjirō of Yasuda, and Ōkura Kihachirō of Ōkura; prominent financiers, including representatives of the leading public sector banks (Bank of Japan, Yokohama Specie Bank, and the Hypothec Bank); and a smattering of individuals from nonfinancial firms in the modern sector (e.g., Tokyo Gas, Fuji Spinning Company, Japan Flour Milling). Also present was that indefatigable fixture of Meiji capitalism, Shibusawa Eiichi. The impetus for the formation of the Yūrakukai harks back to several irregular gatherings involving many of the same people called by the *genrō* cum *seishō* patron Inoue Kaoru[2] in an effort to mobilize their cooperation in economic tasks that were of critical concern in the government's post–Sino-Japanese War *fukoku kyōhei* policy—namely, easing the country's chronic balance-of-payments problems through export promotion and cuts of unnecessary imports and the encouragement of investment on the Chinese mainland. Throughout its life, the Yūrakukai and its activities continued to revolve around Inoue, with the subcommittee-based research and deliberation activities of the association initiated as a rule by Inoue himself or through requests of government agencies mediated by Inoue. In current Japanese political parlance, one could liken the Yūrakukai to a cross between a *kōenkai* (personal support association) and a policy research group *(seisaku shūdan)* attached to Inoue.

At one level, the Yūrakukai represented a rather typical example of a mode of government-business relations that in form traces its roots to the relationship between certain daimyo and Bakufu officials, on the one hand, and merchant houses during the Tokugawa period, on the other. This relationship, which predominated through the early Meiji period, was "personal and unofficial" rather than "formal or official," mediated through "direct contact between one or another of the *(hanbatsu)* oligarchs and an entrepreneur with access to him," and involved an implicit exchange of "special privileges" for "special favors" (Johnson 1982, 85). Although the net result for the political merchants involved was often comparable, the Yūrakukai and similar associations were not lobbying organs or pressure groups in the usual sense of the term.[3] Where lobbying and pressure-group activities involve efforts on the part of private groups to shape the activities of govern-

TABLE 1
Selected Members of the Yūrakukai

Name	Occupation
Amemiya Keijirō	Chairman, Hokkaido Railway and Colliery Co.
Dan Takuma	Managing Director, Mitsui Mining
Hara Rokurō	Chairman, Yokohama Specie Bank
Iwanaga Shōichi	Managing Director, Nippon Yūsen Co.
Iwasaki Hisaya	President, Mitsubishi Gōshi
Magoshi Kyōhei	President, Nippon Beer; Chairman, Imperial Bank of Commerce
Masuda Takashi	Managing Director, Mitsui Bussan
Mitsui Morinosuke	Director, Mitsui Gofukuten
Nezu Kaichirō	Chairman, Yokohama Insurance Company
Ōhashi Shintarō	Owner, Hakubunkan Bookstore
Ōkura Kihachirō	President, Okura Gumi
Shibusawa Eiichi	President, Daiichi Bank
Takahashi Korekiyo	Vice President, Bank of Japan
Takahashi Shinkichi	President, Japan Hypothec Bank
Toyokawa Ryōhei	Chief, Banking Division, Mitsubishi Gōshi
Umemura Seiichi	Managing Director, Tokyo Ishikawajima Shipbuilding
Yamamoto Tatsuo	President, Bank of Japan
Yasuda Zenjirō	Superintendent, Yasuda Bank

Source: Yamashita Naoto, "Nisshin-Nichiro senkan ki ni okeru zaibatsu burjoajii no seisaku shikō: Yūrakukai no dōkō," *Rekishigaku kenkyū* 450 (1878):20.

ment, in the Japanese context of the time the dynamics ran in the opposite direction. A sharp gulf in social status separated state officials from the *seishō,* and in their interactions (in outward form if not always in substance), the latter were expected to show deference, obeisance, and respect to the former. It was always the state-affiliated oligarch who maintained the initiative and on behalf of state purposes sought to shape the activities of private-sector groups. The *seishō* were in effect those private-sector entrepreneurs who were ready, willing, and able to respond to such requests on a regular basis. And while it is clear that over the long term contacts of this sort tended to benefit the clients involved immensely, it was also consistent with this dynamic that the fulfillment of oligarchic requests frequently involved immense risk and costly financial burdens (Morikawa 1976, 38; Kobayashi 1988).

Even as the Yūrakukai exhibited these "traditional" qualities, one can also discern signs of a growing "modernity" beginning to seep into the Japanese government-business relationship. The very fact that this relationship mediated by the Yūrakukai involved a formalized associational format rather than an informal and direct one-on-one encounter reflects the expanded scale and complexity of government-business relations that accompanied the rise of modern enterprise as the Greater Taishō period began. The focus on financial affairs and investment policy can also be seen as reflective of a growing modernity. That is, while it is true that pre-Meiji relationships between samurai officials and merchant houses had always been driven by the desire of the former to mobilize the monetary and financial resources of the latter, what was distinctively "modern" about the unfolding relationship was the increasingly systemic quality of the context in which the relationship was maintained. The concerns of the parties were no longer focused exclusively on the bilateral transaction but on such wider and abstract concerns as the impact of that relationship on the creditworthiness of the state, foreign exchange reserves, and the overall health of the economy. It was precisely these concerns, in fact, that drove the government to convene the High Level Conferences on Agriculture, Commerce, and Industry (Nōshōkō Kōtō Kaigi) in 1896, 1897, and 1898. These represented the first formally organized state commissions in which businessmen were allowed to participate as full delegates.[4]

THE UNAGIKAI

In the summer of 1908, an incident occurred that seemed to signal that the relationship between the state and at least a part of the modern business sector was changing. In preparing the upcoming fiscal year's budget, the government of the soon-to-be *genrō* Saionji Kimmochi found itself with a massive revenue shortfall. Reversing an earlier promise, the government decided to finance the shortfall with a tax hike and additional government borrowing. This decision ignored the prescription of the national banking community, which had recommended budgetary retrenchment and a moratorium on additional government debt. The banking community then joined forces with the small business-based chambers of commerce in orchestrating a wave of nationwide protests against the budget and threatened to boycott the government's bond sales. The Saionji government subsequently resigned and was replaced by the second cabinet of Katsura Tarō, which promptly adopted a policy of budgetary retrenchment in line with the demands of the banking community, thereby reversing the policy of budgetary expansion that had continued since before the Sino-Japanese War of 1894–1895.[5]

This series of events represented the first time that open opposition by a wing of the business community had brought down a reigning cabinet. It also led to changes in the way fiscal policy was made. Among these was the creation of the Unagikai (Eel Society), an informal organization in which leading bankers gathered periodically to discuss fiscal and financial issues with top government finance officials.[6] Also initiated was the practice of presenting government budget drafts to the Bank Clearing House (Tegata Kōkanjo) even before they were sent to the Diet, a policy that seemed to suggest that, symbolically, the power and influence of the banking community was greater than even that of the Diet. By contrast, the chambers of commerce, representing the petite bourgeoisie and demanding tax *cuts* rather than just a moratorium on new debt, had their right to compel legally those qualified for membership to pay dues, a provision critical for maintaining the organizational base of the chambers, revoked by the Katsura government (Fletcher 1989, 12–13).

The sight of the banking community bringing a Satchō government to heel represented a clear reversal of what earlier had been a relationship of subordination between the Japanese business community and the Satchō-dominated state. It is noteworthy, too, that this facing down of a *hanbatsu* government by the financial community preceded by nearly half a decade a comparable public display of power and influence by the political parties in the so-called Taishō Political Crisis of 1912. The basis for this change can be found in the state's growing dependence on the banking community for the absorption of its bond issues domestically and its facilitation of bond sales overseas, and there were signs even prior to the 1908 crisis that state financial concerns were altering the terms of state-business relations. Between 1894 and 1908, Japan fought two major wars, each of which had to be financed through massive borrowing and increased taxes. Victory in the wars created further fiscal burdens in the form of the expenses associated with administering newly won concessions and colonies. Security considerations pushed the government not only to a massive arms buildup but also to a dramatic expansion of government enterprises deemed essential for national security, including the upgrading and expansion of the state's numerous armories, the establishment of the Yawata Steel Works in Kyushu, and railway nationalization.[7] Indeed, by 1907, state enterprise reached the point where it accounted for more than 50 percent of total paid-in capitalization and reserves in the mining, manufacturing, and transport sectors (Nakamura 1975, 94). The ratio highlights not just the sheer size of state enterprise but also the manner in which the *sengo keiei* (postwar management) programs began to act as a major drag on the civilian economy. The fiscal consequences of postwar management came to a head in the wake of the Russo-Japanese War of 1904–1905. Whereas the financial burden of postwar management in the case of the Sino-Japanese War was offset by the windfall of postwar Chinese indemnities, no such relief was to be had from the considerably more costly Russo-Japanese War.

In addition to direct acceptance of state bond issues, the Japanese government needed the banking community's assistance in its effort to refinance these overseas loans on more favorable terms (Kamiyama 1988). On its part, thanks to dramatic growth in private-sector deposits, Japanese

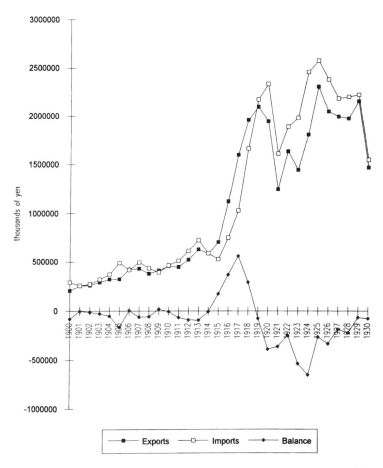

Japan's trade balance, 1900–1930. (Bank of Japan, Hundred Year Statistics of the Japanese Economy, *1996.)*

banking was now built on a foundation of independent deposit banks and was freed of its previous dependence on the Bank of Japan (Takeda 1992). In other areas, an improvement in the business community's status was visible. Earlier, the salaries of even the highest paid Japanese executives were dwarfed by the huge salaries given to government bureaucrats. Now, salary levels in the private sector began to equal or surpass those of officials in comparable levels of the government bureaucracy. The awarding of titles of nobility and various state honors to prominent businessmen reached a zenith during the first decade of this century, helping to elevate the social standings of top members of the business community to the point where they approached that of titled government officials (Takahashi 1973,

106–116; Ando 1976, 197–199). Yet for all the improvements in the status of the business community, there was an essential continuity in the basic format of business-state relations. It was a relationship that directly linked *zaikai* and the *hanbatsu* oligarchs without the mediation of parliament or party. It was first and foremost the needs of the state that defined the issues for action. Although *zaikai*'s concerns were not ignored, they became an issue only to the extent that they affected the realization of state goals. If anything, the scope of participation in these interchanges seems to have narrowed now that the financial community was given virtually exclusive license to constitute *zaikai*.

THE INDUSTRIAL CLUB

The inaugural ceremony for the Japan Industrial Club (Nihon Kōgyō Kurabu) was held in March of 1917. The Industrial Club differed from the Yūrakukai in at least two important ways. First, as enunciated in its inaugural statement and confirmable through a perusal of its membership, the Industrial Club was established to give voice to the concerns of the manufacturing sector and thereby to correct the priority given to banking and finance in government policy. Second, unlike the *kōenkai*-like Yūrakukai, the Industrial Club was not tied to any particular political figure. Composed of individuals associated with larger manufacturing firms based primarily in the Kantō region, the biggest contributors to the Club's finances were the *zaibatsu* houses of Mitsui, Mitsubishi, Yasuda, and Furukawa, all of whom had recently made major investments in the heavy industrial sector. This group also provided the officers of the association.[8] The conventional interpretation of the formation of the Industrial Club is that it was the result of a process in which industrial growth gave rise to a new pressure group (Miyamoto 1988, 25; Takeuchi 1975). That is, it is argued that World War I was the period in which heavy industry first gained a firm foothold in Japan and the Industrial Club represented the voice of this newly rising class of Japanese industrialists. While not incorrect, strictly speaking, a more nuanced interpretation of the historical context of the club's emergence would appear to be in order.

According to Toshitani Nobuyuki and Honma Shigeki (1976), an important modification in the state policy-making process had occurred prior to the club's formation. In response to rising populist pressures and a concomitant decline in *genrō* influence, all of which became amply apparent in the wake of the Taishō Crisis of 1912, a significant concession was made to the demand for greater participation in governance. The concrete institutional mechanism involved was the investigatory council manned by representatives of the political economic elite triumvirate—bureaucracy, the parties, *zaikai*—and, where appropriate, representatives of other relevant societal interests. During the 1910–1920 decade, a series of such councils were set up; these were asked to construct basic guidelines for state policy in such areas as defense, the economy, foreign policy, the legal system, and education. This "opening up" of the system, though, was a quintessentially conservative exercise designed to preserve *hanbatsu* power and autonomy. The aim was to make the state more responsive to its changing socioeconomic base without surrendering formal authority to popular forces. The Diet as an institution was deliberately circumvented, and the oligarchs and bureaucrats drafted the agendas and steered the deliberations of the councils.

The earliest of these councils was the seventy-member Investigatory Council on Production (Seisan Chōsakai), which was established in June 1910 and concluded its work during June 1913. At the outset, fourteen businessmen were on the council (numbers varied over time). As Harada Mikio (1985–1986) shows in a detailed analysis, the council was an outgrowth of the struggle over fiscal policy in the post–Russo-Japanese War period described above (See also Sakamoto 1991). At its most generalized level, the council's mission was to help resolve the fiscal deadlock that was hampering the government's postwar management program. More narrowly, it was assigned the task of finding ways to improve the performance of Japan's export industries in order to ease the balance-of-payments pressures that were hampering the state's military modernization while simultaneously increasing tax revenues for the state and alleviating chronic fiscal crisis.

The focus in deliberation was precisely that which had in the past served as the catalyst for policy dialogue between the Japanese state and business community. Initially, at least, discussion focused on ways to promote Japan's major *export* products, and, in particular, silk. As deliberation proceeded, however, there was an extrapolation of the logic—namely, that the state should promote *import substituting* industries because increased production at home would facilitate *fukoku kyōhei* by cutting down on the outflow of foreign exchange. Although a subtle shift in emphasis that was not developed very systematically at the time, this marked an important step in the conceptual evolution of economic policy in that it was a move away from an exclusive state concern with factors that directly affected government revenues and foreign exchange earnings (i.e., export industries, foreign exchange reserves) to a more macroeconomically sensitive approach to economic management in which the development of nonexport-oriented domestic manufacturing was defined as being in the interest of the state and therefore to be fostered.

The successor Investigatory Council on the Economy (Keizai Chōsakai) established during 1916 took this logic a step further (See Harada 1988–1992). Like its predecessor, it consisted of representatives of big business, public- and private-sector finance capital, various ministries, the *hanbatsu,* and the popular parties. Assigned the task of discussing what the state should do in the economic arena to deal with the disruptions of trade and commerce that were occurring following the outbreak of World War I, the council recommended that the state provide both tariff protection and subsidies to domestic producers in strategic heavy industries. A number of such subsidies were subsequently disbursed, and the *zaibatsu* houses, which had until then been rather coy about investing in the sector, began to move aggressively into manufacturing and heavy industry. The absence of Western competition during World War I, coupled with government subsidization, led to rapid growth of private investment in industries like steel, chemicals, and machinery manufacturing (Nakamura 1983, 144–156; Takeda 1992, 91–111). More than anything else, it was this emergence of heavy industry as a state-recognized strategic sector that provided the impetus for the formation of the Industrial Club.

From an organizational standpoint, the Industrial Club was clearly an innovation in Japanese government-business relations in that it brought an unprecedented degree of formalization and systematization to the expression of big business interests. In other ways, however, the Industrial Club also continued to exhibit features of earlier modes. Despite the rapid diversification of the economy and a mushrooming of new firms during the war years, key officers of the organization were the same individuals who had served as the spokesmen for the big business community since the turn of the century. One gets the sense that the self-image of the Industrial Club was of a manufacturing sector counterpart of financial groups like the Unagi-kai. A careful reading of the record of its activities during the initial years of its operation indicates that even in its new organizational guise the impetus for its activities was largely external. The Industrial Club's twenty-five-year history lists thirty-three separate items on which action was taken on issues relating to governmental policies during the first seven years of the club's existence (Nihon Kōgyō Kurabu 1943, 43–469). Of these, twenty-five, or about three-fourths, can be considered either a response to a governmental agency request for an investigation into an issue of bureaucratic concern (fourteen) or a reaction to a governmental initiative (eleven). Only five could be considered to involve independent initiatives by the Kōgyō Club. Thus, although the personal element may have been diluted and despite a public image to the contrary, the essentially hierarchical, advisory-advisee element remained strong in the state–big business relationship.

On the whole, this bureaucracy-centered orientation of the Industrial Club worked well in generating the policies favored by its core membership. Perhaps the biggest issue to confront the Industrial Club was the deteriorating position of Japan's infant heavy industrial sector as more competitive Western producers returned to the market following the war's end. The state's response initially consisted of ad hoc customs hikes and emergency subsidies that did not cure the fundamental problems involved but did allow the leading firms to stay afloat. The recommendations of the Temporary Investigatory Council on Budgetary Affairs and the Economy (Rinji Zaisei Keizai Chōsakai), another government investigatory council, led to a more systematic fleshing out of customs policy and protection measures (Toshitani and Honma 1976, 221–237). The outcome was a complex of revamped tariff schedules and subsidy arrangements that together represented a nuanced response to the situation confronting Japanese industry. Based heavily on proposals ironed out in the Industrial Club, the new customs rates were designed to impose the minimal level of customs duties required to cover cost differentials between foreign and domestic producers. This approach recognized the fact that much of Japanese heavy industrial production was intermediate processing; thus it was important from a competitive stand-point to keep tariffs low on imported inputs and minimize the costs imposed on consumer firms downstream (Miyajima and Hasegawa 1992). This deft approach in protecting infant industries dovetailed nicely with the interests of the *zaibatsu*, who were at the time still more heavily involved in trade and shipping than in heavy industry. It also is worth noting that these policies, which were worked out in the rarefied air of an investigatory council, contrasted sharply with the wide-gauge tariff walls that typically emerge out of legislative logrolling of the sort that gave birth to the Smoot-Hawley tariffs in the United States.

THE JAPAN ECONOMIC FEDERATION

The Japan Economic Federation (Nihon Keizai Renmei), considered to be the direct antecedent of Japan's current premier *zaikai* association, Keidan-ren, was established on August 1, 1922.[9] The federation proclaimed itself to be a comprehensive organization representing the entire spectrum of busi-ness interests in terms of both geographic scope (i.e., that it also represented business outside of Tokyo) and scale of enterprise (i.e., that it represented small as well as big business). In practice, however, during its first five years its activities were directed by a relatively narrow circle of financiers and *zaibatsu* representatives. Its executive board during this period could be described as an assemblage of Industrial Club types, finance capital, and largely *zaibatsu*-affiliated international trade interests (Takeuchi 1976). The day-to-day operations of the Economic Federation and the drafting of fed-eration opinions are said to have been orchestrated largely by Inoue Junno-suke, president of the Bank of Japan and former (as well as subsequent) minister of finance, and Hijikata Hisaakira of the semipublic Industrial Bank of Japan, with the help of Takashima Seiichi, the director of the organiza-tion's secretariat, and Dan Takuma of Mitsui (Horikoshi 1962, 86–87). Sub-stantively, the federation spoke for the same core group of elites as the *zaikai* associations already discussed.

TABLE 2
Members, Board of Directors, Economic Federation, 1928

Name	Occupation	Other Affiliations
Dan Takuma	Board Member, Mitsui Gōmei	Board Member, Japan Industrial Club
Fujita Ken'ichi	President, South Sakhalin Oil/Nagato Kigyō Coal	President, Tokyo Chamber of Commerce
Fujiyama Raita	Dainippon Flour Milling Company	
Gō Seinosuke	Chairman, Tokyo Electric Light	Managing Director, Japan Industrial Club
Hamaoka Kōtetsu	President, Kyoto Fire Insurance	President, Kyoto Chamber of Commerce
Hijikata Hisaakira	Vice President, Bank of Japan	
Hori Keijirō	President, Osaka Shipping Co.	
Ikeda Seihin	Executive Director, Mitsui Bank	Advisor, Mitsui Gōmei
Inahata Katsutarō	President, Inahata Trading/ Nippon Dyestuffs Manufacturing Co.	President, Osaka Chamber of Commerce
Inoue Junnosuke	President, Bank of Japan	
Isaka Takashi	Yokohama Fire and Marine Insurance	President, Yokohama Chamber of Commerce
Itō Jirōzaemon	President, Matsuzakaya	President, Nagoya Chamber of Commerce
Kikuchi Kyōzō	President, Dainippon Cotton Spinning	
Kimura Kusuyata	Chairman, Mitsubishi Gōshi	Managing Director, Japan Industrial Club
Kodama Kenji	President, Yokohama Specie Bank	
Kushida Manzō	Chairman, Mitsubishi Bank	
Ōhashi Shintarō	Owner, Hakubunkan Bookstore	Managing Director, Japan Industrial Club
Watanabe Chiyosaburō	Managing Director, Osaka Gas	President, Nankai Railways
Yukawa Kankichi	Board Member, Sumitomo Gōshi	

Source: Yamazaki Hiroaki, "Zaikai no rekishi," in *Zaikai: Sei-kan to no yuchaku no kōzō,* edited by Heiwa Keizai Keikaku Kaigi-Dokusen Hakusho Iinkai. *Kokumin no dokusen hakusho* no. 6 (Ochanomizu Shobō, 1982), 26.

The impetus for the formation of the Economic Federation lay in a six-month tour of North America and Europe by twenty-four leading *zaikai* figures during 1921–1922. Included in this group were established *zaikai* titans like Dan, Mitsubishi Bank president Kushida Manzō, Nakajima Kumakichi of the Furukawa *zaibatsu,* and Tokyo Chamber of Commerce president Ōhashi Shintarō, as well as figures like Miyajima Seijirō and Fujiwara Ginjirō, who later were to dominate *zaikai.* Impressed by the social, economic, and political conditions that they had observed, mission members were particularly concerned that the leading industrialized countries had gone through rather drastic postwar retrenchments and deflations. They had reduced their price levels substantially as a result and were preparing to return to the gold standard, thereby, in the view of the delegation, gaining a solid footing for recovery and long-run prosperity in the postwar global economy.

The situation in Japan presented a sharp contrast to what the *zaikai* delegation saw in Europe and the United States. Seiyūkai president Hara Kei became Japan's first "commoner" prime minister in September 1918. The *genrō's* decision to break precedent and hand the government to a "pure" party politician was based on the thinking that "opening up" the prime ministership to the parties would help calm the social instability apparent in the Rice Riots and other incidents of popular unrest that were occurring at that time. Following the same electorally oriented logic that had driven earlier Seiyūkai policy, the Hara government reinstituted fiscal positivism. The same reasoning that drove the *genrō* to back Hara also led them to support his party's economic policy despite misgivings about its potential inflationary consequences, with the added incentive for promilitary elements that an expansionary policy would assure growth in spending on the services (Itō 1987, 33–38).

During the first year of the Economic Federation's life, its policy-related work focused almost exclusively on "price adjustment"—that is, retrenchment—and it is no great exaggeration to say that the primary purpose for establishing the federation was to effect a reversal of the Seiyūkai's fiscal and financial policies, policies federation members saw as detrimental to the long-term viability of the Japanese economy as it reintegrated into the reconstructed gold standard–based postwar global trade and financial system.[10] The first meeting of the federation's executive board set the tone by calling for a search for ways to reduce the country's general price level. A "price adjustment" committee was set up to study the issue. Significantly, and in a manner characteristic of the terms of engagement in business-state relations, a considerable portion of its energy went to the study of measures that the private sector could take to facilitate price adjustment, such as improved operational management, mechanization and simplification of production methods, consolidation of transport operations, the encouragement of coordinated purchasing and marketing across firms, economizing on labor and material usage—in a nutshell, various productivity-enhancing innovations that would later be described as "rationalization." A committee to study issues of industrial organization related to price adjustment was then set up (Horikoshi 1962, 124–130).[11]

THE MAKING OF ECONOMIC POLICY

There was thus latent in the postwar Japanese political economic situation an axis of sociopolitical conflict that pitted a fiscally conservative *zaikai* against fiscally expansionary populist forces pushing for expanded party-based government. The dynamics of the Meiji constitutional structure, however, were such that this latent conflict was deflected and reshaped. The popular parties now mattered in government in a way that they never had before, but even so several factors prevented any particular party from unilaterally imposing its economic agenda on the state. First, as Masumi Junnosuke argues, the rotation of the government between the two established parties during the 1924–1932 period was ultimately a consequence of the willingness of Saionji Kimmochi, the last surviving *genrō*, to enforce this rotation by choosing the heads of the two parties as prime ministers (Masumi 1979, 11–13). Under the selection rules enforced by Saionji ("the normal road of constitutionalism"), a parliamentary majority was neither a sufficient nor a necessary condition for a party to gain control of the government. There were other obstacles as well. Legislative bills would still have to be passed by the nonelected House of Peers. Certain policies could be effectively vetoed by the Privy Council. Normally of more proximate consequence, the state bureaucracy continued during the 1920s to serve as both the primary source of policy initiatives and the agency for implementing state policy. Finance ministers, in particular, were selected less on the basis of their party credentials than on their overall reputation and experience as financiers. Sharing a common technocratic world view, the variation in preferences among these ministers was considerably less than that among the parties and allowed financial policy in particular to sustain a degree of independence despite the large differences in the platforms of the established parties (Hara 1977b). All of these factors served to insulate economic policy from the vicissitudes of party politics.

One sees the significance of these factors in the way by which fiscal retrenchment was ultimately adopted. A move to rein in the "fiscal positivism" of the Hara government was initiated soon after the postwar recession hit the Japanese economy in the spring of 1920 by none other than Hara's own finance minister, Takahashi Korekiyo. A former Ministry of Finance official from the House of Peers who had served as president of the Bank of Japan and had worked on raising foreign loans for the government during the Russo-Japanese War, Takahashi had close connections to the financiers in the Economic Federation. Takahashi subsequently served as prime minister (and finance minister concurrently) for a brief period following Hara Kei's assassination in November 1921. Although he managed to hold down the rate of growth of the budget, pressures from the party and from spending agencies prevented him from instituting full-fledged retrenchment.

A *non-party* government—that of Katō Tomosaburō, a naval officer—which followed Takahashi's interim premiership, did implement retrenchment in the fiscal 1923 budget. In characteristic fashion, pressure from the rank and file of the Seiyūkai for new railroad construction allocations and other pork-barrel items were added to the initial government budget proposal; but in this instance, these budgetary additions were offset by a reduction in military expenditures made possible by the naval arms limitations mandated by the Washington Conference (Itō 1987, 107). The budgetary retrenchment was thus not a clearcut victory for *zaikai's* fiscal conservatism, and the latent tension between it and the Seiyūkai still existed. However, it was, again, in the nature of the Meiji constitutional structure to produce a dynamic that would result in something less than a full-fledged, across-the-board confrontation between *zaikai* and the popular parties. That is, even as the realization of *zaikai's* preference for fiscal conservatism was being undercut by pressures emanating from the Seiyūkai, another important element of the popular parties was making a pitch to supraparliamentary elites for the right to form a government based on a "responsible" stance on fiscal policies. This was the rival Kenseikai (later, Minseitō), which adopted fiscal retrenchment as a pillar of its platform during the fall of 1921.

The practice of deliberating and formulating economic polices through formal government commissions remained standard procedure throughout the 1920s. Perhaps reflecting the difficulty of the problems encountered and the lack of agreement on solutions, the period between the conclusion of World War I and the end of party cabinets in 1932 was punctuated by a large number of high-level investigatory councils on economic issues. The more prominent of these include: the Temporary Investigatory Council on Budgetary Affairs and the Economy (Rinji Zaisei Keizai Chōsakai) of 1918–1924, the Imperial Economic Conference (Teikoku Keizai Kaigi) of 1924, the Investigatory Council on Financial Institutions (Kin'yū Seido Chōsakai) of 1926, the Commerce and Industry Council (Shōkō Shingikai) of 1927–1930, the Economic Council (Keizai Shingikai) of 1927–1930, the Customs Duties Commission (Kanzei Shingikai) of 1929, and the Emergency Commission on Industry (Rinji Sangyō Shingikai) of 1930–1935. A bulk of "real" economic policy debate and decision making occurred in these arenas. Petitions and statements drafted by *zaikai* organizations like the Economic Federation were more often than not a response to council-related activities. Debate in the Diet tended to be rather perfunctory. It was thus rational for *zaikai* organizations—or any interest group that could gain entree into these commissions—to target their efforts toward influencing the councils rather than the Diet. And if forced to choose between the two arenas, the preferred option of *zaikai* would undoubtedly be the council format, where techno-cratic arguments and elite connections would be likely to carry more weight than the quantitative logic of electoral returns.

Students of Taishō party politics widely believe that the *zaibatsu* were a major source of funds for the established parties and that there was an informal division of labor between Mitsui and Mitsubishi, with the former providing funds to the Seiyūkai and the latter the Kenseikai/Minseitō (al-though the nature of political funding is such that definitive empirical evidence is perhaps impossible to obtain).[12] On the other hand, there is little to suggest that the Economic Federation or the Industrial Club channeled funds to the conservative parties in the way that Keidanren channeled funds to the Liberal Democratic Party in the postwar period. No discernible correlation has been found between the policies of the respective parties and the preferences of the respective *zaibatsu* (Masumi 1979; Hara 1977a; Yamazaki 1982). It is often argued that this kind of *zaibatsu* funding of political parties was motivated not by the desire to promote a policy being championed by a party but rather to prevent party platforms from being implemented too fully and disrupting economic policy every time a govern-ment changed (Yamazaki 1982).

As to *what* an Economic Federation–centered *zaikai* might want from economic policy outside of the fiscal policy issues we have been discussing and how successful it was in attaining its preferences, it is useful to highlight the point that the three industrial sectors represented in the Economic Federation's board of directors during its first half-decade of operation corresponded to the three sectors into which the *zaibatsu* expanded most rapidly during the 1920s—namely, heavy industry (iron and steel, petro-chemicals, synthetic fibers, electrical machinery, etc.), banking and finance, and trading companies.[13] *Zaibatsu* expansion in each of the new sectors was facilitated by key pieces of government legislation passed during this period. With respect to heavy industry, the end of the war had left the *zaibatsu* with substantial, uncompetitive investments in a motley set of enterprises in the sector. The significance of the 1926 tariff revisions on the development of Japanese heavy industry has already been noted. With regard to banking and finance, the expansion of *zaibatsu* interests was greatly aided by legislation like the 1926 Trust Bank Law, the 1927 Banking Law, and more generally by a variety of other government policies to promote mergers and consolidation in the banking industry. In tandem with the dramatic reduction in the number of banks, the Big Four *zaibatsu* banks of Mitsui, Mitsubishi, Sumi-tomo, and Yasuda doubled their share of total bank deposits between 1919 and 1929 (Morikawa 1976, 194). Finally, the interests of *zaibatsu* trading houses like Mitsui Bussan, whose activities and profitability were grounded in their control of strategic stages of the distribution process, were facilitated by industrial policies like that embodied in the 1925 Major Export Industries Association Law and the Export Association Law that extended various economic controls and quality-control mechanisms over small-scale exporters (Shibagaki 1965, 403–427).

MASS POLITICS

As the above discussion suggests, the Meiji constitutional structure tended to insulate the economic policy-making process from the vicissitudes of party politics, and because of this, *zaikai,* who had access to a reserved seat on bureaucratic panels, could remain aloof and casual about the way that it organized the representation of its own interests in the face of the explosion of organized interest groups that occurred elsewhere during the same period (Muramatsu, Ito, and Tsujinaka 1986, chap. 1). This, however, began to change significantly during the latter half of the 1920s as universal manhood suffrage and its corollary, mass politics, became a reality. By the 1920s the leaders of the Seiyūkai and Minseitō were very much aware that over the long term their power and influence would depend on the degree to which they could balance the interests of the increasingly politicized middle and lower socioeconomic orders against the conservative leanings of the nonelected elites. Both parties therefore pursued a mixed political economy of co-optation and containment that attempted to balance the interests of conservative elites with the demands of the newly enfranchised orders (Garon 1987, chap. 4). For the Seiyūkai, it was expansionary pork-barrel fiscal policies leavened with conservatism in social policy. The Minseitō chose the opposite. *Zaikai,* whose mainstream favored fiscal *and* social conservatism, thus found itself in conflict with the two established political parties on at least one of these scores. Until the formation of the Tanaka Giichi cabinet in April 1927, the economic policy preferences of the governing party did not matter that much because the cabinets chosen by Saionji were either nonparty, coalition, or minority governments in which party preferences were neutralized. After the installation of Tanaka, however, such preferences did begin to matter (until the fall of party government in 1932) because single-party governance became the norm, and the ruling parties were able to consolidate their hold on the government through elections in which they were returned with a majority. *Zaikai* and Tanaka were at loggerheads as Tanaka proceeded to adopt an archetypal Seiyūkai fiscal positivist policy during a period when Japan's financial and trade situation deteriorated rapidly as a result of the 1927 financial panic (Itō 1987, 218–222). And when the Minseito's Hamaguchi Osachi became prime minister in July 1929 and began a full-fledged drive to pass legislation legalizing labor unions, confrontation grew even more severe.

The details of *zaikai*'s eventually successful campaign to oppose labor legislation has been covered elsewhere and the details need not be repeated here (see Garon 1987, chap. 4; Gordon 1989). What needs to be highlighted is the fact that these developments galvanized *zaikai* into implementing a long-discussed program to add formal organizational substance to the Economic Federation's claim to be the voice of the "general will" of the entire business community (Horikoshi 1962, 152–160). Membership dues were reduced and a nationwide membership drive was initiated under a newly established membership committee in the fall of 1928. The reorganization was reflected in the composition of the board of directors. Added to the representatives of trading companies, finance capital, and trading interests were those of the Big Three *zaibatsu* holding companies and, in a move that expanded geographic scope and brought small businesses into the fold, the heads of the chambers of commerce of the nation's six largest cities (Yamazaki 1982, 25). A second organizational innovation was the creation of a research arm in which staff assistance was contributed to the Economic Federation from such leading firms as Mitsui and Mitsubishi Gōmei, the Bank of Japan, and the South Manchurian Railway Corporation. In addition, an official journal, *Keizai renmei*, began publication. In the process, the Economic Federation evolved into a true peak association (Horikoshi 1962, 157–160).

CONCLUSION

In retrospect it is clear that the Economic Federation's "success" as a fullfledged peak association proved disastrous from the standpoint of *zaikai*'s coming to terms with the political forces unleashed by Taishō *demokurashii*. The federation's drive for fiscal retrenchment eventually culminated in the adoption of stringent deflationary policies and a return to the gold standard under finance minister and ex–Economic Federation leader Inoue Junnosuke. Tragically, this was done just as the Great Depression was beginning to make itself felt in the Japanese economy. *Zaikai*'s rally against the labor union law might have led to the bill's being scrapped, but it also contributed to growing popular dissatisfaction with the unresponsiveness of the existing regime, discrediting both *zaikai* and the established political parties in the process. These developments were clearly contributing factors that helped set the stage for the assassinations of Dan Takuma and Inoue and the advance of militarism and the controlled economy in the decade that followed.

Zaikai was born during a period when business-government relations began to take on an increasingly "modern" quality. It was an institution born in that "space" in a chronically capital-scarce economy where state purposes and private capital intersect. In contexts where the state takes a leading role in modernization it tends, as Meredith Woo-Cumings (1997, 65) recently expressed in a piece on Korea, to *produce* social relations rather than simply respond to them. This dynamic is certainly visible in the creation of *zaikai*, where the unfolding political economy of the Greater Taishō period generated an environment in which *zaikai* and the big business community that it represented were provided with lucrative opportunities and a comfortable niche in the status quo, provided they could be of service in fulfilling state-defined goals.

But, as other contributions to this volume show, the history of Greater Taishō is also a history of social groups in Japan defining modernity on their own terms in those spaces where this was feasible. Taishō Japan, no doubt, generated such spaces in greater abundance than was true of many other "late developers" and certainly more so than in the decades that followed. Even so, one cannot escape the fact that these were circumscribed spaces, particularly where such competing modernities threatened core structures and values embedded earlier in the Meiji political economy. It is not unimaginable that under marginally different conditions, things might have veered in a different direction. But under the conditions that existed in Japan of the Greater Taishō period, and from the standpoint of a group with a solid foothold in the establishment (as was true by the late 1920s for Japan's haute bourgeoisie) the elite-dominated system of decision making produced policy that was more "rational," more technically sophisticated, and more finely attuned to its needs than anything that could be reasonably expected to emerge out of the messier concoctions of parliamentary politics. There was thus little reason for Japanese big business to "buy into" the platforms of the political parties. And by denying the parties the opportunity to mediate their interests, the big business community ultimately helped undermine the ability of established political parties to forge effective social coalitions and thereby take firmer root in an increasingly mass-oriented political order.

NOTES

1. For a useful overview and analysis of the literature, see Wray 1989. Previous studies of *zaikai* during this period include Fletcher 1989, Miyamoto 1988, and Tiedemann 1971.
2. See Kobayashi 1988, 269–288 for a detailed discussion of Inoue and his role.
3. For an analysis using the lobbying organization concept, see Yamada 1980.
4. As formal government councils aimed at discussing a wide range of concerns relating to agriculture, commerce, and manufacturing, the High Level Conferences on Agriculture, Commerce, and Industry represent

somewhat of an exception to the generalization that business-state relations in the modern sector during this period were informal, personalized, and concerned exclusively with the immediate financial concerns of the state. Yet one could also argue that it is this sort of exception that proves the rule in that the meetings were irregular and exceptional, called at the behest of the government, and focused on the subject of how Japan might expand its foreign-exchange earnings in light of the state's "postwar management" plan for strengthening the Japanese military. See Aoki 1994 for related discussion.

5. This discussion is based primarily on Banno 1975 and Takahashi 1973, 99–104.

6. For a description of the Unagajikai, see Wakatsuki 1950, 158–160. I thank Professor Shin'ichi Kitaoka for directing my attention to this source. See also Takeuchi 1975, 8:27.

7. For detailed information, see Nakamura 1985, chap. 4. For a lucid discussion of the relationship between economic and strategic considerations in Japanese imperialism around this time, see Duus 1984, 128–170.

8. Note that the Japanese nomenclature specifically implies an orientation toward manufacturing through the use of the term *kōgyō*, and the name for the organization is literally the Japan Manufacturing Club. However, the standard English translation will be used here. Although the third largest *zaibatsu*, Sumitomo was not active in the Industrial Club due to its location in the Kansai region.

9. See Takeuchi 1976 and Fletcher 1989, 17–23, for detailed treatments of the Economic Federation's formation.

10. The other major item of concern was Japan's entry into the International Chamber of Commerce (see Fletcher 1989, 97–102).

11. Committee activities were suspended following the Great Kantō Earthquake of September 1923.

12. Among the more detailed treatments of party finances during this period is that found in Masumi 1979, 258–275.

13. Throughout the 1920s, depressed conditions characterized the mining and shipbuilding industries, which had earlier been the core sources of revenue for the *zaibatsu*. Maintenance of overall profitability and growth for the *zaibatsu* houses required expansion into new areas. See Shibagaki 1965, 265–428, and Morikawa 1976, 176, for detailed discussion.

REFERENCES

Akita, George. 1967. *The Foundations of Constitutional Government in Modern Japan*. Cambridge: Harvard University Press.

Andō Yoshio. 1976. *Burujoajii no gunzō*. Shōgakkan.

Aoki Kōyō. 1994. "Taisenkan nihon shakai ni okeru bijinesu to gyōsei." *Shakai kagaku* 53:79–105.

Banno Junji. 1975. "Keien naikaku to taishō seihen." In *Iwanami koza, 17: Nihon rekishi (kindai 4)*. Iwanami Shoten.

Bendix, Reinhard. 1974. *Work and Authority in Industry: Ideologies of Management in the Course of Industrialization.* 2d ed. Berkeley: University of California Press.

Duus, Peter. 1984. "Economic Dimensions of Meiji Imperialism: The Case of Korea, 1895–1910." In *The Japanese Colonial Empire, 1895–1945,* edited by Ramon H. Myers and Mark R. Peattie, 128–171. Princeton: Princeton University Press.

Eguchi Keiichi. 1971. *Toshi burujoajii undō shi no kenkyū.* Miraisha.

Fletcher, Miles. 1989. *The Japanese Business Community and National Trade Policy, 1920–1942.* Chapel Hill: University of North Carolina Press.

Garon, Sheldon. 1987. *The State and Labor in Modern Japan.* Berkeley: University of California Press.

Gordon, Andrew. 1989. "Business and the Corporate State: The Business Lobby and Bureaucrats on Labor, 1911–1940." In *Managing Industrial Enterprise,* edited by William D. Wray. Cambridge: Harvard University Press.

Hara Akira. 1977a. "Zaikai." In *Kindai Nihon kenkyū nyūmon,* edited by Nakamura Takafusa and Itō Takashi. Tokyo Daigaku Shuppankai.

———. 1977b. "Zaisei kin'yū." In *Kindai Nihon kenkyū nyūmon,* edited by Nakamura Takafusa and Itō Takashi. Enl. ed. Tokyo Daigaku Shuppankai.

Harada Mikio. 1985–1986. "Nichiro sengo keiei to seisan chōsakai: Waga kuni shihonshugi hatten ki ni okeru keizai seisaku no keisei." *Seinan gakuin daigaku keizaigaku ronshū* 20.2/3:77–114; 21.1:1–27; 21.3:57–120.

———. 1988–1992. "Daiichiji taisen ki ni okeru wagakuni tsūshō sangyō seisaku no keisei: Keizai chōsakai kaigi o chūshin to shite." *Seinan gakuin daigaku keizaigaku ronshū* 23.2:117–159; 24.4:73–128; 25.3:1–88; 27.2:31–66.

Hashimoto Jurō. 1992. "Zaibatsu no kontserunka." In *Nihon keizai no hatten to kigyō shūdan,* edited by Takeda Haruhito. Tokyo Daigaku Shuppankai.

Horikoshi Teizō, ed. 1962. *Keizai dantai rengōkai zenshi.* Keizai Dantai Rengōkai.

Itō Yukio. 1987. *Taishō demokurashii to seitō seiji.* Yamakawa Shuppansha.

Johnson, Chalmers. 1982. *MITI and the Japanese Miracle: The Growth of Industrial Policy, 1925–1975.* Stanford: Stanford University Press.

Kamiyama Tsuneo. 1988. "Kokusai hikiuke shinjikeeto no seiritsu." In *Nichiro sengo no Nihon keizai,* edited by Takamura Naosuke. Hanawa Shobō.

Keizai Renmei Kai. 1932. "Bukka chōsetsu iinkai no chōsa hōkoku ni kakaru seifu no shisetsu jikō ni taisuru seika" (June 21, 1923). In *Zaisei keizai nijūgo nen shi,* edited by Takahashi Kamekichi. Vol. 4, 226–228. Jitsugyō no Sekai Sha.

Kobayashi Masaaki. 1988. *Seishō no tanjō: mō hitotsu no meiji ishin.* Toyo Keizai Shinposha.

Masumi Junnosuke. 1979. *Nihon seitō shi ron,* V. Tokyo Daigaku Shuppankai.

———. 1988. *Nihon seiji shi, II: Hanbatsu shihai, seitō seiji.* Tokyo Daigaku Shuppankai.

Mitani Taichiro. 1988. "The Establishment of Party Cabinets, 1898–1932." In *The Cambridge History of Japan*, edited by Peter Duus. Vol. 6. Cambridge: Cambridge University Press.

Miyajima Hideaki and Hasegawa Shin. 1992. "1920 nendai no jūkagaku kōgyōka to kanzei seisaku." In *Senkanki Nihon no taigai keizai kankei*, edited by Ōishi Kaichirō. Nihon Hyōronsha.

Miyamoto Matao. 1988. "The Development of Business Associations in Prewar Japan." In *Trade Associations in Business History*, edited by Yamazaki Hiroaki and Miyamoto Matao. Vol. 14, The International Conference on Business History. Tokyo University Press.

Morikawa Hidemasa. 1976. *Nihon zaibatsu shi.* Kyōikusha.

Muramatsu Michio, Itō Mitsutoshi, and Tsujinaka Yutaka. 1986. *Sengo Nihon no atsuryoku dantai.* Tōyō Keizai Shinpō Sha.

Najita, Tetsuo. 1967. *Hara Kei and the Politics of Compromise, 1905–1915.* Cambridge: Harvard University Press.

Nakamura Masanori. 1975. "Nihon burujoajii no kōsei." In *Nihon sangyō kakumei no kenkyū*, edited by Ōishi Kaichirō. II. Tokyo Daigaku Shuppankai.

Nakamura Takafusa. 1983. *Economic Growth in Prewar Japan.* New Haven: Yale University Press.

———. 1985. *Meiji taishō ki no keizai.* Tokyo Daigaku Shuppankai.

Nihon Kōgyō Kurabu. 1943. *Nihon kōgyō kurabu nijūgo nen shi.* Nihon Kōgyō Kurabu.

Sakamoto Yūichi. 1991. "'Nichiro sengo keiei' to seisan chōsakai." In *Nihon teikokushugi no keizai seisaku*, edited by Gotō Yasushi. Kashiwa Shobō.

Shibagaki Kazuo. 1965. *Nihon kin'yū shihon bunseki.* Tokyo Daigaku Shuppankai.

Takahashi Kamekichi. 1973. *Nihon kindai keizai hattatsu shi.* Vol. 2. Tōyō Keizai Shinpōsha.

Takeda Haruhito. 1992. "Takakuteki jigyō bumon no teichaku to kontserun soshiki no seibi." In *Nihon keizai no hatten to kigyō shudan*, edited by Takeda Haruhito. Tokyo Daigaku Shuppankai.

Takeuchi Shōichi. 1975. "Nihon kōgyō kurabu no setsuritsu no haikei to sono shutai." *Chiba shōdai ronsō* 13-1b:25–49.

———. 1976. "Nihon keizai renmeikai no setsuritsu to setsuritsuki no kaiin." *Chiba shōdai ronsō* 13-4b:91–118.

Tiedemann, Arthur E. 1971. "Big Business and Politics in Prewar Japan." In *Dilemmas of Growth in Prewar Japan*, edited by James Morley. Princeton: Princeton University Press.

Toshitani Nobuyuki and Honma Shigeki. 1976. "Tennōsei kokka kikō-hō taisei no saihen: 1910–20 nendai ni okeru ichi danmen." In *Taikei nihon kokka shi 5: Kindai 2*, edited by Hara Yuzaburō, Minegishi Sumio, Sasaki Junnosuke, and Nakamura Masanori. Tokyo Daigaku Shuppankai.

Wakatsuki Reijirō. 1950. *Kofūan kaikoroku.* Yomiuri Shimbunsha.

Woo-Cumings, Meredith. 1997. "Slouching Toward the Market: The Politics of Financial Liberalization in South Korea." In *Capital Ungoverned: Liberalizing Finance in Interventionist States,* edited by Michael Loriaux, Meredith Woo-Cumings, Kent E. Calder, Sylvia Maxfield, and Sofia A. Perez. Ithaca: Cornell University Press.

Wray, William D. 1989. "Afterword: The Writing of Japanese Business History." In *Managing Industrial Enterprise: Cases from Japan's Prewar Experience,* edited by William D. Wray. Cambridge: Harvard University Press.

Yamada, Makiko. 1980. "The Emergence of Organized Lobbying." In *Government and Business: Proceedings of the Fifth Fuji Conference,* edited by Keiichiro Nakagawa. University of Tokyo Press.

Yamashita Naoto. 1978. "Nisshin-Nichiro senkan ki ni okeru zaibatsu burjoajii no seisaku shikō: Yūrakukai no dōkō." *Rekishigaku kenkyū* 450:12–26.

Yamazaki Hiroaki. 1982. "Zaikai no rekishi." In *Zaikai: Sei-kan to no yuchaku no kōzō,* edited by Heiwa Keizai Keikaku Kaigi-Dokusen Hakusho Iinkai. Kokumin no dokusen hakusho no. 6. Ochanomizu Shobō.

❥ 14 ❧

Fashioning a Culture of Diligence and Thrift: Savings and Frugality Campaigns in Japan, 1900–1931

Sheldon Garon

Historians, being historians, love to periodize. For several decades, they have been fascinated by the problem of "Taishō" and its evocations of "Taishō democracy" and "Taishō culture." Defining the beginning and end of Taishō has itself been contentious. Should it be confined to the Taishō emperor's reign (1912–1926) or perhaps commence in 1905 with the mass protests known as the Hibiya Riots? Or, as many American scholars assert, is it more useful to locate "Taishō" in the years from 1918 to roughly 1932—that is, the period between World War I and Japan's "Fifteen Years' War"?

Regardless of how they periodize, historians generally treat "Taishō" as a time sandwiched between eras that were its antitheses. Political and social historians describe a transition from the oligarchic-bureaucratic Meiji order to "Taishō democracy," which in turn succumbed to the repression and authoritarianism of the 1930s. For them, what distinguished Taishō was the rise and subsequent fall of new political and social forces—notably political parties, labor and tenant organizations, progressive intellectuals, women's groups, and *burakumin* activists.

The newer field of cultural history tends to identify "Taishō culture" with the advent of a "mass-consumption society" and the Americanization of popular culture. Like many Japanese scholars, Donald Roden explains the transition from Meiji to Taishō in terms of a shift in emphasis from production, "civilization," and Victorian character-molding institutions to consumption and a "new obsession for culture and personality" (Roden 1990, 41–42, 52, 55; see also Harootunian 1974, 15–18; Takemura 1980;

312

Minami 1965). The consumer culture of Taishō appears all the more distinctive in these accounts in view of its impending demise during the 1930s and war years, as the state launched wave after wave of punishing austerity drives.

In recent years, political historians have grown wary of depicting the interwar years as an oasis of democracy and toleration surrounded by Meiji and early Shōwa illiberalism. Their work suggests instead that many of the authoritarian aspects of the 1930s evolved from processes at work during the preceding 1920s—including democratization itself (Fletcher 1982; Smith 1983; Mitchell 1976). The Diet's passage of both universal manhood suffrage and the repressive Peace Preservation Law in 1925 was no coincidence, explains Gregory Kasza, for example. Rather, democratization may have broadened the base of support for suppressing far-left elements considered beyond the boundaries of the newly expanded political community (Kasza 1988, 20–27).

Cultural historians, on the other hand, are just beginning to explore the transition from Taishō to the 1930s. As such, the image persists of "Taishō" as an age of unrestrained consumption and raucous self-expression.

The case of interwar savings and frugality campaigns accordingly confounds prevailing characterizations of Meiji, Taishō, and Shōwa cultures. At first glance, the government's drives appear to be curious anachronisms in a rapidly changing Japan. The very titles of the campaigns—"encouragement of diligence and thrift" and "moral suasion mobilization"—hark back to the neo-Confucian vocabulary of premodern China and Tokugawa Japan. Yet like other twentieth-century campaigns to manage society (see Garon 1997), savings-promotion efforts followed a strikingly linear path. They emerged on the national scale in the late Meiji era, became institutionalized during the 1920s and early 1930s, and ultimately reached down to shape the daily habits of nearly every Japanese amid the China and Pacific wars (1937–1945). Moreover, savings campaigns steadily incorporated middle-class social reformers, educators, and women's leaders during the interwar period—at the very time when these new social forces are commonly represented as carving out autonomous spheres of political and cultural activity vis-ň-vis the state.

The 1920s must therefore be seen as an era when movements to consume and movements to save expanded concurrently, and, perhaps more surprising, frequently coincided. Indeed, the persistently high rates of personal savings, for which postwar Japan is famous, began their rise during the late 1920s. Reluctant to boost savings solely through material incentives (for example, higher interest rates), the state and allied groups actively promoted habits of thrift throughout the twentieth century. This essay traces the early development of these campaigns as a study in the complex interactions between consumption and thrift and between state and society.

MODERNIZING "MORAL SUASION"

As present-day Japanese officials are wont to tell us, the nation's "spirit of thrift" has a long history, dating back to the Tokugawa period (1600–1868). It is also true that efforts to promote frugality and savings by means of "moral suasion" *(kyōka* or *fūka)* predated Japan's modern era. The Tokugawa shogunate and domain authorities regularly exhorted peasants to avoid extravagance. But the real heroes of the twentieth-century promoters of savings were a group of late-Tokugawa agrarian reformers, the most famous of whom was Ninomiya Sontoku (1787–1856). Aiming to extend the resources of impoverished villages and maintain popular welfare, Ninomiya and others preached the importance of "diligence" *(kin)* and "thrift" *(ken)* (Toyama n.d., 2). Later savings and frugality campaigns inherited not only the language of these efforts, but also the confidence that persuasion would effectively increase household savings.

Nonetheless, the modern campaigns emerged after 1868 within a rapidly changing environment and differed significantly from previous hortatory activities. No longer were injunctions against consumption intended primarily to maintain people within their statuses or to preserve the taxpaying ability of communities. The new priorities of industrialization and military strengthening required modern taxation but also the efficient channeling of popular wealth to enterprises and the central state through a nationwide network of financial institutions. The need to mobilize the savings of one's own people was made all the more urgent by the regime's decision to avoid foreign loans during the late nineteenth century. Other departures occurred in the *means* of persuading the populace to save. Newspapers, motion pictures, and a centralized bureaucracy gradually served to standardize the messages. At the same time, the state experimented with new forms of intermediary organizations that would supersede or supplement traditional communal units. Many, though not all, of these innovations resulted from the conscious emulation of savings-promotion programs in contemporary Western nations.

Institution building in fact preceded effective social mobilization by several decades. Desperately short of capital and eager to attract small savers throughout the nation, the new regime introduced the postal savings system as one of its first financial reforms in 1875. This innovation was yet another example of the young state's adoption of the latest in Western policies. The British had recently established the first postal savings network in 1861, and only a handful of nations had followed—notably Germany, Belgium, and Canada. Savings banks, which Japanese officials similarly modeled after European and American institutions, were introduced during the early 1880s. As in the West, savings banks were designed to lure small savers (see Tucker 1991, chap. 4). Postal savings, nonetheless, remained the principal

Poster from Campaign to Encourage Diligence and Thrift,
1925. The schoolboy writes: "Diligence and Thrift (kinken),
It's for My Own Good and the Good of the Nation."
(Naimushō Shakaikyoku, 1927.)

venue for household savings until the late twentieth century. Reflecting the
Western rhetoric of the time, Finance Minister Matsukata Masayoshi in
1882 proclaimed: "The wealth of a nation lies in its labor and thrift" (quoted
in Chochiku Zōkyō Chūō Iinkai 1983, 3, 1).

Although savings institutions expanded in scale during the late nineteenth century, officials frequently expressed dissatisfaction with the slow
growth in household savings. Postal savings actually declined in the years
immediately following the Sino-Japanese War of 1894–1895 (Sugiura 1990,
31). One problem was the difficulty of persuading people to entrust their
savings to the radically new financial institutions. Equally serious was the
absence of effective intermediaries that the government could marshal to
disseminate its messages at the grass roots. The Meiji regime initially at-

tempted to encourage national savings as part of the Great Promulgation Campaign (1870–1884), which aimed at creating a national religion. Relying on Shinto and Buddhist priests to explain the intricacies of postal savings, however, proved less than successful (Chochiku Zōkyō Chūō Iinkai 1983, 2; Hardacre 1986, 45–46). Moreover, in contrast to contemporary Germans, Japanese administrators did little to mobilize the most obvious intermediary—the nationally controlled schools—even though Paul Mayet, an influential German advisor to the government, drafted a 300-page proposal for "postal school savings banks" in 1886 (Mayet 1893, vii–viii; Chochiku Zōkyō Chūō Iinkai 1983, 5).

The first concerted drive to mold popular economic behavior on a national basis occurred in the opening decade of the twentieth century. A new generation of bureaucrats in the Home Ministry and ministries of Communications and Finance regarded national saving as indispensable to Japan's military and economic competitiveness. Influenced by "national efficiency" thinking in the West, officials sought to demonstrate Japan's alarming weakness vis-ň-vis the other powers—as measured by various indices of "national strength" (see Searle 1971). Cross-national tables telegraphed Japan's high rates of death, suicide, divorce, and imprisonment, while calling attention to the extremely small number of livestock per one thousand Japanese. Prominent among these measures was the relatively low level of Japanese saving. In 1908–1909, Japanese saved per capita a mere 5 yen, as compared to 172 yen in both the United States and Germany and 110 yen in Britain (Inoue 1913, 66–68). Special savings-promotion songs exhorted the populace to make greater efforts if Japan were to catch up and surpass the "civilized countries" of Britain, America, Germany, Belgium, and the Netherlands (Chochiku Zōkyō Chūō Iinkai 1983, 6).

Early twentieth-century officials strove to augment national savings for more immediate reasons, as well. In the aftermath of the Russo-Japanese War (1904–1905), by itself a costly venture, the Japanese government committed the nation to several ambitious undertakings that demanded massive amounts of finance—namely, an enormous military build-up, administration of newly acquired territories in Northeast Asia, and the modernization of industrial infrastructure. There were recognized limits as to how much these projects could be financed from increased taxation and foreign loans, both of which had risen to unprecedented levels during the war. The solution, agreed Home Ministry officials, lay in launching a pervasive moral suasion campaign to encourage "diligence and thrift" throughout the country.

The ensuing Local Improvement Campaign (1906–1918) saw the government managing daily life in many realms (Pyle 1973). One of its major components was the promotion of popular savings and the active discouragement of consumption. Statistics reveal that major changes occurred in economic behavior at the time of the campaigns. The number of people who opened postal savings accounts rose dramatically. Most had never before held deposits in financial institutions. Between 1905 and 1914, postal savings depositors more than doubled from 5,537,000 to 11,974,000 (from 12 percent to 23 percent of the population). In just five years (1905–1910), total assets in the postal savings system rose 205 percent while per capita income increased only 20 percent. Institutionalized thrift, in short, was becoming a habit, and one recent economic history singles out the Local Improvement Campaign as the primary explanation for the burst in saving (Sugiura 1990, 31, 33, 35, 44).

The bureaucracy promoted thrift on several fronts. At the ideological level, the state systematically disseminated messages of diligence and thrift. In the Boshin Imperial Rescript of 1908, the emperor instructed his subjects to be "frugal in the management of their households . . . to abide by simplicity and avoid ostentation, and to inure themselves to arduous toil without yielding to any degree of indulgence" (*Japan Year Book* 1911, 496). The Boshin Rescript would later serve as the canon of the interwar savings campaigns. At the grass-roots level, officials not only encouraged villagers to save money. Working closely with local "customs reform" (*fūzoku kairyō*) groups, they also moved forcefully to eliminate wasteful consumption on festivals, drinking, weddings, and funerals. The Home Ministry's well-known drive to consolidate the numerous hamlet shrines into one state-supported Shinto shrine per administrative village was, in part, intended to rationalize and reduce expenditures on ceremonial life (Fridell 1973, 46–48).

In an effort to create intermediaries to assist the state in its campaigns, the Home Ministry's Bureau of Local Affairs incorporated many communal groups into national, hierarchically organized federations covering agricultural cooperatives, young men's and young women's associations, and military reservists' associations. One such federation, the Central Hōtokukai (established 1906), absorbed indigenous *hōtokusha* (repaying virtue societies), which had been founded by the followers of Ninomiya Sontoku. The semiofficial federation thereupon introduced similar self-help and mutual-aid societies throughout the rest of rural Japan. In so doing, the Home Ministry adapted Ninomiya's teachings of "diligence and thrift" to the more modern needs of national saving.

Although the Local Improvement Campaign aimed at mobilizing household savings to strengthen the nation-state, the heightened commitment to savings-promotion also reflected official and private interest in improving the welfare of Japanese subjects. Inoue Tomoichi, the Home Ministry's leading specialist on savings programs, was also the architect of the government's policies toward poor relief during the first two decades of the twentieth century. Officials in the early Meiji years generally regarded poverty as resulting from natural calamities or the absence of family members who could provide support. By the early twentieth century, however,

Inoue and many other bureaucrats commonly attributed destitution to individual failings (Garon 1997, 36–37, 42–45). The best means of preventing poverty, they insisted, was not the provision of relief after the fact but rather policies "to improve the general morals of the poor and develop their industry while establishing programs to encourage their diligence, thrift, and vigorous efforts." Frugality became central to maintaining "independence" and "managing one's own life" (*jiei*). In his search for methods of inducing Japanese to save more, Inoue exhaustively surveyed Western thrift programs. Ultimately he recommended the greater use of postal savings and the expansion of communal savings arrangements run by agricultural cooperatives and the *hōtokusha* (Inoue 1909, 172–173, 199; also Inoue 1904).

Home Ministry officials did not develop their policies on savings in a vacuum. The growing emphasis on thrift as a form of individual self-reliance owed much to the influence of Japanese Christians and other nongovernmental figures. Working as a commissioned officer of the government, the Protestant minister Kanamori Michitomo unabashedly preached the virtues of thrift throughout Japan in a series of official savings campaigns running from 1900 to 1913. Tomeoka Kōsuke, a well-known Protestant social worker and another one of the Home Minister's commissioned officers, played the central role in rediscovering the local cult of Ninomiya Sontoku. It was on the basis of Tomeoka's report that the ministry institutionalized the *hōtokusha* and propagated Ninomiya's teachings. The late-Meiji-era campaigns to encourage saving and frugality were propelled by a complex mix of inherited hortatory impulses, new statist objectives, and the imported "character-molding" project of contemporary Anglo-American societies (Garon 1994, 355).

"MASS CONSUMPTION" AND ITS CRITICS

The Local Improvement Campaign encouraged national saving on an unprecedented scale between 1906 and 1914, but its limits were apparent. Excepting some Protestants and other middle-class activists, state officials dominated both the campaigns and the thinking behind them. Early twentieth-century campaigns, moreover, targeted towns and villages, rather than the big cities where much of the nation's wealth was concentrated.

While the subsequent savings drives of the 1920s preserved the hortatory features of the Local Improvement Campaign, the interwar campaigns differed from previous efforts in several respects. They also responded to a new set of circumstances. To begin with, the promotion of thrift became bound up with renewed pressures to maintain Japan's great-power status and economic position in the wake of World War I. Having surveyed the wartime policies of the Western belligerents, top Army officers drafted plans for comprehensive "mobilization" of the nation before the anticipated next war

(Barnhart 1987, 23). Economic and social bureaucrats, for their part, grew concerned that the Western powers were strengthening themselves for the "coming peacetime economic war" in international trade. Many warned that the Japanese economy, which had enjoyed favorable trade balances during World War I, was being crippled by growing deficits following the war. Rapidly rising prices made Japanese goods uncompetitive and—coupled with increased consumer demand at home—sapped potential savings, raised the costs of capital, and contributed to a sharp slowdown in economic growth in 1920 (Naimushō Shakaikyoku 1922b, 1–2). Household savings rates plummeted from a high of 18.7 percent in 1918 to 0.8 percent in 1922 and finally into negative territory (−4.9 percent) in 1923 (Horioka 1993, 282).

In an effort to boost savings, Japanese authorities surveyed the newest methods and technologies employed by Western governments in national savings campaigns during World War I. In one report on "The Thrift Campaign in the United States," the Home Ministry commented in glowing terms on the sale of twenty-five-cent "Thrift Stamps" and five-dollar "War Savings Certificate Stamps" in 1918. Japanese officials were particularly impressed by the nationwide sales of the stamps to elementary school pupils and the campaign's success in teaching American children the "relationship between the sense of thrift and patriotism." The sale of Thrift Stamps—noted the bureaucrats with obvious interest—"contributed to the campaign to assimilate the many Americans born in other countries" and "succeeded in inculcating a sense of the State *(kokkateki kannen)*" in large numbers of citizens (Naimushō Shakaikyoku 1922a, 1–2; Cohen 1990, 77–78).

The campaigns after 1918 were also distinctive for their criticism of urban patterns of consumption. The earlier Local Improvement Campaign had concentrated on discouraging the more traditional forms of consumption, especially those related to ceremonial life. Spearheading the new campaign for "restraint in consumption" in 1922, the Home Ministry's Social Bureau instead singled out the spread of the "consumer economy," terming it a major cause of Japan's postwar inflation and trade deficits. The nation's industrial boom during World War I, asserted officials, had given rise to habits of "luxury and self-indulgence" *(shashi hōitsu),* which "have not changed in the least" amid the postwar recession (Naimushō Shakaikyoku 1922b, 1–2).

Indeed, economic expansion and rapid urbanization during the latter half of the 1910s spawned a highly visible style of mass consumption that appeared impervious to messages of "diligence and thrift." There was, to put it simply, more money around and a greater abundance of goods and services on which to spend it. The *narikin*, the nouveaux riches created by the wartime boom, became notorious for their free spending. Less provocative, albeit more numerous, were growing legions of "salarymen," whose families were affluent enough to purchase what Takemura Tamio has termed "consumer status symbols," such as imported pens, gold watches, or Kodak cameras. By the early 1920s, department stores, which in the past catered primarily to the wealthy's desire for luxury goods, were also appealing to the broader middle classes with everyday items. The advent of nationwide advertising facilitated the growth of large-scale markets for mass-produced goods. Widely read magazines for middle-class women surfaced to promote the consumption of fashion and household goods. Established in 1917, *Shufu no tomo* (Housewife's Friend) alone reported a monthly circulation of 600,000. The proliferation of movie theaters, restaurants, cafés, and bars offered further outlets for consumption.

Although members of the working class lacked the means to participate fully in this new culture, they, too, were affected by changing patterns of consumption. In the course of the Taishō years, most Japanese men, including workers, abandoned Japanese clothing in favor of ready-made Western clothes. The tremendous growth of young working women in the service industry similarly increased demand for Western clothing (Takemura 1980, 85, 91–94, chap. 4; Sato 1995).

If officials were to restrain such consumption, they recognized that their campaigns must focus more on the cities. Nevertheless, formulating a persuasive message was not an easy matter. In March 1919, Home Minister Tokonami Takejirō launched the Campaign to Foster National Strength (Minryoku Kan'yō Undō). Officials encouraged saving as part of a far-reaching drive to cultivate in the people a "sound sense of the State" *(kenzen naru kokka kannen),* "public-spiritedness," and the "spirit of sacrifice." In a departure from the unalloyed statist imperatives of the past, however, this postwar campaign also presented saving and frugality as effective means of improving one's own welfare. Tokonami instructed prefectural governors to encourage the "beautiful customs of diligence, thrift, and vigorous efforts" with an eye toward stabilizing people's livelihoods, in addition to strengthening the national economy (directive of March 1, 1919, cited by Nakajima 1974, 58).

The Campaign to Foster National Strength became known for its forceful interventions into daily life. In Toyama prefecture, the flash point of the nationwide Rice Riots of 1918, officials blamed the outbreak of disturbances on the people's infatuation with luxury. Acting on central directives, local authorities exhorted residents to cease exchanging New Year's cards, sending funeral wreaths, practicing flower arranging, holding lavish weddings, and other allegedly wasteful rituals (Lewis 1990, 35). Nor were officials content merely to issue injunctions to the populace. Responding to the Home Ministry's request for reports on "programs to encourage consumer thrift" in 1922, district chiefs *(gunchō)* commonly returned detailed village-by-village surveys of the time spent on weddings, funerals, and other gatherings. In the case of weddings, reports included data for each village and town on the type of ceremony, who attended, and even what was served at the banquets ("Shōhi setsuyaku shōrei shisetsu ni kansuru ken" 1922).

Such interventions required more manpower than the small Japanese bureaucracy could muster, and the Campaign to Foster National Strength increasingly incorporated intermediary groups to help advance its messages. At first, the Home Ministry worked through young men's associations and local household heads' associations *(koshukai)*, which were composed overwhelmingly of males. Officials also enlisted the support of semiofficial national federations, such as the Central Hōtokukai, and they secured the cooperation of representatives of Buddhist, Shinto, and Christian organizations. In October 1920, the Home Ministry announced plans to promote the formation of local women's associations *(fujinkai)* throughout the nation in order to mobilize married women behind its campaign. The state's incorporation of women's groups was something quite new, for adult women had generally been neglected as objects and subjects in previous savings campaigns. Although we commonly think of the present-day Japanese housewife, with her tight control over family finances, as a permanent feature of the landscape, wives were just beginning to emerge as the recognized managers of the household in the early twentieth century (Garon 1997, 126–129; Nakajima 1974, 58–59; Abe 1982, 78; see also Uno 1991).

Within the cities, the bureaucracy found new allies in the thousands of community activists who arose after World War I to deal with the problems of poverty, public hygiene, political radicalism, and crime. Most were shopkeepers, proprietors of workshops, and others who made up the "old middle class." Many of the volunteers concurrently served as state-supervised "district commissioners" *(hōmen iin)*, whose job it was to visit the homes of the poor. To address the perceived breakdown in urban order following the Great Kantō Earthquake of 1923, the Home Ministry also strongly encouraged the expansion of "moral suasion groups." These organizations encompassed the district commissioners, youth associations, private charities, and religious groups. In 1924, the Home Ministry oversaw the formation of a national Federation of Moral Suasion Groups (Kyōka Dantai Rengōkai). Judging that the "winds of extravagance and the habits of luxury have actually gotten stronger" after the earthquake, the federation worked closely with the Ministry of Finance and Ministry of Communications (postal savings) to institutionalize savings-promotion at the neighborhood level (Kyōka Dantai Rengōkai 1924, 41–42). Within the countryside, women's associations and agricultural cooperatives tended to encourage saving among their members as a mutual endeavor. District commissioners and other moral suasion activists in the cities, on the other hand, spent much of their time instructing lower-class individuals in the habits of diligence and thrift and careful household budgeting (Ōmori 1982, 71–72; Garon 1997, 11, 52–55).

The Campaign to Foster National Strength's emphasis on austerity did not go uncontested. Many intellectuals, left-liberals, and women's leaders expressed distaste for the government's blandishments against consumption. Kōno Hironaka, a veteran member of parliament, ridiculed Home Minister Tokonami's reliance on "makeshift antiquated methods," such as hiring wandering storytellers *(naniwabushi)* who left the people with little more than platitudes (Kōno 1922, 2).

The most fundamental challenge to the campaign for frugality came from those who advocated greater consumption as a means of improving living standards and human happiness. Their positive appraisal of consumption was summed up in the popular phrase "cultured living" *(bunka seikatsu)* during the early 1920s. The movement became closely identified with the Society for the Study of Cultured Living (Bunka Seikatsu Kenkyūkai), a forum organized by the influential commentators Morimoto Kōkichi, Yoshino Sakuzō, and Arishima Takeo. The first issue of the society's magazine *Bunka seikatsu* sold out immediately in 1921. Lectures by the organizers reportedly drew big crowds (Akazawa 1985, 19–20).

As Akazawa Shirō observes, the movement for "cultured living" rested on a very different set of assumptions than those underlying the Campaign to Foster National Strength. Whereas the Home Ministry sought to dampen consumption in order to strengthen the nation, the proponents of cultured living equated national strength with improvements in the consumer lives of millions of individuals. Morimoto Kōkichi charged that few Japanese had benefited from their nation's rise as one of the Big Five powers after 1918, remarking that Japan remained among the "world's poor nations" (Akazawa 1985, 20). Others condemned the official morality of denying desires; readers were instead advised to affirm "the pleasures in life" (Tezuka 1921). They were especially critical of the Home Ministry's call for greater thrift and "restraint in consumption." It did "more harm than good" for the government to encourage "those below the middle classes who lack the margin to live" to save more and be diligent and thrifty, judged Morimoto. He did not disagree with the need to curtail "wasteful expenditures" *(kūhi)*, but he opposed the official campaign to promote saving at the cost of curbing "rational" expenditures on essential foods and desirable housing (Akazawa 1985, 20).

"RATIONALIZING" DAILY LIFE
AND CONSUMPTION

Historians of interwar Japan often portray the proponents of enhanced consumer life and the bureaucratic champions of "diligence and thrift" as intractable foes. In both thought and behavior, however, the two camps intersected in significant areas, and in the course of the decade they cooperated in various campaigns to promote thrift. The key to understanding this convergence lies in the concept of "rationalization." We err in representing consumption as unrestrained expenditure—that is, as the antithesis of saving. In the case of the United States during the 1920s, the growth of mass consumption was accompanied by calls for prudent family budgeting and consumer education from prominent home economists. According to Mary Hinman Abel, editor of the *Journal of Home Economics* in 1925, thrift entailed the "wise spending of money" (Tucker 1991, 116). Even more so in Japan, several leading advocates of Western-style consumption simultaneously lectured consumers on the need to save.

The best known of these publicists was Hani Motoko, who had begun linking consumption and saving a full decade before comparable official campaigns in the 1920s. A Protestant educator, Hani published *Fujin no tomo* (Women's Friend; established in 1903 as *Katei no tomo* and renamed in 1908). This was one of the earliest Japanese magazines aimed at middle-class women who were taking on the role of household manager. She also popularized her views through nationwide women readers' groups known as *tomonokai* (friends' societies). *Fujin no tomo* introduced women to labor-saving household items, efficient Western-style kitchens, and more nutritious foods (for example, bread in place of rice). The new consumer goods were presented not as luxuries, but as higher-quality, simpler, and sometimes less expensive replacements for traditional, wasteful expenditures on maids or lavish ceremonial occasions. During the early 1910s, Hani's magazine launched the first major campaigns to encourage wives to record income, expenditures, and savings in household account books (Saitō 1978, 144, 157). Tips on how to economize and save money also became a standard feature of the later mass-circulation magazines for housewives.

While the Home Ministry's Campaign to Foster National Strength pounded away at consumption per se after World War I, the consumer-centered ideas of Hani Motoko and others had a greater impact within the Ministry of Education. Rather than condemn the consumption of Western-style goods, officials in charge of "social education" became convinced that "improvements" (usually Westernization) in food, clothing, and shelter would strengthen Japan and raise living standards. In 1920, the Ministry of Education launched its first "daily life improvement campaign," and it organized a coordinating organ, the League of Daily Life Improvement (Seikatsu Kaizen Dōmeikai). Composed of academic specialists and prominent male and female educators, the league's investigative committees went beyond the usual bromides to recommend practical changes that would reduce the costs of housing, food, clothing, and ceremonial life. With respect to housing, the experts echoed the thinking of the "cultured living" school. They urged the construction of both multifamily apartment buildings *(kyōdō jūtaku)* and basic single-family dwellings—the latter popularly known as "culture homes" *(bunka jūtaku).* Such homes enabled consumers to "avoid housing built just for the sake of guests and ostentation" (Nakajima 1974, 62–64; Minami 1965, 250).

From the start, notes Nakajima Kuni, the daily life improvement campaigns appealed to many urban consumers because they offered practical instruction in how to economize while recognizing the benefits of the new consumer culture. Between 1918 and 1926, the Ministry of Education—often in conjunction with women's groups—sponsored a series of well-attended public lectures and exhibitions. There one could learn about ways of simplifying weddings or the "Ikeda method of conserving rice" by mixing in cheaper, yet nutritious, grains and beans (Nakajima 1974, 69–71). Despite her close ties to leading socialists, Hani Motoko repeatedly lent the support of the *Fujin no tomo* to the government's daily life campaigns. At the Domestic Science Exhibition sponsored by the Ministry of Education in 1918, Hani prominently displayed Western clothes made from Japanese-produced silk. During the latter half of the 1920s, she stepped up her magazine's campaign to inculcate thrift and account-keeping among Japanese women, declaring: "A simple household, a rich society" (Saitō 1978, 166–167, 172–173).

The daily life improvement campaigns offered the government opportunities to persuade urban groups and individuals as never before. Younger officials in the Home Ministry's Social Bureau soon adopted the Ministry of Education's strategy of promoting savings in the name of "daily life improvement." As the agency charged with upgrading housing and ameliorating poverty, Social Bureau officials found themselves encouraging saving in terms of benefits to the individual (Minami 1965, 249). In 1925, the Social Bureau sponsored a six-day "Study Course on Home Economics" for teachers (mostly women), as well as leaders of the semiofficial young women's associations. Savings-promotion occupied center stage as bureaucrats and educators lectured on such topics as "the budgeted life," "rational consumption" of food, and "scientific diligence and thrift." The contemporary American language of scientific management further suffused the government's message. Ueno Yōichi, Japan's leading exponent of Taylorism, trumpeted the benefits of bringing industrial "efficiency" to domestic life (Nakajima 1974, 59–60).

The theme of rationalizing consumption became a major element in the interwar governments' most focused savings drive, the Campaign to Encourage Diligence and Thrift (1924–1926). Invoking the Boshin Rescript of 1908, this seemingly anachronistic crusade was, in many respects, a product of the era of "Taishō democracy" and "Taishō culture." The campaign was closely identified with Home Minister (later prime minister) Wakatsuki Reijirō and Finance Minister Hamaguchi Osachi, two bureaucrats-turned-politicians in the relatively liberal Kenseikai party. In an age of mass politics, they believed, the national economy could be strengthened only if the state was willing to mobilize all of its people—men and women, adults and schoolchildren, farmers and urban dwellers. Kenseikai leaders resisted pressures from backbenchers for women's suffrage in the mid-1920s, but they, like many bureaucrats, endeavored to involve women more fully in the nonpartisan aspects of "civic life," including social work and propagating norms of "rational" economic behavior (Garon 1997, 126–130). To promote diligence and thrift nationwide, the Home Ministry organized a central coordinating council and prefectural and municipal liaison councils while overseeing the formation of 3,897 campaign committees in towns and villages. In addition, 7,144 private or semiofficial groups assisted the bureaucracy in urging the populace to save.

The application of modern technologies and mass media to moral suasion was equally remarkable. The Campaign to Encourage Diligence and Thrift blanketed trains, trams, temples, and public buildings with a staggering 2,313,500 posters. The government also relied upon newspaper and magazine advertisements, pamphlets, and even motion pictures. Emulating World War I campaigns in Western nations, the Home Ministry conducted seven nationwide "Diligence and Thrift Weeks" to stimulate the opening of savings accounts and the purchase of bonds and life insurance. On June 10, 1925, Home Minister Wakatsuki kicked off the third Diligence and Thrift Week with a plea transmitted via the newest medium, the radio (Naimushō Shakaikyoku 1927, 1, 17–19).

There was, moreover, something democratic about the Campaign to Encourage Diligence and Thrift's efforts to appeal both to individual self-interest and to urban middle-class groups that were not officially sponsored. The drive's colorful, eye-catching posters reiterated earlier themes that Japan woefully lagged behind the Western powers in national and per capita wealth and would continue to do so until "We all work together" to toil and save. At the same time, posters propagated newer messages: "Diligence and Thrift, It's for Your Own Good and the Good of the Nation," and "Diligence and Thrift: The Bases of Stabilizing [the People's] Livelihood and Augmenting National Strength."

In addition, departing from previous practice, the government actively sought the understanding and cooperation of a broad array of women's groups in its campaign. On April 26, 1926, Prime Minister Wakatsuki and Finance Minister Hamaguchi hosted more than one hundred representatives of women's organizations, proclaiming that it was the nation's women "who are in charge of the consumer economy" ("Kinken shōrei kyōgikai" 1926). Although most of the participating groups were semiofficial women's associations, some operated quite independently of state control. The Japanese Women's Christian Temperance Union was at the time challenging the government in other drives to abolish licensed prostitution and

Poster from Campaign to Encourage Diligence and Thrift, 1925.
Caption reads: "Step by step, Fuji is attained. Rin by rin, wealth is
gained." A rin was worth one-thousandth of a prewar yen. The
characters for "Diligence and Thrift" appear in the upper corners.
(Naimushō Shakaikyoku, 1927.)

bring about women's suffrage. Similarly the prominent suffragist, Dr. Takeuchi Shigeyo, headed a women's association in Tokyo's Yotsuya ward that eagerly participated in the government's campaign and achieved sixty thousand yen in new savings. In 1926, more than five hundred women attended one of the Yotsuya association's savings rallies, capped off by the showing of a hortatory motion picture provided by the Tokyo prefectural government (*Fujo shinbun* 1926).

Finally, the Campaign to Encourage Diligence and Thrift was innova-

*Poster from Campaign to Encourage Diligence and Thrift, 1926.
Caption reads: "Diligence and Thrift, the Seeds of Human
Happiness." The depicted division of labor conveys the gendered
message that women's domestic roles contribute to the national
economy no less than males' productive labor. (Naimushō
Shakaikyoku, 1927.)*

tive in attempting to measure the impact of moral suasion on savings behavior. For the period between late 1924 and early 1927, the Social Bureau reported sharp increases in all forms of savings and, of course, attributed most of the rise to the campaign. Whether moral suasion was the primary stimulus is not easy to determine. Yet officials did convincingly demonstrate that total savings and the number of savers rose noticeably after each of the Diligence and Thrift Weeks. Without singling out the campaign as a cause, present-day economists detect a steady increase in household savings rates during the period, from *minus* 4.6 percent in 1924 to a positive 2.4 percent in 1927 (Horioka 1993, 282). Social Bureau officials also remarked on the campaign's "indirect" achievements in influencing greater numbers of Japanese to eliminate "empty formalities," take up by-employments, and engage in "service to society" (Naimushō Shakaikyoku 1927, 35–36).

The succeeding Seiyūkai cabinet of Tanaka Giichi (1927–1929) gave less attention to savings-promotion, but large-scale campaigns reappeared soon after the Minseitō (successor to the Kenseikai) came to power under Prime Minister Hamaguchi Osachi in July 1929. Hamaguchi immediately announced plans to return Japan to the gold standard. Choosing to peg the yen at its higher, pre–World War I value, the cabinet embarked on an ambitious program to deflate the economy in short order. Moral suasion became an important tool, with the government launching the Campaign for Retrenchment in the Private and Public Economies. Calling once again for "restraint in consumption," the cabinet broadened its appeal to autonomous women's groups in an effort to bring about "thrift in the kitchen of every home," in the words of Finance Minister Inoue Junnosuke (Saji 1986, 3). The thrift campaign overlapped with the Ministry of Education's Moral Suasion Mobilization Campaign (Kyōka Dōin Undō), which was unparalleled in incorporating religious organizations, moral suasion groups, and youth and women's associations—including the Council of Women's Groups Encouraging Diligence and Thrift (Monbushō 1930, 732).

To the surprise of contemporary observers, many women's organizations, conservative and progressive, enthusiastically participated in Hamaguchi's frugality drive (Garon 1997, 136). The socialist parties' women's sections and consumer cooperatives remained aloof, having steadfastly opposed official savings campaigns in the past (*Fujo shinbun* 1928). Other overtly political women's groups joined the thrift offensive but did so tactically to persuade the Hamaguchi cabinet to sponsor women's-suffrage legislation in exchange. Most women's organizations, however, cooperated in pursuit of what they believed to be a consumerist position. They looked upon the campaign to boost savings and reduce expenditures as a positive force in bringing rationality to household consumption. Women's groups had been in the forefront of a consumers' movement to reduce public-utility and transportation prices earlier in 1929. The state's program to deflate the prices of necessities—albeit by discouraging demand—struck many activists as beneficial to improving daily life (Saji 1986, 4–5).

This type of thinking prevailed within the three-million-member Federation of Women's Associations of Western Japan, whose progressive leadership was agitating for women's suffrage at the time. Closely aligning itself with Hamaguchi's retrenchment drive, the federation hosted a day of "Consumer Economy Lectures" on August 15, 1929. The umbrella organization sponsored the first annual All-Japan Women's Economic Conference later that autumn. To be sure, federation leaders pledged to protect consumer interests. The Women's Economic Conferences likewise deliberated on taking collective action to fight price-fixing, reduce consumption taxes, and cut tariffs on imported necessities. Nonetheless, rather than press the government to bring down consumer prices, the women generally took it upon themselves to avoid purchasing unnecessary commodities, shun imported luxury goods, and conserve water, electricity, and gas. As the federation's journal proudly noted, "The question of consumer thrift is an appropriate issue on which women have for the first time organized together, achieved success, and demonstrated women's power" (*Fujin* 1929, 1, 2–3).

The Hamaguchi cabinet's drive to dampen consumption worked all too well. Aggregate demand fell by early 1930, just as Japan began suffering the effects of the worldwide Depression. One might have expected the self-proclaimed consumers' groups to repudiate the ongoing thrift campaign under such circumstances. Yet at the following All-Japan Women's Economic Conferences in November 1930 and 1931, women's leaders reaffirmed their desire to cooperate with the government to "rationalize the kitchen" (*Osaka asahi shimbun* 1930; also "Dai 3-kai Zen Nihon fujin keizai taikai" 1931, 15). The continued commitment by organized women to encouraging thrift was surely a factor in the significant growth in household savings rates during the Depression, from 1.7 percent (1928) to 4.8 percent (1930) and 6.3 percent (1931).

CONCLUSIONS

The growth of interwar savings and frugality campaigns compels us to reexamine many of our assumptions concerning Japanese history and economic behavior. First, the state's determined efforts to mold a culture of diligence and thrift suggests that moral suasion played a major role in encouraging Japanese to save in the course of the twentieth century. Regrettably, few scholars have rigorously discussed relationships between the state and culture in analyzing how Japan attained and maintained high levels of household savings after World War II. Economists tend to emphasize such factors as the postwar growth in real income, whereas political scientists often point to Japanese institutions that have facilitated savings—notably the postal savings system (Sato 1987; Anderson 1990). Yet neither set of factors adequately explains why Japan's household savings rates have exceeded 7 percent since 1932 (excepting 1934, 1937, and 1945–1949) under a variety of economic circumstances—Depression, the industrial boom of the mid-1930s, wartime austerity, and the postwar years of recovery, high growth, and stagnation following the Oil Shock of 1973–1974. Indeed, the state's capacity to coax savings out of the people reached remarkable levels during the

Pacific War, when household savings rates rose to 33 percent in 1941 and an astounding 44 percent in 1944. In 1952, the postwar government built upon interwar and wartime innovations to create the Central Council for Savings Promotion, which continues to coordinate nationwide campaigns (since 1987, under the name of the Central Council for Savings *Information*).

Second, this case demonstrates that "Taishō democracy" and "Taishō culture" should not be equated simply with the liberation of society from state management. The 1920s witnessed a tremendous expansion of organizations within society, it is true. Some emerged totally outside of official supervision; many others, such as local women's associations and the district commissioner system, developed through a mix of popular initiatives and state patronage. We generally think of "Taishō" in terms of new organizations of workers, tenant farmers, and *burakumin*. Quantitatively speaking, however, the most significant organization occurred among the new and older middle classes in cities and towns and among middling farmers in the countryside (Ōmori 1982; Waswo 1988). From their ranks came the district commissioners and leaders of various women's organizations, moral suasion groups, youth associations, and agricultural cooperatives. Ironically the state emerged from the relatively democratic 1920s far more capable of promoting savings and otherwise managing society than it had been in 1918. Its new strength, I argue, lay in large part in the ability to secure the cooperation of these middle-class groups in the expanding moral suasion campaigns of the era.

Third, changes in gender roles and their representation were central to the state's growing capacities. Officials refrained from involving adult women in their savings campaigns until the 1920s, when the state, media, and women themselves began gendering wives as the nation's savers, consumers, and keepers of "daily life." Women's groups might have coalesced into an assertive consumers' movement that demanded lower prices and enhanced consumption. Instead most women's and consumers' organizations tacitly accepted the status quo of high prices, and they turned to instructing the populace in how to "rationalize" consumption and save money within those constraints. The state's reliance on women in its savings and "daily life improvement" campaigns grew steadily during the 1920s, becoming the norm by the time of the China and Pacific Wars (1937–1945). Hani Motoko, the liberal suffragist Ichikawa Fusae, and countless local women served the wartime state by exhorting ordinary women to save money and drastically curb consumption. If anything, the identification of women with saving and consumption strengthened after World War II. Postwar savings drives depended almost entirely on women's groups as intermediaries (Garon 1997, chaps. 4–6). These included such prominent "consumers'" groups as the Japan Housewives Association (Shufuren).

Finally, we might rethink our portrayal of "Taishō" as the repudiation of

Meiji-style attempts at character-building. If one gazed beyond the neon lights of the Ginza, one would have seen the profusion of middle-class groups that eagerly allied with the state to mold an industrious, thrifty, and orderly populace. The proponents of "rational consumption" and "daily life improvement" were no more averse to employing moral suasion than were state officials. In 1938, the Ministry of Finance hired Hani Motoko to give lectures as a part of its wartime national savings and austerity campaign. Japan's foremost proponent of "rationalized" living spoke, as she had long done, of the need to eliminate waste and encourage accurate account-keeping among the families of factory workers and villagers, and she explained: "A simple life is far from an impoverished life, but rather is a truly comfortable life in terms of both the human spirit and one's body. The simple life therefore is one in which there is no waste whatsoever." And who, according to Hani, were to be the teachers in this newest campaign to get by on less? None other than "*our* sound middle class," which would do its utmost to guide "the masses" toward the simple life (Hani 1938, 243, 248, 245–246; my emphasis).

ACKNOWLEDGMENTS

Research for this essay was funded by a Fulbright-Hays Faculty Research Grant. The author wishes to thank Janet E. Hunter and members of Princeton University's Davis Seminar for their helpful comments.

REFERENCES

Abe Tsunehisa. 1982. "1920 nendai no fujinkai." In *Nihon joseishi*, vol. 5, edited by Joseishi Sōgō Kenkyūkai, 75–113. Tokyo Daigaku Shuppankai.
Akazawa Shirō. 1985. *Kindai Nihon no shisō dōin to shūkyō tōsei.* Azekura Shobō.
Anderson, Stephen J. 1990. "The Political Economy of Japanese Saving: How Postal Savings and Public Pensions Support High Rates of Household Saving in Japan." *Journal of Japanese Studies* 16.1:61–92.
Barnhart, Michael A. 1987. *Japan Prepares for Total War: The Search for Economic Security, 1919–1941.* Ithaca: Cornell University Press.
Chochiku Zōkyō Chūō Iinkai. 1983. *Chochiku undōshi: Chozōi 30 nen no ayumi.* Chochiku Zōkyō Chūō Iinkai.
Cohen, Lizabeth. 1990. *Making a New Deal: Industrial Workers in Chicago, 1919–1939.* Cambridge: Cambridge University Press.
"Dai 3-kai Zen Nihon fujin keizai taikai." 1931. *Fujin* 8.11:14–19.
Fletcher, William Miles, III. 1982. *The Search for a New Order: Intellectuals and Fascism in Prewar Japan.* Chapel Hill: University of North Carolina Press.

Fridell, Wilbur M. 1973. *Japanese Shrine Mergers 1906–12: State Shinto Moves to the Grass Roots.* Sophia University.

Fujin (Zen Kansai Fujin Rengōkai). 1929. 6.10:1–3.

Fujo shinbun. 1926. No. 1377 (October 31):14.

———. 1928. No. 1450 (March 25):2.

Garon, Sheldon. 1994. "Rethinking Modernization and Modernity in Japanese History: A Focus on State-Society Relations." *Journal of Asian Studies* 53.2:346–366.

———. 1997. *Molding Japanese Minds: The State in Everyday Life.* Princeton: Princeton University Press.

Hani Motoko. 1938. "Warera no mezasu kan'i seikatsu." In Kokumin Chochiku Shōreikyoku, *Kokumin chochiku shōrei kōenshū.* Kokumin Chochiku Shōreikyoku, 243–48.

Hardacre, Helen. 1986. "Creating State Shinto: The Great Promulgation Campaign and the New Religions." *Journal of Japanese Studies* 12.1:29–63.

Harootunian, H. D. 1974. "Introduction: A Sense of an Ending and the Problem of Taishō." In *Japan in Crisis,* edited by Bernard Silberman and H. D. Harootunian, 3–28. Princeton: Princeton University Press.

Horioka, Charles Yuji. 1993. "Consuming and Saving." In *Postwar Japan as History,* edited by Andrew Gordon, 259–292. Berkeley: University of California Press.

Inoue Tomoichi. 1904. *Kinken shōrei gyōsei oyobi hōsei.* Seibunkan.

———. 1909. *Kyūsai seido yōgi.* Hakubunkan.

———. 1913. "Kyūsai jigyō ni tsuki kibō sūsoku." *Jizen* 4.3:48–68.

The Japan Year Book. 1911. Japan Year Book Office.

Kasza, Gregory. 1988. *The State and the Mass Media, 1918–1945.* Berkeley: University of California Press.

Kinken Shōrei Kyōgikai. 1926. *Fujin shinpō* 338:22.

Kōno Hironaka. 1922. "Futsū senkyo dankō no kyūmi." *Kensei* 5.2:1–4.

Kyōka Dantai Rengōkai. 1924. "Kokuryoku shinkō undō shuisho." *Shakai jigyō* 8.5:41–53.

Lewis, Michael. 1990. *Rioters and Citizens: Mass Protest in Imperial Japan.* Berkeley: University of California Press.

Mayet, P[aul]. 1893. *Agricultural Insurance, in Organic Connection with Savings-Banks, Land-Credit, and the Commutation of Debts,* translated by Authur Lloyd. London: Swan Sonnenschein.

Minami Hiroshi, ed. 1965. *Taishō bunka.* Keisō Shobō.

Mitchell, Richard H. 1976. *Thought Control in Prewar Japan.* Ithaca: Cornell University Press.

Monbushō. 1930. *Kyōka dōin jisshi gaikyō.* Monbushō.

Naimushō Shakaikyoku. 1922a. *Beikoku ni okeru setsuyaku undō.* Naimushō Shakaikyoku.

———. 1922b. "Shōhi setsuyaku ni tsuite." *Shakai jigyō* 6.7:1–11.

———. 1927. *Kinken shōrei undō gaikyō.* Shakaikyoku Shakaibu.

Nakajima Kuni. 1974. "Taishō-ki ni okeru 'seikatsu kaizen undō.'" *Shisō* (Nihon Joshi Daigaku Shigaku Kenkyūkai) 15:54–83.

Ōmori Makoto. 1982. "Toshi shakai jigyō seiritsu-ki ni okeru chūkansō to min-ponshugi—Osaka-fu hōmen iin seido no seiritsu o megutte." *Hisutoria* 97:58–74.

Osaka asahi shimbun. 1930. November 10, 2.

Pyle, Kenneth B. 1973. "The Technology of Japanese Nationalism: The Local Improvement Movement, 1900–1918." *Journal of Asian Studies* 33.1:51–65.

Roden, Donald. 1990. "Taishō Culture and the Problem of Gender Ambivalence." In *Culture and Identity: Japanese Intellectuals during the Interwar Years,* edited by J. Thomas Rimer, 37–60. Princeton: Princeton University Press.

Saitō Michiko. 1978. "Hani Motoko no shisō—kaji kakeiron chūshin ni." In *Onnatachi no kindai,* edited by Joseishi Kenkyūkai, 144–170. Kashiwagi Shobō.

———. 1988. *Hani Motoko: Shōgai to shisō.* Domesu Shuppan.

Saji Emiko. 1986. "Hamaguchi naikaku no fujin kōminken mondai." *Nihonshi kenkyū* 292:1–25.

Sato, Barbara. 1995. "Women and Reading in the 1920s." Paper presented to Modern Japanese History Workshop, New York University.

Sato, Kazuo. 1987. "Saving and Investment." In *The Political Economy of Japan,* edited by Kozo Yamamura and Yasukichi Yasuba, 1:137–185. Stanford: Stanford University Press.

Searle, G. R. 1971. *The Quest for National Efficiency.* Berkeley: University of California Press.

"Shōhi Setsuyaku Shōrei Shisetsu ni Kansuru Ken, Shakaikyokuchō yori Shōkai Kaitō." 1922 (October). Document: Taishō 1292-50, Shakai, Saitama-ken gyōsei monjo. Urawa city, Saitama prefecture: Saitama Kenritsu Bunshokan.

Smith, Henry D., II. 1983. "The Nonliberal Roots of Taishō Democracy." In *Japan Examined: Perspectives on Modern Japanese History,* edited by Harry Wray and Hilary Conroy, 191–198. Honolulu: University of Hawai'i Press.

Sugiura Nariyuki. 1990. "Nichirō sengo no yūbin chokin no tenkai to chochiku shōrei seisaku." *Shakai keizai shigaku* 56.1:31–61.

Takemura Tamio. 1980. *Taishō bunka.* Kodansha.

Tezuka Kaneko. 1921. "Ryōri no kompon seishin." *Bunka seikatsu* 1.2. Reprinted in Akazawa Shirō, *Kindai Nihon no shisō dōin to shūkyō tōsei* (Azekura Shobō, 1985), 20.

Toyama Shigeru. n.d. "Wagakuni ni okeru chochikushin." *Seikatsu no sekkei* 124 (June 1986). Reprinted in Toyama Shigeru, *Chochiku zuisō.* N.p.

Tucker, David M. 1991. *The Decline of Thrift in America: Our Cultural Shift from Saving to Spending.* New York: Praeger.

Uno, Kathleen S. 1991. "Women and Changes in the Household Division of Labor." In *Recreating Japanese Women 1600–1945*, edited by Gail Lee Bernstein, 17–41. Berkeley: University of California Press.

Waswo, Ann. 1988. "The Transformation of Rural Society, 1900–1950." In *The Cambridge History of Japan*, vol. 6, edited by Peter Duus, 541–605. Cambridge: Cambridge University Press.

❦ 15 ❧

Visions of Women and the New Society in Conflict: Yamakawa Kikue versus Takamure Itsue

E. Patricia Tsurumi

By the end of World War I, the Japanese left wing included individuals with a wide range of viewpoints. But by 1921 most of them had lined up on one side or the other of the fledgling labor movement's famous *ana-boru* (anarchism vs. Bolshevism) debate between champions of anarcho-syndicalism and advocates of Marxian socialism. Like so much of "Taishō democracy," the mainstream of the *ana-boru* controversy regarding the postrevolutionary society leftists hoped to build defined human needs in terms of society's male members.

In a parallel discourse a few years later, female anarchists and socialists argued about the kind of postrevolutionary society women needed (Ogata 1980). Participants in the feminists' version of the *ana-boru* fight deplored the social construction known as "woman" in the Japan of their day and sought to construct "woman" for a postrevolutionary Japan that would embrace gender equality. But their constructions of the new woman and the new society were radically different. Despite some crossover between anarchist and socialist camps, anarchist feminists generally espoused gynocentric or woman-centered feminism while socialist feminists adhered to a version of humanist feminism.[1]

This essay is about the most famous segment of the women's *ana-boru* conflict: the dispute between humanist feminist Yamakawa Kikue (1890–1980) on the Marxian socialist side and gynocentrist Takamure Itsue (1894–1964) in the anarchist camp. It occurred mainly during 1928. Since I am interested in their ideas as articulations of the two major streams of left-wing feminism during the Taishō era rather than as representations of

335

ana and *boru* positions of the time, a major aim of this essay is to shed light on the constructedness of "woman" and of "postrevolutionary Japan" in the debate. Absorbed and refined by later writers and activists, their arguments became central parts of the inheritance of all future generations of Japanese feminist theorists, including those active in Japan today.

The essay first investigates notions of "woman" and "postrevolutionary society" offered by Yamakawa and Takamure before 1928. In Yamakawa's case these appeared in her contributions to the "motherhood protection" debate of 1918–1919 in which she confronted bourgeois feminists Hiratsuka Raichō (1886–1971), Yamada Waka (1879–1957), and Yosano Akiko (1878–1942). In Takamure's case these were laid out at length in this poet's first published prose work on women, *The Genesis of Love (Ren'ai no sōsei)* in 1926. The essay then examines the animosity-laden exchange between Yamakawa and Takamure in 1928 that appeared as articles in a number of women's periodicals. The essay concludes with a brief consideration of the meaning of the debate for later generations of Japanese feminists and the global significance of the ideas of Takamure and Yamakawa today.

YOUNG KIKUE AND HER CONCEPT OF "WOMAN" IN THE 1918–1919 MOTHERHOOD DEBATE

Born and reared in Tokyo, both before and after her graduation from Tsuda College (Josei Eigaku Juku) in 1912, the young woman then named Aoyama Kikue got her "real education" reading socialist and anarchist writings, attending public lectures, and talking to activists. A serious student of ideas, she often read the works of Western theorists in the original languages. At the end of 1916 she married Yamakawa Hitoshi (1880–1958), a prison-seasoned Marxist theorist widely respected in left-wing circles.[2]

Exchanges in print regarding motherhood protection had been going on since 1915, but they were savagely hostile by the time Yamakawa Kikue jumped into the fray with "Women's Opinion that Stabs Women in the Back" (Fujin o uragiru fujin ron) in the August 1918 issue of *New Japan (Shin Nihon)*. This article was aimed squarely at Yamada Waka, who had recently published "A Discourse on Women's Problems from Now On" (Kongo no fujin mondai o teishō su).[3] A former prostitute turned Christian educator, Yamada Waka was the most conservative of the three prominent bourgeois feminists in the motherhood debate; she supported the "good wife and wise mother" ideology of the Japanese state, maintaining that the roles of women and men were equal but different. Kikue scornfully denounced Waka for her "exaggeration of biological differences between the sexes" (Yamakawa 1918a, 156). Waka's claim that women should devote themselves to their families while men worked outside of their homes, noted Kikue, was an

Yamakawa Kikue, 1921. (Experience of Women.
Asahi Shimbunsha, 1995, 67).

arrangement only possible for those in the middle classes and above. According to Kikue, Waka, who used "biology as an excuse to defend male absolutism" (Yamakawa 1918a, 156), offered no proof or logic regarding women's nature.

Kikue asked, "What is woman's true nature? Those who know the answer are women themselves. Yamada Wakako is not the sole person who knows the answer . . . " (Yamakawa 1918a, 172). Attacking Waka's arrogant proclamations about woman's nature, Kikue did not directly offer her own definition of woman's nature. She was content to express her hopes for the future in terms of the awakening of women, the building of a women's movement, a changed economic system, and equality of men and women (Yamakawa 1918a, 173).

Next Kikue took on the brilliant poet Yosano Akiko and the *Bluestocking* editor, Hiratsuka Raichō. Akiko had written that individual women like individual men must take responsibility for supporting the children they bring into the world. To be able to support their children, argued Akiko, women must have better education than currently available to them, must be able to enter gainful occupations now closed to them, and must enjoy political suffrage equally with men. This mother of eleven, with a husband who had ceased making significant economic contributions to their family, was totally confident that she could support her children largely from the proceeds she earned with her pen. She saw motherhood as only a small part of her rich life (Yosano 1916, 234; Mackie 1988b, 37). Totally opposed to state support for mothers, Akiko saw dependence upon state or society as demeaning to a woman as dependence upon a man (Yosano 1918, 85; Mackie 1988b, 37; Molony 1993, 128).[4]

Akiko's rejection of state support for motherhood had been aimed at Hiratsuka Raichō, founder of the literary feminist group, Bluestocking (Seitō), and the journal of the same name. Raichō argued for state support for Japanese mothers along lines advocated in the writings of her current heroine, the gynocentric Swedish reformer Ellen Key (1849–1926). Back in her early *Bluestocking* days, Raichō had written that she did not want to be a mother, that motherhood would only impede perfection of the full potential of her selfhood (Hiratsuka 1914). But overwhelmed by the unbridled maternalism of the young Itō Noe (1895–1923), her co-worker on the *Bluestocking* journal, and stimulated by Key's book about "the rights of motherhood" (Key 1911), Raichō changed her mind. Yet fearing that the heavy demands of motherhood might violate her individuality or hinder perfection of her self, she welcomed the idea of state support that she found in Key's writings (Hiratsuka 1916; Nishikawa 1985, 164–167).

Since being a mother was part of being a woman, society should support motherhood, concluded Raichō. "We are not to be liberated from being 'women'; as 'women' we must be liberated" Raichō maintained (Nishikawa 1985, 167). She also argued for public financial support of mothers on the grounds that mothers produce and rear children for the benefit of state and society (Hiratsuka 1918, 232; Mackie 1988, 37). Raichō noted that the kind of support a genius of superior talent and energy like Akiko could give to her children was beyond the capability of ordinary women (Hiratsuka 1918, 231; Rodd 1991, 192).

In a September 1918 article in *Fujin kōron (Women's Review)*, Yamakawa Kikue leveled her sights at both Yosano Akiko and Hiratsuka Raichō. She addressed them with much more sympathy and respect than she had given Yamada Waka—even if some of her politeness was tongue in cheek.[5]

Calling Yosano Akiko the Mary Wollstonecraft of Japan, Kikue identified the source of Akiko's argument as "women's rights-ism" born in late eighteenth-century Europe. In this stream of feminism "woman" is essentially defined as "man ² humanity" and the emphasis is upon women's admittance to the male-controlled activities of industry, politics, art, and science. While she agreed with Akiko that women's need for more and better education was urgent, Kikue found Akiko's hopes for individual effort to achieve education, employment, financial independence, and political suffrage illusory within a society that systematically denied equal opportunity to the vast majority of its members. She pointed out that in the capitalist labor market women were paid very little, and their presence there was manipulated to lower remuneration for all laborers, while women's work within the family was entirely unremunerated. Like Raichō before her, she pointed out that Yosano Akiko's agenda was only possible for a few Japanese women.

Yamakawa Kikue recognized Raichō's argument as an offshoot of European maternalist theories of Ellen Key and German gynocentric feminists in the late nineteenth and early twentieth centuries. Yet despite the acknowledgment that capitalism damaged women and children, this line of thinking ignored the harm the same system did to men. Recognition of motherhood as service to state and society in this thought and Raichō's offshoot of it was just another version of Good Wife and Mother-ism. Mothers who were unable to bring up their children without help should indeed have state support, said Kikue. But this aid should be given not because the needy women were mothers raising children for society and state. It should be given for the same reason that society supported the institutional care of elderly, infirm, and disabled members who could not look after themselves.

Yamakawa Kikue reminded readers that neither Yosano Akiko nor Hiratsuka Raichō challenged the country's existing economic structure. The implicit definition of "woman" in Yosano Akiko's polemics was a social construction that could serve as a blueprint only for extremely talented and confident middle-class and upper-class women. Hiratsuka Raichō's definition was no more encouraging: in motherhood for the sake of society and state "woman" was an entity that for a modest price agreed to be an instrument of male-dominated society. And in January 1919 Raichō revealed that she too offered solutions for only a minority of women: "The Agony of Contemporary Housewives" (Gendai katei fujin no nayami) asks maids to subsidize middle-class motherhood (Hiratsuka 1919).

Kikue's answer was that the fundamental barrier to development of the full potential of "woman" was the existing economic system; it must be completely destroyed and replaced with something else. Her September and December 1918 articles described the ways in which Japanese capitalism was failing women but said little about how a new economic system would improve women's lot. Kikue did not offer solutions to important questions like women's unpaid reproductive labor—how women currently doing unpaid labor within capitalist families would be compensated in a postrevolutionary economy that embraced gender equality. She never discussed how responsibility for children was to be shared equally by men and women. While calling for a revolutionary change in economic relations, she never directly said that socialist revolution will lead to women's liberation. It is true that she was still young, but she was well read and was a keen student of the Russian Revolution, then offering a new model to progressive people all over the world.[6]

Even though she rejected humanist feminism that tolerated capitalism, Kikue herself was part of the historical humanist feminist stream that she claimed "Japan's Mary Wollstonecraft" represented. During the next decade as an activist within the labor movement she sometimes advocated stopgap measures to help women become closer in equality to men, even when to do so did not directly challenge capitalism.[7] For short-term gain she was not always unwilling to work with bourgeois reformers in the women's suffrage movement,[8] nor in the birth control movement.[9] She even cooperated with anarchists she respected—like Itō Noe and Ōsugi Sakae (1885–1923). But such cooperation involved only temporary truces in her war against bourgeois enemies willing to settle for gender equality within the status quo or anarchist rivals with hopelessly utopian concepts of postrevolutionary society.[10]

TAKAMURE ITSUE, *GENESIS OF LOVE*, AND NEW WOMAN-ISM

While in 1918 young Yamakawa Kikue was injecting socialist logic into the motherhood protection debate, young Takamure Itsue, a poet from a small village in Kumamoto, was on a Buddhist-inspired pilgrimage to eighty-eight temples in Shikoku.[11] In August of 1920 she set off for Tokyo. The next few years were eventful for her: her published poetry found appreciative readers; she gave birth to a stillborn child; and she experienced and resolved domestic friction with her spouse, Hashimoto Kenzō (1897–1976). With him, she joined activists including the anarchist intellectual Ishikawa Sanshirō (1876–1956) and social activists Shimonaka Yasaburō (1877–1961) and Shibuya Teisuke (1905–?), who by the middle of the decade were founding the Peasant Self-Rule Society (Nōmin Jiji Kai).

A poor peasant from Saitama prefecture, Shibuya, like Takamure, was a poet. And like her too he was appalled by the nation's capital, which to both of them signified urban privilege in a boundless sea of rural suffering. With sympathy they watched laid-off factory workers leaving Tokyo for home villages that could not support them while desperate refugees from the countryside poured into the capital. Itsue enthusiastically took part in the

Takamure Itsue, 1930. (Experience of Women. *Asahi Shimbunsha*, 1995, 68).

Peasant Self-Rule Society's organization of tenant farmers and of women. While thus involved, she wrote *Genesis of Love,* which was to become the point of departure for all her future ideas (Takamure 1965, 216; Kano and Horiba 1977, 146; Tsurumi 1985, 7).

Takamure Itsue's engagement with the peasant anarchists is reflected in this thoroughly anticapitalist book. For instance, in a long passage on syndicalism, anarcho-syndicalist thought and organization are approvingly described as "natural" or "spontaneous" (Takamure 1926, 125–128), while in the brief passage that follows Marxism is given short shrift as a "theory of economic principles that cannot solve women's problems or farmers' problems" (128). Repudiation of modern industrialism is a strong theme—Itsue repeatedly contrasts idyllic portraits of rural life of past eras with the evils of contemporary urban Japan. In *Genesis of Love* she offers her definitions of "woman" and the postcapitalist world.[12]

In this book Takamure Itsue identifies humanist feminism both as "women's rights-ism" of England and the United States (with Mary Wollstonecraft and Charlotte Perkins Gilman as representatives of it) and "new women's rights-ism" in revolutionary Russia (Alexandra Kollontai is cited). Gynocentric feminism is identified as the "woman-ism" of maternal feminists in Germany and Scandinavia with Ellen Key singled out as a key figure. Itsue spends thirty-three pages attacking Key's views of women and motherhood (82–111). Gynocentric feminism is also identified as "new womanism," but in contrast to "women's rights-ism" and European "woman-ism," this identification is positive—Itsue claims she is the first pioneer of "new woman-ism" in Japan.

As such, she champions two related goals: community care for mothers and the abolition of marriage. She argues that because women reproduce, they are closer to nature's nonhuman order than are men. Therefore women rather than institutionalized matrimony, the patriarchal family, state, or society should make decisions regarding reproduction and child care. "Society's government officials (*yakunin*) may say 'Mothers, we don't necessarily want to take your adorable children away from you. Bringing them up yourself is also an option.' Now to me 'option' is a negative (*shōkyoku teki*) word I do not like. Mothers don't like to be parted from children. . . . We must have a system rooted in nature" (97). She defined such a system as one that does not take children away from mothers nor make mothers bear their reproductive and child-care burdens as isolated individuals. Reproduction and child care were to be supported by a self-governing, nonhierarchical community in which men and women would be equal producers and womanhood highly esteemed. A corollary of this was abolition of institutionalized marriage. The purpose of both was to allow woman to enjoy passionate carnal and spiritual loving that, along with motherhood, was part of her basic nature.

Opposed to concentration of power and authority in any form, she criticized modern society in which men competed for power and status and kept women subordinate to themselves. According to Takamure Itsue, this was a production of the "survival of the fittest principle" developed by Western civilization. Thus she linked men, modern society, and the West and found them all equally hateful. In premodern Japanese history—especially in early Japanese history—she felt that she had found a world in which women were highly respected beings who received appropriate reproductive and child-care support and loved passionately without the harmful restrictions of matrimony. At a time when the vast majority of female and male intellectuals of the right, left, and middle were infatuated with the West, Takamure Itsue's critical negation of Western civilization was highly original. The social construct of her "natural" woman was strongly rooted in what she perceived to be the specific, concrete Japanese past.

ANA-TAKAMURE VERSUS BORU-YAMAKAWA

Ten years after the motherhood debate and two years after the publication of *Genesis,* the feminists' *ana-boru* encounter began. During 1928 Yamakawa and Takamure's exchanges in three magazines, *Fujin undō (The Woman's Movement), Fujin kōron,* and *Nyonin geijutsu (Women's Arts),* dominated; but other women soon joined them to take up positions on both sides, filling many pages in *Nyonin geijutsu* and *Fujin sensen (The Woman's Front)* up until 1931, when these two journals ceased publication.[13]

In her five articles published in 1928, Takamure Itsue constructed "woman" as a free being close to nature. Men were not so "natural" as women, so efforts to make female naturalness a part of the male nature were necessary (Takamure 1928e, 112). Unfettered love was at the core of women's naturalness (Takamure 1928b, 65; 1928c, 74, 81, 83; 1928d, 86). Itsue reported that in her talks with researchers regarding revolutionary Russia she was told that one example of the kindness shown women in Russia was Russian fathers' assumption of child-rearing responsibilities. Itsue saw a father's claiming a woman's offspring as his child as an unfortunate negation of that woman's freedom to love; and to Itsue, free loving was an essential part of woman's nature (Takamure 1928b, 65). Private property, with its intimate ties to the patriarchal family system, must be abolished along with other inhibitors of free love (Takamure 1928b, 61; 1928c, 81). Her favorite image of a natural woman undistorted by modern industrialism was a freely loving peasant maiden working, singing, and dancing in the fields and mountains of ancient Japan (Takamure 1928c, 74).[14]

The other important part of a woman's nature was motherhood, a category that for Itsue included reproduction and child rearing. To her, raising children was as innately part of being a woman as was giving birth to them. Individual women were to be in control of both functions, but they were not to perform them unaided. The entire community—a small self-governing rural community—was to support women as mothers. Here again her model was "ancient society in which women freely brought up their children with the cooperation of the entire village" (Takamure 1928a, 9). Totally opposed to the socialization of child care that the Marxist feminists advocated, Itsue maintained that what mothers wanted was somewhere between having to bear the entire burden of child care and having child care done entirely by state-appointed professionals (Takamure 1928d, 86). To Marxist assurances that in their new society women would be the ones making choices about child care, Itsue replied, "When [Alexandra] Kollontai says that those [women in Russia] who want bring up their children themselves should go ahead and do so, this is like saying today to [Japanese] women that those women who want to get an education should go ahead and do so" (Takamure 1928a, 11).

Since it was only small, self-governing communities of agricultural producers loosely linked in free association that could enable women to be true to their "nature," Itsue had thrown her lot in with the anarchist movement that advocated such arrangements. "I am an opponent of Marxism's consciousness concerning motherhood first and an anarchist second. Put another way, it is because a movement toward anarchism is at the same time a movement toward consciousness [of the needs] of motherhood that my point of departure is different from yours," she told Yamakawa Kikue (Takamure 1928d, 87). When Itsue talked about the nature or the needs of women, she felt she was talking about all women. Thus she claimed there existed no differences that had to separate bourgeois and proletarian women (Takamure 1928b, 68). She called upon all women to join with working people who would support and cherish them in small communities of primary producers.

Her ideal for the future Japan was a coalition of agricultural villages. The citizens of this country would all be primary producers concerned with consumption (providing all members of the self-ruling villages with the basics for daily life) rather than production (of increasing amounts of goods by means of ever-advancing science and large-scale industrial organization). All citizens would respect and support women as lovers and mothers. Her main model for this new society was ancient Japan, which, according to her, had been a world of egalitarian cooperative agricultural communities that esteemed women. This was a good world not only because it was egalitarian but also because it was female centered and thus the opposite of contemporary male-centered, Westernized, authoritarian, hierarchical, industrial, urban Japan. Her other model was poor peasants of her day, especially those who were organizing to fight landlords. If you want a glimpse of the self-governing manual workers of the postrevolutionary future, she told Yamakawa Kikue, "Look at gatherings of peasant women. They are people with no education but they know all about injustice. They were anarchists when they were born" (Takamure 1928d, 89).

Yamakawa Kikue did not attempt to define "woman," yet she was very aware that the concept of "woman" was an artificial construction. As her first verbal thrust at Itsue articulated, the content of this concept was determined by the economic system that shaped it and other identities. In "Women as Bargain Goods with Giveaway Premiums" (Keihin tokkahin toshite no onna), Kikue argued that in capitalist society "married woman" was constructed by the capitalist marriage relationship. Within it wives, as economic dependents of husbands, were prostitutes just like women who sold sexual services for cash to a variety of male customers (Yamakawa 1928a). Kikue was shrewd enough to recognize that different individuals constructed "woman" differently. Bourgeois advocates of women's rights saw "woman" as a class-blind entity that sought political suffrage, education, and employment to put herself on terms of equality with men (Yamakawa 1928d, 168). And to members of women's peace groups, "woman" was the intrinsically peaceful gender while 'man' made war (Yamakawa 1928d, 172–174).[15]

Such social constructions of "woman" Kikue introduced only to denounce. She denied the existence of "woman" as an entity shaped by gender. As a good Marxist of her times she insisted that problems "are class problems not women's problems" and that progressive women needed to put their energies into class organizations not women-only organizations (Yamakawa 1928b, 20–21). There are some "in-the-short-run" exceptions to this rule: Marxist women may work in all-women's groups including non-Marxist women for some specific special purpose like political suffrage (Yamakawa 1928b, 22) or in the Red Wave Society (Sekiran Kai), 1921–1925, the single-gender group that Yamakawa and other left-wing women organized because Article Five, Clause Two, of the Police Security Regulations did not permit women to participate in political organizations (Yamakawa 1921b; Shapcott 1987, 11–21). Another reason for condoning such "exceptions" to class solidarity—one that she might not have been willing to make public during the 1920s—may well have been the fierce struggle she waged in 1925 with male socialist and labor activists who arrogantly refused to champion female as well as male proletarian needs. As she later acknowledged, not all barriers to women organizing as full-fledged warriors in the class struggle were erected by the state and the capitalist economy (Yamakawa 1956, 273–275).

Yamakawa Kikue developed her argument against a gender identity at great length in her last lunge at Itsue in 1928, titled "An Investigation of Feminism" (Fueminizumu no kentō) (Yamakawa 1928d).[16] In this she denied the existence of a single-sex culture. A country's "high society culture" (*kōkyū shakai no bunka*) may appear to be male culture, but it is only the culture of the small number of males who belong to the ruling class. Ruling-class males have a monopoly on learning and knowledge that excludes women, but it must be remembered that this also excludes nonruling-class males. In contemporary society what is called women's culture are the demands made by women-only groups for female admission to formal rights and equalities that are but empty pretenses under capitalism. Reviewing women's support of their nations' male armies, she noted the sharp contradictions between Japanese women organizing for world peace while condoning Japanese imperialism in China. Kikue concluded that claims that women are the peace-loving gender cannot be taken seriously.

The crux of her arguments in this article is that the "woman" and "man" she constructs are equal in ability, morality, and every other measure that matters to society. She has no time for those who argue that women must participate in public life because women's superior morality will improve politics (171). "We women are the same human beings as men. What men can do we can do. I do not think that by virtue of our sex we can do what men cannot do. Women are not deities; neither are they devils. In essence, women are just human beings" (172).

Kikue dealt very little with the ultimate postrevolutionary society that would bring fulfillment to women. When she mentioned it, she seems to have done so mainly out of exasperation at Itsue's "ignorance" of Marxism. In "The Apparition that Emerged from Dogma: Takamure Itsue's Newly Discovered 'Marxist Society'" (Doguma kara deta yūrei: Takamure Itsue shi shin hakken no 'marukusu shakai' ni tsuite) she reasonably complained that the "Marxist society" that Itsue criticized as being like capitalism with its centralized power and industrial production processes was not *the* Marxist society but only Marxism's "dictatorship of the proletariat" on the way to the ultimate postrevolutionary society. In so protesting, Kikue made a few comments about the society that was the ultimate goal: it would be a society in which the slogan "to each according to his or her need" would be a reality. But such remarks are few and general. She is much more interested in discussing work and life under "the dictatorship of the proletariat." During that period, large-scale industry propelled by science and management aimed at ever-increasing production would be an economic system directed by centralized political power. In that ever-modernizing economy the division of labor would be applied "as necessary" and "a person will contribute [labor] according to his or her abilities" (Yamakawa 1928c, 151). And Kikue certainly thought the division of labor—especially between intellectual workers and manual workers—would be very necessary. If it is fair to take this penultimate Marxist society about which Kikue writes in concrete detail as her vision of the new social fabric, then her model reflected much that was part of the urban, industrialized, centralized societies of capitalist countries, including Japan. To Itsue this marked Kikue's postrevolutionary vision as but a slightly kinder monster than capitalism. To Kikue, since the rulers of her new society would work on behalf of the oppressed and exploited, this world was only distantly and temporarily related to capitalism.

THE TWO VISIONS IN PRESENT AND FUTURE JAPAN AND BEYOND

In the late 1920s, the arguments of Yamakawa Kikue and Takamure Itsue shaped as well as reflected feminist thinking and activism. Their *ana-boru* contentions did much to turn the gaze of anarchist and socialist women (whose leaders and mentors were usually men) toward "woman" as well as "women." The not-always-acknowledged influence upon feminists outside of the left wing was also substantial. Later, feminists who (re)emerged after the era of repression and war from 1931 to 1945 absorbed the ideas of these two women, carrying them into their own feminist praxis.[17]

True to European humanist and socialist lineages in which humankind was equated with the male, Yamakawa Kikue defined gender equality as women's full participation in a world created by and for men; but for her research, analysis, and debate were always the first steps in the long march needed to bring the female half of humanity closer to the equality starting line.[18] So it is not surprising that—as Morosawa Yokō reminds us—Kikue was the first person in Japan to use social science to study women's problems from a woman's point of view (Morosawa 1994, 132). Since so many Japanese feminists are scholars, including private scholars working outside of the academy, this intellectual legacy has been far-reaching. Her prewar socialist feminism was strong in women's participation in the 1960 struggle against Japan's security treaty with the United States, that leader of the capitalist-imperialist world.[19] From the 1960s up through the 1980s, when Japanese women repeatedly went to court to sue employers who discriminated against female employees, Yamakawa's emphasis on paid labor as the key to equal treatment of women and men went with them (Itō 1995; Upham 1993, 129–165). Both the internationalism of the Japanese women's movement (particularly conspicuous during and since the United Nations International Women's Decade) and the research and educational orientation of domestic campaigns of internationally active groups bear Kikue's imprint (Mackie 1988a, 61).

Takamure Itsue's gynocentric feminism was a celebration of women's culture emphasizing maternalism, rural-community support, and female sexuality with models for this culture drawn from what Itsue insisted was the historical Japanese past. Her historical research into that past came later, but it too provided a model for later feminists, notwithstanding the fact that it has received severe criticism from some feminists (Ogino 1980; Kurihara 1994). Certainly the importance she gave to motherhood in her definition of "woman" has been continued in the maternalism debates that have dominated the postwar Japanese women's movement, although not always in ways that would have met with Itsue's approval (Kōuchi 1984; Moloney 1993; Sakurai 1987). Strong echoes of her belief that rural women were "natural anarchists" can be found in the protests of the grandmothers who led the struggles at Kitafuji at the foot of Mount Fuji against appropriation of common lands by United States forces and the Japanese Self-Defense forces and in the strategies and organization chosen by women who fought in the Sanrizuka struggles against appropriation of farm land to build Narita airport (Mackie 1988a, 61; Tomura 1975; Apter and Sawa 1984, 192–194).

Itsue's spirit also can be found among those postwar women who are trying to establish alternative agricultural communities (Hikata 1995). Initiatives of the mostly female leadership and rank-and-file supporters in Japan's highly localized environmental movement echo Itsue's declaration that women are the gender closest to nature's nonhuman order. As Nishikawa Yūko notes, in Takamure Itsue's compassion for and solidarity with suffering peasants, Minamata Disease activist Ishimure Michiko found strength that helped sustain her commitment to the tragically ill, dying, and dead Minamata fisherfolk (Nishikawa 1985, 182–188).[20] And the still faint but increasingly heard demands that Japanese women have rights to sexual independence hark back to Itsue's construction of woman as a spontaneously loving being who must be freed from monogamous marriage fetters.[21]

In postwar Japan feminists have made a number of judgments about the life choices of Yamakawa and Takamure. Itsue's defiance of Japanese patriarchal norms in her personal life and in her historical research made her the darling of the women's movement during the 1970s, but many of the younger generation of feminist activists and scholars now condemn her for her active collaboration in the prosecution of the war.[22] Some are challenging her woman-centered scholarship. Kikue was celebrated less during the first two postwar decades, but now she has admirers from various hues in the feminist rainbow who point to her consistent criticism of militarism throughout the war. Undoubtedly, perceptions of the two will undergo further changes as the controversies regarding prewar and wartime feminists rage on.

In the *ana-boru* debate, Yamakawa Kikue, intellectual, logician, and teacher as well as agitprop expert, laid out her carefully researched arguments in the orderly fashion that was her trademark. Unabashedly a mental laborer (she was not the least bit apologetic about being an intellectual in a working-class movement), she had science, reason, and sociology on her side. "I felt that it was not my fault I was not born working class. . . . An intellectual who does not belong to a class independent of the capitalists is not by that very fact a running dog of the capitalists" (Yamakawa 1956, 242). What could be a more rational way to build a new equalitarian world for both women and men than advancing step by step against hunger and want, using economies of scale and the division of labor to increase and distribute wealth efficiently? Since cities possessed amenities that rural areas lacked, was it not humane as well as logical to increase urban populations? Since the young Russian Revolution had fostered some promising consequences for women and did include feminists like Alexandra Kollontai who were fighting gender discrimination (Kollontai 1977; Porter 1980), Kikue's optimism on that front was not at all unreasonable. One can certainly understand why she saw Takamure Itsue's vision as an obscure haze that contributed nothing positive to preparation for a new society that would meet women's needs.

It was not only Yamakawa Kikue who found Takamure Itsue's picture of the future far from reason and reality. Writing in the same September 1928 issue of *Fujin kōron* that carried Itsue's "The Way of the Newly Arisen Woman: Politics and Autonomy" (Shinkō fujin no michi: seiji to jiji), proletarian novelist Hirabayashi Taiko (1905–1972) lashed out at Itsue's worship of peasant life in "Romanticism and Realism: A Criticism of the Debate between Mme. Yamakawa Kikue and Mme. Takamure Itsue" (Romanchishizumu to riarizumu: Yamakawa Kikue Takamure Itsue ryōshi no ronsō no hihyō). "What about the suffering of [peasants'] daily lives? [What about] the agony of severely chapped hands, hookworms, and trachoma? How can she [Takamure] declare beautiful the hopeless lives of peasant women who have no chance to know anything about freedom in their own slave lives!" (Hirabayashi 1928, quoted in Nishikawa 1985, 1787).

Itsue's own anarchist comrade in the Proletarian Women Artists' League, Matsumoto Masae, repeatedly expressed doubts about Itsue's other bucolic model. Masae was skeptical about the matriarchal society supposedly revealed by the glorious female-centered Japanese past Itsue repeatedly praised. Where was the hard evidence for such a woman-centered past, Matsumoto Masae asked (Matsumoto 1931a, 1931b; Tsurumi 1985, 13). Koto Kanno has even suggested that it may have been difficult for Itsue herself to believe in what must have seemed to be such a hopelessly utopian future (Koto 1981, 13).

Is it even more difficult for us to take her new society seriously? Two decades ago, perhaps even ten years ago, my answer would have been that I found her utopia attractive but totally unrealizable. But today we cannot ignore the consequences of our adoption of much of the other model. We can no longer pretend not to see the havoc that continues to be created by our industrial, urban, centralized societies with production processes that spew throw-away goods and political processes that exclude the vast majority of our citizens. Yamakawa's twins for endless good, science and the division of labor, have become the youngest two riders in the apocalypse. As Donna Haraway urges, "We must find another relationship to nature besides reification, possession, appropriation, and nostalgia" (Haraway 1995, 70). And as Vandana Shiva and others have begun to show us, in the Third World women are indeed finding another relationship as they use traditional subsistence production practices to resist the unarticulated assumptions of "development," the grand inheritance of Yamakawa's vision. The women in India who unite in such ventures as Chipko (hug the tree) nonviolent direct action do so for survival—their own and the planet's. When they do so, they deny assumptions that nature itself is unproductive, that organic agriculture based on nature's cycles of renewability is unproductive, and that subsistence producers who work together in cooperation are unproductive (Shiva 1988; Mies and Shiva 1993; Schücking and Anderson 1991). The modest successes of such Third World resisters and the unhappy fruits of the Yamakawa vision that today we see all over the globe should prompt us to take another look at Takamure's insistence that the New Society is to be found in small, rural, self-sufficient, autonomous, cooperative communities striving to remain in tune with nature.

NOTES

I would like to acknowledge the support for this essay that I received from the faculty and staff of the International Center for Research in Japanese Studies, Kyoto, in 1994; a Japan Foundation Fellowship 1992–1993; and my fellow members of the Kyoto-based Kindai Josei Shi Bunka Kai (Modern Women's History Subcommittee) of the Nihon Josei Gaku Kenkyū Kai.

1. In her "Humanism, Gynocentrism, and Feminist Politics," American philosopher Iris Morgan Young writes that humanist feminism "defines women's oppression as the inhibition and distortion of women's potential by a society that allows the self-development of men" (Young 1985, 73), while it considers "femininity as the primary vehicle of women's oppression and calls upon male dominated institutions to allow women the opportunity to participate fully in public world-making activities of industry, politics, art, and science" (74). In gynocentric feminism "the oppression of women consists not of being prevented from participating in full humanity, but of the denial and devaluation of specifically feminine virtues and activities by an overly instrumentalized and authoritarian masculine culture" (79). More than five decades earlier, Japan's Takamure Itsue came up with similar definitions, labeling "humanist feminism" as "women's-right-ism" (*joken-shugi*) and "gynocentricism" as "woman-ism" (*joseishugi*) (Takamure 1926, 9). I too see feminism as historically running in these two major streams that include numerous variations but are all thought or action aimed at eliminating gender-based injustice.
2. I used three autobiographical books (Yamakawa [1956] 1972, 1978a, 1978b). Others have written about her life and work (Shapcott 1987; Mackie 1988b, 1994; Sotozaki and Okabe 1979; Sugaya 1988; Yamakawa Kikue Tanjō Hyaku Nen wo Kinen suru Kai 1990).
3. It is not clear when or where Yamada Waka first published this article, although the date seems to have been sometime between April and July of 1918 (see Nishikawa 1985, 170; Suzuki 1981, 285). Yamada Waka's "Bosei hogo mondai" (The Motherhood Protection Question) in the September 1918 issue of *Taiyō* may have been more or less a reprint of the same article.
4. In a November 1918 article Yosano Akiko did support payments to working mothers who lost income due to pregnancy and childbirth, but she viewed these as health insurance funds paid to any ill or disabled worker (Rodd 1991, 197; Molony 1993, 127).
5. She prefaced her criticism of Akiko's contention that individual effort will

solve motherhood problems with acknowledgment of Yosano Akiko's impressive talents and praise for her earlier demonstrations of equalitarian and progressive thinking. She also recommended Akiko's current admonitions as a "good stimulus to women of the middle class and above who are indecisive and indolent" (Yamakawa 1918b, 181).

6. In an interview with Shapcott, Yamakawa Kikue said that the Russian Revolution made a deep impact on her and that the revolution had encouraged her to study Marxist theory seriously (Shapcott 1987, 7).

7. I do not agree with Barbara Molony that "by 1925 Yamakawa modified her position and came to accept in the absence of socialist revolution, the desirability of improving work conditions to facilitate mothers' access to work" (Molony 1993, 128). In 1925 Kikue tried to get her male colleagues who came together to organize a nonanarchist proletarian party to accept the "Women's Demands" she drew up. She saw these demands as a Marxist, working-class program for justice as well as aid to those in weak positions. The demands were: (1) abolition of the family headship system and abolition of all laws that do not treat men and women equally; (2) equal educational and employment opportunities for both sexes; (3) abolition of the system of prostitution; (4) a minimum wage system to apply equally to all regardless of gender or ethnicity (to apply to Koreans and Taiwanese as well as Japanese); (5) equal wages for men and women doing the same work; and (6) protection of motherhood, including postnatal care and prohibition of dismissals of pregnant women. As she made clear, these were demands for which the entire proletariat should be fighting. They were not the program of a special women's group within the labor movement (Yamakawa 1928b, 22–24; [1956] 1972, 275–276).

8. Sharon H. Nolte perceptively noted that regarding the women's suffrage movement "Yamakawa treated bourgeois feminism with contempt in theory and cooperation in practice" (Nolte 1986, 701). Nolte also pointed out that other women in proletarian organizations took a similar approach: "The organizational separation of women according to class was often mediated by cooperation and, I believe, by mutual sympathy. . . . More than their male counterparts, progressive women were united by a consciousness of their restricted place in Japanese society and their gender, which was the formal basis of their exclusion and of the civil code limitations affecting them" (701–702). We know from one of her autobiographies (Yamakawa [1956] 1972) that Kikue found the enforced organizational separation frustrating and that she was aware of it when she weighed the costs of taking energy from the supposedly genderless class fight to put it into activism on behalf of women.

9. See, for example, her "Josei no hangyaku" (Women's Treason) in the January 1921 issue of *Kaihō (Liberation)* (Yamakawa 1921a).

10. One battle in this war was her attack on bourgeois women's organization in a July 1921 article titled "Shin Fujin Kyōkai to Sekirankai" (The New Woman's Association and the Red Wave Society) (Yamakawa 1921b).

11. She has left us an autobiographical version of a life that has attracted a good

number of biographers. See Takamure 1965; Akiyama 1973; Konō 1977, 1990; Kano and Horiba 1977; Hashimoto and Horiba 1981; Nishikawa 1982; Yamashita 1988.

12. She apparently wrote this book spontaneously, following where genius led her for pages and pages of unbroken text. Even after her husband, a professional editor at Heibonsha, edited this seemingly endless prose poem, it remained difficult to approach analytically; but from start to finish, it is a work about feminism.

13. After 1928 Yamakawa wrote in *Fujin kōron,* but she did not debate the *ana-boru* question in *Nyonin geijutsu* any more. She did not write in *Fujin sensen,* a publication of which Takamure Itsue was a major editor. As Vera Mackie reminds us, although *Nyonin geijutsu* and *Fujin sensen* "are usually presented as anarchist women's arts journals, both journals published contributions from a broad spectrum of the left, including Communist Sata Ineko, Marxist Yamakawa Kikue, maternalist feminist Hiratsuka Raichō, as well as anarchists Yagi Akiko and Takamure Itsue" (Mackie 1994, 81; see also Ogata 1980).

14. For later examples, see various issues of *Fujin sensen,* 1930 to 1931.

15. Such social constructions by women were of course products of their economic systems. The bourgeois women's rights movement, for example, occurred because capitalism took women out of their isolated homes to work for pay alongside men, thus acquiring independent thoughts to match their newly increased economic independence. Itsue retorted that this was true for only a few women because for thousands of years peasant women had been working alongside their menfolk (Takamure 1928d, 89).

16. In this article Kikue uses "feminism" and "feminist" as derogatory labels that she and her comrades applied to non-Marxist, nonproletarian-linked champions of women's causes.

17. Space does not permit me to acknowledge all the fine work on postwar Japanese feminism in which one can trace the Yamakawa and Takamure heritages, but some excellent English-language studies are Buckley and Mackie 1986; Buckley 1993; Mackie 1988a; Ueno 1987, 1988; Upham 1993; and Uno 1993. In Japanese, see Ochiai 1989 and Ueno 1990.

18. After 1945 she did not for a minute agree with another humanist feminist, Sanpei Takako (1903–1978), who claimed that with the postwar reforms Japanese women no longer faced heavy gender-based discrimination (Sanpei 1958, 222).

19. During this struggle in 1960 more than forty women's organizations joined left-wing groups, students, and trade unions in protest against American military bases in Japan.

20. Ishimure Michiko is such a strong champion of Takamure Itsue that when in 1994 a scholar published a book suggesting that some of Itsue's findings regarding the history of ancient Japan were fabrications, Ishimure retorted that Itsue presented her truth as poetry if not as "scholarship" and that the prewar male historians also had fabrications in their work (Ueno 1995; see also Kurihara 1994).

21. There are still strong taboos inhibiting discussion of female sexuality. As Matsui Yayori put it: "If we look at the issue of 'women's independence' historically, we see that up until the 1970s this mainly meant economic independence, or the right to work. When women began to demand sexual independence, however, the pressure brought against them by men increased suddenly" (1995, 17).
22. Space limitations preclude a discussion here of the question of prewar feminist leaders and wartime collaboration and cooperation.

REFERENCES

Akiyama Kiyoshi. 1973. *Jiyū onna ronsō: Takamure Itsue no anakizumu.* Shisō no Kagakusha.
Apter, David E., and Nagayo Sawa. 1984. *Against the State, Politics and Social Protest in Japan.* Cambridge: Harvard University Press.
Buckley, Sandra. 1993. "Altered States: The Body Politics of 'Being-Woman.'" In *Postwar Japan as History*, edited by Andrew Gordon. Berkeley: University of California Press.
Buckley, Sandra, and Vera Mackie. 1986. "Women in the New Japanese State." In *Democracy in Contemporary Japan*, edited by Gavan McCormack and Yoshio Sugimoto. Armonk, New York: M. E. Sharp.
Fujin sensen. March 1930–June 1931. Reprinted in a facsimile of the original, Rokuinbō, 1983.
Haraway, Donna. 1995. "Otherworldly Conversations, Terran Topics, Local Terms." In *Biopolitics*, edited by Vandana Shiva and Ingunn Moser. London: Zed Books.
Hashimoto Kenzō and Horiba Kyoko. 1981. *Waga Takamure Itsue.* Asahi Shimbunsha.
Hikata Mitsuko. 1995. "Women and Alternatives to Agricultural Decline." *AMPO* 25-26.1.
Hirabayashi Taiko. 1928. "Romanchishizumu to riarizumu: Yamakawa Kikue Takamure Itsue ryōshi no ronsō no hihyō." *Fujn kōron* (September).
Hiratsuka Raichō. 1914. "Dokuritsu suru ni tsuite ryōshin ni." *Seito* (February). Reprinted in *Hiratsuka Raichō hyōron shū*, edited by Kobayashi Tomie and Yoneda Sayoko. Iwanami, 1987.
———. 1916. "Bosei no shuchō ni tsuite Yosano Akiko ni atau." *Bunshō sekai* (May). Reprinted in *Hiratsuka Raichō hyōron shū.*
———. 1918. "Yosano Kaetsu ryōshi e: Bosei hogo no shuchō wa iraishugi ka." *Fujin kōron* (May). Reprinted in *Hiratsuka Raichō hyōron shū.*
———. 1919. "Gendai katei fujin no nayami." *Fujin kōron* (January). Reprinted in *Hiratsuka Raichō hyōron shū.*
Itō Yasuko. 1995. "Josei ni totte no sengo 50 nen." *Rekishi hyōron* 545 (September).

Kano Masanao and Horiba Kyoko. 1977. *Takamure Itsue*. Asahi Shimbunsha.

Key, Ellen. 1911. *Love and Marriage*, translated by Arthur C. Chater. London: G. P. Putnam's Sons.

Kollontai, Alexandra. 1977. *Selected Writings of Alexandra Kollontai*, translated by Alix Holt. New York: W. W. Norton.

Kōno Nobuko. 1977. *Hi no kuni no onna: Takamure Itsue*. Shin Hyōron.

———. 1990. *Takamure Itsue: Reinō no josei shi*. Riburopoto.

Koto Kanno. 1981. "Takamure Itsue and Her Decision to Embark upon the Matriarchal Systems Research." Paper given at Canadian Asian Studies Association Conference, Halifax, Nova Scotia, May.

Kōuchi Nobuko, ed. 1984. *Shiryō: Bosei hogo ronsō*. Domesu Shuppan.

Kurihara Hiromu. 1994. *Takamure Itsue no kon'in josei shi zō no kenkyū*. Kōryō Shoten.

Mackie, Vera. 1988a. "Feminist Politics in Japan." *New Left Review* 167.

———. 1988b. "Motherhood and Pacifism in Japan, 1900–1937." *Hecate* 14:2.

———. 1994. "Socialist Women and the State in Taishō and Early Showa Japan." *Japanese Studies Bulletin* 14:1.

Matsui Yayori. 1995. "The Movement at a Crossroad." *AMPO* 25–26.1.

Matsumoto Masae. 1931a. "Ren'ai to keizaigaku: josei chūshin setsu no kentō." *Fujin sensen* (May).

———. 1931b. "Ninshin no keizaigaku." *Fujin sensen* (June).

Mies, Maria, and Vandana Shiva. 1993. *Ecofeminism*. London: Zed Books.

Molony, Barbara. 1993. "Equality Versus Difference: The Japanese Debate over 'Motherhood Protection', 1915–50." In *Japanese Working Women*, edited by Janet Hunter. London: Routledge.

Morosawa Yōko. 1994. *Orutanateibu no onna ron*. Domesu Shuppan.

Nishikawa Yūko. 1982. *Takamure Itsue: mori no ie no miko*. Shinchō.

———. 1985. "Hitotsu no keifu: Hiratsuka Raichō, Takamure Itsue, Ichimure Michiko." In *Bosei wo tou: rekishi teki hensen*, edited by Wakita Haruko, 2. Kyoto: Jinbun Shoin.

Nolte, Sharon H. 1986. "Women's Rights and Society's Needs: Japan's 1931 Suffrage Bill." *Comparative Studies in Society and History* 28.1.

Ochiai Emiko. 1989. *Kindai kazoku to fueminizumu*. Keisō Shobō.

Ogata Akiko. 1980. *Nyonin geijutsu no sekai: Hasegawa Shigure to sono shuhen*. Domesu Shuppan.

Ogino Miho. 1980. "Takamure Itsue no kenkyū ni miru Nihon no kon'in sei no hensen." *Josei gaku nenpō*, inaugural issue.

Porter, Cathy. 1980. *Alexandra Kollontai, a Biography*. London: Virago.

Rodd, Laurel Rasplica. 1991. "Yosano Akiko and the Taishō Debate over the 'New Woman.'" In *Recreating Japanese Women, 1600–1945*, edited by Gail Lee Bernstein. Berkeley: University of California Press.

Sakurai Kinue. 1987. *Bosei hogo undō shi*. Domesu Shuppan.

Sanpei Takako. 1958. *Aru onna no hansei*. San'ichi Shobō.

Schücking, Heffa, and Patrick Anderson. 1991. *Biodiversity, Social and Ecological Perspectives*. London: Zed Books.

Shapcott, Jennifer. 1987. "The Red Chrysanthemum: Yamakawa Kikue and the Socialist Women's Movement in Pre-War Japan." In *Papers on Far Eastern History* 35.

Shiva, Vandana. 1988. *Staying Alive: Women, Ecology and Development*. London: Zed Books.

Sotozaki Mitsuhiro and Okabe Masako, eds. 1979. *Yamakawa Kikue no kōseki: Watakushi no Undō Shi to chosaku mokuroku*. Domesu Shuppan.

Sugaya Naoko. 1988. *Fukutsu no onna: Yamakawa Kikue no gohansei*. Kaien Shobō.

Suzuki Yūko. 1981. "Kaisetsuni." In *Yamakawa Kikue shū*, edited by Tanaka Sumiko and Yamakawa Sinsaku, 1. Iwanami, 1981–1982.

Takagi Sumiko. 1986. "Women in the Labor Front." *AMPO* 18:2–3.

Takamure Itsue. 1926. *Ren'ai no sōsei*. Reprinted in *Takamure Itsue zenshū*, edited by Hashimoto Kenzō, 7. Rironsha, 1965–1967.

———. 1928a. "Fujin undō no tan'itsu taikei no shin teishō." *Fujin undō* (January). Reprinted in *Fujin undō no tan'itsu taikei*, edited by Josei Shi Kenkyūkai. Seigabo, 1975.

———. 1928b. "Musan kaikyū to fujin: tsutsushinde Yamakawa Kikue joshi ni tatematsuru." *Fujin undō* (March). Reprinted in *Fujin undō no tan'itsu taikei*.

———. 1928c. "Yamakawa shi no ren'ai kan o nanzu." *Fujin kōron* (May). Reprinted in *Fujin undō no tan'itsu taikei*.

———. 1928d. "Fumareta inu ga hoeru: futatabi Yamakawa Kikue shi e." *Fujin kōron* (June). Reprinted in *Fujin undō no tan'itsu taikei*.

———. 1928e. "Shinkō fujin no michi: seiji to jiji." *Nyonin geijutsu* (September). Reprinted in *Fujin undō no tan'itsu taikei*.

———. 1965. *Hi no kuni no onna no nikki*. Reprinted in *Takamure Itsue zenshū*, edited by Hashimoto Kenzō, 10. Rironsha, 1965–1967.

Tomura Issaku. 1975. "Ten Years of Struggle: Sanrizuka and Its Links in Asia." *AMPO* 7.4.

Tsurumi, E. Patricia. 1985. "Feminism and Anarchism in Japan: Takamure Itsue, 1894–1964." *Bulletin of Concerned Asian Scholars* 17.2.

Ueno Chizuko. 1987. "The Position of Japanese Women Reconsidered." *Current Anthropology* 28.4.

———. 1988. "The Japanese Women's Movement: The Counter-Values to Industrialism." *The Japanese Trajectory: Modernization and Beyond*. Cambridge: Cambridge University Press.

———. 1990. *Kafuchōsei to shihonsei: marukusu shugi fueminizumu no chihei*. Iwanami.

———. 1995. "'Takamure josei shi' dō uketsugu ka." *Asahi shimbun*, December 12.

Uno, Kathleen S. 1993. "The Death of 'Good Wife and Wise Mother'?" In *Postwar Japan as History*, edited by Andrew Gordon. Berkeley: University of California Press.

Upham, Frank K. 1993. "Unplaced Persons and Movements for Place." In *Postwar Japan as History*, edited by Andrew Gordon. Berkeley: University of California Press.

Yamada Waka. 1918. "Bosei hogo mondai." *Taiyō* (September). Reprinted in *Shiryō: Bosei hogo ronsō*, edited by Kōuchi Nobuko. Domesu Shuppan, 1984.

Yamakawa Kikue. 1918a. "Fujin no uragiru fujin ron." *Shin Nihon* (August). Reprinted in *Yamakawa Kikue shū*, edited by Tanaka Sumiko and Yamakawa Shinsaku, 1. Iwanami, 1981–1982.

_____. 1918b. "Bosei hogo to keizai teki dokuritsu." *Fujin kōron* (September). Reprinted in *Yamakawa Kikue shū*, 1.

_____. 1918c. "Yosano Akiko shi ni kotae." *Fujin kōron* (December). Reprinted in *Yamakawa Kikue shū*, 1.

_____. 1921a. "Josei no hangyaku." *Kaihō* (January).

_____. 1921b. "Shin fujin kyōkai to Sekirankai." *Taiyō* 7 (September). Reprinted in *Nihon fujin mondai shiryō shūsei*, 8. Domesu Shuppan. 1977–1980.

_____. 1928a. "Keihin tsuki tokkahin toshite no onna." *Fujin kōron* (January). Reprinted in *Yamakawa Kikue shū*, 5.

_____. 1928b. "Musan fujin undō ni tsuite tachiba wo akira ka ni suru." *Fujin undō* (February). Reprinted in *Yamakawa Kikue shū*, 5.

_____. 1928c. "Doguma kara deta yūrei: Takamure Itsue shi shin hakken no 'marukusu shugi shakai' ni tsuite." *Fujin kōron* (June). Reprinted in *Yamakawa Kikue shū*, 5.

_____. 1928d. "Fueminizumu no kentō." *Nyonin geijutsu* (July). Reprinted in *Yamakawa Kikue shū*, 5.

_____. [1956] 1972. *Onna nidai no ki*. Nihon hyōron shinsha. Heibonsha.

_____. 1978a. *Nijū seki wo ayumu: aru onna no ashiato*. Daiwa Shobō.

_____. 1978b. *Watakushi no undō shi*. Reprinted in *Yamakawa Kikue no kōseki: Watakushi no Undō Shi to chosaku mokuroku*, edited by Sotozaki Mitsuhiro and Okabe Masako. Domesu Shuppan, 1979.

Yamakawa Kikue Tanjō Hyaku Nen Wo Kinen Suru Kai. 1990. *Gendai fueminizumu to Yamakawa Kikue*. Daiwa Shobō.

Yamashita Etsuko. 1988. *Takamure Itsue ron: haha no arukeoroji*. Kawade Shinsha.

Yosano Akiko. 1916. "Nendo jizō." *Taiyō* (July). Reprinted in *Nihon fujin mondai shiryō shūsei*, 8. Domesu Shuppan, 1977–1980.

———. 1918. "Josei no tettei shita dokuritsu." *Fujin kōron* (March). Reprinted in *Shiryō: Bosei hogo ronsō*, edited by Kōuchi Nobuko. Domesu Shuppan, 1984.

Young, Iris Morgan. 1985. "Humanism, Gynocentrism, and Feminist Politics, "*Women's Studies Internationalist Forum* 8:3. Reprinted in *Throwing Like a Girl and Other Essays in Feminist Philosophy and Social Theory.* Bloomington: Indiana University Press, 1990.

❧ 16 ❧

Broadcasting in Korea, 1924–1937:
Colonial Modernity and
Cultural Hegemony

MICHAEL E. ROBINSON

In February of 1927, under the call sign JODK, the newly established Kyŏngsŏng Broadcast Corporation (KBC) began regular programming in Korea. By the end of the colonial period, an estimated 305,000 radio permits had been granted for use in private homes, tea rooms, restaurants, public markets, schools, and village meeting halls, and KBC had brought every nook and cranny of the colony within range of its network of stations and relay facilities for exchanging programming with Japan, Manchukuo, and China.[1] In the twentieth century, no other colony was tied to its metropole with such an extensive communications net (Fanon 1965, chap. 2).[2]

Standard nationalist histories of the colonial period, if they mention radio at all, interpret the phenomenon as another part of the extensive Japanese information control system that served its propaganda and cultural assimilation programs.[3] This was, of course, true. All communications in the colony were tightly controlled at the center, and Japanese officials recognized immediately the potential of broadcasting to further the long-range goals of spreading Japanese language use and cultural values. In the mid-1930s, the Japanese intensified their information controls and cultural assimilation campaigns under the banner of *naisen ittai* (Japan and Korea as one body). Radio played an important role in *naisen ittai* and the later Movement to Create Imperial Citizens *(kōminka)*. After 1937, KBC became an increasingly important vehicle for transmitting sanitized war news from Tokyo throughout the colony. Indeed, the domestic Japan Broadcasting Corporation (Nihon Hōsō Kyōkai, or NHK) played an equally important propaganda role; while it did not have to negotiate between two languages as in Korea, its programming became similarly dominated by central censors by 1941.

Upon closer inspection, however, the story of colonial radio is much more ambiguous. While closely controlled at the center, the problems of creating and expanding colonial radio required the Government General of Korea (GGK) to make some significant cultural policy concessions. Most notably, Japanese authorities were confronted with the necessity of creating a second, all-Korean-language system in order to disseminate receivers and create a mass audience. Moreover, financing the system required a broad fee-paying audience. And as the experience of the first six years of broadcast (1927–1933) demonstrated, this could be done only if Koreans were attracted to buying and using radios. Thus, within six years of the inception of colonial broadcasts, the initial mixed-language channel was supplemented by the addition of an all-Korean-language channel, and sales of radios soared.

While still tightly controlled by Ministry of Communication officials, the existence of all-Korean radio created a cultural space within the diverse information, educational, economic, and pure entertainment programming forming the public airwaves—a space that contradicted the cultural/political logic (if there was one) of assimilation. From 1933 until the outbreak of the Pacific War in 1941 and the imposition of severe censorship (Korean-language broadcasting ceased entirely in 1944), Korean radio stimulated a revival of traditional music genres, created new forms of dramatic arts, introduced Western classical music and jazz, fed its audience's insatiable appetite for modern, popular song (*yuhaengga*), and became a vehicle for Korean vernacular standardization. Indeed, Korean radio became an important productive force in the creation of a modern, popular culture in colonial Korea; and while this culture was a product of Japanese colonial political, cultural, and economic ascendancy, it also played a role in subverting Japanese cultural hegemony.

This essay will attempt to recast the story of Korean radio as a part of a dynamic colonial cultural hegemony. It is not simply the story of the creation of another Japanese-dominated, modern institution foisted upon the agencyless Korean people in order to serve its domination. Radio should be seen as part of a more complicated colonial hegemony constructed of both physical coercion and cultural/political attraction. Japanese cultural hegemony worked so well because it provided limited spaces for Korean cultural autonomy (Robinson 1994, 54–73).[4] In the end, allowing a space for cultural autonomy acted to both sustain and subvert the ultimate goals of Japanese cultural assimilation. I avoid calling radio a "space of resistance" because this implies that Korean-language broadcasting directly contested Japanese cultural assimilation; it did not. Korean radio did, however, construct culture and in doing so resisted by creating and maintaining Korean art forms with strong emotive ties to Koreans of all classes. Therefore, even within a tightly controlled, censored, colonial medium dominated by Japanese programming (particularly after 1937), Koreans made of it something of their own.

This study focuses on the creation of Korean radio insofar as it illuminates the problems and difficulties inherent within the Japanese effort to "assimilate" their colony. The central problem for the Japanese was to create and spread the new medium of radio in order to use it as a tool for acculturating Koreans to Japanese values. Ultimately, they inadvertently created a space for Korean cultural construction that undermined their original intent.

ESTABLISHING BROADCASTING IN KOREA
1924–1927

After the massive uprisings in the spring of 1919, the GGK altered the original military control policies in the colony. Under Governor General Saitō Makoto (1919–1927, 1929–1931) the GGK instituted a policy of cultural rule *(bunka seiji)* in order to ameliorate Korean resistance and co-opt Korean elites by encouraging active participation in the cultural and political affairs of the colony (Baldwin 1969). After 1920, the GGK allowed Korean newspapers and magazines, permitted political participation, and granted permits for cultural, academic, student, and citizen associations. The 1920s witnessed, therefore, a renaissance of cultural and political activism in the colony. While granting these concessions, the Japanese strove to tighten their control apparatus by using more indirect means and by strengthening intelligence gathering and oversight functions in an expanded, reorganized police system. The ultimate goal of cultural rule was to encourage active participation in the life of the colony while slowly intensifying their long-range program to culturally assimilate Korea (Baldwin 1982, 162).[5]

Broadcasting began in Japan in 1926 and in Korea in 1927, and policies created in Japan established precedents for the colony. By 1924, the GGK had created the basic policy framework for colonial broadcasting, and officials were enthusiastic about the potential of radio as an easily controlled, centralized medium for information and education. Indeed, early radio regulations (GGK Administrative Orders of 1924) were modeled after the Japanese 1915 Wireless Telegraphic Communications Law. This transferred the Japanese government's assumptions about broadcasting (a statist public interest option) and its bureaucratic controls directly to Korea (Kasza 1988, 72–83).[6] In spite of the limits on private investment, government regulations, and a very limited market, eleven separate applications for broadcasting permits representing both Japanese and Korean investors were submitted to the Ministry of Communications between 1923 and 1924. Following the pattern established with the creation of NHK in 1924, the original petitioners were amalgamated into one public interest juridical person *(kōeki hōjin)* and a separate permit granted permission to erect transmission facilities between 1925 and 1927 (Kasza 1988, 80).[7]

GGK testing began as early as 1924. A spate of newspaper articles in the colonial press followed the testing program closely, and there was tremendous public enthusiasm for the project *(Tonga ilbo* [Eastern Daily], December 17, 1924, and *Chosŏn ilbo* [Korea Daily] December 17, 1924). The colonial press presented the story of radio testing as a science lesson for its readers while effusively celebrating Korea's inclusion in the emerging future of electronic communications. Ignoring the reality of government controls that would constrict programming freedom, the papers provided free advertising and cultivated public awareness of and excitement for the new medium. The newspapers followed KBC's slow gestation through GGK bureaucratic red tape, tracked the numbers of radio owners (in 1925 there were only eight hundred receivers operating), advertised broadcast demonstrations in public parks and in their own offices, and announced the locations of mobile testing units *(Chosŏn ilbo,* July 2, 1925; April 20, 1926; July 8, 1926; *Tonga ilbo,* June 26, 1925; July 15, 1926; November 6, 1926).

The testing period between 1924 and the creation of KBC in 1927 coincided with a burst of Korean cultural activity in Seoul and the growing provincial centers of the colony. It was also a period of political transition. In the early 1920s moderate nationalists used the new Korean press and organizational "freedoms" to expand the space for cultural autonomy in the colony. Without directly challenging Japanese rule, the so-called cultural nationalists mounted educational, journalistic, economic, and cultural programs designed to strengthen Korean cultural identity and economic autonomy (Robinson 1988, chap. 3). The advent of radio in Korea fit into this larger movement. Cultural nationalists viewed radio as an indication of cultural and technological growth in Korea. They saw it as a means for spreading Korean cultural consciousness in Korea and, more broadly, to the world. As one newspaper paean to the new medium put it: "through the miracle of radio waves we can introduce our culture, music, and the sounds of our language to the world" *(Chosŏn ilbo,* January 12, 1927).

After February 16, 1927, this was, technically, possible. On that date the newly chartered KBC began formal broadcasts after two years of testing. Using a Marconi Q-type six-kilowatt transmitter at 690 KHz, KBC was on the air sixteen hours a day; its range, however, was limited to Seoul and its environs, and it was broadcasting in Korean less than 30 percent of the time (HPK 1977, 18–20). For the next six years, KBC struggled with financial, technical, and programming problems that inhibited its expansion and cultural potential. It is in this period that the conflict over the new cultural space of radio emerged.

PROBLEMS WITH EARLY BROADCASTING
1927–1933

A dual-language broadcasting policy prevailed at KBC for its first six years.[8] The original mix of language was based on a three (Japanese) to one (Korean) ratio. This meant that the overwhelming majority of broadcasting was in Japanese (with some Korean translation of certain news items). KBC hired, with great fanfare, two Korean announcers in late 1926. They assumed the very difficult job of providing on-the-spot translations (early programming used two microphones, side by side) for general announcements, programming schedules, short news items, financial reports (market, stock prices, etc), and GGK bulletins. The Japanese staff designed and wrote most of the programming, and the two Korean announcers were responsible for only several hours of "entertainment" programming in Korean.

The dual-language policy came under immediate criticism in the Korean-language press; it also stirred up the Japanese community.[9] Both communities were annoyed by the use of the other's language, each for predictable reasons. That the GGK would respond is another illustration of how such cultural issues were negotiated during the period of cultural rule. By July of 1927 Korean language use was increased to 40 percent and different methods of alternating programming began (HPK 1977, 38–40). While this helped, the original conception of using two languages within a single broadcast day continued to fragment and discombobulate the listening audience.

The original dual-language policy was predicated on the idea that Korean should be used as a bridge language to introduce the Japanese-language reports. With short news items, market reports, and GGK announcements, this was probably effective for Japanese-speaking Koreans and not too bothersome for Japanese listeners. Responding to Korean complaints, however, within six months KBC started to alternate Japanese and Korean versions of the same programs. This diluted by half the amount of information that could be presented and forced non-Japanese speakers and Japanese listeners (only a small fraction of the Japanese community ever learned Korean) to "wait their turn" in getting information.

The situation with regard to radio's most popular programming—entertainment—was equally volatile. Entertainment (music, radio drama) occupied only 30 percent of the broadcast day, but it was clearly the main attraction of radio from its inception. Koreans complained about the lack of Korean music and the odd scheduling of entertainment programs. Eventually, the station created a schedule in which entertainment programs (Korean music and Japanese music) alternated every other day to provide some unity for nighttime listeners. The dual-language policy, however, continued to confuse the programming schedule. The Korean newspapers had to run detailed, daily schedules so the radio audience could plan their listening around the mixture of different shows, some repeated in both languages, different programs in either Korean or Japanese—all compounded by the even/odd day alternation.

In 1928, KBC introduced relay programming from Japan to Korea. In combination with the early hard-wire connections from NHK, relays increased the percentage of Japan-based radio in Korea. The construction of a ten-kilowatt relay transmitter on Kōshima in 1928 effectively jammed the distant KBC signal from Seoul in the middle and southern Korean regions. By 1931, NHK agreed to stop transmission from Kōshima between 9:40 and 11:00 P.M. in order to avoid blocking KBC Korean entertainment programming that reached the small, out-of-Seoul audience; KBC also began devoting this entire time slot to Korean music.

It was clear that KBC's dual-language policy inhibited the spread of radio use in the Korean community while also angering the Japanese audience. Indeed, the audience for radio was still predominantly Japanese in this early period. If the GGK thought that radio dominated by Japanese language, controlled information, and Japanese music would ultimately spread to the Korean community, it was sorely mistaken. As research in this field deepens, it will be interesting to speculate about the effects of alternate-language broadcasting on language acquisition or resistance. A case can be made that Japanese-dominated radio encouraged Japanese language comprehension. An equally valid interpretation might be that alternating use, as in bad foreign-language teaching, provided instant translation and therefore no incentive to acquire Japanese. But clearly the dual-language model failed; it fragmented programming, irritated listeners, inhibited the spread of radio use, and reduced revenues in the first six years of broadcasting.

FINANCING RADIO AND BUILDING AN AUDIENCE

The lack of a broad audience was the largest problem faced by KBC in its early years. KBC had to finance its operations on registration and listener fees. The GGK spent 30,000 yen for equipment and testing in 1924 and between 1925 and 1927 ultimately increased its investment in KBC to 400,000 yen. Private investment provided less than 10 percent of the 400,000-yen initial capitalization.[10] The law governing the charter of KBC limited profits for private investors to 7 percent, but the KBC did not turn a profit until the late 1930s.[11] In the early period, simple enthusiasm for the project and perquisites for investors, including exemption from all fees and participation in KBC governance, were the main incentives for KBC's Korean and Japanese investors.

Having chosen a noncommercial option for radio, KBC had to be supported by listener fees. The first rates established an initial two-wŏn registration fee and a monthly two-wŏn listener fee. There were 1,440 registered users in February 1927 (the inauguration of KBC); after three months this number had increased to 3,318. This provided a mere 6,638 wŏn monthly income for the station, which was carrying a 300,000-wŏn debt on construction and equipment, not to mention its current operations obligations running at 10,000 wŏn a month. Clearly, income had to be increased if the station was to continue, let alone expand. KBC offered a number of incentives to attract listeners. The manipulation of the language content and different strategies of alternate day, Japanese/Korean programming and music hours at night (introduced in Korean) responded to the need to attract Korean listeners. In 1927, KBC reduced the monthly listener fee to one wŏn per month and created installment plans for rural listeners, who found monthly payment inconvenient. It dispatched autos with radios to rural markets to promote radio sales and created a mobile radio sales unit to bring radios to rural villages. And KBC established free radio service centers in Seoul and P'yŏngyang; they also scheduled regular traveling service units that circulated in the provinces (HPK 1977, 33–35). Ultimately, KBC focused on spreading its geographical coverage by installing more powerful transmitters as an additional strategy for expanding its listener base. This, however, would required more funds for equipment and construction.

In spite of these efforts, radio sales remained flat. Moreover, the Japanese community continued to represent the overwhelming majority of the radio audience. In the mid-to-late 1920s, radios were still expensive consumer items. The cheapest crystal sets cost as much as ten wŏn and vacuum tube radios cost more than 100 wŏn. By the early 1930s, however, cheaper vacuum radios suitable for home use appeared, followed quickly by the development of more powerful units built for larger audiences (tea rooms, offices, restaurants, etc.) (Chŏng 1992b, 54–61; HPK 1977, 122–130). Cost alone cannot account for stagnant sales. In the end, the fragmented programming and language confusion on KBC remained its biggest problem. This conclusion is supported by the fact that radio sales and audience expansion increased after the announcement in 1931 of plans for a second all-Korean language station (Station 2). Table 1 provides figures for registered radios in Korea.

In the first four years of radio, the listening audience had increased to only 10,831, 83.8 percent of whom were Japanese users. Between 1930 and 1931, the size of the Korean audience even fell in terms of percentage share from 13.3 to 12.2. KBC's announcement of its intent to create an all-Korean station in early 1931 clearly had some effect on radio sales to Koreans. After 1931, radio sales to Koreans expanded steadily with large increases in percentage share in 1933 (the first year of Station 2) and again in 1935 and 1937.

TABLE 1
Registered Radio Receivers in Korea, 1926–1940

Year	Total	Korean (%)	Japanese (%)	Foreign (%)
1926	1,829	386 (21)	1,431 (78)	12
1927	5,122	949 (18.5)	4,161 (81.2)	12
1928	8,469	1,353 (15.9)	7,102 (83.8)	14
1929	10,153	1,573 (15.4)	8,558 (84.2)	22
1930	10,831	1,448 (13.3)	9,410 (86.8)	23
1931[a]	14,309	1,754 (12.2)	12,493 (87.3)	62
1932	20,479	2,738 (13.3)	17,641 (86.1)	100
1933	26,340	4,517 (17.1)	21,690 (82.3)	131
1934	28,021	5,111 (18.2)	22,786 (81.3)	124
1935	37,500	8,775 (23.4)	28,503 (76)	222
1936[b]	64,821	16,324 (25.1)	48,089 (74.1)	408
1937	86,891	29,683 (34.1)	56,570 (65.1)	638
1938	120,901	45,490 (37.6)	74,790 (61.8)	621
1939	146,637	60,917 (41.5)	85,720 (58.4)	n/a
1940	191,180	95,153 (49.7)	96,027 (50.2)	n/a
1942[c]	277,281	126,047	149,653	1,581

Source: Chōsen Sōtokufu tōkei nenpō (1926–1940); Han'guk Pangsong Chinhŭnghoe, *Han'guk pangsong ch'onggam* (Seoul: Han'guk Pangsong Chinhŭnghoe, 1991), 176, 222–223; see also Chŏng Chin-sŏk, "Ilcheha ŭi radio pogŭp kwa ch'ŏngchwija," *Sinmun kwa pangsong* (October 1992):62.

Notes: These figures are for illustration only. There is much to be done with balancing different counts. The figures for registered receivers in the *GGK Ministry of Communication Annual*, the *GGK Statistical Annual*, and the privately published *Maeil sinbo's Korea Annual (Chosŏn nyŏngam)* vary from year to year. Numbers in parentheses are percent of total. Months for figures in the table vary.
[a]KBC announced its intention to create a second all-Korean-language station in May 1931.
[b]These figures represent a year-and-a-half interval. All other year figures vary in date less than three months.
[c]Wartime figures are taken from an estimate in *Han'guk pangsong ch'onggam*, 222–223.

By 1940, Korean radio use had reached parity with that of the Japanese community. While the totals are unimpressive, the fact remains that Korean radio use increased 36.8 percent (1932), 39 percent (1933), and 41 percent (1935) after 1931.

Overall, radio sales were also increasing rapidly. The Manchurian Incident of 1931 and excitement within both the Korean and Japanese communities for news about Japan's advance in China stimulated these sales. With the beginning of the war in China in 1937, the radio audience increased dramatically. By 1940, it hovered near the 200,000 mark, and best estimates of radio distribution at the end of the colonial period indicate approximately 305,000 (slightly more than 1 percent of the Korean population) radios in use. This number was quite modest compared to the vast radio audience of the metropole. In 1944 there were 6.6 million radios in use in Japan, the fourth largest audience in the world behind only the United States, Germany, and Great Britain (Kasza 1988, 88).

While the increase in radio distribution between 1931 and 1936 can be attributed to the Korean response to the new all-Korean station, the doubling of the audience after 1937 reflected GGK interests in expanding the information net during the war. And they were willing to directly finance the expansion with considerable investment in facilities. The second infusion of money into the system in 1931 (a 430,000-wŏn loan from NHK) helped build facilities for Station 2 as well as more powerful transmitters to increase the station's reach. A network of regional stations was added after 1935 with an additional 543,000-wŏn loan to KBC, again squeezed out of Japanese radio revenues. The expansion of the colonial radio audience also meant increased revenues available for expansion. By 1939, a total 1,397,000 wŏn had been invested in the colonial system. Ironically, its listener fees drew disproportionately from the Japanese community throughout the 1930s. In a sense, the radio listeners in the metropole and the Japanese audience in the Korean colony were forced to pay for the system—a system supporting a Korean-language station (HPK 1977, 30–35).[12]

OVERSIGHT AND RADIO AS
AN ASSIMILATION TOOL

The Japanese considered this investment a good one in spite of the ironies inherent in providing a cultural space for Koreans as well as financing it on the backs of Japanese listeners. It was clear that the GGK decided to provide a Korean-language station in tandem with the move to intensify cultural assimilation in the colony after 1931. Japanese educational, linguistic, and cultural control policies shifted toward promoting in Koreans an active identification with Japanese cultural values, and these programs were soon amalgamated under the banner of *naisen ittai*. The program was designed to spread Japanese language use, restrict the use of the Korean language in schools and government offices, rewrite Korean history, and spread Japanese cultural values more generally.

In 1931, the Japanese looped their hopes for radio through the internal policy committee responsible for the emerging *naisen ittai* program, and the issue of whether it was wise to provide Koreans with their own station was the cause of heated debate (HPCH 1991, 198–199). In the end, the contradictory interests were balanced by a decision to centralize programming controls, to originate more programming in Japan, and, finally, to increase the number of Japanese culture and language lectures aired on the new station. Thus the Japanese restricted the new station's programming autonomy from its inception. Over time, more and more programs were simple translations of Japanese news, government reports, and cultural/educational lectures.

The Ministry of Communications created a new programming oversight committee (Hōsō Hensei I-inkai) in 1931 to monitor the new station. To insure total control of output, they created a "cut-off" switch for Station 2 that augmented the already functioning direct phone lines to the broadcast booths at KBC.[13] In 1935, radio controls were also integrated with the powerful Korean Information Coordinating Committee (Chōsen Hōjō I-inkai) that coordinated all information and censorship in the colony (HPCH 1991, 159, 195–197).[14] The controls were virtually airtight, and there is little mention of direct censorship of politically or morally offensive items over colonial radio.

The Japanese increased the percentage of Japanese-originated programming on both channels after 1931. With new relay stations and improved relay technology, direct broadcasts to Korea from Japan began in the early 1930s. This saved money on program production and fed the Japanese audience's appetite for news and familiar sounds from home. It also supported the assimilation program by creating an illusion of unified cultural programming while binding the colony electronically to the metropole.

There was also an effort to effect directly a transformation of cultural forms on the radio. The Japanese progressively encouraged the playing of Japanese songs, martial music, and even the Japanization of Korean music genres during the war years. Beginning in the late 1930s, KBC ran contests publicized in the colonial press that awarded substantial prizes and the promise of air time for Japanized Korean popular songs as well as patriotic songs in Korean (HPK 1977, 45–50; HPCH 1991, 190–195).[15] This was particularly evident after the beginning of the war with China; after 1941 and the reduction of Korean-language time slots, music programming was devoted entirely to military and patriotic songs.

After 1937, Ministry of Communications officials required KBC to devote more time in their educational programs to lectures on ethics (*simjŏn*), agricultural improvement (*nongch'ŏn chinhŭng*), and women's education (*puin kyoyuk*). These three categories of lectures were integral to the formal Movement to Create Imperial Subjects (Kōminka Undō) begun in 1935 by Governor General Ugaki Kazushige and intensified by Governor General Minami Jirō after 1936. Japanese-language lectures and language "radio classroom" programs were added in 1938 along with the decision to force exclusive use of Japanese in schools and government facilities. The increase in the numbers of these required programs left less time for autonomous Korean-language programs in the education and lecture category, but some Korean-produced cultural and educational shows remained. Finally in

July 1941, the GGK banned lectures and lessons on the Korean language altogether. This anticipated the elimination of Station 2 in April 1942 as Korean-language broadcasts were folded back into the Japanese station. All Korean-language broadcasting ended in December of 1944 (HPCH 1991, 206, 220–221).

KOREAN RADIO AND CULTURAL CONSTRUCTION

Radio in Korea certainly supported Japanese cultural and political hegemony. This was inherent in the original policy that shaped its structure, restrained programming, controlled information, and self-consciously insinuated Japanese cultural and assimilationist content into broadcasting from its inception. It is, however, still possible to find within the world of broadcasting, spaces in which cultural construction evolved toward different purposes. While this construction could not directly resist Japanese rule, it could and did serve a positive function to maintain and create Korean cultural traditions. Centered within an important Japanese assimilationist institution, Korean radio created a counterhegemonic niche in and of itself and stimulated other nodes of cultural construction in the colony. Its counterhegemonic aspects were, however, ambiguous: radio also drew Korean elites (artists, writers, programmers) into the modern sphere, thus further enmeshing them within colonial cultural hegemony.

One of the most important features of Korean radio resided in its language maintenance/development function. The advent of Korean-language broadcasting in the late 1920s added an additional weapon to the movement to organize and standardize the Korean vernacular language. The permission to publish Korean vernacular newspapers after 1920 stimulated a Korean nationalist movement to create a unified grammar and orthography. Radio played an important role in this process by begging questions of standard pronunciation (*p'yojunmal*). Intellectuals scrutinized the choice of announcers and their use of language throughout the history of colonial broadcasting (*Chosŏn ilbo* January 7, 1927; January 9, 1927; July 31, 1940).[16] The advent of the all-Korean station in 1933 coincided with the publication of the first *Unified Korean Orthography* (Matchumbŏp t'ongil an) and, later, the *Unified Korean Grammar* (Chosŏn munbŏp t'ongil an) (*Han'gŭl hakhoe 50 nyŏnsa* 1971, 89–97; Robinson 1988, 89–92). And, in 1933, one of the first series of cultural lectures produced by Station 2 was on Korean language (*Chosŏn ilbo*, November 7, 1933). These lectures were not for the masses (indeed, radio distribution was still in its infancy); they were, however, intended to serve the Korean intelligentsia's agenda of standardizing the modern Korean vernacular and elevating its use in modern discourse (*Tonga ilbo*, December 14, 1938).

The lectures on the Korean language were combined in Korean programmers' minds with other lectures on Korean history, traditional arts, and more modern topics such as science, economics, and world affairs (Yun 1934, 120). While Korean radio producers labored under the censor's control of the cut-off button, the Korean press self-consciously celebrated these lectures as a forum to demonstrate the capacity of vernacular Korean to deal with modern abstract thought. They were also seen as projecting the very "sounds and cadences" of the ancient language on the global airwaves (*Tonga ilbo,* November 10, 1929). One can view such commentary as a self-conscious dialogue about making Korean language modern, like Japanese. Here is a glimpse of Korean elites, working in the language movement, competing to place the use of Korean on a par with Japanese language use in articulating abstract thought (in lectures and the like on the radio). Their efforts were both to maintain the use and existence of the Korean vernacular and to prove it was equal to Japanese as an instrument of the modern. This supports a broad, nationalist reading of such activity, namely, that the Korean language not be subordinated to Japanese within the cultural universe of the empire. Their efforts seem clearly directed against the assimilation program's putative goal of reducing Korean language use to (as one Japanese commentator put it) "a simple expression of the rusticated aspects of peninsular culture in the colony, while maintaining Japanese *(kokugo)* as the argot of modern life" (Tsuda 1940, 57).

While this language "resistance" can be read in simple nationalist terms, it also reveals the workings of colonial cultural hegemony. Japanese dominance of the modern sphere required Koreans to justify their own language, to "elevate" or perfect its utility as a modern language. It seems clear that further work on this issue can revise our understanding of how and how far linguistic assimilation evolved. The story of radio seems to indicate that language resistance was not just an issue of the survival of Korean (the usual charge) but over its actual use within the modern sphere of discourse. One could read this struggle as one that was the more narrow concern of Korean colonial elites, fighting for a particular aspect of their dual cultural identity as cosmopolitans within the broader frame of the empire.

Station 2 complemented the rather intellectualized discussion of Korean with children's lessons in *han'gŭl* and grammar during their popular "Radio School" *(Radio hakkyo)* program in the late afternoon after regular school. This program served to augment the dwindling attention to formal Korean language study in the state-run schools after 1931. Ironically, both the "Radio School" and linguistics lectures continued after the formal crackdown on Korean language use in schools, offices, and semigovernment corporations beginning in 1938. As late as February 1940, Station 2 was running a series on the purification of the Korean language (*Chosŏn ilbo,* February 9, 1922). The very existence of such programming in 1940 confounds the postcolonial shibboleth of forced Japanese language use. Further research will be necessary on the impact of these campaigns on language use and how these programs were interpreted in the depressed atmosphere of forced assimilation, but the contradiction remains.[17]

Of equal relevance to the issue of cultural construction was Korean radio's effect on reviving and reshaping traditional music and dramatic art genres. In its beginning, musical entertainment was broadcast "live." There was no library of phonograph recordings to draw upon, and music programming had to find artists (Yi 1989). Station 2 also had to make choices about what kinds of music were suitable for broadcast. Early music programs were a combination of performances of traditional Yi dynasty court music *(aak)* and folk songs drawn from different regional traditions (HPK 1977, 42, passim).[18] In the early years, only small ensembles and individual singers could be featured because of the limited studio space at the station. Between 1927 and 1933, KBC broadcast much of its music from theaters using direct-wire feeds to the station. Live performances over the radio stimulated attendance at and excitement for music performances and reviews that had become a permanent feature of Seoul's burgeoning entertainment industry (Yu 1992).[19]

Radio's use of traditional performers stimulated a revival of traditional music genres, and radio exposure created new singing stars in the late 1920s and early 1930s. The traditional music programming was not without controversy within the Korean community. There were objections to radio's use of *kisaeng* entertainers from the four great *kisaeng* schools in P'yŏngyang as well as disagreements over which folk songs were "representative" of certain regions. The discussion broadened in the first years of broadcasting to a debate over radio's role in favoring certain regional (the *sŏdo*, western, or *namdo*, southern, for instance) styles over others. The following excerpt from the *Tonga ilbo* of December 17, 1933, illustrates this struggle:

> . . . all walks of life are brought together in listening to the radio. . . in this period of transition between new and old ideas [we can detect] a collision. Anonymous letters detail struggles in households all over Korea . . . between fathers who hate the sounds of the new songs *sinsik yuhaeng* and want more traditional songs and their sons—or between those who want only the Korean zither [*kayagŭm*] and those who want to hear Western music. The old are arrayed against the young who hate the "old stinking traditional songs" or "old fashioned instruments." There is also regional strife as listeners complain: "can't we have more music from the western provinces [*sŏdoga*]?" Or, "can't we have more songs from the south [*namdoga*]?"

Radio clearly stimulated a debate over the canonization of traditional Korean music, stimulated public performances of obscure genres, and, ultimately, led to the resuscitation of endangered art forms on phonograph records.

In dramatic arts, radio also played an important catalytic function. Radio melodramas and translations of Western plays became a staple on Korean-language radio. Starting with selected readings of traditional novels and stories, KBC soon established its own Radio Drama Research Association (Radio Yŏnguk Yŏn'guhoe) to adapt novels and stories for radio actors (HPK 1977, 20, 66–67, 71–74). This association worked with Korean writers who were both producing new-style plays based on Western forms as well as translating directly classic works in the Western dramatic canon. Early radio featured a number of Western works (Isben, Shakespeare) as well as adaptations of longer traditional Korean works such as the *Tale of Ch'unhyang* (Ch'unhyangjŏn). By 1933 and the advent of the Korean-language station, the "Radio Drama Hour" (7:00–8:00 P.M.) that preceded the most popular late-night music program had become a radio staple. The Korean press provided summaries of radio drama programs that served to further advertise activity in the urban live theater scene.

In the first six years of dual-language broadcasting, popular music was eclipsed by Western and traditional, high culture, Korean music. By 1933, however, new forms of popular song were clearly establishing themselves as the most popular radio fare. Korean popular song *(yuhaengga)* had evolved after 1900 as a mixture of Korean folk idioms and imported Japanese *torotto* ("fox trot") music. Akin to contemporary Korean *ppongjjak nori,* these pop songs were a mixture of gliding Korean tonal scales, folk singing technique, and a standard Western beat in both 2/4 and 3/4 time. By the mid-1920s, the early Korean recording industry had already created a star system and a market for new recordings of this idiom. In the early 1930s, radio began to use more and more records for their programs, and the explosion of phonograph and record sales coincides with this phenomenon.[20] The Korean-language press ran daily advertisements, bought by record companies, of new records, and new recording releases were often timed with performance of the record on radio. By 1935, the recording industry was big business and the linkage between the press, the recording industry, and radio was obvious to all.

The spectacular rise in the popularity of pop songs in the early and mid-1930s placed radio in the center of controversy. There were complaints from radio's middle-class audience that pop music was unsuitable for family listening: barroom music should stay in the bars. One vaguely leftist cultural critic put it this way in the December 1934 issue of *Creation (Kaebyŏk):*

> Recently, on the streets of Seoul, all we hear are the same sounds from the same people. Its a monotone/tedium like in walking in a desert. Ever day the same flutes, oboes, violins, comedy stories, etc. . . . everyone listening [because of the novelty of radio]. Drunken songs with corrupt lyrics from the mouths of *kisaeng* come into our homes every night . . . to great harm and spiritual corruption . . . noisy, incessant

songs of the failed Chosŏn dynasty, songs of vagrants . . . all [come into] in the sanctity of the home. Should we not be cultivating the cultural consciousness of the masses more than [worrying about] business?

Korean intellectuals also worried that the "vulgar" pop idiom was replacing an appreciation for traditional music. Soon, the Japanese authorities began to take notice of the message within pop songs—tales of tragedy, unrequited love, laments of lost traditions, partings at the Shimonoseki ferry, paeans to a sense of Korean place—all overly melodramatic, spiritually unhealthy, and vaguely unpatriotic. The GGK's Song Purification Movement of the late 1930s (following a similar campaign in Japan) was an attempt to counteract the tremendous emotive hold of this music on the Korean population.[21] Yet, as far as I can tell, Japanese censors began to create black lists and directly ban songs only after 1941, both in Korea and Japan.

While only sketched here in brief, the story of Korean pop songs on the radio is clearly multilayered. Korean radio had a catalytic effect on the creation and expansion of an important popular cultural medium of song. This music was "consumed" in records and radio broadcasts, but it also became the staple of, and possibly reinforced, restaurant, wine shop, and home singing—a continuation of an earlier and more "participatory" form of popular culture. It also underscored a tension within the Korean elite's program to create a national cultural identity. It is clear in the press that radio programmers and cultural elites were worried that popular song would divert from their project to canonize and preserve traditional Korean music as part of a modern Korean high culture. The usual reading of why such popular music was attractive is that it was nationalist; that is, popular music was one of the last vestiges of cultural resistance in the face of Japanese cultural suppression. The Korean cultural elites' debate over the meaning of popular song, however, might indicate another possibility. As with language, elites' conception of cultural construction within the modern sphere "resisted" by attempting to emulate cultural norms in the metropole through the establishment and deepening of a Korean high, modern culture co-equal to that of their colonial masters. In this sense, the debates in the 1930s in Korea over culture anticipated postcolonial debates over the same issue in South Korea, with modern Western rock representing the new enemy to a "true" Korean music culture.[22]

RETHINKING JAPANESE ASSIMILATION AND KOREAN RESPONSE

This brief synopsis of radio in colonial Korea is meant to open up the discussion of the meaning and effects of colonial modernity and Japanese hegemony in 1920s and 1930s Korea. The dichotomizing repression-resistance thesis, the staple of existing Korean nationalist histories of the period, interprets radio as another in a long list of impositions. The Japanese imposed radio on the Korean population just as it imposed Japanese history, language, cultural values, and Shinto worship at the height of the forced assimilation campaigns after 1937. At its most extreme, this view goes on to vilify all modern cultural production (radio included) in colonial Korea as dominated either by the GGK directly, or, as in the case of the recording industry, indirectly by Japanese and Western monopoly capital (Yi 1989, passim). This view privileges the productive forces behind the construction of modern, consumption-oriented, mechanically reproduced popular culture.

We know less, however, about how radio was consumed by its audience. Were the endless lectures on how to be good imperial citizens, patriotic songs, and mind-numbing GGK news and policy reports really effective in inculcating Japanese values in the Korean population? Were the Korean intellectual elite's efforts to codify the Korean language as a "language of the modern" successful despite the decreasing amount of time devoted to such programming after 1937? This survey of radio focuses on production; even the original content of radio programs is difficult to determine. We can use reviews of lectures and secondhand commentary from the newspapers, but this is still a biased source. Even as we uncover transcripts and recordings of the original lectures, we will still have to struggle to determine how they were "read" by contemporary listeners.

The colonial intellectual elite who ran the newspapers had their own spin on the significance of Korean-language radio; they also were driven by the same commercialism that spurred Japanese and Western investment in cinema and the phonograph and recording industry. On the one hand, Korean intellectuals saw Korean radio as part of a cultural maintenance and canonization project; on the other, they decried radio's role in helping erode cultural values by popularizing "vulgar" popular song genres. It is important to recognize here that both interpretations hold; Korean radio did have a role in cultural maintenance, and it also represented a locus of cultural construction that neither nationalist ideologues nor GGK officials could control. Therefore, the story of Korean radio is more than one of a single Korean culture resisting Japanese assimilation. It was also a space of intra-Korean elite struggle over how their culture should evolve in modern form. The cultural and political structures of colonialism decisively shaped this struggle.

Finally, the story of Korean radio during the colonial period must also be seen as part of a more complex system of cultural construction. Colonial radio was not placed in a vacuum. While it did represent another modern technology transferred to Korea by the its colonial overlords, this new medium evolved in an already developing modern, popular culture (Yu

1992, passim). By 1900, Koreans had begun to create a modern, consumer popular culture. Music performances in theaters for fees, modern adaptation of Western drama held in new theaters, cinema, and pulp fiction—all new forms of entertainment—had appeared before the advent of radio.[23] Indeed, radio reinforced the consumption of leisure in all of these arenas. Most dramatically, radio was quickly linked with the development of new music genres, and it served to popularize the consumption of music in record form after 1927.

It is a gross oversimplification to assert that Japanese radio was just another in a series of coercive, modern technologies exported to Korea to serve Japanese political control and, ultimately, assimilation. That it did serve these purposes does not negate the possibilities that it had other effects on Korean society. Radio, like other Japanese "investments" in colonial Korea, became part of a dynamic system of new cultural forms, technologies, and habits that transformed cultural life there between 1910 and 1945. These had tremendous power and shaped, while Japanizing, the structure of an emerging Korean modernity. But within selected spaces of autonomous development, Koreans struggled to make part of that modernity their own. To this end, the experience of Korean radio is instructive. Further work on this subject will help shape our understanding of cultural construction in the colony, and, more importantly perhaps, it will also illuminate important continuities between Korea's colonial past and its contemporary cultural debates.

NOTES

Research for this paper was supported, in part, by a Korea Foundation Fellowship for research in Korea during the summer of 1994.

1. Table 1 (pp. 561–562) contains yearly statistics on radio receivers (permits) by ethnicity in Korea.
2. French Algeria is the closest analogue to Japanese-dominated Korea. However, French Radio Algeria remained focused on broadcasts in the urban centers and immediate hinterland where the French population was centered. Only during the end of French rule did they spread the net to counter-resistance broadcasts (also in French language).
3. Andrew Nahm put it this way: "A vast majority of Korean families had no radios, and to them the wireless communication system was irrelevant" (Nahm 1988, 247). The exhaustive histories of communications published in Korea generally share this sentiment while piling up data that if different questions are asked, might support new interpretations (HPK 1977; HPCH 1991).
4. Other spaces I have in mind are the Korean-language press, recording industry, and cinema.

5. The period of cultural rule is generally set at 1919–1931, ending with the Manchurian Incident and an intensification of Japanese assimilation programs. I would argue that cultural rule set important parameters within the overall Japanese cultural hegemony in Korea. While the policy co-opted Korean cultural, social, and political leaders, it also created autonomous cultural spaces that undermined later assimilation programs of the middle-to-late 1930s.

6. For a description of GGK policy linkages and administrative orders on radio, see HPCH 1991, 137–139.

7. Formal permission was granted on November 30, 1926; broadcasts began February 16, 1927.

8. Standard Korean histories of broadcasting assert that the dual-language policy of KBS was unique to the pre-1945 colonial world.

9. Even before formal broadcasts began, there was sniping in the press (see *Maeil sinbo,* December 8, 1926). In 1927 criticism focused on how the language mix inhibited the spread of radios (*Chosŏn ilbo,* January 7–9, 1927; March 23, 1927; *Tonga ilbo,* May 21, 1927; December 16, 1927).

10. Figures on the financing of KBC before 1933 are drawn from the secondary histories, HPK 1977 and HPCH 1991. More detailed year-by-year budgets for KBC are contained in the GGK Ministry of Communications annual, *Chōsen Sōtokufu Teishin Kyoku nenpō,* yearly after 1933.

11. Government Directive (*furei*) 380, *Chōsen Sōtokufu kampō,* (February 1926). This directive set profits, registration, and listener fees.

12. The expansion of the radio audience meant that listener fees could be reduced. The basic monthly fee was lowered again to seventy-five chŏn in 1939.

13. Early Korean broadcasts were monitored by an official of the Ministry of Communications in the studio. This official had an open telephone line to the ministry and could stop broadcasting on the spot. Later, a cut-off button wired to the ministry itself replaced the need of an official in the control booth. There is no evidence that the button was ever used.

14. This committee had been established in 1920 as part of the cultural policy reorganization. It gradually assumed control of all printing, journalism, cinema, radio, and advertising media. The committee was charged to coordinate all information surveillance as well as production of propaganda after 1937.

15. Singled out for particularly vehement denunciation in postwar writing on assimilation programs was the Japanese attempt to "recast" Korean folk song genres (*minyo, kasa*) in a traditional Japanese narrative song (*naniwabushi*) style.

16. Radio announcers became stars during the period. The inclusion of women announcers, following the Japanese pattern, contradicted traditional roles for women in public life. KBC received thousands of letters to the female announcers, among them proposals of marriage.

17. An important part of this research, as yet only beginning, will be to investigate the issue of Japanese language use by the colonial population. The

Japanese boasted that by 1943 23.2 percent of the population understood some Japanese, 12.3 percent "without difficulty." The Korean population in 1944 stood at 25,133,352 (there were 712,587 Japanese in the colony that year). Further research on Korean use of radio and consumption of Japanese-language publications in the colony will help us assess these claims.

18. Indeed, the regional mixture of material was deliberately fostered through a popular programming device of remote broadcasts from provincial cities—the "Night in P'yŏngyang" or "Night in Kwangju" broadcasts. These began during the period of dual-language radio and continued after 1933. It is interesting to speculate about how these broadcasts represented or stimulated regional identity during the period.

19. Ch'ae Namsik (1993) satirized the popularity of "live" music reviews in his serialized novel, *Peace Under Heaven,* personified by the listening habits of the novel's odious protagonist, Master Yun.

20. According to *Wŏlgan ŭmak (Music Monthly)*, December 1935, 449–450, "[e]ven poor farmers can identify major record companies and different popular records." This article claims that there were 30,000 phonographs in Korea at the time. Other sources indicate 50,000 records sold in Korea as a "best-seller," as in the case of "The Tears of Mokp'o Harbor" (Mokp'o ŭi nunmul) in 1935. The same source reminds us of the popularity of Korean singers and their songs in the Japanese market. In Japan, a record selling 300,000 copies was not uncommon (Pak 1992).

21. For one description of the Song Purification Movement (Kayo Chŏnghwa Undong), see *Chosŏn ilbo,* December 21, 1939. The movement took a number of forms, including sponsoring song-and-radio-drama writing contests with cash prizes (*Chosŏn ilbo,* September 1, 1937).

22. Contemporary struggles over the issue of Western popular culture and its corrosive influences in Korea are played out at both the state and grassroots levels. The state holds Western rock music as responsible for the corruption of Korean youth—its hedonism, materialism, and "untraditional" attitudes toward the older generation. Youthful cultural nationalists are also trying to revive Korean folk music, dance, and participatory theater.

23. The bibliography on these separate elements of popular culture is restricted to informal "histories" of various music genres, the Korean (not all cinema) cinema, and modern literature. Mainstream historians dominating history writing in the Republic of Korea have not yet embraced this topic as relevant. Among younger scholars, however, the field is growing and ultimately will challenge and reshape modern history in Korea.

REFERENCES

Baldwin, Frank. 1969. "The March First Movement: Korean Challenge and Japanese Response." Ph.D. diss., Columbia University.

———. 1982. "The March First Movement" (in Korean). In *Ilche ŭi Taehan ŏllon sŏnjŏn chŏngch'aek,* edited by Kim Kyu-hwan, 162. Seoul: Iu ch'ulp'ansa.

Ch'ae Namsik. 1993. *Peace Under Heaven,* translated by Chun Kyung-ja. Armonk, New York: M. E. Sharpe.

Chogwang. March 1939. "Rek'o-dŭ kye ŭi naemak tŭtnŭn." 5.3:314–323.

Chŏng Chin-sŏk. 1992a. *Han'guk pansong kwangye kisa moŭm.* Seoul: Kwanhŭn K'ŭlŏp Sinyŏng Yŏn'gu Kigŭm.

———. 1992b. "Ilcheha ŭi radio pogŭp kwa ch'ŏngchwija." *Sinmun kwa pangsong* (October):54–61.

Chōsen. February 1939. "Chōsengo setsuji mondai." 285:93.

Chōsen Sōtokufu Bunshoka. 1938. "Chōsen ni ōkeru kokugo fukyu jōtai." Keijō.

Chōsen Sōtokufu kampō. February 1926. No. 380.

Chōsen Sōtokufu Teishin Kyoku nenpō.

Dong, Wonmo. 1965. "Japanese Colonial Policy and Practice in Korea, 1905–1945: A Study in Assimilation." Ph.D. diss., Georgetown University.

Fanon, Frantz. 1965. *A Dying Colonialism.* New York: Grove Press.

Han'gŭl hakhoe 50 nyŏnsa. 1971. Seoul: Han'gŭl Hakhoe.

Henderson, Gregory. 1968. *Korea: The Politics of the Vortex.* Cambridge: Harvard University Press.

(HPK) Han'guk Pangsong Kongsa. 1977. *Han'guk pangsongsa.* Seoul: Han'guk Pangsong Kongsa.

(HPCH) Han'guk Pangsong Chinhŭnghoe. 1991. *Han'guk pangsong ch'onggam.* Seoul: Han'guk Pangsong Chinhŭnghoe.

Kasza, Gregory. 1988. *The State and Mass Media in Japan 1918–1945.* Berkeley: University of California Press.

Kim Kyu-hwan. 1982. *Ilche ŭi Taehan ŏllon sŏnjŏn chŏngch'aek.* Seoul: Iu ch'ulp'ansa.

Kyebyŏk. December 1934. "Radio." 2.1:94.

Lee, Chong-Sik. 1964. *The Politics of Korean Nationalism.* Berkeley: University of California Press.

Nahm, Andrew. 1988. *Korea: Tradition and Transformation.* Seoul: Hollym Press.

Nihon Hōsō Kyōkai. 1967. *The History of Broadcasting in Japan.* Nihon Hōsō Kyōkai.

———. 1965. *Nihon Hōsōshi 1.* Nihon Hōsō Shuppan Kyōkai, 544–545.

Pak Ch'an-ho. 1992. *Han'guk kayosa.* Seoul: Hyŏnamsa.

Robinson, Michael. 1994. "Mass Media and Popular Culture in 1930s Korea: Cultural Control, Identity, and Colonial Hegemony." In *Korean Studies: New Pacific Currents,* edited by Dae-Sook Suh, 54–73. Honolulu: University of Hawai'i Press.

———. 1988. *Cultural Nationalism in Colonial Korea 1920–1925.* Seattle: University of Washington Press, 89–92.

Suh, Dae-Sook. 1967. *The Korean Communist Movement.* Princeton: Princeton University Press.

Tsuda Takeshi. 1940. "Hantō bunka no seikaku." *Chōsen,* no. 299 (April):57.

Yi Ch'ang-Hyŏn. 1989. "Ilcheha munhwa sanŏp ŭi taejung ŭmak saengsan e kwanhan chŏngch'i kyŏngjehak." *Sahoe pip'yng* 3 (December).

Yu Sŏnyŏng. 1992. "Han'guk taejung munhwa ŭi kŭndaejŏk kusŏng e taehan yŏn'gu: Chosŏn hugi esŏ ilche sidae kkaji rŭl chungsim ŭro." Ph.D. diss., Korea University.

Yun Paeknam. 1934. "Sinsedae ŭi sahoejŏk yŏkhal." *Sindonga* (March):120.

❧ Contributors ❦

Barbara J. Brooks is assistant professor of history at the City College of the City University of New York. She is working on a book on citizenship and colonial society in the Japanese empire, having recently completed a book manuscript titled *Japan's Imperial Diplomacy: Treaty Ports, Consuls, and War in China, 1895–1938.*

Lonny E. Carlile is assistant professor in the Center for Japanese Studies and Asian Studies Program at the University of Hawai'i at Mānoa. Recent publications include "Economic Development and the Evolution of Japanese Overseas Tourism" (1996), a translation titled *Contemporary Politics in Japan* by Masumi Junnosuke (1995), and "Party Politics and the Japanese Labor Movement" (1994).

Kevin Doak is associate professor of modern Japanese history at the University of Illinois at Urbana-Champaign. He is the author of *Dreams of Difference: The Japan Romantic School and the Crisis of Modernity* as well as various articles on nationalism and romanticism in twentieth-century Japan.

Joshua A. Fogel is professor of history and East Asian languages and cultural studies at the University of California at Santa Barbara and founding editor of *Sino-Japanese Studies,* an interdisciplinary journal. His recent publications include *The Cultural Dimension of Sino-Japanese Relations: Essays on the Nineteenth and Twentieth Centuries* (1994) and *The Literature of Travel in the Japanese Rediscovery of China, 1862–1945* (1996).

Sheldon Garon is professor of history and East Asian studies at Princeton University. He is the author of *Molding Japanese Minds: The State in Everyday Life* (1997) and *The State and Labor in Modern Japan* (1987). He is currently working on a book on savings and frugality campaigns in twentieth-century Japan.

Elaine Gerbert is associate professor of Japanese literature at the University of Kansas. She has translated novellas by Uno Kōji *(Love of Mountains)* and written on Satō Haruo in *Beautiful Town: Stories and Essays by Satō Haruo* and on Uno Kōji in a festschrift for Edwin McClellan. Some of her other writings are "The Suwa Pillar Festival Revisited" (1996) and "Lessons from the Kokugo Readers"(1993), for which she received the George Z. Bereday award.

Jeffrey E. Hanes teaches history and Asian studies at the University of Oregon. His recent publications include "From Megalopolis to Megaroporisu" (1993) and "Taishū bunka/ka'i bunka/minshu bunka" ("Mass Culture/Subcultures/Popular Culture," 1996), and "Contesting Centralization? Space, Time, and Hegemony in Meiji Japan" (1997).

Helen Hardacre is Reischauer Institute Professor of Japanese Religions and Society, Harvard University. Her major publications include *Lay Buddhism in Contemporary Japan: Reiyukai Kyōdan* (1984), *The Religion of Japan's Korean Minority* (1986), *Kurozumikyō and the New Religions of Japan* (1986), *Shinto and the State, 1868–1988* (1989), and *Marketing the Menacing Fetus in Japan* (1997).

Sharon A. Minichiello is associate professor of Japanese history and director of the Center for Japanese Studies at the University of Hawai'i at Mānoa. Her publications include "Chishikijin to seiji: Takagi Yasaka to Matsumoto Shigeharu, 1931–1941" (Intellectuals and politics: Takagi Yasaka and Matsumoto Shigeharu, 1931–1941) in *Kindai Nihon no seiji kōzō* (The Political Structure of Modern Japan, 1993), and *Retreat from Reform: Patterns of Political Behavior in Interwar Japan* (1984).

Tessa Morris-Suzuki holds a chair in Japanese history in the Research School of Pacific and Asian Studies, Australian National University. Her research focuses on the social effects of technological change and on issues of national identity in modern Japan. Her most recent books are *The Technological Transformation of Japan* and *Reinventing Japan: Time, Space, Nation*.

Jonathan M. Reynolds completed his Ph.D. at Stanford University in 1991 and is assistant professor in the History of Art Department at the University of Michigan. His primary research focus is Japanese modernist architecture.

He is the author of *Maekawa Kunio and the Emergence of a Japanese Modernist Architecture.*

Michael E. Robinson is associate professor of Korean history in the Department of East Asian Languages and Cultures at Indiana University. He is the author of *Cultural Nationalism in Colonial Korea* (1988) and numerous articles on modern Korean history and culture.

Roy Starrs, who holds a Ph.D. in modern Japanese Literature from the University of British Columbia, is head of the Department of Japanese of the University of Otago, New Zealand. His main interests lie in East-West comparative literature and culture, as reflected in his study of Nietzschean philosophy in Mishima's novels, *Deadly Dialectics: Sex, Violence and Nihilism in the World of Yukio Mishima* (1994). His newest work is *Soundings in Time: The Fictive Art of Yasunari Kawabata* (1998).

Mariko Asano Tamanoi is assistant professor in anthropology at the University of California at Los Angeles. Her publications include articles in the *Journal of Asian Studies, Annual Review of Anthropology,* and *Comparative Studies in Society and History.* She is the author of *Under the Shadow of Nationalism: Politics and Poetics of Rural Japanese Women* (1998).

Julia Adeney Thomas is an assistant professor in history at the University of Wisconsin at Madison. She is completing a book manuscript titled "Reconfiguring Nature: Japan's Confrontation with Modernity" and is pursuing a new project on photography and nationalism in Japan.

E. Patricia Tsurumi is professor emerita of Japanese history at the University of Victoria, British Columbia. She is the author of *Japanese Colonial Education in Taiwan, 1895–1945* (1977); *Factory Girls, Women in the Thread Mills of Meiji Japan* (1990), which won the Canada Council's 1991 Canada-Japan Book Prize; and a number of shorter studies.

Christine Yano is an assistant professor in anthropology at the University of Hawai'i. During 1996–1997, she was a postdoctoral fellow at the Reischauer Institute of Harvard University, where she completed a book manuscript, "Tears of Longing: Nostalgia and the Nation in Japanese Popular Song."

❧ Index ❧

Page numbers in **boldface** refer to illustrations.